MW00838022

# The CISM™ Prep Guide
## Mastering the Five Domains
## of Information Security
## Management

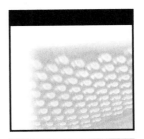

# The CISM™ Prep Guide
## Mastering the Five Domains of Information Security Management

Ronald L. Krutz
Russell Dean Vines

WILEY

Wiley Publishing, Inc.

**Executive Publisher:** Robert Ipsen
**Executive Editor:** Carol Long
**Developmental Editor:** Kenyon Brown
**Editorial Manager:** Kathryn A. Malm
**Senior Production Editor:** Angela Smith
**Media Development Specialist:** Angie Denny
**Text Design & Composition:** Wiley Composition Services

This book is printed on acid-free paper. ∞

Copyright © 2003 by Ronald L. Krutz, Russell Dean Vines. All rights reserved.

Published by Wiley Publishing, Inc., Indianapolis, Indiana
Published simultaneously in Canada

No part of this publication may be reproduced, stored in a retrieval system, or transmitted in any form or by any means, electronic, mechanical, photocopying, recording, scanning, or otherwise, except as permitted under Section 107 or 108 of the 1976 United States Copyright Act, without either the prior written permission of the Publisher, or authorization through payment of the appropriate per-copy fee to the Copyright Clearance Center, Inc., 222 Rosewood Drive, Danvers, MA 01923, (978) 750-8400, fax (978) 646-8700. Requests to the Publisher for permission should be addressed to the Legal Department, Wiley Publishing, Inc., 10475 Crosspoint Blvd., Indianapolis, IN 46256, (317) 572-3447, fax (317) 572-4447, E-mail: permcoordinator@wiley.com.

Limit of Liability/Disclaimer of Warranty: While the publisher and author have used their best efforts in preparing this book, they make no representations or warranties with respect to the accuracy or completeness of the contents of this book and specifically disclaim any implied warranties of merchantability or fitness for a particular purpose. No warranty may be created or extended by sales representatives or written sales materials. The advice and strategies contained herein may not be suitable for your situation. You should consult with a professional where appropriate. Neither the publisher nor author shall be liable for any loss of profit or any other commercial damages, including but not limited to special, incidental, consequential, or other damages.

For general information on our other products and services please contact our Customer Care Department within the United States at (800) 762-2974, outside the United States at (317) 572-3993 or fax (317) 572-4002.

**Trademarks:** Wiley, the Wiley Publishing logo and related trade dress are trademarks or registered trademarks of Wiley Publishing, Inc., in the United States and other countries, and may not be used without written permission. CISM is a trademark of Information Systems Audit and Control Association. All other trademarks are the property of their respective owners. Wiley Publishing, Inc., is not associated with any product or vendor mentioned in this book.

Wiley also publishes its books in a variety of electronic formats. Some content that appears in print may not be available in electronic books.

*Library of Congress Cataloging-in-Publication Data:* Is available from the Publisher

ISBN: 0-471-45598-9

Printed in the United States of America

10 9 8 7 6 5 4 3 2

*I want to dedicate this book to our grandchildren—Patrick, Ryan, and Aaron. Seeing the world through their eyes makes it appear new and wondrous.*

*RLK*

*This book is dedicated to my parents, James and Marian. May the posse never catch you.*

*RDV*

# Contents

# Acknowledgments

I want to thank my family for their loyalty, support, and encouragement during the writing of this work. I also want to thank Carol Long, our executive editor, for her guidance and recommendations on this project.

**RLK**

I would like to thank my friends, particularly Louis Schneider and Maria Kaleja, for their support; the able and astute Wiley editors, including Carol Long; and the continued support from my wife, Elzy Kolb.

**RDV**

# Introduction

The Information Systems Audit and Control Association (ISACA) has developed the Certified Information Security Manager (CISM) certification for experienced information security managers. The CISM emphasizes risk and security management while covering technical and design security topics at a conceptual level. As stated by ISACA, the CISM "defines the core competencies and international standards of performance that information security managers are expected to master."

## Certification Requirements

The requirements for obtaining the CISM are to pass the CISM examination, subscribe to a code of professional ethics, and provide verifiable evidence of a minimum number of years of information security work experience, with a minimum number in the appropriate job analysis domain. Specifically, the candidate must have the following:

- A minimum of five years' work experience in information security with a minimum of three years' information security management experience in three or more of the job practice areas.

- Security-related certifications can provide a two-year waiver for the information security work experience. These certifications include CISA and CISSP. A postgraduate degree in information systems security or a related field also qualifies the candidate for this waiver.

- Non-security-related information system management experience or skill-based certifications such as SANS GIAC, MCSE, CBCP, or Comp-TIA Security+ qualify for a one-year experience waiver.

There is also a grandfathering provision for information security managers with appropriate experience and for professionals with related information security certifications such as CISSP and CISA.

A detailed listing of the CISM job practice areas and their corresponding tasks and knowledge statements is given in Appendix B. These areas list the topics that will be tested in the CISM certification examination. A summary of the five CISM job practice areas is given as follows:

1. Information Security Governance
   - Develop strategy
   - Obtain management commitment
   - Define roles
   - Establish reporting and communication channels
   - Identify legal and regulatory issues
   - Develop security policies
   - Develop and maintain practices and guidelines
   - Develop business case for security

2. Risk Management
   - Develop management processes
   - Develop life cycle processes
   - Conduct risk identification and analysis
   - Define strategies
   - Report changes

3. Information Security Program Management
   - Plans
   - Baselines
   - Procedures and Guidelines
   - Integrating information security
   - Methods to meet policy requirements
   - Accountability
   - Metrics
   - Identification of resources

4. Information Security Management
   - Policy compliance
   - Metrics
   - Change management issues

- Vulnerability assessments
- Noncompliance issues
- Awareness and training

5. Response Management
   - Detecting, identifying, and analyzing events
   - Response and recovery plans
   - Testing
   - Execution of response and recovery
   - Procedures
   - Postevent reviews

## The Prep Guide Approach

This book incorporates the proven and successful approach taken by the authors in their other information security certification guides. The material is compiled and presented in a fashion that is conducive to assimilation of the essential knowledge. It eliminates divergent, unnecessary, and unrelated material that is found in general information security texts that tends to impede the learning process. This guide is focused on the critical information that ISACA has deemed appropriate for the CISM candidate to master and necessary to pass the CISM examination.

The sample questions and answers and the enclosed CD-ROM are designed to test the candidate's knowledge as well as serve as a learning and reinforcing mechanism for the subject matter in the book.

## Approach and Hints

The approach recommended by the authors to prepare for the CISM examination using the CISM Prep Guide is to do the following:

- Absorb the key concepts presented for each of the domains
- Answer the sample questions at the end of each chapter
- Reinforce the learning process by studying the correct answers and explanations in Appendix C
- Using the Boson CD, take multiple practice examinations that can be generated by the Boson test engine
- Note the answers and explanations provided by the Boson test engine while taking the practice examinations

As with any multiple-choice examination, there are techniques that can be used to increase the chances of selecting the correct answers. For example, in a question with four multiple-choice answers, a well-prepared candidate can usually identify two of the answers as incorrect. Subsequently, the candidate must choose from the better of the two remaining answers. This process narrows the field of solutions and supports a candidate who has done a thorough job of studying for the examination.

One mistake that many exam takers make is not reading the question carefully and deliberately. A quick scan of the question may result in the candidate missing a key word or phrase that is instrumental in selecting the correct answer. Also, in many instances, some questions in the examination might provide the answers or clues to answers for other questions in the exam.

Obviously, nothing can replace experience, hard work, and careful preparation in getting ready to take the CISM Examination. These efforts, coupled with structured guidance and information provided by the *CISM Prep Guide,* will stand the candidate in good stead in achieving the CISM Certification.

# About the Authors

**RONALD L. KRUTZ, Ph.D., P.E., CISSP.** Dr. Krutz is a Senior Information Security Consultant with the Information Assurance Solutions (IAS) operation of BAE Enterprise Systems. He is also the lead for all Capability Maturity Model (CMM) engagements for IAS, and he developed IAS's HIPAA-CMM assessment methodology. He has more than 30 years of experience in distributed computing systems, computer architectures, real-time systems, information assurance methodologies, and information security training. He has been an Information Security Consultant at Realtech Systems Corporation, an Associate Director of the Carnegie Mellon Research Institute (CMRI), and a professor in the Carnegie Mellon University Department of Electrical and Computer Engineering. He was also a lead instructor for ISC2 in its CISSP training seminars. Dr. Krutz founded the CMRI Cybersecurity Center and was founder and Director of the CMRI Computer, Automation, and Robotics Group. Dr. Krutz conducted sponsored-applied research and development in the areas of computer security, artificial intelligence, networking, modeling and simulation, robotics, and real-time computer applications.

Dr. Krutz is the author of three textbooks in the areas of microcomputer system design, computer interfacing, and computer architecture and has published more than 40 technical papers. He co-authored the *CISSP Prep Guide;* the *Advanced CISSP Prep Guide, Q&A;* the *CISSP Prep Guide, Gold Edition;* and the *Security+ Prep Guide* for John Wiley and Sons. Dr. Krutz is a Certified Information Systems Security Professional (CISSP), a Registered Professional Engineer, and a Senior Member of the IEEE. He is a also a Distinguished Visiting Lecturer in the University of New Haven Computer Forensics Program and a consulting editor for John Wiley and Sons for its information security series.

Dr. Krutz holds B.S., M.S., and Ph.D. degrees in Electrical and Computer Engineering.

**RUSSELL DEAN VINES, CISSP, Security+, CCNA, MCSE, MCNE.** President and founder of The RDV Group Inc., a New York City-based security consulting services firm, Mr. Vines has been active in the prevention, detection, and remediation of security vulnerabilities for international corporations, including government, finance, and new media organizations, for many years. He is the author of *Wireless Security Essentials,* and he co-authored the *CISSP Prep Guide;* the *Advanced CISSP Prep Guide, Q&A;* the *CISSP Prep Guide, Gold Edition;* and the *Security+ Prep Guide* for John Wiley and Sons. He is a consulting editor for John Wiley and Sons for its information security book series.

Mr. Vines has been active in computer engineering since the start of the personal computer revolution. He holds high-level certifications in Cisco, 3Com, Ascend, Microsoft, and Novell technologies and is trained in the National Security Agency's ISSO Information Assessment Methodology. He has headed computer security departments and managed worldwide information systems networks for prominent technology, entertainment, and nonprofit corporations based in New York. He formerly directed the Security Consulting Services Group for Realtech Systems Corporation; designed, implemented, and managed international information networks for CBS/Fox Video, Inc.; and was director of MIS for the Children's Aid Society in New York City.

Mr. Vines' early professional years were illuminated not by the flicker of a computer monitor but by the bright lights of Nevada casino show rooms. After receiving a *Down Beat* magazine scholarship to Boston's Berklee College of Music, he performed as a sideman for a variety of well-known entertainers, including George Benson, John Denver, Sammy Davis Jr., and Dean Martin. Mr. Vines composed and arranged hundreds of pieces of jazz and contemporary music recorded and performed by his own big band and others. He also founded and managed a scholastic music publishing company and worked as an artist-in-residence for the *National Endowment for the Arts* (NEA) in communities throughout the West. He still performs and teaches music in the New York City area and is a member of the American Federation of Musicians Local #802.

# The CISM™ Prep Guide
## Mastering the Five Domains of Information Security Management

# CHAPTER 1

# Information Security Governance

The first area of CISM study we will examine is the area of Information Security Governance. The goal of this domain is to establish and maintain a framework to provide assurance that information security strategies are aligned with business objectives and consistent with applicable laws and regulations. The fundamental areas that develop this framework are the following:

- Basic information security concepts
- Polices and procedures
- Legal and regulatory issues

## Basic Information Security Concepts

Let's start by examining fundamental security concepts. Obviously, this will be a refresher course for some of you, but we feel we should all be on the same page with the basics.

### Confidentiality, Integrity, and Availability

Information systems security is defined in terms of protecting the confidentiality, integrity, and availability of information systems.

*Confidentiality* ensures that the information is not disclosed to unauthorized persons or processes. The concept of confidentiality attempts to prevent the intentional or unintentional unauthorized disclosure of a message's contents. Loss of confidentiality can occur in many ways, such as through the intentional release of private company information or through a misapplication of network rights.

*Integrity* is addressed through the following three goals:

- Prevention of the modification of information by unauthorized users
- Prevention of the unauthorized or unintentional modification of information by authorized users
- Preservation of the internal and external consistency

Internal consistency ensures that internal data is consistent. For example, assume that an internal database holds the number of units of a particular item in each department of an organization. The sum of the number of units in each department should equal the total number of units that the database has recorded internally for the whole organization. External consistency ensures that the data stored in the database is consistent with the real world. Continuing with the example, external consistency means that the number of items recorded in the database for each department is equal to the number of items that physically exist in that department.

*Availability* ensures that a system's authorized users have timely and uninterrupted access to the information in the system. In other words, availability guarantees that the systems are up and running when needed. In addition, this concept guarantees that the security services that the security practitioner needs are in working order.

These concepts represent the three fundamental principles of information security. All of the information security controls and safeguards and all of the threats, vulnerabilities, and security processes are subject to the C.I.A. yardstick. Figure 1.1 shows the triangle concept of C.I.A.

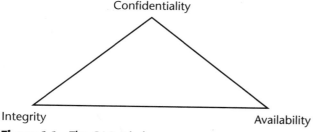

**Figure 1.1**   The C.I.A. triad.

# Information Classification

The information that an organization produces or processes must be classified according to the organization's sensitivity to its loss or disclosure. Information loss can have an impact on a business globally, not just on the business unit or line operation levels.

There are several reasons for classifying information:

- To demonstrate an organization's commitment to security protections
- To help identify which information is the most sensitive or vital to an organization
- To support the tenets of confidentiality, integrity, and availability as it pertains to data
- To help identify which protections apply to which information
- To meet possible requirements for regulatory, compliance, or legal reasons

The basic classification levels are Unclassified, Confidential, Secret, and Top Secret. There are a number of other levels of additional protection categories built on top of these classification levels. The definitions of the major classification levels are as follows:

**Unclassified information.**   Any information that need not be safeguarded against disclosure, but must be safeguarded against tampering, destruction, or loss due to record value, utility, replacement cost, or susceptibility to fraud, waste, or abuse.

**Confidential information.**   Information that, through unauthorized disclosure, reasonably could be expected to cause damage to national security. Examples of such information are the strength of military forces and design, production, and performance data on classified weapons systems and munitions.

**Secret information.**   Information that, if disclosed to unauthorized parties, could be expected to cause serious damage to the national security. Examples include revelation of significant military plans or intelligence operations, disruption of foreign relations significantly affecting the national security, and the compromise of significant scientific or technological developments relating to national security.

**Top Secret information.**   Information that, if disclosed to unauthorized parties, could be reasonably expected to cause exceptionally grave damage to national security. Examples include the compromise of complex cryptology and communications intelligence systems, the revelation of sensitive intelligence operations, armed hostilities, and the disclosure of vital scientific or technological developments.

Other categories of classified material that build on the four major classification areas are the following:

**For Official Use Only (FOUO) information.**   Unclassified information that may be exempt from mandatory release under the Freedom of Information Act (FOIA) if it meets additional stringent requirements.

**Sensitive But Unclassified (SBU) information.**   Information originated within the Department of State that warrants a degree of protection and administrative control and meets the criteria for exemption from mandatory public disclosure under the Freedom of Information Act.

**Unclassified Controlled Nuclear Information (DoD UCNI).**   Unclassified information on security measures (including security plans, procedures, and equipment) for the physical protection of DoD Special Nuclear Material (SNM), equipment, or facilities.

A special classification that is "above" Top Secret is *Sensitive Compartmentalized Intelligence* (SCI). SCI information usually comes from intelligence systems such as reconnaissance satellites, aircraft, and submersibles.

In addition, the following classification terms are commonly used in the private sector (see Table 1.1):

- *Public* information is similar to unclassified information; all of a company's information that does not fit into any of the next categories can be considered public. If disclosed, it is not expected to seriously or adversely affect the company.

- *Sensitive* information requires a higher level of classification than normal data. This information is protected from a loss of confidentiality as well as from a loss of integrity due to an unauthorized alteration.

- *Private* information is considered of a personal nature and is intended for company use only. Its disclosure could adversely affect the company or its employees. For example, salary levels and medical information are considered private.

- *Confidential* information is considered very sensitive and is intended for internal use only. This information is exempt from disclosure under the Freedom of Information Act. Its unauthorized disclosure could seriously and negatively affect a company. For example, information about new product development, trade secrets, and merger negotiations is considered confidential.

**Table 1.1**   Simple Information Classification Scheme

| DEFINITION | DESCRIPTION |
| --- | --- |
| Public Use | Information that is safe to disclose publicly |
| Internal Use Only | Information that is safe to disclose internally but not externally |
| Company Confidential | The most sensitive need-to-know information |

### Classification Criteria

Several criteria are used to determine the classification of an information object:

**Value.**   Value is the number one commonly used criteria for classifying data in the private sector. If the information is valuable to an organization or its competitors, it needs to be classified.

**Age.**   The classification of the information might be lowered if the information's value decreases over time. In the Department of Defense, some classified documents are automatically declassified after a predetermined time period has passed.

**Useful life.**   If the information has been made obsolete due to new information, substantial changes in the company, or other reasons, the information can often be declassified.

**Personal association.**   If information is personally associated with specific individuals or is addressed by a privacy law, it might need to be classified. For example, investigative information that reveals informant names might need to remain classified.

There are several steps in establishing a classification system. A common process is the following:

1. Identify the administrator/custodian.
2. Specify the criteria for how to classify and label the information.
3. Classify the data by its owner, who is subject to review by a supervisor.
4. Specify and document any exceptions to the classification policy.
5. Specify the controls that you will apply to each classification level.
6. Specify the termination procedures for declassifying the information or for transferring custody of the information to another entity.
7. Create an enterprise awareness program about the classification controls.

## *Distributing Classified Information*

External distribution of classified information is often necessary, and you will need to address the inherent security vulnerabilities. Some of the instances when this distribution is necessary are the following:

**Court order.**   Classified information might need to be disclosed to comply with a court order.

**Government contracts.**   Government contractors might need to disclose classified information *in accordance with* (IAW) the procurement agreements that are related to a government project.

**Senior-level approval.**   A senior-level executive might authorize the release of classified information to external entities or organizations. This release might require the signing of a confidentiality agreement by the external party.

## *Classification Roles*

Individuals have different defined roles in information classification schemes, and it is important to understand these roles. The system must clearly define the roles and responsibilities of all participants in the information classification program. A key element of the classification scheme is the role that the users, owners, or custodians of the data play in regard to the data.

### Owner

An information owner may be an executive or manager of an organization. This person is responsible for the information that must be protected. An owner is different from a custodian. The owner has the final corporate responsibility for data protection, and under the concept of due care, the owner may be liable for negligence for failing to protect sensitive information. The day-to-day function of protecting the data, however, is assigned to a custodian. Some of the responsibilities of an owner are these:

- Making the original determination to decide what level of classification the information requires, which is based on the business needs for the protection of the data

- Reviewing the classification assignments periodically and making alterations as the business needs change

- Delegating the responsibility of the data protection duties to the custodian

### Custodian

An information custodian is delegated the responsibility of protecting the information by its owner. This role is executed typically by IT systems personnel. The duties of a custodian are these:

■ Running regular backups and routinely testing the validity of the backup data

■ Performing data restoration from the backups when necessary

■ Maintaining those retained records in accordance with the established information classification policy

■ Occasionally administering the classification scheme

### User

An end user is considered to be one that routinely uses the information as part of his or her job. Users can also be considered consumers of the data, who need daily access to the information to execute their tasks. Users must follow the operating procedures that are defined in an organization's security policy, and they must adhere to the published guidelines for its use. In addition, users must practice "due care" to secure sensitive information according to the information security and use policies. Users must use the company's computing resources only for company purposes, and not for personal use.

## Network Security

Network security is clearly a major area of information security governance. Let's examine the elements of the network that require information security governance, as they affect the overall security posture of an organization.

### Network Address Translation (NAT)

Generically, NAT (Network Address Translation) describes the process of converting an IP address valid in one network to a different IP address valid in another network. More specifically, NAT converts a private IP address on the inside, trusted network to a registered "real" IP address seen by the untrusted, outside network.

The Internet Assigned Numbers Authority (IANA) has reserved three blocks of the IP address space for private Intranets: 10.0.0.0 to 10.255.255.255, 172.16.0.0 to 172.31.255.255, and 192.168.0.0 to 192.168.255.255. Employing these internal addresses through NAT enhances security by hiding the true IP address of the origination of the packet. As each incoming or outgoing packet is converted by NAT, the request may be authenticated.

Also, NAT helps conserve the number of global IP addresses that a company requires, and it allows the company to use a single IP address for its outside communications.

NAT can be statically defined, or it can be configured to dynamically use a group of IP addresses. For example, Cisco's version of NAT lets an administrator create policies that define the following:

- A static one-to-one relationship between one local IP address and one global IP address

- A relationship between a local IP address to any of one of a dynamic group of global IP addresses

- A relationship between a local IP address and a specific TCP port to a static or dynamic group of global IP addresses

- A conversion from a global IP address to any one of a group of local IP addresses on a round-robin basis

NAT is described in general terms in RFC 1631, which discusses NAT's relationship to Classless Interdomain Routing (CIDR) as a way to reduce the IP address depletion problem. NAT is often included as part of a router, and most firewall systems now include NAT capability.

### Virtual Private Networking (VPN)

A virtual private network (VPN) is created by building a secure communications link between two nodes by emulating the properties of a point-to-point private link. A VPN can be used to facilitate secure remote access to a network, securely connect two networks together, or create a secure data tunnel in a network.

The portion of the link in which the private data is encapsulated is known as the tunnel. It may be referred to as a secure, encrypted tunnel, although it's more accurately defined as an encapsulated tunnel, as encryption may or may not be used. To emulate a point-to-point link, data is encapsulated, or wrapped, with a header that provides routing information. Most often the data is encrypted for confidentiality. This encrypted part of the link is considered the actual virtual private network connection.

A VPN tunnel is created by dynamically building a secure communications link between two nodes by using a secret encapsulation method (see Figure 1.2). This link is commonly called a secure encrypted tunnel, although it is more accurately defined as an encapsulated tunnel because encryption may or may not be used.

Tunneling is a method of transferring data from one network to another network by encapsulating the packets in an additional header. The additional header provides routing information so that the encapsulated payload can traverse the intermediate networks.

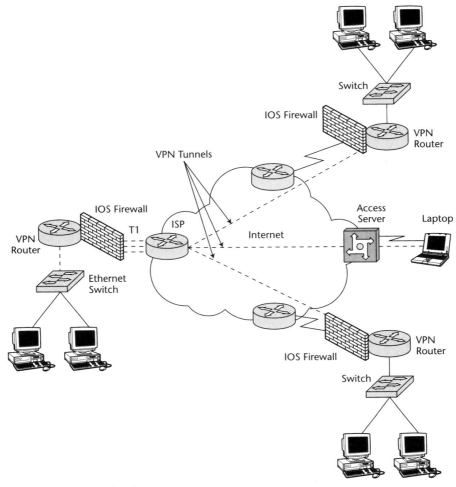

**Figure 1.2**   Example of a VPN.

For a tunnel to be established, both the tunnel client and the tunnel server must be using the same tunneling protocol. Tunneling technology can be based on either a Layer 2 or a Layer 3 tunneling protocol. These layers correspond to the Open Systems Interconnection (OSI) Reference Model.

Tunneling, and the use of a VPN, is not intended as a substitute for encryption/decryption. In cases where a high level of security is necessary, the strongest possible encryption should be used within the VPN itself, and tunneling should serve only as a convenience.

Common VPN and remote access protocols are as follows:

**Point-to-Point Tunneling Protocol (PPTP).**   Works at the Data Link Layer of the OSI model. This standard is very common with asynchronous connections that use Win9x or NT clients. PPTP uses native Point-to-Point Protocol (PPP) authentication and encryption services.

**Layer 2 Tunneling Protocol (L2TP).**    A combination of PPTP and the earlier Layer 2 Forwarding (L2F) Protocol and works at the Data Link Layer like PPTP. It has become an accepted tunneling standard for VPNs. L2TP supports TACACS+ and RADIUS, but PPTP does not.

**Internet Protocol Security (IPSec).**    Operates at the Network Layer and enables multiple and simultaneous tunnels, unlike the single connection of the previous standards. IPSec has the functionality to encrypt and authenticate IP data, but it is not multiprotocol.

**Serial Line Internet Protocol (SLIP).**    A TCP/IP protocol and early de facto standard for asynchronous dial-up communication. An ISP for Internet access may provide a SLIP connection. PPP is now preferred over SLIP because it can handle synchronous as well as asynchronous communication. PPP can share a line with other users, and it has error detection that SLIP lacks.

**Point-to-Point Protocol (PPP).**    Defines an encapsulation method to transmit multiprotocol packets over Layer 2 point-to-point links, such as a serial interface. PPP is a full-duplex protocol that can be used on various physical media, including twisted pair or fiber optic lines or satellite transmission. It uses a variation of High Speed Data Link Control (HDLC) for packet encapsulation.

**Password Authentication Protocol (PAP).**    A basic clear-text authentication scheme. The NAS requests the username and password, and PAP returns them in clear text, unencrypted. PAP user authentication is often used on the Internet, which simply sends a username and password to a server where they are compared with a database of authorized users. While the user database may be kept in encrypted form, each ID and password are sent unencrypted.

**Challenge-Handshake Authentication Protocol (CHAP).**    An encrypted authentication mechanism that avoids transmission of the actual password on the connection. The NAS sends a challenge, which consists of a session ID and an arbitrary challenge string, to the remote client. The remote client must use the MD5 one-way hashing algorithm to return the username and an encryption of the challenge, session ID, and the client's password. The username is sent unhashed. CHAP is an improvement over PAP because the clear-text password is not sent over the link.

**Microsoft Challenge-Handshake Authentication Protocol (MS-CHAP).** An encrypted authentication mechanism very similar to CHAP. As in CHAP, the NAS sends a challenge, which consists of a session ID and an arbitrary challenge string, to the remote client. The remote client must return the username and an encrypted form of the challenge string, the session ID, and the MD4-hashed password. This design, which uses a hash of the MD4 hash of the password, provides an additional level of security because it allows the server to store hashed passwords instead of cleartext passwords.

**MS-CHAP version 2 (MS-CHAP v2).** An updated encrypted authentication mechanism that provides stronger security. The NAS sends a challenge to the access client that consists of a session identifier and an arbitrary challenge string. The remote access client sends a response that contains the username, an arbitrary peer challenge string, and an encrypted form of the received challenge string, the peer challenge string, the session identifier, and the user's password.

**Extensible Authentication Protocol (EAP).** This was designed to allow the dynamic addition of authentication plug-in modules at both the client and server ends of a connection. EAP is an extension to PPP that allows for arbitrary authentication mechanisms for the validation of a PPP connection. This allows vendors to supply a new authentication scheme at any time, providing the highest flexibility in authentication uniqueness and variation. EAP is supported in Microsoft Windows 2000 and defined in RFC 2284.

## *Firewalls*

Firewalls act as perimeter access-control devices and are classified into three common types:

- *Packet filtering firewalls* examine both the source and destination address of the incoming data packet. This firewall either blocks or passes the packet to its intended destination network. The firewall can allow or deny access to specific applications and/or services based on the Access Control Lists (ACLs). ACLs are database files that reside on the firewall, are maintained by the firewall administrator, and tell the firewall specifically which packets can and cannot be forwarded to certain addresses.

- *Proxy firewalls* work by transferring a copy of each accepted data packet from one network to another, thereby masking the data's origin. A proxy server can control which services a workstation uses on the Internet, and they are commonly application-level or circuit-level firewalls.

- *Stateful inspection firewalls* intercept incoming packets at the network level, then use an "inspection engine" to extract state-related information from upper layers. A stateful inspection firewall maintains the information in a dynamic state table and evaluates subsequent connection attempts. Stateful inspection firewalls keep low-protocol records at the IP level.

### Bastion Host

A bastion host is any computer that is fully exposed to attack by being on the public side of the demilitarized zone (DMZ), unprotected by a firewall or filtering router. Firewalls and routers, anything that provides perimeter access-control security, can be considered bastion hosts. Other types of bastion hosts can include Web, mail, DNS, and FTP servers. Often a bastion host is used as a sacrificial lamb. Due to their exposure, a great deal of effort must be put into designing and configuring bastion hosts to minimize the chances of penetration.

### *VLANs*

A Virtual LAN (VLAN) is a collection of nodes that are grouped together in a single broadcast domain in a switch, and that are based on something other than physical segment location. A VLAN creates an isolated broadcast domain*, and a switch with multiple VLANs creates multiple broadcast domains, similar to a router. VLANs, however, can't route between each other. Such routing would defeat the purpose of the VLAN: to isolate the traffic from the general traffic flow.

Some advantages of VLANs are these:

- VLANs can aid in isolating segments with sensitive data from the rest of the broadcast domain and increase security assurance.
- VLANs can reduce the number of router hops and increase the usable bandwidth.
- VLANs reduce routing broadcasts as ACLs control what stations receive what traffic.
- VLANs may be created to segregate job or department functions that require heavy bandwidth, without affecting the rest of the network.
- A single VLAN can span across multiple switches.
- Multiple VLANs can exist in a single switch.

## Access Control

A principal concern in the practice of information security is controlling what *subjects* (persons or programs) have access to which *objects* (files, programs, databases). In addition, the privileges that a subject has to an object must be defined. For example, Bob may be permitted to read File A, but he may not have the privilege to write to it.

---

* A broadcast domain is a network (or portion of a network) that will receive a broadcast packet from any node located within that network. Normally everything on the same side of the router is all part of the same broadcast domain.

In planning and implementing access control systems, the following three items must be considered:

**Threat.**   An event or activity that has the potential to cause harm to the information systems or networks.

**Vulnerability.**   A weakness or lack of a safeguard, which may be exploited by a threat, to cause harm to information systems or networks.

**Risk.**   The potential for harm or loss to an information system or network; the probability that a threat will materialize.

## Controls

In order to reduce the risk and the potential for loss, *controls* are used. Controls fall into the categories of preventive, detective, and corrective. *Preventive* controls attempt to inhibit harmful occurrences; *detective* controls are used to find situations that may cause harm to the information system; and *corrective* controls are used to restore the information system to the state that existed prior to an attack.

Preventive, detective, and corrective controls can be implemented using administrative techniques, technical (logical) means, and physical devices. Examples of *administrative* controls are security awareness training, establishment of policies and procedures, personnel background checks, and increased supervision. *Technical* controls include smart cards, encryption, and access control lists (ACLs). *Physical* controls include the securing of laptops to desks, locking file cabinets, employing guards, locking doors, and protecting cable runs.

The objective of controls is to provide accountability for individuals who are accessing sensitive information. *Accountability* is another facet of access control that is based on the premise that individuals accessing and using an information system are responsible for their actions. Thus, any activities conducted on an information system by an individual should be traceable to that individual. Accountability is accomplished through means that require the subject requesting access to provide identity and authentication information. Familiar examples of these two items are presenting an identity (ID) to log on to a computer and then providing a password as the authentication means to verify the identity.

## Authentication

The key component in granting access of a subject to an object is the authentication of the subject requesting access to an information system. *Authentication* is the reconciliation of evidence that attests to a user's identity. It establishes the identity of the users and verifies that they are who they say they are. A related concept is non-repudiation. *Non-repudiation* is the prevention of a sender of a message from denying that he or she sent the message. Authentication can be accomplished in a number of ways, including passwords, tokens, and the physical characteristics of an individual, biometrics.

### Passwords

In applying a password for authentication, a user presents an identification (ID) to a workstation or authentication server. Then, a corresponding password is entered to authenticate the ID and verify that the user is the person he or she professes to be.

Passwords can be compromised and must be protected. Choices for passwords should not be intuitive and related to the user's name, occupation, pets, birthday, and so on. The password should be a random sequence of numbers, letters, or symbols and should be at least eight characters in length.

Passwords should be changed at intervals proportional to value of the information to be protected. Typical time frames range from one month to six months. This type of password is called a *static password* because it is the same for each logon in the interval before it is changed. The more times the same password is used, the more chance there is of its being compromised.

In the ideal case, a password should be used only once. This *"one-time password"* provides maximum security because a new password is required for each new logon. Such a password is termed a *dynamic password* because it changes as a function of time.

A *passphrase* is a sequence of characters that is usually longer than the allotted number of characters for a password. It can be a sentence or phrase that the user can remember. This passphrase is converted into a virtual password by the system by using transformations such as a one-way hash function.

*Tokens* are used to supply static and dynamic passwords and are in the form of credit card-sized memory cards or smart cards. For example, an ATM card is a memory card that stores your specific information. Smart cards provide even more capability by incorporating additional processing power on the card. Tokens come in four main types:

- Static password tokens
- Synchronous dynamic password tokens
- Asynchronous dynamic password tokens
- Challenge-response tokens

### Static Password Tokens

With this type of token, the user authenticates himself or herself to the token, and then the token authenticates the user to the authentication server or workstation.

### Synchronous Dynamic Password Tokens

A synchronous dynamic password token generates a new unique password value at fixed time intervals. This password is time-synchronized with the authentication server and must be presented to the authentication server along with a PIN (known to the authentication server) within a fixed time window to be accepted. For example, each new password could be generated by encrypting the time of day with a secret key that is known to the token and to the authentication server.

### Asynchronous Dynamic Password Tokens

This token generates the new password asynchronously; thus, entry of the password into the authentication server does not have to fit into a fixed time interval for authentication. The new password is entered into the authentication server along with the user's PIN.

### Challenge-Response Tokens

The challenge-response token is based on the user supplying a valid response to a challenge number presented by the authentication server or workstation. Specifically, the authentication server generates a random challenge string, and the user enters the string into the token along with the user's PIN. The token takes the challenge string and user's PIN and generates a response string of characters. This response string is usually the result of an encryption process. The user enters the response string into the authentication server, which verifies that it is the valid response based on the user's PIN and the key used in the encryption process. The challenge-response approach is also used in remote access protocols, such as the Challenge Handshake Authentication Protocol (CHAP). CHAP uses a non-replayable challenge-response protocol that verifies the identity of the node attempting to initiate the remote session. CHAP is commonly used by remote access servers and xDSL, ISDN, and cable modems. CHAP is an improvement over an earlier remote authentication protocol called the Password Authentication Protocol (PAP). PAP uses a static password for authentication. PAP is considered a weak protocol because the password is subject to replay and the user ID and password are not encrypted during the logon session.

In all these token-based schemes, a front-end authentication device or a back-end authentication server, which services multiple workstations or the host, can perform the authentication.

## Multifactor Authentication

In order to provide additional access protection for an information system, multifactor authentication can be employed. *Multifactor authentication* requires more than one authentication method. For example, in addition to a password, the authentication entity may require a fingerprint. In general, authentication is based on the following three factor types:

- Type 1: Something you know (PIN, password)
- Type 2: Something you have (ATM card, smart card)
- Type 3: Something you are (fingerprint, retina scan)

*Two-factor authentication* requires two of the three factors to be used in the authentication process. For example, withdrawing funds from an ATM machine requires two-factor authentication in the form of the ATM card (something you have) and your PIN number (something you know). The "something you are" Type 3 factor is the domain of the area of biometrics.

*Biometrics* is defined as an automated means of identifying or authenticating the identity of a living person based on physiological or behavioral characteristics. Biometrics is used for identification in physical access control and for authentication in technical (logical) access. In biometrics, *identification* is a "one-to-many" search of an individual's characteristics from a database of stored images. *Authentication* in biometrics is a "one-to-one" search to verify a claim to an identity made by a person. The three main performance measures in biometrics are the following:

**False Rejection Rate (FRR) or Type I Error.**    The percentage of valid subjects that are falsely rejected.

**False Acceptance Rate (FAR) or Type II Error.**    The percentage of invalid subjects that are falsely accepted.

**Crossover Error Rate (CER).**    The percent in which the False Rejection Rate equals the False Acceptance Rate.

In most cases, the sensitivity of the biometric detection system can be increased or decreased during an inspection process. If the system's sensitivity is increased, such as in an airport metal detector, the system becomes increasingly selective and has a higher FRR. Conversely, if the sensitivity is decreased, the FAR will increase. Thus, to have a valid measure of the system performance, the CER is used. These concepts are shown in Figure 1.3.

Other important factors that have to be evaluated in biometric systems are enrollment time, throughput rate, and acceptability. *Enrollment time* is the time it takes to initially "register" with a system by providing samples of the biometric characteristic to be evaluated. An acceptable enrollment time is about two minutes.

The *throughput rate* is the rate at which individuals, once enrolled, can be processed and identified or authenticated by a system. Acceptable throughput rates are in the range of 10 subjects per minute.

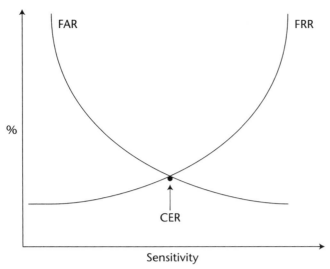

**Figure 1.3** Crossover Error Rate.

*Acceptability* refers to considerations of privacy, invasiveness, and psychological and physical comfort when using the system. For example, a concern with retina scanning systems may be the exchange of body fluids on the eyepiece. Another concern would be the retinal pattern that could reveal changes in a person's health, such as diabetes or high blood pressure.

Acquiring different data elements reflecting a biometric characteristic can greatly affect the storage requirements and speed of operation of a biometric identification or authentication system. For example, in *fingerprint* systems, the actual fingerprint is stored and requires approximately 250kb per finger for a high-quality image. This level of information is required for one-to-many searches in forensics applications on very large databases. In *finger-scan* technology, a full fingerprint is not stored—the features extracted from this fingerprint are stored using a small template that requires approximately 500 to 1000 bytes of storage. The original fingerprint cannot be reconstructed from this template. Finger-scan technology is used for one-to-one verification using smaller databases. Updates of the enrollment information may be required because some biometric characteristics, such as voice and signature, may change with time.

The following are typical biometric characteristics that are used to uniquely identify or authenticate an individual:

- Fingerprints
- Retina scans
- Iris scans

- Facial scans
- Palm scans
- Hand geometry
- Voice
- Handwritten signature dynamics

Once a subject has been authenticated to an information system, there are a number of possible ways to assign rights for these subjects to access objects. The approaches range from a straightforward, tabular method to formal models that also incorporate restrictions on information transfer. The main access privilege assignment methods are discussed in the following sections.

### The Access Matrix

The access matrix is a table with the subjects listed in the row headings and the objects listed in the column headings. The common cell in the table between a subject and object contains the access privilege of the subject to that object. A simple illustration of an access matrix is given in Table 1.2.

A row in the access matrix is called a *capability list* because it specifies all the rights or capabilities of a subject. A column in the access matrix is referred to as an *access control list* because it lists the rights that all subjects have to an object. The access matrix implements discretionary access control. Discretionary access control will be discussed in more detail later in this chapter.

The access matrix is straightforward and easy to use, but it can become unwieldy if large numbers of subjects and objects are involved and if frequent changes have to be made to the matrix.

### Access Control Models

Additional models have been developed to formalize access control rules and concepts and to address situations that are more complex and require stricter controls than can be achieved with an access matrix. Examples of such models are the Bell-LaPadula confidentiality model and the Biba and Clark Wilson integrity models.

The Bell-LaPadula model was developed to formalize the U.S. Department of Defense (DoD) multilevel security policy. The model formalizes mandatory access control based on labels and the employment of classifications and clearances. Mandatory access control will be discussed later in this chapter. The model does also permit, under special circumstances, a discretionary access control mode. The Bell-LaPadula model deals only with the confidentiality of classified material; it does not address integrity or availability.

**Table 1.2**  An Access Matrix

|  | FILE C | FILE D | PROGRAM E |
|---|---|---|---|
| Mr. Jones | Read | Write | Execute |
| Ms. Adams | Read/Write | None | None |
| Process A | Write | Write | Execute |
| Process B | Read | Read/Write | None |

The Bell-LaPadula model defines three multilevel properties. The first two properties implement mandatory access control, and the third one permits discretionary access control.

**The Simple Security Property (SS Property).**   This property states that reading of information by a subject at a lower sensitivity level from an object at a higher sensitivity level is not permitted (no read up).

**The * (star) Security Property.**   The star property states that writing of information by a subject at a higher level of sensitivity to an object at a lower level of sensitivity is not permitted (no write down).

**The Discretionary Security Property.**   This property uses an access matrix to specify discretionary access control.

In some instances, a property called the *Strong * Property* is cited. This property states that reading or writing is permitted at a particular level of sensitivity, but not to either higher or lower levels of sensitivity.

The discretionary portion of the Bell-LaPadula model is based on the access matrix. The system security policy defines who is authorized to have certain privileges to the system resources. *Authorization* is concerned with how access rights are defined and how they are evaluated. Some discretionary approaches are based on context-dependent and content-dependent access control. *Content-dependent* control makes access decisions based on the data contained in the object. *Context-dependent* control is related to the environment or context of the data and is a function of factors such as location, time of day, and previous access history.

The Biba model was developed in 1977 to address the first goal of integrity, which is to protect data from modification by unauthorized users. The model is the integrity analog of the Bell-LaPadula confidentiality model. The Biba model classifies objects into different levels of integrity, similar to the Bell-LaPadula model's classification of different sensitivity levels. The model specifies the three following integrity axioms:

**The Simple Integrity Axiom.**    This axiom states that a subject at one level of integrity is not permitted to observe (read) an object of a lower integrity (no read down).

**The * (star) Integrity Axiom.**    The star axiom states that an object at one level of integrity is not permitted to modify (write to) an object of a higher level of integrity (no write up).

**Axiom Three.**    This axiom states that a subject at one level of integrity cannot invoke a subject at a higher level of integrity.

The approach of the Clark-Wilson model (1987) was to develop a framework for use in the real-world, commercial environment. This model addresses the three integrity goals and defines the following terms:

**Constrained Data Item (CDI).**    A data item whose integrity is to be preserved.

**Integrity Verification Procedure (IVP).**    A process that confirms that all CDIs are in valid states of integrity.

**Transformation Procedure (TP).**    A process that manipulates the CDIs through a well-formed transaction, which transforms a CDI from one valid integrity state to another valid integrity state.

**Unconstrained Data Item (UDI).**    Data items outside of the control area of the modeled environment such as input information.

The Clark-Wilson model requires integrity labels to determine the integrity level of a data item and to verify that this integrity was maintained after an application of a TP. This model incorporates mechanisms to enforce internal and external consistency, a separation of duty, and a mandatory integrity policy.

## Security Architecture and Technologies

An organization's information system security architecture is a function of multiple technologies, policies, and hardware and software organization. Some of the key aspects of a security architecture are concerned with signing on to multiple resources, assigning access privileges, protecting information from compromise, confirming the identity of the person sending a message, and ensuring that the sender cannot repudiate the sending of a message. These concepts are discussed in the following sections.

### Single Sign-On (SSO)

Single Sign-On (SSO) addresses having to log on multiple times to access different resources in an information system. With this situation, a user must remember numerous passwords and IDs and may take shortcuts in creating passwords that may be open to exploitation. In SSO, a user provides one ID and password per work session and is automatically logged on to all the required applications. For SSO security, the passwords should not be stored or transmitted in the clear. SSO applications can run either on a user's workstation or on authentication servers. The advantages of SSO include having the ability to use stronger passwords, easier administration of changing or deleting the passwords, and requiring less time to access resources. The major disadvantage of many SSO implementations is that once a user obtains access to the system through the initial logon, the user can freely roam the network resources without any restrictions.

SSO authentication mechanisms may include items such as smart cards and biometric devices. Strict controls must be placed to prevent a user from changing configurations that are set by another authority.

SSO can be implemented by using scripts that replay the users' multiple logins, or by using authentication servers to verify a user's identity and encrypted authentication tickets to permit access to system services.

Enterprise Access Management (EAM) provides access control management services to Web-based enterprise systems that include SSO. SSO can be provided in a number of ways. For example, SSO can be implemented on Web applications in the same domain residing on different servers by using nonpersistent, encrypted cookies on the client interface. This is accomplished by providing a cookie to each application that the user wishes to access. Another solution is to build a secure credential for each user on a reverse proxy that is situated in front of the Web server. The credential is, then, presented at each instance of a user attempting to access protected Web applications.

Kerberos is one of the principal means of implementing SSO.

### Kerberos

Kerberos was developed under Project Athena at MIT and named for the three-headed dog that guards the entrance to the underworld in Greek mythology.

Kerberos uses symmetric key cryptography to authenticate clients to other entities on a network from which the client requires services. Some basic assumptions that assist in understanding the rationale behind Kerberos are the following:

- Numerous networked clients, servers, and network resources are available.
- The client location and computers are not necessarily secure.
- The network cabling cannot be assumed to be secure.
- Messages are not secure from interception.

A few specific locations and servers can be secured and can serve as trusted authentication mechanisms for every client and service on the network. (These centralized servers implement the Kerberos trusted *Key Distribution Center* [KDC], *Kerberos Ticket Granting Service* [TGS], and *Kerberos Authentication Service* [AS].)

In a Kerberos implementation, all network clients and servers have a secret key. These secret keys are known by the KDC and used by the KDC to perform authentication and to provide for symmetric key encryption of messages sent on the network. Kerberos authenticates a client to a requested service on a server through special messages called tickets and by issuing temporary symmetric session keys. The symmetric session keys are valid for a specified period of time and are used for communications between the client and KDC, the server and the KDC, and the client and the server.

Kerberos addresses confidentiality and integrity of information. It does not directly address availability and attacks such as frequency analysis. Also, because all the secret keys are held and authentication is performed on Kerberos TGS and Authentication servers, these servers are vulnerable to both physical attacks and attacks from malicious code. Replay can be accomplished on Kerberos if the compromised tickets are used within the allotted time window. Because the client password is used in the initiation of the Kerberos request for service protocol, password guessing can be used to impersonate a client.

The keys used in the Kerberos exchange are also vulnerable. The client's secret key is stored temporarily on the client workstation and is susceptible to compromise, as are the session keys that are stored at the client's computer and at the servers.

Kerberos will be explained using the terminology and symbols given in Table 1.3.

**Table 1.3**  Kerberos Items and Symbols

| KERBEROS ITEM | SYMBOL |
|---|---|
| Client | $C$ |
| Client secret key | $K_c$ |
| Client network address | $A$ |
| Server | $S$ |
| Client/TGS session key | $K_{c, tgs}$ |
| TGS secret key | $K_{tgs}$ |
| Server secret key | $K_s$ |
| Client/server session key | $K_{c, s}$ |
| Client/TGS ticket | $T_{c, tgs}$ |
| Client to server ticket | $T_{c, s}$ |
| Client to server authenticator | $A_{c, s}$ |

**Table 1.3** *(continued)*

| KERBEROS ITEM | SYMBOL |
|---|---|
| Starting and ending time ticket is valid | V |
| Timestamp | T |
| M encrypted in secret key of x | $[M] K_x$ |
| Ticket Granting Ticket | TGT |
| Optional, additional session key | Key |

### Kerberos Client-TGS Server Initial Exchange

To initiate a request for service from a server, s, the user enters an ID and password on the client workstation. The client temporarily generates the client's secret key, $K_c$, from the password using a one-way hash function. The client sends a request for authentication to the TGS server using the client's ID in the clear. Note that no password or secret key is sent. If the client is in the Authentication Server database, the TGS server returns a client/TGS session key, $K_{c,tgs}$, encrypted in the secret key of the client and a Ticket Granting Ticket (TGT) encrypted in the secret key of the TGS server. Thus, neither the client nor any other entity except the TGS server can read the contents of the TGT because $K_{tgs}$ is known only to the TGS server. The TGT is made up of the client ID, the client network address, the starting and ending time the ticket is valid, and the client/TGS session key. Symbolically, these initial messages from the TGS server to the client are represented as follows:

$$[K_{c,tgs}]K_c$$
$$TGT = [c, a, v, K_{c,tgs}]K_{tgs}$$

The client decrypts the message containing the session key, $K_{c,tgs}$, with its secret key, $K_c$, and will now use this session key to communicate with the TGS server. The client then erases its stored secret key to avoid compromise of the secret key.

### Kerberos Client to TGS Server Request for Service

When requesting access to a specific service on the network from the TGS server, the client sends two messages to the TGS server. For one message, the client submits the previously obtained TGT that is encrypted in the secret key of the TGS server and an identification of the server, s, from which service is requested. The other message is an authenticator encrypted in the assigned session key, $K_{c,tgs}$. The authenticator contains the client ID, a timestamp, and an optional additional session key. These two messages are as follows:

$$TGT = s, [c, a, v, K_{c,tgs}]K_{tgs}$$
$$Authenticator = [c, t, key]K_{c,tgs}$$

### Kerberos TGS Server to Client Issuing of Ticket for Service

After receiving a valid TGT and authenticator from the client requesting a service, the TGS server issues a ticket, $T_{c,s}$, to the client encrypted in the server's secret key, $K_s$, and a client/server session key, $K_{c,s}$, encrypted in the client/TGS session key. These two messages are as follows:

Ticket $T_{c,s} = s, [c, a, v, K_{c,s}]K_s$

$[K_{c,s}]K_{c,tgs}$

### Kerberos Client to Server Authentication Exchange and Providing of Service

To receive service from the server, s, the client sends the Ticket, $T_{c,s}$, and an authenticator to the server. The server decrypts the message with its secret key, $K_s$, and checks the contents. The contents contain the client's address, the valid time window, v, and the client/server session key, $K_{c,s}$, which will now be used for communication between the client and server. The server also checks the authenticator and, if that timestamp is valid, will provide the requested service to the client. The client messages to the server are as follows:

Ticket $T_{c,s} = s, [c, a, v, K_{c,s}]K_s$

Authenticator $= [c, t, key]K_{c,s}$

In addition to SSO, another important aspect of a security architecture is the implementation of policies specifying the access rights of subjects to objects. Three popular approaches to implementing access policies are discussed in the following section.

## DAC/MAC/RBAC

Discretionary access control (DAC), mandatory access control (MAC), and role-based access control (RBAC) are important mechanisms used to define the access privileges that subjects have to objects.

### Discretionary Access Control

In discretionary access control, an authority, within limitations, can specify what objects can be accessed by a subject. A common approach is using access control lists (ACLs), as discussed earlier in this chapter. With an ACL, subjects and objects are listed along with the privileges that the subjects are assigned with respect to the objects. Access control lists are applicable when the designated authority needs the discretion to specify the resources that certain subjects are permitted to access.

When a user, within certain limitations, has the right to alter the access control to certain objects, this is termed a *user-directed* discretionary access control.

*Identity-based* access control is a type of discretionary access control that is based on the identity of the individual.

### Mandatory Access Control

In *mandatory access control*, a subject's access to an object is dependent on labels. In the military context, a subject has a *clearance* and an object has a *classification*. (In a nonmilitary environment, the word *sensitivity* is usually used instead of classification.) Thus, the subject's clearance can be compared to the object's classification to determine if the subject can access the object. For example, the military labels documents as Unclassified, Confidential, Secret, and Top Secret. Similarly, an individual can receive a clearance of Confidential, Secret, or Top Secret and can have access to documents classified at or below his or her specified clearance level. Thus, an individual with a clearance of Secret can have access to Secret documents, Confidential documents, and Unclassified documents, with a restriction. This restriction is that the individual must have a need-to-know relative to the classified documents involved. *Need-to-know* refers to the restriction that the subject must have the information in order to complete the subject's assigned task. Even if the individual is cleared for a classification level, unless there is a need-to-know, the individual should not access the information. A detailed discussion of document classification is presented later in this chapter in the "National Security" section.

A type of mandatory access control is rule-based access control. In *rule-based* access control, access is determined by rules (such as the correspondence of clearance labels to classification labels) and not by the identity of the subjects and objects alone.

A method of implementing mandatory access control is through the use of the concept known as the *Trusted Computing Base* (TCB). The TCB is the total combination of protection mechanisms in a computer system, which includes the hardware, software, and firmware that are trusted to enforce a security policy. The *security perimeter* is the boundary that separates the TCB from the remainder of the system. A *trusted path* must also exist so that a user can access the TCB without being compromised by other processes or users. A *trusted computer system* is one that employs the necessary hardware and software assurance measures to enable its use in processing multiple levels of classified or sensitive information. This system meets the specified requirements for reliability and security.

A related concept to the TCB is the reference monitor. The *reference monitor* is a system component that enforces access controls on an object. It is an abstract machine that mediates all access of subjects to objects. The *security kernel* is defined as the hardware, firmware, and software elements of a trusted computing base that implement the reference monitor concept. The security kernel must do the following:

- Mediate all accesses
- Be protected from modification
- Be verified as correct

### Role-Based Access Control (RBAC)

In *role-based* access control, a central authority determines what individuals can have access to which objects based on the individual's role or title in the organization. This approach is especially useful in an organization where there are frequent personnel changes. Thus, role-based access control privileges do not need to be changed whenever a new person takes over a role or title in the organization.

*Task-based* access is control is similar to role-based access control, but the controls are based on the subject's responsibilities and duties.

A third type of control that is similar to that of role-based is *lattice-based* access control. This type of control is based on the lattice model, in which there are pairs of elements that have a least upper bound of values and a greatest lower bound of values. Relative to access control, the pair of elements is the subject and object, and, accordingly, the subject has the greatest lower bound and the least upper bound of access rights to an object.

Role-based, task-based, and lattice-based access controls are sometimes grouped under the heading of *nondiscretionary* access controls.

## Cryptographic Techniques

Cryptography is the art and science of hiding the meaning of a communication from unintended recipients. The word "cryptography" comes from the Greek, *kryptos* (hidden) and *graphein* (to write). A message in unencrypted form is called *plaintext* and is called *ciphertext* after it has been encrypted. An unintended receiver of the message tries to obtain the plaintext from the ciphertext or tries to determine the *key* or *cryptovariable* that is used to encipher the plaintext message. These acts are defined as *cryptanalysis*. The amount of effort that is required to recover the plaintext from the ciphertext is called the *work factor*. The higher the work factor, the more difficult is the recovery process.

Cryptography and cryptanalysis make up the field of *cryptology*. The encryption and decryption processes can be summarized in the following equations, where E is the encryption transformation, D is the decryption transformation, M is the plaintext message, and C is the ciphertext. The letter K shows that encryption and decryption are a function of the key or cryptovariable, K.

Encryption    $E(M,K) = C$

Decryption    $D(C,K) = D[E(M,K),K] = M$

The transformations described in these equations are called a *cryptosystem*. It is also important to note the difference between a cipher and a code. A *cipher* is a transformation that operates on bits, and a *code* operates on phrases or words.

If the encrypted message is sent from the point of origin to its final destination, it is termed an *end-to-end encryption*. Another approach, called *link encryption*, requires that each sender/receiver node have keys in common with its two neighboring nodes in a transmission chain. In operation, a node receives an encrypted message from its predecessor node, decrypts the message, and then re-encrypts it with a different key that is common to the successor node. Then, the encrypted message is sent on to the successor node, where the process is repeated until the final destination is reached. Link encryption does not protect the information if the nodes along the transmission path are compromised.

The encryption system that has been used over the centuries requires that the sender and receiver share a common secret key. That key is used to encrypt the message and is also needed to decrypt the message. This type of encryption is called *symmetric key* or *private key* encryption. The problem that has to be addressed with secret key encryption is secure distribution of the key. The keys for particular days can be distributed in codebooks, by courier, specifying letters in particular pages of a book, or other out-of-band messaging schemes. *Out-of-band messaging* refers to sending information, such as a key, by different means than the encrypted message. For example, the secret key could be sent by conventional mail while the encrypted message is sent electronically. As one might expect, there are numerous ways that a message can be encrypted.

A straightforward means of encryption that is used in a number of symmetric key algorithms is the *Exclusive Or (XOR)* function. In binary logic systems, the XOR function operates as follows:

- If two input bits are identical, the output of the XOR function is a logical 0.
- If two input bits are different, the output of the XOR function is a logical 1.

Thus, if a plaintext message is made up of the string of bits 11010110 and we apply the cryptovariable string of 11101101 to the plaintext message through an XOR function, the ciphertext is produced as follows:

```
Plaintext        11010110
Cryptovariable   11101101
Ciphertext       00111011
```

A useful characteristic of the XOR function is that if the XOR function using the same cryptovariable is applied to the ciphertext, the original plaintext will be generated. This feature is illustrated as follows using the previous example:

```
Ciphertext        00111011
Cryptovariable    11101101
Plaintext         11010110
```

Therefore, the same hardware and/or software can be used for encryption and decryption. The XOR function lends itself to hardware implementation because it is simple to implement using basic Boolean operations.

Cryptographers have long theorized about the possibility of the sender and receiver having different keys such that each key of the pair could be used to encrypt or decrypt a message. If one of these keys was made public, then anyone could encrypt a message with the public key and send it to the person with the other corresponding key of the pair. If the receiver's key were kept private, then the receiver would be the only person who could decrypt the ciphertext. Thus, the problem of transmitting secret keys would not exist. This approach is called *asymmetric key* or *public key* cryptography. In 1976, Whitfield Diffie and Martin Hellman published a seminal paper [Whitfield Diffie and Martin Hellman, "New Directions in Cryptography," IEEE Transactions on Information Theory, Vol. IT-22 (November 1976), pp. 644–54]. This paper described a method whereby two users could securely exchange a secret key over a nonsecure medium. This paper laid the groundwork for the development of public key cryptography. Symmetric key and asymmetric key cryptography will be discussed in the following sections.

### Symmetric Key Cryptography

Symmetric key cryptography uses a secret key to encrypt a message, and the same secret key has to be used by the receiver to decrypt the message. Thus, the key is a shared secret between the sender and the receiver. Symmetric key encryption has the following general characteristics:

- Faster than asymmetric (public key) encryption, which will be discussed in the next section (approximately 1000 to 10,000 times faster).
- Useful in encrypting large volumes of data.
- Because the sender and receiver must share the same secret key, the sender must have a different secret key for use with each different receiver.
- A secure means has to be used to transmit the secret key from the sender to the receiver.

Symmetric key encryption algorithms have evolved and gained in sophistication over the centuries. The following discussions provide an overview of the most common symmetric algorithms, including the latest cryptosystems in use today.

The *substitution cipher* simply involves substituting one letter of the alphabet for another. In the classic Caesar cipher, the key is shifting the alphabet three letters to the right. Thus, the letter A would be encrypted into the letter D, the letter B would be encrypted into the letter E and so on. Thus, the word FIG would be encrypted into the word ILJ. To decrypt the message, the reverse procedure would be followed. Because only one alphabet is used, this type of substitution is called a *monoalphabetic substitution*. A substitution cipher is attacked using frequency analysis. In this approach, the frequency of occurrence of particular letters in a language can be used to deduce the letters in the plaintext message from the ciphertext.

In an improvement over the monoalphabetic substitution cipher, the *polyalphabetic substitution* cipher uses multiple alphabets in the substitution process. The French diplomat Blaise de Vigenère, born in 1523, developed a very effective polyalphabetic cipher comprising 26 alphabets. Because multiple alphabets are used, the polyalphabetic cipher counters frequency analysis because the same letter in the plaintext is not always converted into the same letter in the ciphertext. Attacks on polyalphabetic ciphers, however, are based on determining the period when the substitution repeats by starting over with the first alphabet.

The German Enigma rotor machine that was used in World War II employed rotors to effect a polyalphabetic substitution cryptosystem.

*Transposition, or permutation* as it is sometimes called, simply involves the transposition of the plaintext letters. By transposing the letters, an anagram is generated. A simple example of transposition is rearranging the letters of the plaintext HOW ARE YOU into OAYHURWEO. Deciphering this short sentence is fairly easy, but the difficulty of rearranging the transposed text back to its original order increases drastically as the sentences get longer and longer. Keep in mind that the longer the plaintext that is subject to transposition, the more difficult it is to communicate the key to the intended receiver. Two examples of transposition in which the key is easy to understand are the rail fence transposition and columnar transposition. In rail fence transposition, the plaintext is written on two lines. For example, applying the rail fence transposition to the plaintext message NOW IS THE TIME yields:

```
N   W   S   H   T   M
  O   I   T   E   I   E
```

Then, the lower part of the text is concatenated onto the upper text to yield the enciphered message

```
NWSHTMOITEIE
```

The ciphertext is converted back into the plaintext by reversing the process.

In columnar transposition, the plaintext message is written in horizontal fashion and read vertically to generate the ciphertext. Thus, the sentence NOW IS THE TIME can be written horizontally:

```
N O W I
S T H E
T I M E
```

By reading the letters vertically, the ciphertext of NSTOTIWHMIEE is produced.

The *one-time pad* is an unbreakable symmetric cipher that has the following characteristics:

- The key is a series of letters that is as long as the message.
- The sequence of letters in the key is truly random, and there are no repeating patterns.
- A particular key should be used once and only once.

The principle of the one-time pad was developed around 1918 by Major Joseph Mauborgne, who was in charge of cryptographic research for the U.S. Army. A machine that implemented the one-time pad using the XOR function was developed by Gilbert S. Vernam at AT&T. The one-time pad is sometimes known as the Vernam cipher. If the key to the one-time pad is random and the key is used only once, the one-time pad is unbreakable.

Most approaches to symmetric or secret key cryptography use complex algorithms that are made up of a series of substitutions, transpositions, Exclusive Or operations, and various shifting and rotating of key components and plaintext. In general, most symmetric key cryptosystems assume the following information is known to the public:

- The algorithm used to encrypt the plaintext message
- A copy of plaintext and the associated ciphertext
- In some cases, an encipherment of plaintext chosen by a possible attacker

Information that has to be protected from disclosure is the key or crypto-variable and the particular cryptographic transformation that is used out of the many possible transformations using the specified algorithm.

The *Data Encryption Standard* (DES) was adopted in 1977 as the U.S. government cryptosystem for use in commercial, nonclassified applications. DES uses a symmetric key algorithm called the Data Encryption Algorithm (DEA). DEA is based on the Lucifer algorithm developed by Horst Feistel and his team at IBM. DES and DEA are described in the U.S. Federal Information Processing Standard (FIPS) Publication 46-1.

DES is a block cipher because it segregates the plaintext into 64-bit blocks and applies the key and encryption algorithm to each block. The DEA of DES uses a 56-bit key plus 8 additional parity bits. DES uses 16 rounds of substitution and transposition in the DEA.

DES was recertified by the U.S. National Institute of Standards and Technology (NIST) in 1993, but it has not been used by the U.S. government since 1998. DES has been replaced by the Advanced Encryption Standard (AES) as a result of the vulnerability of DES to brute force attacks. With a 56-bit key, one would have to try $2^{56}$ or 70 quadrillion possible keys in this attack. This trial-and-error approach can be accomplished by using networks of very large numbers of computers. Even though DES has been replaced by AES, DES variants are still in use, and DES employs many fundamental concepts of symmetric key algorithms. A version of DES, called Triple-DES, uses three encryptions. Triple-DES is very secure and is used in many nonclassified applications.

The *Advanced Encryption Standard* (AES) is a block cipher that has replaced DES, but it is anticipated that Triple-DES will remain an approved algorithm for U.S. government use. The AES initiative was announced in January 1997 by the National Institute of Standards and Technology (NIST), and candidate encryption algorithm submissions were solicited. On August 29, 1998, 15 AES candidates were announced by NIST. In 1999, NIST announced 5 finalist candidates. These candidates were MARS, RC6, Rijndael, Serpent, and Twofish. NIST closed Round 2 of public analyses of these algorithms on May 15, 2000.

On October 2, 2000, NIST announced the selection of *the Rijndael Block Cipher*, developed by the Belgian cryptographers Dr. Joan Daemen and Dr. Vincent Rijmen, as the proposed AES algorithm. Rijndael was formalized as the Advanced Encryption Standard (AES) on November 26, 2001 as Federal Information Processing Standard Publication 197. FIPS PUB 197 states "This standard may be used by Federal departments and agencies when an agency determines that sensitive (unclassified) information (as defined in P.L. 100-235) requires cryptographic protection. Other FIPS-approved cryptographic algorithms may be used in addition to, or in lieu of, this standard." AES is made up of the three key sizes, 128, 192, and 256 bits, with a fixed block size of 128 bits. Depending on which of the three keys is used, the standard may be referred to as "AES-128," "AES-192," or "AES-256." It is expected that AES will be adopted by other private and public organizations inside and outside of the United States.

The Rijndael algorithm was designed to have the following properties:

- Resistance against all known attacks
- Design simplicity
- Code compactness and speed on a wide variety of platforms

The Rijndael Block Cipher is suited for the use in high-speed chips and in a compact coprocessor on a smart card.

In decimal terms, for the Rijndael algorithm, there are approximately $3.4 \times 10^{38}$ possible 128-bit keys, $6.2 \times 10^{57}$ possible 192-bit keys, and $1.1 \times 10^{77}$ possible 256-bit keys.

The *International Data Encryption Algorithm* (IDEA) cipher is another symmetric key cryptosystem. It operates on 64-bit plaintext blocks and uses a 128-bit key. It employs a block encryption algorithm that was developed by James Massey and Xuejia Lai. (X. Lai, "On the Design and Security of Block Ciphers," *ETH Series on Information Processing*, v.1, Konstanz: Hartung-Gorre Verlag, 1992).

The IDEA algorithm performs 8 rounds and operates on 16-bit sub-blocks using algebraic calculations that are amenable to hardware implementation. With its 128-bit key, an IDEA cipher is much more difficult to crack than DES. IDEA operates in the modes described for DES and is applied in the Pretty Good Privacy (PGP) email encryption system that was developed by Phil Zimmerman.

### Asymmetric Key Cryptography

In asymmetric key cryptography, there are two separate, different keys that are related mathematically. One key is held by the sender, and the other is held by the receiver. This key pair has the characteristic that a message encrypted with one of the keys can be decrypted by the other and vice versa.

As discussed earlier in this section, in its development of the key exchange method over a nonsecure medium, the Diffie-Hellman paper provided the foundation for the development of asymmetric or, as it also known, public key cryptography.

A fundamental concept in public key cryptography is that of the one-way function. A *one-way function* is a function that is easy to compute in one direction, but very difficult or impossible to reverse. If the function $y = f(z)$ is a one-way function, it would be very easy to compute y given z, but very difficult to compute z given y. For some one-way functions, a *trapdoor* exists, that enables one to easily calculate z, given y. One-way functions are used to generate the key pairs used in asymmetric key cryptography.

As we discussed previously, in asymmetric or public key cryptography, the sender and receiver have two different keys. These keys, though, are related mathematically. For example, if Alice and Bob wish to send encrypted messages to each other, Alice will have a public key, known to everybody, and a private key, known only to her. Similarly, Bob will have his own private key that is known only to him and a corresponding public key that is known to everyone. The public and private keys have the properties that if a plaintext message is encrypted with one of the keys, the message can be decrypted using the other key. Because the public and private keys are generated using a one-way function, it is very difficult or impossible to derive a private key from its corresponding public key.

For Alice to send a secret message to Bob, Alice would encrypt the message with Bob's public key, which is known to everybody, and send it to Bob. Because Bob has the private key that is mathematically related to his public key, Bob can decrypt the message. No one else can decrypt the message unless he or she knows Bob's private key. Also, the encryption process using the public key is a one-way function in that the public key cannot decrypt the message that was encrypted with the public key. In thinking about this process, a number of questions and issues arise. One question is, how do I know that the public key posted for everyone to read as Bob's public key is really Bob's? It could be someone else who says it is Bob's and has the corresponding private key to read messages that people think they are sending to Bob. One solution is to have a trusted certificate authority (CA) that verifies Bob's identity and his corresponding public key. This topic will be discussed in a later section. Also, the relationship between a public and private key can also serve to authenticate the source of a message. If Bob uses his private key to encrypt a plaintext message, his public key is the only other key that can decrypt the message. Therefore, if his public key does decrypt the message, the message had to be sent by Bob. Again, we are assuming the Bob's public key has been certified to be his public key. This operation does not protect the message because anyone can read it using Bob's public key, but it does authenticate Bob as the source of the message.

A number of popular algorithms are used to generate the public and private keys used in public key cryptography that have the desired properties. The principal ones are discussed in the following sections.

The *RSA algorithm* is based on the difficulty of factoring a number that is the product of two prime numbers. As a one-way function, it is easy to multiply two large prime numbers to obtain their product, but it is difficult to factor a very large number to obtain its prime factors. Thus, the difficulty of obtaining the public key from the private key is based on the difficulty of obtaining the prime factors of a large number. There is a general-purpose factoring algorithm, the Number Field Sieve (NFS), which can be used to factor large numbers. A version of NFS has successfully factored a 155-digit number. So, if the product of two prime factors is on the order of 200 digits, at least as of this writing, the RSA algorithm is safe from factoring attacks.

RSA is derived from the last names of its inventors, Rivest, Shamir, and Addleman (R. L. Rivest, A. Shamir, and L. M. Addleman, "A Method for Obtaining Digital Signatures and Public -Key Cryptosystems," *Communications of the ACM*, v. 21, n.2, February 1978, pp. 120–126). RSA can be used for encryption, key exchange, and digital signatures.

Building on the Diffie-Hellman key exchange method, Dr. T. El Gamal developed a public key cryptosystem based on the difficulty of finding discrete logarithms in a finite field. In a simplified example, given g and x, it is not difficult to find $y = g^x$. Given y and g, however, it is much more difficult to find x. The *El Gamal algorithm* can be used for encryption and digital signatures. It is described in T. El Gamal, "A Public-Key Crypto System and a Signature Scheme Based on Discrete Logarithms," *Advances in Cryptography: Proceedings of CRYPTO 84*, Springer-Verlag, 1985, pp. 10–18.

The *elliptic curve algorithm* is another approach to a one-way function that implements public key cryptography. It is based on the following equation for an elliptic curve:

$y^2 = x^3 + ax + b$ along with a single point O, the point at infinity

Elliptic curves are analogous to the discreet logarithm problem and are usually defined over finite fields. The elliptic curve has the properties that the operation of addition performed in the elliptic curve space is analogous to modular multiplication and the operation of multiplication is analogous to modular exponentiation.

The elliptic curve public key cryptography system was developed independently by Neal Koblitz (N. Koblitz, "Elliptic Curve Cryptosystems," *Mathematics of Computation*, v. 48, n. 177, 1987, pp. 203–209) and V.S. Miller (V.S. Miller, "Use of Elliptic Curves in Cryptography," *Advances in Cryptology-CRYPTO '85 Proceedings*, Springer-Verlag, 1986, pp. 417–426).

One of the main advantages of elliptic curve systems is that equivalent levels of security to RSA and discreet logarithm implementations can be achieved with a smaller key size. This characteristic is a result of the increased difficulty in finding discreet logarithms using elliptic curves as opposed to finding conventional discreet logarithms or factoring the product of prime numbers. For example, a 160-bit key using the elliptic curve cryptosystem is equivalent to a 1024-bit key in the RSA cryptosystem. The elliptic curve approach lends itself to implementation in hardware in applications such as smart cards.

The *Merkle-Hellman Knapsack* is a one-way function that is based on the difficulty of determining which combination of available weights will total a specific weight. A good way to visualize this problem is to assume that there exists a fixed set of balls of different weights. If we place a subset of the balls into a knapsack, we can easily determine the total weight of the balls in the knapsack by summing the weights of those balls. However, the reverse operation can be much more difficult. Given the total weight of the balls in the knapsack, the problem would be to find which subset of balls must be in the knapsack.

The Merkle-Hellman Knapsack one-way function is described in R.C. Merkle and M. Hellman, "Hiding Information and Signatures in Trapdoor Knapsacks," *IEEE Transactions on Information Theory*, v.24, n. 5, September 1978, pp. 525–530.

### Digital Certificates

Whatever algorithm is used in public key cryptography, it is critical that the public key for an individual that is available to all is really the public key of the stated individual. A digital certificate from a trusted, third-party CA can verify that the public key is that of the named individual. The CA accomplishes this certification by digitally signing the individual's public key and associated information. Digital signatures are discussed in detail later in this chapter.

A CA acts as notary by verifying a person's identity and issuing a certificate that vouches for a public key of the named individual. This certification agent signs the certificate with its own private key. The certificate is then sent to a Repository, which holds the certificates and Certificate Revocation Lists (CRLs) that denote the revoked certificates. To verify the CA's signature, its public key must be cross-certified with another CA.

The integration of digital signatures and certificates, and the other services required for e-commerce, is called the *Public Key Infrastructure* (PKI). These services provide integrity, access control, confidentiality, authentication, and non-repudiation for electronic transactions. The PKI includes the following elements:

- Digital certificates
- Certificate Authority (CA)
- Registration authorities
- Policies and procedures
- Certificate revocation
- Non-repudiation support
- Timestamping
- Lightweight Directory Access Protocol (LDAP)
- Security-enabled applications
- Cross-certification

In PKI, a repository is usually referred to as a directory. The directory contains entries associated with an object class. An object class can refer to individuals or other computer-related entities. The class defines the attributes of the object. Attributes for PKI are defined in RFC 2587, Internet X.509 Public Key Infrastructure LDAP v2 Schema by Boeyen, Howes and Richard, published in 1999. Additional information on attributes can be found in RFC 2079, Definition of an X.500 Attribute Type and an Object Class to Hold Uniform Resource Identifiers (URLs) by M. Smith, published in January 1997.

The X.509 certificate standard defines the authentication basis for the X.500 Directory. The X.500 Directory stores information about individuals and objects in a distributed database residing on network servers. Some of the principal definitions associated with X.500 are the following:

- Directory User Agents (DUAs)—clients
- Directory Server Agents (DSAs)—servers
- Directory Service Protocol (DSP)—enables information exchanges between DSAs
- Directory Access Protocol (DAP)—enables information exchanges from a DUA to a DSA
- Directory Information Shadowing Protocol (DISP)—used by a DSA to duplicate or "shadow" some or all of its contents

DSAs accept requests from anonymous sources as well as authenticated requests. They share information through a chaining mechanism.

The *Lightweight Directory Access Protocol* (LDAP) provides a standard format to access the certificate directories. These directories are stored on LDAP servers on a network, and the servers on these networks provide public keys and corresponding X.509 certificates for the enterprise. A directory contains information such as the individuals' names, addresses, phone numbers, and public key certificates. LDAP enables a user to search these directories over the Internet. A series of standards under X.500 defines the protocols and information models for computer directory services that are independent of the platforms and other related entities.

The primary security concerns relative to LDAP servers are availability and integrity. For example, denial of service attacks on an LDAP server could prevent access to the Certification Revocation Lists and, thus, permit the use of a revoked certificate for transactions.

The Lightweight Directory Access Protocol was developed as a more efficient version of DAP and has evolved into a version 2 (Yeong, Y., T. Howes, and S. Killie, Lightweight Directory Access Protocol, RFC 1777, 1995). LDAP servers communicate through referrals—that is, a directory receiving a request for information it does not have will query the tables of remote directories. If it finds a directory with the required entry, it sends a referral to the requesting directory. LDAP v2 does not have chaining and shadowing capabilities, but additional protocols can be obtained to provide these functions.

The DAP protocol in X.500 was unwieldy and led to most client implementations using LDAP. LDAP version 3 is under development with extensions that will provide shadowing and chaining capabilities.

The original X.509 certificate (CCITT, The Directory–Authentication Framework, Recommendation X.509, 1988) was developed to provide the authentication foundation for the X.500 Directory. Since then, a version 2, a version 3, and a recent version 4 have been developed. Version 2 of the X.509 certificate addresses the reuse of names, version 3 provides for certificate extensions to the core certificate fields, and version 4 provides yet additional extensions. These extensions can be used as needed by different users and different applications. A version of X.509 that takes into account the requirements of the

Internet was published by the IETF (Housley, R., W. Ford, W. Polk, and D. Solo, Internet X.509 Public Key Infrastructure Certificate and CRL Profile, RFC 2459, 1999).

A basic format of an X.509 Certificate has been defined by the Consultation Committee, International Telephone and Telegraph, International Telecommunications Union (CCITT-ITU)/ International Organization for Standardization (ISO).

Some of the different types of certificates that are issued are the following:

**CA certificates.**   Issued to CAs and that contain the public keys used to verify digital signatures on CRLs and certificates.

**End entity certificates.**   Issued to entities that are not CAs and that contain the public keys that will be needed by the user of the certificate to perform key management or verify a digital signature.

**Self-issued certificates.**   Issued by an entity to itself to establish points of trust and to distribute a new signing public key.

**Rollover certificates.**   Issued by a CA to transition from an old public key to a new public key.

### Key Management and Control

As noted earlier, distribution of secret keys in symmetric key encryption poses a problem. Secret keys can be distributed using asymmetric key cryptosystems. Other means of distributing secret keys are face-to-face meetings to exchange keys and sending the keys by secure messenger or some other, secure, alternate channel. Another method is to encrypt the secret key with another key, called a *key encryption key*, and send the encrypted secret key to the intended receiver. These key encryption keys can be distributed manually, but they need not be distributed often. The X9.17 Standard (ANSI X9.17 [Revised], "American National Standard for Financial Institution Key Management [Wholesale]," American Bankers Association, 1985) specifies key encryption keys as well as data keys for encrypting the plaintext messages.

Key distribution can also be accomplished by splitting the keys into different parts and sending each part by a different medium. In large networks, distribution of keys can become a large problem because in an N-person network, the total number of key exchanges is $N(N-1)/2$. Using public key cryptography or the creation and exchange of session keys that are valid only for a particular session and time are useful mechanisms for managing the key distribution problem.

Keys can be updated by generating a new key from an old key. If two people share a secret key, they can apply the same transformation function, say a hash algorithm, to their common secret key and obtain a new secret key.

Another aspect of key management is revocation of keys. A digital certificate contains a timestamp or period for which the certificate is valid. Also, if a key is compromised or must be made invalid because of business or personnel-related issues, it must be revoked. Therefore, the CA maintains a certificate revocation list of all invalid certificates; users should examine this list regularly. Because continued use of the same key makes it vulnerable to compromise, keys should be changed at specified intervals. The frequency of changing the key is a direct function of the value of the data being encrypted and transmitted. Also, if the same secret key is used to encrypt valuable data over a relatively long period of time, the larger the volume of data that will be compromised when the key is broken. Another important concern if the key is not changed frequently is that an attacker can intercept and change messages and, therefore, send different messages to the receiver. When keys have been in use for long periods of time and are replaced by others, they should be destroyed. Keys that are stored on disks or EEPROMS should be overwritten numerous times, or the storage device itself should be destroyed. Older keys stored by the operating system in various locations in memory also have to be searched out and destroyed.

Managing the distribution of public keys is another critical issue that has to be addressed. As discussed earlier in this section, a CA is a form of centralized key management. It is a central location that issues certificates and maintains CRLs. An alternative is distributed key management where a "chain of trust" or "web of trust" is set up among users who know each other. Because they know each other, they can trust that each one's public key is valid. Then, some of these users may know other users and verify their public key. Thus, the "chain" will spread outward from the original group. This arrangement results in an informal verification procedure that is based on people knowing and trusting each other.

For national security and crime-fighting purposes, governments want the ability to "listen in" to encrypted transmissions. To avoid privacy and civil liberties issues, the *escrowing* of encryption keys with "trusted" agencies has been proposed. The keys could then be retrieved to monitor encrypted transmissions only after obtaining a valid court order. Most approaches involve dividing the secret key into multiple parts and escrowing each part with a different agency.

A specific example of escrowed encryption is the U.S. Escrowed Encryption Standard (National Institute of Standards and Technology, NIST FIPS PUB 185, "Escrowed Encryption Standard," U.S. Department of Commerce, February 1994). This standard proposed the adoption of the Clipper cryptosystem for telephone communications and the Capstone cryptosystem for computer communications. The telephone-related standard is implemented in tamper-proof hardware as the Clipper chip. The Clipper chip uses the declassified Skipjack symmetric key algorithm for encryption. The Skipjack key is 80 bits in length, which is weak in terms of the computational power available with today's technology.

The U.S. government used the Clipper and Capstone standards for its own communications and required organizations doing business with the U.S. government to use these standards. It was hoped that other businesses would use the standards on a voluntary basis. Because of privacy and civil liberty concerns, the Escrowed Encryption Standard was not a success and was not widely adopted as hoped for by the U.S. government. The obvious concern related to escrowed encryption in general is the possibility of the escrow agencies divulging the private keys under government pressure or by corrupt employees.

In order to address some of these concerns, Sylvio Micali proposed a key escrow system that would be administered by voluntary trustees or businesses in different countries rather than by government agencies. His approach (S. Micali, "Fair Cryptosystems," MIT/LCS/TR-579.b, MIT Laboratory for Computer Science, November 1993) also provides for a validity test of each escrowed portion of the key without requiring the other parts of the key.

Because symmetric key cryptosystems are faster than asymmetric key cryptosystems, they are excellent for encrypting and transmitting large volumes of data—for example, a digitized motion picture. Symmetric key cryptosystems, though, suffer from the problem of securely distributing the secret key(s). Asymmetric key cryptosystems have eliminated the problem of distributing secret keys because two keys, public and private, are used for encrypting and decrypting the transmissions. The drawback of the asymmetric key cryptosystem is that it is computationally intensive and not well suited for transmitting large amounts of data. By combining private and public key cryptosystems in one application, we can have the best of both worlds. The public key cryptosystem can be used to securely distribute the secret key of a symmetric key cryptosystem. Then, the data can be encrypted and decrypted using the symmetric key algorithm. This approach is called a *hybrid* cryptosystem.

An excellent example of such a hybrid system is Pretty Good Privacy (PGP) developed by Phil Zimmerman in the late 1980s. The name was derived from Ralph's Pretty Good Groceries, a sponsor of the radio show, "Prairie Home Companion," hosted by Garrison Keillor. Zimmerman put together a hybrid system using the RSA asymmetric key algorithm to encrypt and distribute the secret key of the IDEA symmetric key cipher that, in turn, was used to encrypt and transmit the data. Zimmerman developed a user-friendly interface that did not require the user to understand cryptography in detail and that handled the key generation issues in a manner transparent to the user. Zimmerman was concerned about the ability of governments to monitor the transmissions of ordinary citizens and saw PGP as a tool that these citizens could use to protect their privacy. In 1991, Zimmerman gave his PGP system to a friend to post on a Usenet bulletin board. From there, it spread all over the world and was praised by human rights groups as a godsend in protecting private information from government monitoring. In 1993, however, the U.S. government investigated Zimmerman and accused him of illegally exporting software that was on the government's munitions list. Items on this required an export license from the U.S. State Department. Eventually, the issue was resolved, and Zimmerman was not punished because, technically, he had not exported the software but gave it to a friend who posted it on an Internet bulletin board.

Instead of using a certification agency for validation of a person's public key, PGP uses a "web of trust" where users and groups can certify keys to each other.

## Cryptographic Attacks

An attacker applies cryptanalysis to obtain the plaintext or the key from the ciphertext. The following is a list of some common attacks:

**Birthday attack.**   Usually applied to the probability of two different messages using the same hash function that produces a common message digest, or given a message and its corresponding message digest, finding another message that when passed through the same hash function generates the same specific message digest. The term "birthday" comes from the fact that in a room with 23 people, the probability of two or more people having the same birthday is greater than 50 percent.

**Brute force.**   Trying every possible combination of key patterns—the longer the key length, the more difficult it is to find the key with this method.

**Chosen ciphertext.**   Portions of the ciphertext that are selected for trial decryption while having access to the corresponding decrypted plaintext.

**Adaptive chosen ciphertext.**   A form of a chosen ciphertext attack where the selection of the portions of ciphertext for the attempted decryption is based on the results of previous attempts.

**Chosen plaintext.**   Chosen plaintext that is encrypted, and the output ciphertext is obtained.

**Adaptive chosen plaintext.**   A form of a chosen plaintext attack where the selection of the plaintext is altered according to the previous results.

**Ciphertext only.**   An attack in which only the ciphertext is available.

**Differential cryptanalysis.**   Applied to private key cryptographic systems by looking at ciphertext pairs, which were generated through the encryption of plaintext pairs, with specific differences and analyzing the effect of these differences.

**Linear cryptanalysis.**   Using pairs of known plaintext and corresponding ciphertext to generate a linear approximation of a portion of the key.

**Differential linear cryptanalysis.**   Using both differential and linear approaches.

**Factoring.**   Using a mathematical approach to determine the prime factors of large numbers.

**Known plaintext.**   An attack in which the attacker has a copy of the plaintext corresponding to the ciphertext.

**Man-in-the-middle.**   An attacker taking advantage of the store-and-forward nature of most networks by intercepting messages and forwarding modified versions of the original message while in between two parties attempting secure communications.

**Meet-in-the-middle.**   Is applied to double encryption schemes by encrypting known plaintext from one end with each possible key (K) and comparing the results "in the middle" with the decryption of the corresponding ciphertext with each possible K.

**Statistical.**   Exploiting the lack of randomness in key generation.

### Steganography

Where cryptography attempts to protect a message by encryption, steganography attempts to pass information by hiding the existence of a message. The word *steganography* comes from the Greek words *steganos*, meaning "covered," and *graphein*, meaning "to write." Examples of steganography are the use of invisible ink; the microdot, which compresses a message into the size of a period or dot; and changing the least significant bit of each word in a digital image. The image is essentially unaffected, but the secret information is transmitted. Steganography can also be used to make a digital "watermark" to detect the illegal copying of digital images.

One major problem with steganography is that, if the hidden message is somehow found, it is easily read and the secret information is available to anyone.

## *Digital Signatures*

In addition to encryption, public key algorithms can be used to develop digital signatures that verify the integrity and source of a message. To accomplish this signing, *hash functions* are used. The hash function has been used extensively in computer science applications. It takes an input of variable length and generates an output of fixed length called a message digest (MD). Symbolically, this operation can be represented as

$$H(M)=MD$$

in which M is the message, H is the hash function applied to the message, and MD is the output message digest.

For a hash function to be useful in cryptography, the output should uniquely represent the input. Thus, if the message input to the hash function changes, the message digest should change also. In addition, the hash function should be one-way in that it should be easy to generate the MD from the message, but very difficult or impossible to generate the message from the MD. Therefore, in summary, a strong hash algorithm should have the following characteristics:

1.  It should be computationally infeasible to find two messages that produce a common message digest—that is, $H(M1) \neq H(M2)$.

2.  If there exists a message and its corresponding message digest, it should be computationally infeasible to find another message that generates that specific message digest.

3.  It should be computationally infeasible to find a message that corresponds to a given message digest.

4.  The message digest should be calculated using all of the data in the original message.

Items 1 and 2 seem to be identical, but there is a subtle difference between them. Item 1 describes the case where two messages can hash to ANY common message digest. This situation is usually referred to as a *collision*. Item 2 refers to the situation where a message and its specific message digest exist and an attacker attempts to find another message that hashes to that specific message digest. These two items are important because message digests are used in digital signatures to uniquely represent the messages from which they were generated. If another message could be found that generates the same message digest as the original message, then this other message could be substituted for the original message to deceive the receiver. In item 3, the message digest is generated by a one-way function in that the original message should not be able to be generated from its corresponding message digest.

Attacks relating to items 1 and 2 are referred to as *birthday attacks*. The birthday analogy to item 1 would state that "If there is a room filled with N people, what is the value of N that would result in a better than 50/50 chance of two people having a common birthday?" Again, we are not looking for a specific birth date, but ANY birthday shared by two individuals. The answer to this question is N = 23. With 23 people in a room, there are $N(N-1)/2$ or 253 pairs of individuals in the room.

Similarly, the attack represented by item 2 would require 253 people in the room to have a better than 50/50 chance of another person having the same birthday as a specific individual in the room.

To resist birthday attacks, a hash function should generate a message digest of at least 128 bits. For example, the Secure Hash Algorithm—1 (SHA-1) defined in FIPS 180 (National Institute of Standards and Technology, NIST FIPS PUB 180, "Secure Hash Standard, " U.S. Department of Commerce, May 1993) generates a message digest of 160 bits for any message less than 264 bits in length. Another example of a hash algorithm is Message Digest 5 (MD5) developed by Ron Rivest (R.L. Rivest, "The MD5 Message Digest Algorithm," RFC 1321, April 1992). MD5 generates a 128-bit message digest. A third hash algorithm that produces a variable-length message digest is HAVAL (Y. Zheng, J Pieprzyk, and J. Seberry, "HAVAL-A One-Way Hashing Algorithm with Variable Length of Output," *Advances in Cryptology-AUSCRYPT '92 Proceedings*, Springer-Verlag, 1993). HAVAL can produce message digests of 128, 160, 192, 224, or 256 bits in length.

Hash algorithms can also use keys to control the generation of the message digest from the input message. Then, only an individual with the key used in the generation of the message digest can verify that the hash function sent with an original message is correct. An example of a keyed hash algorithm is a *message authentication code* or MAC. MACs are used to verify that files sent between users have not been altered en route. To accomplish this authentication, a hash or MAC of a message is generated using a keyed hash algorithm, and the MAC is appended to the message prior to transmission. At the receiving end, the MAC is generated from the received message and compared to the MAC sent with the message. If the MACs generated at the transmitting and receiving ends are identical, the message is authenticated.

By applying hash functions with public key encryption, digital signatures can be generated. Digital signatures, which are implemented with public key algorithms, provide for detection of unauthorized or accidental modifications of the transmitted message as well as authentication of the identity of the sender. Thus, digital signatures support non-repudiation. The concept of Bob sending a digitally signed message to Alice is summarized as follows:

Using a one-way hash algorithm, Bob generates a message digest, MD, of the plaintext message. Recall that a strong hash algorithm will generate a fixed-length message digest that uniquely characterizes the message from a message input of variable length. Typical message digests are 128, 160, or 256 bits in length.

- Bob encrypts MD with his private key.
- Bob attaches MD to his original plaintext message.
- Bob sends the message with the appended MD digest to Alice.
- Alice decrypts MD using Bob's public key. If Bob's public key "opens" the message digest, this verifies that Bob was the originator of the message. (We assume that Bob's public key was certified to be his by an independent certification agency.)

- Alice then takes the message that was sent with MD and generates a message digest, MD', using the same hash algorithm used by Bob to generate MD at the transmitting end.

- If MD' = MD, then the message integrity has been preserved, indicating that the message was not modified en route.

The U.S. National Institute of Standards and Technology (NIST) describes its digital signature standard, DSS, in FIPS PUB 186, "Digital Signature Standard," U.S. Department of Commerce, May 1994. The standard states "Digital signatures are used to detect unauthorized modifications to data and to authenticate the identity of the signatory. In addition, the recipient of signed data can use a digital signature in proving to a third party that the signature was in fact generated by the signatory." DSS uses either the RSA digital signature algorithm or the Digital Signature Algorithm (DSA). DSA was developed by Claus Schnorr (C. P. Schnorr, "Efficient Signature Generation for Smart Cards," *Advances in Cryptology-CRYPTO '89 Proceedings*, Springer-Verlag, 1990, pp. 239–252).

The RSA digital signature algorithm and the DSA use the Secure Hash Algorithm (SHA-1) described in FIPS 180 (National Institute of Standards and Technology, NIST FIPS PUB 180, "Secure Hash Standard," U.S. Department of Commerce, May 1993).

SHA-1 sequentially processes blocks of 512 bits and generates a message digest of 160 bits in length when any message less than 264 bits is provided as an input. As with any good, strong hash algorithm, SHA-1 has the properties that do the following:

- It is computationally infeasible to find a message that corresponds to a given message digest.

- It is computationally infeasible to find two different messages that produce the same message digest.


# Roles and Responsibilities

Controls are often defined by the job or role an employee plays in an organization. A role refers to an individual's title, position, and responsibilities in the organization. The human resources director is a role in an organization. A group is a subset of the organization that operates under a common policy and management. For example, the organization's human resources department is a group.

In addition to the information classification roles defined earlier in the chapter, each of these roles and groups has data security rights and responsibilities. Roles and responsibilities are central to the concept of "separation of duties"— the concept that security is enhanced through the division of responsibilities in the production cycle. It is important that individual roles and responsibilities are clearly communicated and understood (see Table 1.4).

**Senior or executive management.** Assigned the overall responsibility for the security of information. Senior management might delegate the function of security, but they are viewed as the end of the food chain when liability is concerned.

**Information systems security professionals.** Delegated the responsibility for implementing and maintaining security by the senior-level management. Their duties include the design, implementation, management, and review of the organization's security policy, standards, guidelines, and procedures.

**Owner.** A manager who is responsible for specific organizational information. The owner should not be an IT person, but a manager with business responsibilities. The owner is responsible for ensuring that the appropriate security controls are in place, for assigning the initial classification to the data to be protected, for approving access requests from other parts of the organization, and for periodically reviewing the data classifications and access rights. Data owners are primarily responsible for determining the data's sensitivity or classification levels. They can also be responsible for maintaining the information's accuracy and integrity.

**Information custodian.** Has responsibilities for backup, retention, and recovery of data. The information owner delegates these responsibilities to the custodian.

**User supervisor.** The immediate manager of a user. This manager has the responsibilities for user information, including user IDs, informing other relevant organizational entities of a change in status of the individual, reporting of security incidents, and coordinating security awareness training.

**Table 1.4** Common Roles and Responsibilities

| ROLE | DESCRIPTION |
| --- | --- |
| Senior manager | Has the ultimate responsibility for security |
| InfoSec officer | Has the functional responsibility for security |
| Owner | Determines the data classification |
| Custodian | Preserves the information's C.I.A. |
| User/operator | Performs in accordance with (IAW) the stated policies |
| Auditor | Examines security |

**Users.**   Responsible for following the procedures set out in the organization's security policy during the course of their normal daily tasks.

**Information systems auditors.**   Responsible for providing reports to the senior management on the effectiveness of the security controls by conducting regular, independent audits. They also examine whether the security policies, standards, guidelines, and procedures effectively comply with the company's stated security objectives.

## Polices and Procedures

Computer security policy is often defined as the "documentation of computer security decisions." The term "policy" has more than one meaning. Policy is senior management's directives to create a computer security program, establish its goals, and assign responsibilities. The term "policy" is also used to refer to the specific security rules for particular systems. Additionally, "policy" may refer to entirely different matters, such as the specific managerial decisions setting an organization's email privacy policy or fax security policy.

A security policy is an important document to develop while designing an information system, early in the System Development Life Cycle (SDLC). The security policy begins with the organization's basic commitment to information security formulated as a general policy statement. The policy is then applied to all aspects of the system design or security solution.

Security policies are the basis for sound security implementation. Often organizations will implement technical security solutions without first creating a foundation of policies, standards, guidelines, and procedures, which results in unfocused and ineffective security controls.

### Policy Statements

A good, well-written policy is an essential and fundamental element of sound security practice. A policy, for example, can literally be a lifesaver during a disaster, or it might be the result of a requirement of a governmental or regulatory function. A policy can also provide protection from liability due to an employee's actions or can form a basis for the control of trade secrets.

When we refer to specific polices rather than a group "policy," we generally refer to those policies that are distinct from the standards, procedures, and guidelines. As you can see from the policy hierarchy chart in Figure 1.4, policies are considered the first and highest level of documentation, from which the lower-level elements of standards, procedures, and guidelines flow. This order, however, does not mean that policies are more important than the lower elements. You should create these higher-level policies, which are the more general policies and statements, first in the process for strategic reasons, and then the more tactical elements can follow.

**Figure 1.4**  Policy hierarchy.

An organizational security policy is a general statement of management's intent, and its implementation is mandatory. This high-level policy comprises the following:

- An acknowledgment of the importance of the computing resources to the business model
- A statement of support for the information security throughout the enterprise
- A commitment to authorize and manage the definition of the lower-level standards, procedures, and guidelines

Below the general organization policies are the *functional policies* guiding implementation. *Standards* are compulsory and define the use of specific hardware and software technologies in a uniform manner. *Procedures* are detailed, step-by-step actions that are required to be accomplished. *Baselines* describe how to implement security mechanisms to ensure that security is being accomplished in a uniform manner on the various platforms and operating systems throughout the enterprise. The use of adopted baselines is compulsory. *Guidelines* are noncompulsory, recommended actions and take into account the different types of information systems.

Let's look a little more closely at these policy distinctions.

### Senior Management Statement of Policy

The first policy of any policy creation process is the senior management statement of policy. This text is a general, high-level statement of a policy that contains the following elements:

- An acknowledgment of the importance of the computing resources to the business model

- A statement of support for information security throughout the enterprise

- A commitment to authorize and manage the definition of the lower-level standards, procedures, and guidelines

Fundamentally important to any security program's success is the senior management's high-level statement of commitment to the information security policy process and a senior management's understanding of how important security controls and protections are to the enterprise's continuity. Senior management must be aware of the importance of security implementation to preserve the organization's viability (and for their own "due care" protection) and must publicly support that process throughout the enterprise.

### Regulatory Policy

Regulatory policies are security policies that an organization must implement due to compliance, regulation, or other legal requirements. These companies might be financial institutions, public utilities, or some other type of organization that operates in the public interest. These policies are usually very detailed and are specific to the industry in which the organization operates.

Regulatory policies commonly have two main purposes:

- To ensure that an organization is following the standard procedures or base practices of operation in its specific industry.

- To give an organization the confidence that it is following the standard and accepted industry policy.

### Advisory Policy

Advisory policies are security policies that are not mandated to be followed but are strongly suggested, perhaps with serious consequences defined for failure to follow them (such as termination, a job action warning, and so forth). A company with such policies wants most employees to consider these policies mandatory. Most policies fall under this broad category.

These policies can have many exclusions or application levels. Thus, these policies can control some employees more than others, according to their roles and responsibilities within that organization. For example, a policy that requires a certain procedure for transaction processing might allow for an alternative procedure under certain, specified conditions.

### Informative Policy

Informative policies are policies that exist simply to inform the reader. There are no implied or specified requirements, and the audience for this information could be certain internal (within the organization) or external parties. This situation does not mean that the policies are authorized for public consumption, but that they are general enough to be distributed to external parties (vendors accessing an extranet, for example) without a loss of confidentiality.

Penalties might be defined for the failure to follow a policy, however, such as the failure to follow a defined authorization procedure without stating what that policy is and then referring the reader to another more detailed and confidential policy.

### System Security Policy

As per NIST, managerial computer system security policies may be categorized into three basic types:

**Program policy.**    Used to create an organization's computer security program.

**Issue-specific policies.**    Used to address specific issues of concern to the organization.

**System-specific policies.**    Technical directives taken by management to protect a particular system.

Program policy and issue-specific policy both address policy from a broad level, usually encompassing the entire organization. They do not provide sufficient information or direction, for example, to be used in establishing an access control list or in training users on what actions are permitted. System-specific policy fills this need. System-specific policy is much more focused because it addresses only one system. Table 1.5 helps illustrate the difference between these three types of policies.

**Table 1.5**   System Security Policy

| POLICY TYPE | DESCRIPTION | EXAMPLE |
| --- | --- | --- |
| Program policy | High-level program policy | Senior-level management statement |
| Issue-specific policy | Addresses single issue | Email privacy policy |
| System-specific policy | Single-system directives | Router access control lists |

**Password Management Policy**

The management of passwords is key to the protection of sensitive information held on computers. Passwords are the primary means of authentication for most users. Best practices have evolved for managing and using passwords, and these practices should be applied in a networked computing environment. The following list summarizes these practices:

- An organization should have a clear password policy, and the employees should know this policy.
- The organization should enforce the password policy.
- A password should be a minimum of eight random alphanumeric characters. No common words, names, or phrases should be used that are associated with the user.
- After a specified number of unsuccessful logon attempts, usually three, the logon session should be terminated or the time to allow the next logon attempt should be increased.
- Passwords should be protected and not written down and placed in easily observable locations.
- Passwords should be changed at specified periods. The frequency of the changing of passwords is a function of the sensitivity of the information to be protected. On the average, a password should be changed every 90 days.
- When there is an extended period of inactivity in a session, the session should be terminated and the logon process repeated to regain entry into the system.
- The date and time of the last successful logon should be displayed. This information can alert the user to an unauthorized logon when the user was absent from the workstation.
- Passwords and IDs should not be shared and should be unique for each user.
- When an employee is terminated, his or her account on the system should be terminated. Also, the passwords of other employees who have worked with this individual should also be changed because the terminated employee may know their passwords.
- For increased security, dynamic password generators should be used.
- For remote logon situations, authentication protocols such as CHAP should be used.

### Disposal/Destruction Policy

Storage media such as disks or tapes can be a source of compromise of sensitive information if they are not disposed of in the correct manner. Proper disposal of media after use is required to prevent *data remanence*. Remanence is defined as the residual information remaining on the media after erasure, which may be subject to restoration by another user.

Computer forensics experts can retrieve data from disks that have been formatted, broken, or even burned. Such techniques are used by law enforcement personnel to discover evidence and to construct a trail of misuse. Anytime a storage medium is reused (and also when it is discarded), there is the potential for the media's information being recovered. Methods must be employed to properly destroy the existing data to ensure that no residual data is on the media.

**Clearing.** Refers to the overwriting of data media (primarily magnetic) intended to be reused in the same organization or monitored environment.

**Purging.** The degaussing or overwriting media intended to be removed from a monitored environment, such as during resale (laptops) or donations to charity.

**Destruction.** Refers to completely destroying the media and, therefore, the residual data. Paper reports, diskettes, and optical media (CD-ROMs) need to be physically destroyed before disposal.

It should be noted that erasing the data through an operating system does not remove the data; it just changes the File Allocation Table and renames the first character of the file. This is the primary method used by computer forensics investigators to restore files. Also, damaged sectors of a disk may not be overwritten by the format utility. Degaussing may have to be used, or formatting seven times is recommended.

Another vulnerability associated with media is that rewriting files on top of old files may not overwrite all data areas on the disk. This situation may occur because the new file may not be as long as the older file and data may be able to be retrieved past the file-end control character. Other concerns are the improper operation of degaussing equipment and the failure to format media with sensitive information at least seven times.

### Human Resources Policy

Information security can be severely affected by human resource and administrative policies. For example, a good human resource policy is to have an individual working in a sensitive area take vacation time in large increments instead of one day here and a day there. The reason is that if someone is involved in unauthorized activities, the chances of being discovered are increased if that individual is away for an extended period and someone else has to take over his or her duties. Similarly, background checks before hiring an individual are a must. Background checks are common sense, but it is startling to find out how many organizations do not conduct these checks or conduct weak ones. Individuals with criminal records, bad conduct at other places of employment, or other telltale signs should not be considered for work in places where they may have access to sensitive information.

Another extremely important area is having well-thought-out policies and procedures in place to handle termination of employees. The termination could be friendly or unfriendly. In the termination interview, the employee should be reminded of the conditions in the employment agreement document that he or she signed when he or she first started working for the organization. These conditions usually include nondisclosure of proprietary information, possible restrictions on working for a direct competitor for a period of time, returning all documents and related material to the organization when leaving, turning in keys, and so on. In reference to keys, cryptographic keys have to be taken into account. If the individual being terminated has encrypted files on his or her computer, the individual must provide the employer with the decryption keys so that the information can be retrieved. All computer accounts assigned to the individual must be closed, and all passwords that the individual knows for information system accounts must be changed.

## Standards, Guidelines, and Procedures

The next level down from policies is the three elements of policy implementation: *standards*, *guidelines*, and *procedures*.

These three elements contain the actual details of the policy, such as how they should be implemented and what standards and procedures should be used. They are published throughout the organization via manuals, the intranet, handbooks, or awareness classes.

It is important to know that standards, guidelines, and procedures are separate yet linked documents from the general policies (especially the senior-level statement). Unfortunately, companies will often create one document that satisfies the needs of all of these elements. This situation is not good. There are a few good reasons why you should keep them separate:

- Each of these elements serves a different function and focuses on a different audience. Also, physical distribution of the policies is easier.

- Security controls for confidentiality are different for each policy type. For example, a high-level security statement might need to be available to investors, but the procedures for changing passwords should not be available to anyone who is not authorized to perform the task.

- Updating and maintaining the policy is much more difficult when all the policies are combined into one voluminous document. Mergers, routine maintenance, and infrastructure changes all require that the policies be routinely updated. A modular approach to a policy document will keep the revision time and costs down.

*Standards* specify the use of specific technologies in a uniform way. Standardizing operating procedures can benefit an organization by specifying the uniform methodologies to be used for the security controls. Standards are usually compulsory and are implemented throughout an organization for uniformity. Examples of standards are IEEE 802.11, EIA RS-232, and RS-422. Standards are mandatory.

*Baselines* take into consideration the difference between various operating systems, for example, to ensure that the security is being uniformly implemented throughout the enterprise. If adopted by the organization, baselines are compulsory. A uniform technical baseline specified across the enterprise can be institutionalized and can become a standard.

*Guidelines* are similar to standards. They refer to the methodologies of securing systems, but they are recommended actions only and are not compulsory. Guidelines are more flexible than standards and take into consideration the varying nature of the information systems. Guidance or guidelines are normally provided to the staff members to direct and clarity how the policy can be followed. You can use guidelines to specify the way standards should be developed, for example, or to guarantee the adherence to general security principles.

*Procedures* embody the detailed steps that you follow to perform a specific task. Procedures are the detailed actions that personnel must follow. They are considered the lowest level in the policy chain. Their purpose is to provide the detailed steps for implementing the policies, standards, and guidelines previously created.

## Administrative Policy Controls

In the information security arena, policies require administrative controls to protect information systems. These controls can be very effective in screening personnel, controlling access to sensitive information, and detecting violations of the security policies.

### Acceptable Use

An acceptable or appropriate use policy details the conditions that a user must agree to in order to use an account on an information system. The account might have access to an organization's network or be with an outside organization, such as an Internet Service Provider (ISP). Users signing up for an account must agree to the stated policy provisions. Examples of such provisions are the following:

- The user must be at least 18 years of age and legally able to agree to the terms of the acceptable use policy.

- The user must agree to use the account for the uses permitted by the account. For example, an employee of a company usually has to agree not to use the account for purposes other than company business.

- The user must take full responsibility for his or her actions in using the account and accepts all recourses for his or her actions.

- The owner of the account is fully responsible for any charges incurred by the use of the account.

- The user must agree not to use the account to obtain materials that are found to be illegal or contravene acceptable use policies and standards.

### Due Care

The concept of due care or due diligence requires that an individual or organization engage in good business practices relative to the organization's industry. The practice of due diligence for an individual is related to the legal, *prudent man rule* that requires senior officials to perform their duties with the care that ordinary, prudent people would exercise under similar circumstances. Due care may be a legal requirement in some cases.

### Separation of Duties

Separation of duties divides responsibility among a number of different individuals. For example, a check issued by a company for over a certain amount would require the signatures of three different individuals. Thus, for fraud to take place, collusion among the three individuals must occur. To put it in different terms, collusion must be forced to occur if a violation of policy is to take place.

In many organizations, the same individual is the systems administrator and information security director. This arrangement gives the individual almost total control of the information systems and makes the systems vulnerable to actions that could be taken by this individual. Following the doctrine of separation of duties, one individual should be assigned the systems administrator role and another should be assigned the information security responsibilities. Separation of duties is sometimes called *segregation of duties*.

A related concept is that of *least privilege*. The principle of least privilege states that an individual should be given the minimum amount of privileges required for that person to perform his or her assigned job. Also, these privileges should be assigned for the minimum amount of time necessary for performance of the assigned tasks.

**Need to Know**

The concept of need to know is usually associated with government classifications of materials and the clearances of individuals to access those materials. It is similar to the least privilege principle. Even though an individual has the proper clearance to access documents of a particular classification, that individual is not permitted to access that information if he or she does not have a need to know the information. For example, a military personnel officer may have a Secret clearance and, thus, can access documents that are classified as Secret or below. If that officer does not have a need to know certain types of Secret information, the officer is not permitted to access that information. In our example, the military personnel officer would be authorized access to personnel records classified as Secret but would not be authorized access to Secret information describing a new air defense weapons system. That officer does have a need to know the Secret material describing the new weapons system to perform his or her job.

## Policies and Ethics

An individual's ethics are a function of his or her cultural heritage, homeland, religion, and numerous other intangibles. People violate ethical computing standards by making assumptions that they really are not harming anyone.

Many crackers rationalize intrusions and illegally gaining access to proprietary information as harmless because no physical property is stolen. Their credo is "information should be free." Others are of the opinion that hacking into an organization's information systems is performing a service by alerting the organization to weaknesses in its system safeguards. Such thinking is wrong because it is difficult to predict what can happen to information if unauthorized persons gain access to networks and browse files. Breaches of security can result in millions of dollars in losses to an organization through the destruction or unavailability of critical data and resources or through stock devaluation. From the national perspective, destructive cracker behavior could seriously affect a nation's critical infrastructure, economic health, and national security.

In an attempt to formalize ethical behavior relative to information systems and information systems security, a number of organizations have developed and published ethical guidelines. Certified professionals in any field and, particularly, in the field of information systems security are held to higher standard of ethical conduct. In order to instill proper computing behavior, ethics should be incorporated into an organizational ethical computing policy.

Some typical ethical codes follow.

### The Computer Ethics Institute's Ten Commandments of Computer Ethics

1. Thou shalt not use a computer to harm other people.

2. Thou shalt not interfere with other people's computer work.

3. Thou shalt not snoop around in other people's computer files.

4. Thou shalt not use a computer to steal.

5. Thou shalt not use a computer to bear false witness.

6. Thou shalt not copy or use proprietary software for which you have not paid.

7. Thou shalt not use other people's computer resources without authorization or the proper compensation.

8. Thou shalt not appropriate other people's intellectual output.

9. Thou shalt think about the social consequences of the program you are writing for the system you are designing.

10. Thou shalt use a computer in ways that ensure consideration and respect for your fellow humans.

### (ISC)² Code of Ethics

Certified Information Systems Security Professionals (CISSPs) shall:

1. Conduct themselves in accordance with the highest standards of moral, ethical, and legal behavior.

2. Not commit or be a party to any unlawful or unethical act that may negatively affect their professional reputation or the reputation of their profession.

3. Appropriately report activity related to the profession that they believe to be unlawful and shall cooperate with resulting investigations.

4. Support efforts to promote understanding and acceptance of prudent information security measures throughout the public, private, and academic sectors of our global information society.

5. Provide competent service to their employers and clients, and shall avoid any conflicts of interest.

6. Execute responsibilities in a manner consistent with the highest standards of their profession.

7. Not misuse the information in which they come into contact during the course of their duties, and they shall maintain the confidentiality of all information in their possession that is so identified.

### The Internet Activities Board (IAB) Ethics and the Internet (RFC 1087)

The IAB states that "Access to and use of the Internet is a privilege and should be treated as such by all users of the system."

Any activity is defined as unacceptable and unethical that purposely:

1. Seeks to gain unauthorized access to the resources of the Internet.
2. Destroys the integrity of computer-based information.
3. Disrupts the intended use of the Internet.
4. Wastes resources such as people, capacity, and computers through such actions.
5. Compromises the privacy of users.
6. Involves negligence in the conduct of Internet-wide experiments.

### The U.S. Department of Health, Education, and Welfare Code of Fair Information Practices

The United States Department of Health, Education, and Welfare has developed the following list of fair information practices that focuses on the privacy of individually, identifiable personal information.

1. There must not be personal data record-keeping systems whose very existence is secret.
2. There must be a way for a person to find out what information about them is in a record and how it is used.
3. There must be a way for a person to prevent information about them, which was obtained for one purpose, from being used or made available for another purposes without their consent.
4. Any organization creating, maintaining, using, or disseminating records of identifiable personal data must ensure the reliability of the data for their intended use and must take precautions to prevent misuses of that data.

# Legal and Regulatory

As stated in the goal for this domain, business objectives and strategies must be aligned with applicable laws and regulations. For example, the Federal Sentencing Guidelines address information security and the associated responsibilities of senior management as follows:

- Provide punishment guidelines for those found guilty of breaking federal law.

- Treat the unauthorized possession of information without the intent to profit from the information as a crime.

- Address both individuals and organizations.

- Make the degree of punishment a function of the extent to which the organization has demonstrated due diligence (due care or reasonable care) in establishing a prevention and detection program.

- Place responsibility on senior organizational management for the prevention and detection programs with fines of up to $290 million for nonperformance.

## Information Security Management Due Diligence

The concept of *due diligence* or *due care* requires that an individual or organization engage in good business practices relative to the organization's industry. The practice of due diligence for an individual is related to the legal, *prudent man rule* that requires senior officials to perform their duties with the care that ordinary, prudent people would exercise under similar circumstances. Another, similar definition of due diligence is the level of judgment, care, and prudence that a person would reasonably be expected to do under particular circumstances.

A typical information security-related due diligence checklist would include the following items:

- Does the organization have an information security policy that is up to date and known by the members of the organization?

- Has the organization conducted security awareness training programs at regular intervals?

- Is the organization's intellectual property adequately protected? In particular, are trade secrets given the protections required and are the individuals who handle these secrets adequately trained?

- Have the confidentiality, integrity, and availability of critical information been adequately protected by physical, administrative, and technical means?

## Privacy

Privacy is the right of an individual to protection from unauthorized disclosure of the individual's personally identifiable information (PII). For example, the Health Insurance Portability & Accountability Act (HIPAA) lists the following 16 items as a person's individual identifiers:

- Names
- Postal address information, other than town or city, state, and zip code
- Telephone numbers
- Fax numbers
- Electronic mail addresses
- Social security numbers
- Medical record numbers
- Health plan beneficiary numbers
- Account numbers
- Certificate/license numbers
- Vehicle identifiers and serial numbers, including license plate numbers
- Device identifiers and serial numbers
- Web Universal Resource Locators (URLs)
- Internet Protocol (IP) address numbers
- Biometric identifiers, including finger and voice prints
- Full face photographic images and any comparable images

An individual's right to privacy is embodied in the following fundamental principles of privacy:

- *Notice* regarding collection, use, and disclosure of PII
- *Choice* to opt out or opt in regarding disclosure of PII to third parties
- *Access* by consumers to their PII to permit review and correction of information
- *Security* to protect PII from unauthorized disclosure
- *Enforcement* of applicable privacy policies and obligations

## Privacy Policy

Organizations develop and publish privacy policies that describe their approach to handling PII. Web sites of organizations usually have their privacy policies available to read online, and these policies usually cover the following areas:

- Statement of the organization's commitment to privacy
- The type of information collected, such as name, address, credit card number, phone numbers, etc.
- Retaining and using email correspondence

- Information gathered through cookies and Web server logs and how that information is used
- How information is shared with affiliates and strategic partners
- Mechanisms to secure information transmissions, such as encryption and digital signatures
- Mechanism to protect PII stored by the organization
- Procedures for review of the organization's compliance with the privacy policy
- Evaluation of information protection practices
- Means for the user to access and correct PII held by the organization
- Rules for disclosing PII to outside parties
- Providing PII that is legally required

### Privacy-Related Legislation and Guidelines

The following list summarizes some important legislation and recommended guidelines for privacy:

- The *Cable Communications Policy Act* provides for discretionary use of PII by cable operators internally, but it imposes restrictions on disclosures to third parties.
- The *Children's Online Privacy Protection Act* (COPPA) is aimed at providing protection to children under the age of 13.
- *Customer Proprietary Network Information Rules* apply to telephone companies and restricts their use of customer information both internally and to third parties.
- The *Financial Services Modernization Act (Gramm-Leach-Bliley)* requires financial institutions to provide customers with clear descriptions of the institution's policies and procedures for protecting the PII of customers.
- The *Telephone Consumer Protection Act* restricts communications between companies and consumers, such as in telemarketing.
- The *1973 U.S. Code of Fair Information Practices* states that:
  1. There must not be personal data record-keeping systems whose very existence is secret.
  2. There must be a way for a person to find out what information about him or her is in a record and how it is used.
  3. There must be a way for a person to prevent information about him or her, which was obtained for one purpose, from being used or made available for another purposes without his or her consent.

4. Any organization creating, maintaining, using, or disseminating records of identifiable personal data must ensure the reliability of the data for their intended use and must take precautions to prevent misuses of that data.

■ The *Health Insurance Portability and Accountability Act* (HIPAA), Administrative Simplification Title, includes Privacy and Security Rules and standards for electronic transactions and code sets.

■ The *European Union* (EU) has defined privacy principles that include the following:

1. Data should be collected in accordance with the law.

2. Information collected about an individual cannot be disclosed to other organizations or individuals unless authorized by law or by consent of the individual.

3. Records kept on an individual should be accurate and up to date.

4. Individuals have the right to correct errors contained in their personal data.

5. Data should be used only for the purposes for which it was collected, and it should be used only for a reasonable period of time.

6. Individuals are entitled to receive a report on the information that is held about them.

7. Transmission of personal information to locations where "equivalent" personal data protection cannot be assured is prohibited.

■ The *Organization for Economic Cooperation and Development* (OECD) has issued guidelines that are summarized as follows:

1. There should be limits to the collection of personal data, and any such data should be obtained by lawful and fair means.

2. Personal data should be relevant to the purposes for which it is to be used, and, to the extent necessary for those purposes, should be accurate, complete, and kept up-to-date.

3. The purposes for which personal data are collected should be specified not later than at the time of data collection.

4. Personal data should not be disclosed, made available, or otherwise used for purposes other than those specified.

5. Personal data should be protected by reasonable security safeguards against such risks as loss or unauthorized access, destruction, use, modification, or disclosure of data.

6. There should be a general policy of openness about developments, practices, and policies with respect to personal data.

7. An individual should have the right to obtain information from a data controller concerning data that the controller might be holding relative to the individual.

8. A member country should refrain from restricting transborder flows of personal data between itself and another member country except where the latter does not yet substantially observe these guidelines or where the re-export of such data would circumvent its domestic privacy legislation.

9. A member country may also impose restrictions in respect of certain categories of personal data for which its domestic privacy legislation includes specific regulations in view of the nature of those data and for which the other member country provides no equivalent protection.

## Electronic Monitoring

Additional privacy issues involve keystroke monitoring, email monitoring, surveillance cameras, badges, and magnetic entry cards. Key points in electronic monitoring are that the monitoring is conducted in a lawful manner and that it is applied in a consistent fashion. With email, for example, an organization monitoring employees' email should do the following:

- Inform all that email is being monitored by means of a prominent logon banner or some other frequent notification. This banner should state that by logging on to the system, the individual consents to electronic monitoring and is subject to a predefined punishment if the system is used for unlawful activities or if the user violates the organization's information security policy. It should also state that unauthorized access and use of the system is prohibited and subject to punishment.

- Ensure that monitoring is uniformly applied to all employees.

- Explain what is considered acceptable use of the email system.

- Explain who can read the email and how long it is backed up.

- Not provide a guarantee of email privacy.

## The Platform for Privacy Preferences (P3P)

The Platform for Privacy Preferences was developed by the World Wide Web Consortium (W3C) to implement privacy practices on Web sites. The W3C P3P Specification states "P3P enables Web sites to express their privacy practices in a standard format that can be retrieved automatically and interpreted easily by user agents. P3P user agents will allow users to be informed of site practices (in both machine- and human-readable formats) and to automate decision-making based on these practices when appropriate. Thus users need not read the privacy policies at every site they visit."

The latest W3C working draft of P3P is P3P 1.0, January 28, 2002 (www. w3.org/TR). With P3P, an organization can post its privacy policy in machine-readable form (XML) on its Web site. This policy statement should include the following:

- Who has access to collected information
- The type of information collected
- How the information is used
- The legal entity making the privacy statement

The specification of P3P 1.0 contains the following items:

- A standard vocabulary for describing a Web site's data practices
- A set of data elements that Web sites can refer to in their P3P privacy policies
- A standard schema for data a Web site may wish to collect, known as the "P3P base data schema"
- A standard set of uses, recipients, data categories, and other privacy disclosures
- An XML format for expressing a privacy policy
- A means of associating privacy policies with Web pages or sites and cookies
- A mechanism for transporting P3P policies over HTTP

A useful consequence of implementing P3P on a Web site is that Web site owners are required to answer multiple-choice questions about their privacy practices. This activity will cause the organization sponsoring the Web site to think about and evaluate its privacy policy and practices in the event that it has not already done so. After answering the necessary P3P privacy questions, an organization can then proceed to develop its policy. A number of sources provide free policy editors and assistance in writing privacy policies. Some of these resources can be found at www.w3.org/P3P/ and http://p3ptoolbox.org/.

P3P also supports user agents that allow a user to configure a P3P-enabled Web browser with the user's privacy preferences. Then, when the user attempts to access a Web site, the user agent compares the user's stated preferences with the privacy policy in machine-readable form at the Web site. Access will be granted if the preferences match the policy. Otherwise, either access to the Web site will be blocked or a pop-up window will appear notifying the user that he or she must change his or her privacy preferences. Microsoft's

Internet Explorer 6 (IE6) Web browser supports P3P and can be used to generate and display a report describing a particular Web site's P3P-implemented privacy policy.

Another P3P implementation is provided by AT&T's Privacy Bird software that is an add-on to a browser and inserts an icon of a bird in the top right corner of a user's Web browser. The AT&T software reads the XML privacy policy statements from a Web site and causes the bird to chirp and change color to inform the user if the user's listed privacy preference settings are satisfied by the Web site's P3P policy statements. Clicking on the bird provides more detailed information concerning mismatches between the Web site's policy practices and the user's provided preferences.

## Restrictions on Cryptography

Governments and law enforcement agencies are concerned that the unrestricted availability of strong encryption products will make it more difficult to monitor the communications of criminals and terrorists and gather evidence to thwart their activities and bring them to justice. The United States had stringent export restrictions on certain cryptographic systems to prevent encryption from being widely used as a means to conceal communications of terrorists and lawbreakers. In January of 2000, the United States issued a document describing the revision of export controls (Revisions to Encryption Items, RIN: 0694-AC11, U.S. Department of Commerce, Bureau of Export Administration, January 10, 2000). This document described new rules that eased the export restrictions on encryption systems. To quote the summary section of this document:

"This rule amends the Export Administration Regulations (EAR) to allow the export and reexport of any encryption commodity or software to individuals, commercial firms, and other non-government end-users in all destinations. It also allows exports and reexports of retail encryption commodities and software to all end-users in all destinations. Post-export reporting requirements are streamlined, and changes are made to reflect amendments to the Wassenaar Arrangement. This rule implements the encryption policy announced by the White House on September 16 and will simplify U.S. encryption export rules. Restrictions on terrorist supporting states (Cuba, Iran, Iraq, Libya, North Korea, Sudan or Syria), their nationals and other sanctioned entities are not changed by this rule."

As a result of this change in the EAR, in July of 2000, the United States announced a relaxation of its encryption export policy. To quote the President's Chief of Staff, John D. Podesta, "Under our new policy, American companies can export any encryption product to any end user in the European Union and eight other trading partners. We're also speeding up the time to market by eliminating the thirty-day waiting period when exporting encryption goods to these countries."

# Warranties, Patents, Copyrights, Trade Secrets

Information security managers have to be familiar with warranty and intellectual property laws and issues in order to effectively safeguard an organization's critical information. Mishandling of data that is the lifeblood of an organization and that has great value in the marketplace and to competitors can severely damage an organization and open its officers to liability suits. In this section, basic information will be provided on the laws relating to intellectual property and the serviceability of a product provided to a customer.

## *Warranties*

A warranty is a contract that commits an organization to stand behind its product. There are two types of warranties, implied and express. An *implied* warranty is an unspoken, unwritten promise created by state law that goes from a manufacturer or merchant to the customer. Under implied warranties, there are two categories—the implied warranty of fitness for a particular purpose and the implied warranty of merchantability. The implied warranty of *fitness for a particular purpose* is a commitment made by the seller when the consumer relies on the advice of the seller that the product is suited for a specific purpose. The implied *warranty of merchantability* is the seller's or manufacturer's promise that the product sold to the consumer is fit to be sold and will perform the functions that it is intended to perform. An *express* warranty is a warranty that is explicitly offered by the manufacturer or seller to the customer at the time of the sales transaction. This type of warranty contains voluntary commitments to remedy defects and malfunctions that some customers may encounter in using the product. An express warranty can be made orally or in writing. If it is in writing, it falls under the Magnuson-Moss Warranty Act.

The Magnuson-Moss Warranty Act is the 1975 U.S. federal law that governs warranties on consumer products. The act requires manufacturers and sellers of consumer products to provide consumers with detailed information concerning warranty coverage. In addition, the FTC adopted three rules under the act. These rules are the Rule on Disclosure of Written Consumer Product Warranty Terms and Conditions (the Disclosure Rule), the Rule on Pre-Sale Availability of Written Warranty Terms (the Pre-Sale Availability Rule), and the Rule on Informal Dispute Settlement Procedures (the Dispute Resolution Rule). These rules and the act detail three basic requirements that apply to a warrantor or seller. These requirements are as follows:

1. A warrantor must designate, or title, the written warranty as either "full" or "limited."

2. A warrantor must state certain specified information about the coverage of the warranty in a single, clear, and easy-to-read document.

3. The warrantor or seller must ensure that warranties are available at the site of sale of the warranted consumer products so that consumers can read them before purchasing a product.

Regarding used products, an implied warranty can be disclaimed by the seller if a written warranty is not provided. This disclaimer must be made in a conspicuous manner, preferably in writing, so that the consumer is aware that there is no warranty on the product. Terms such as this product is being sold "with all faults" or "as is" should be used. Some states do not permit disclaiming of the implied warranty.

## Patents

A patent provides the owner of the patent with a legally enforceable *right to exclude* others from practicing the invention covered by the patent for a specified period of time. It is of interest to note that a patent does not necessarily grant the owner the right to make, use, or sell the invention. The patent obtained by an individual, A, may build on other patents and, thus, A would have to obtain permission from the owner(s) of the earlier patent(s) to exploit A's patent.

There are four criteria that an invention must meet in order to be patentable. These criteria are as follows:

- The invention must fall into one of the following five classes:
  - Processes
  - Machines
  - Manufactures (objects made by humans or machines)
  - Compositions of matter
  - New uses of any of the above
- The invention must be useful. One aspect of this test for utility is that the invention cannot be only a theoretical phenomenon.
- The invention must be novel; it must be something that no one has developed before.
- The invention must not be obvious to "a person having ordinary skill in the art to which said subject matter pertains."

Patent law protects inventions and processes ("utility" patents), ornamental designs ("design" patents), and new varieties of plants ("plant patents"). In the United States, as of June 8, 1995, utility patents are granted for a period of 20 years from the date the application was filed. For patents in force prior to June 8, 1995, and patents granted on applications pending before that date, the patent term is the greater of 17 years from the date of issue (the term under prior law) or 20 years from the date of filing. Design patents are granted for a period of 14 years, and a plant patent has a term of 17 years. Once the patent on an invention or design has expired, anyone is free to make, use, or sell the invention or design.

## Copyrights

A copyright protects "original works of authorship" and protects the right of the author to control the reproduction, adaptation, public distribution, and performance of these original works. Copyrights can also be applied to software and databases. The copyright law has two provisions that address uses of copyrighted material by educators, researchers, and librarians. These provisions do the following:

- Codify the doctrine of "fair use," under which limited copying of copyrighted works without the permission of the owner is allowed for certain teaching and research purposes
- Establish special limitations and exemptions for the reproduction of copyrighted works by libraries and archives

The length of time that a copyright remains in effect varies. Based on the 1998 Sonny Bono Copyright Term Extension Act, a copyright, in general, is extended for an additional 20 years.

The Sonny Bono Copyright Term Extension Act, signed into law on October 27, 1998, amends the provisions concerning duration of copyright protection. Effective immediately, the terms of copyright are generally extended for an additional 20 years. Two specific example provisions of the Sonny Bono Copyright Term Extension Act are as follows:

- Works originally created on or after January 1, 1978, are protected from the time of their creation and are usually given a term of the author's life plus an additional 70 years after the author's death.
- Works originally created before January 1, 1978, but not published or registered by that date are covered by the statute, also with a duration of the author's life plus an additional 70 years after the author's death. In addition, the statute provides that in no case will the term of copyright for these types of works expire before December 31, 2002. For works published on or before December 31, 2002, the term of copyright will not expire before December 31, 2047.

Materials might fall into other copyright categories depending on the age of the work, if the copyright was renewed, if it was developed as work for hire, and so on. Detailed information can be found in the following publications of the U.S. Copyright Office:

- Circular 15, "Renewal of Copyright"
- Circular 15a, "Duration of Copyright"
- Circular 15t, "Extension of Copyright Terms"

### The Digital Millennium Copyright Act (DMCA)

The Digital Millennium Copyright Act, H.R. 2281, was enacted into law on October 28, 1998. DMCA addresses licensing and ownership information and prohibits trading, manufacturing, or selling in any way that is intended to bypass copyright protection mechanisms. For example, Sec. 1201of the Act, Circumvention of Copyright Protection Systems, states:

*(a) VIOLATIONS REGARDING CIRCUMVENTION OF TECHNOLOGI-CAL MEASURES- (1)(A) No person shall circumvent a technological measure that effectively controls access to a work protected under this title. The prohibition contained in the preceding sentence shall take effect at the end of the 2-year period beginning on the date of the enactment of this chapter.*

DMCA also addresses Internet Service Providers (ISPs) that unknowingly support the posting of copyrighted material by subscribers. If the ISP is notified that the material is copyrighted, the ISP must remove the material. Additionally, if the posting party proves that the removed material was of "lawful use," the ISP must restore the material and notify the copyright owner within 14 business days.

Two important rulings regarding the DMCA were made in 2001. The rulings involved DeCSS, which is a program that bypasses the Content Scrambling System (CSS) software used to prevent viewing of DVD movie disks on unlicensed platforms. In a trade secrecy case [DVD-CCA v. Banner], the California appellate court overturned a lower court ruling that an individual who posted DeCSS on the Internet had revealed the trade secret of CSS. The appeals court has reversed an injunction on the posting of DeCSS, stating that the code is speech protected by the First Amendment.

The second case [Universal City v. Reimerdes] was the first constitutional challenge to DMCA anti-circumvention rules. The case involved Eric Corley, the publisher of the hacker magazine *2600 Magazine*. Corley was covering the DeCSS situation and, as part of that coverage, posted DeCSS on his publication's Web site. The trial and appellate courts both ruled that the posting violated the DMCA and was, therefore, illegal. This ruling upheld the DMCA. It appears that there will be more challenges to DMCA in the future.

## Trade Secrets

A trade secret secures and maintains the confidentiality of proprietary technical or business-related information that is adequately protected from disclosure by the owner. Corollaries to this definition are that the owner has invested resources to develop this information, it is valuable to the business of the owner, it would be valuable to a competitor, and it is not obvious.

## National Security

In today's environment, there is a tension between protecting our nation and preserving the privacy rights of citizens. Some of the recent laws pertaining to national security, their effect on privacy, and means to protect confidential documents are discussed in the following sections.

### *Privacy Rights versus National Security*

In order to balance the privacy rights of individuals with the need to apprehend lawbreakers through the use of wiretaps, the U.S. Congress passed The Federal Intelligence Surveillance Act (FISA) of 1978, the Electronic Communications Privacy Act (ECPA) of 1986, and the Communications Assistance for Law Enforcement Act (CALEA) of 1994. These laws reflected different views concerning wiretapping as technology progressed. The Federal Intelligence Surveillance Act (FISA) of 1978 limited wiretapping for national security purposes as a result of the record of the Nixon Administration in using illegal wiretaps. The Electronic Communications Privacy Act (ECPA) of 1986 prohibited eavesdropping or the interception of message contents without distinguishing between private or public systems. The Communications Assistance for Law Enforcement Act (CALEA) of 1994 required all communications carriers to make wiretaps possible in ways approved by the FBI.

An example of a related technology that, if improperly used, can compromise the privacy of individuals is the pen register. A *pen register* is a device that records all the numbers dialed from a specific telephone line. Other devices, programs, or acts that create a tension between ensuring the security of the United States and the privacy rights of the individual are the following:

**Carnivore.**   A device used by the U.S. FBI to monitor ISP traffic. (S.P. Smith et. al., *Independent Technical Review of the Carnivore System – Draft report*, U.S. Department of Justice Contract # 00-C-328 IITRI, CR-022-216, November 17, 2000).

**Echelon.**   A cooperative, worldwide signal intelligence system that is run by the NSA of the United States, the Government Communications Head Quarters (GCHQ) of England, the Communications Security Establishment (CSE) of Canada, the Australian Defense Security Directorate (DSD), and the General Communications Security Bureau (GCSB) of New Zealand.

**U.S. Patriot Act.**   Signed into law on October 26, 2001, giving the government new powers to subpoena electronic records and to monitor Internet traffic. Based on this act, the U.S. government can require the assistance of ISPs and network operators and allows investigators to gather information about electronic mail without having to show probable cause that the person to be monitored had committed a crime or was intending to commit a crime. Also, under the Patriot Act, if it is suspected that notification of a search warrant would cause a suspect to flee, a search can be conducted before notification of a search warrant is given. In addition, in a November 18, 2002, ruling, a special appeals court confirmed that the U.S. Department of Justice has broad powers under the Patriot Act to use wiretaps for intelligence gathering to prosecute terrorists. The United States Foreign Intelligence Court of Review, the three-person appeals court that made the ruling, was created to administer the 1978 law that permitted the U.S. government to engage in wiretaps for intelligence purposes inside the United States. The Court of Review overturned the ruling of a lower court, the Foreign Intelligence Surveillance Act court. The lower court upheld the "wall' between wiretapping for intelligence purposes and wiretapping for criminal investigation. The reasoning of the lower court was that it was more difficult to obtain a court order for wiretapping for a criminal investigation than for intelligence gathering. Therefore, the court was concerned that agencies such as the FBI would obtain authorization for wiretapping using the lower threshold requirements for intelligence gathering when the wiretap was really part of a criminal investigation. The intelligence surveillance law requires only that there is probable cause that the individual under surveillance is an agent of a foreign power. The Foreign Intelligence Court of Review ruled that the U.S. Patriot Act did away with this wall and that officials of the Justice Department criminal and intelligence branches could work together to obtain wiretap information to protect the United States from terrorist attacks.

### U. S. Department of Defense Security Clearance

Intelligence information and information on projects and equipment must be protected from unauthorized disclosure. In order to specify what individual can have access to what documents, individuals are assigned security clearances and the documents are assigned classification labels. An additional requirement for an individual to have access to classified documents is that the individual must have a need –to know the information contained in that document in order to carry out his or her legal and authorized tasks.

In order to obtain a clearance, the individual must submit to a background investigation conducted by the Defense Security Service (DSS.) Individuals seeking a Top Secret or SCI clearance are required to undergo a more strict background investigation, the Single Scope Background Investigation (SBI), and polygraph testing. When the background testing is completed, the resultant data is sent to the Central Clearance Facility, which will determine if the requested clearance will be issued.

Top Secret clearances require review and reinvestigation every 5 years, and Secret or Confidential clearances must be reviewed and reinvestigated every 10 years.

## Document Retention

It is good practice for an organization to have a document retention policy in place. In addition to giving all relevant employees requirements for handling, retaining, and disposing of sensitive documents, a document retention policy might be required to comply with federal and state laws. Improper or early disposal of records and leakage of sensitive material may open corporate officers to civil damage.

The document retention policy should take into account the type of organization involved and the types of documents generated by the organization. The policy should be made known to the relevant employees of an organization, and it should be applied in a consistent manner.

Outside customers or clients of an organization may specify their document retention requirements at the beginning of an engagement. Audit organizations and CPAs may be required to retain a client's documents for a period of five years or more in the event any legal proceedings relating to the client might require the client's records. On the other hand, the organization cannot afford to become an off-site document storage facility for a client's documents. Similarly, in-house documents cannot be kept indefinitely. Therefore, a specific retention time should be established for documents and should be adhered to except in the case of legal activities.

Electronic communications, such as email, might be reviewed at a later time by lawyers and prosecutors if a legal proceeding is brought against an organization. Similarly, competitors as well as insiders might employ corporate espionage to discover an organization's trade secrets, bid prices, and other critical information. Again, an organizational document retention and destruction policy will mitigate the loss of critical information and defend against possible liability of the organization and its officers. The retention time of electronic documents and email should, at a minimum, cover the audit period of such material. For example, an organization may be given notice to provide accounting records, computer-generated books of original entry, general ledgers, journal entries, or depreciation schedules. Again, what has to be kept and for what period of time it has to be kept are usually specified in statutes. Compliance with the appropriate statutes protects the organization from liability for damages.

An extremely important consideration in document disposal is the method of disposal. An organization can choose to destroy the documents itself or outsource the task. The latter option is attractive if one considers the large volumes of paperwork generated by an organization daily. On the other hand, if document destruction were outsourced to another party, it would be embarrassing, at the least, if documents that were supposed to be destroyed surfaced later. An outside organization should be trusted and be insured and bonded. This outside company should provide distinctive containers around the organization in which to deposit sensitive documents that must be destroyed. The outside company should provide a "chain of custody" of the materials from the receptacles in offices to the destruction facility.

# Sample Questions

Answers to the Sample Questions for this and other chapters are found in Appendix C.

1. The difficulty of finding the prime factors of very large numbers is the strong, one-way function used in which of the following public key cryptosystems?

   a. El Gamal

   b. Diffie-Hellman

   c. RSA

   d. Elliptic curve

2. Elliptic curve cryptosystems:

   a. Have a higher strength per bit than an RSA cryptosystem

   b. Have a lower strength per bit than an RSA cryptosystem

   c. Cannot be used to implement digital signatures

   d. Cannot be used to implement encryption

3. Digital certificates, certification authority, timestamping, Lightweight Directory Access Protocol (LDAP), and non-repudiation support a portion of what services?

   a. Cryptanalysis

   b. Public Key Infrastructure

   c. Steganography

   d. Disaster recovery

4. A *reference monitor* is a system component that enforces access controls on an object. Specifically, the *reference monitor concept* is an abstract machine that mediates all access of subjects to objects. What do you call the hardware, firmware, and software elements of a Trusted Computing Base that implement the reference monitor concept?

   a. The authorization database

   b. Identification and authentication (I & A) mechanisms

   c. The auditing subsystem

   d. The security kernel

5. Access control that is based on an individual's duties or title in an organization is known as:

    a. Rule-based access control

    b. Discretionary access control

    c. Role-based access control

    d. Mandatory access control

6. The * (star) property of the Bell-LaPadula model states what?

    a. Reading of information by a subject at a lower sensitivity level from an object at a higher sensitivity level is not permitted (no read up).

    b. Writing of information by a subject at a higher level of sensitivity to an object at a lower level of sensitivity is not permitted (no write down).

    c. An access matrix is used to specify discretionary access control.

    d. Reading or writing is permitted at a particular level of sensitivity, but not to either higher or lower levels of sensitivity.

7. An ATM card and a PIN are an example of what?

    a. Multi-factor identification

    b. Single-factor authentication

    c. Two-factor authentication

    d. Single-factor identification

8. A token that generates a unique password at fixed time intervals is called:

    a. An asynchronous dynamic password token

    b. A time-sensitive token

    c. A synchronous dynamic password token

    d. A challenge-response token

9. Elliptic curves, which are applied to public key cryptography, employ modular exponentiation that characterizes the:

    a. Elliptic curve discrete logarithm problem

    b. Prime factors of very large numbers

    c. Elliptic curve modular addition

    d. Knapsack problem

10. In the discretionary portion of the Bell-LaPadula model that is based on the access matrix, how the access rights are defined and evaluated is called:

   a. Authentication

   b. Authorization

   c. Identification

   d. Validation

11. The Biba model axiom "an object at one level of integrity is not permitted to modify (write to) an object of a higher level of integrity (no write up)" is called:

   a. The Constrained Integrity Axiom

   b. The * (star) Integrity Axiom

   c. The Simple Integrity Axiom

   d. The Discretionary Integrity Axiom

12. A trade secret:

   a. Provides the owner with a legally enforceable right to exclude others from practicing the art covered for a specified time period

   b. Protects "original" works of authorship

   c. Secures and maintains the confidentiality of proprietary technical or business-related information that is adequately protected from disclosure by the owner

   d. Is a word, name, symbol, color, sound, product shape, or device used to identify goods and to distinguish them from those made or sold by others

13. The chain of evidence relates to:

   a. Securing laptops to desks during an investigation

   b. DNA testing

   c. Handling and controlling evidence

   d. Making a disk image

14. The concept of due care states that senior organizational management must ensure that:

    a. All risks to an information system are eliminated

    b. Certain requirements must be fulfilled in carrying out their responsibilities to the organization

    c. Other management personnel are delegated the responsibility for information system security

    d. The cost of implementing safeguards is greater than the potential resultant losses resulting from information security breaches

15. Which one of the following items is NOT TRUE concerning the Platform for Privacy Preferences (P3P) developed by the World Wide Web Consortium (W3C)?

    a. It allows Web sites to express their privacy practices in a standard format that can be retrieved automatically and interpreted easily by user agents.

    b. It allows users to be informed of site practices in human-readable format.

    c. It does not provide the site privacy practices to users in machine-readable format.

    d. It automates decision-making based on the site's privacy practices, when appropriate.

16. Kerberos is an authentication scheme that can be used to implement:

    a. Public key cryptography

    b. Digital signatures

    c. Hash functions

    d. Single Sign-On

17. In biometrics, a "one-to-one" search to verify an individual's claim of an identity is called:

    a. Audit trail review

    b. Authentication

    c. Accountability

    d. Aggregation

18. Biometrics is used for identification in the physical controls and for authentication in the:

    a. Detective controls

    b. Preventive controls

    c. Logical controls

    d. Corrective controls

19. What part of an access control matrix shows one user's capabilities to multiple resources?

    a. Columns

    b. Rows

    c. Rows and columns

    d. Access control list

20. The Secure Hash Algorithm–1 (SHA–1) is specified in the:

    a. Data Encryption Standard

    b. Digital Signature Standard

    c. Digital Encryption Standard

    d. Advanced Encryption Standard

21. The Digital Signature Standard (DSS) uses which digital signature algorithm(s)?

    a. Either the RSA digital signature algorithm or the Digital Signature Algorithm (DSA)

    b. DSA only

    c. RSA only

    d. Either the El Gamal digital signature algorithm or the Digital Signature Algorithm (DSA)

22. The U.S. Escrowed Encryption Standard employed which of the following symmetric key algorithms?

    a. IDEA

    b. DES

    c. 3 DES

    d. SKIPJACK

23. Key clustering is:

    a. The condition where many keys in use are very similar

    b. When one key encrypts a plaintext message into two different ciphertexts

    c. When two different keys encrypt a plaintext message into the same ciphertext

    d. Escrowing of keys

24. Which of the following is NOT an asymmetric key algorithm?

    a. Knapsack

    b. RSA

    c. Diffie-Hellman

    d. Rijndael

25. A hybrid cryptosystem employs which of the following methodologies?

    a. Private key encryption to encrypt and send the secret key that will be used to encrypt and send the message using public key encryption

    b. Public key encryption to encrypt and send the secret key that will be used to encrypt and send the message using private key encryption

    c. Public key encryption to encrypt and send the secret key that will be used to encrypt and send the message using public key encryption

    d. Private key encryption to encrypt and send the secret key that will be used to encrypt and send the message using private key encryption

26. In public key cryptography, which of the following statements is NOT true?

    a. A message encrypted with Bob's public key can be decrypted only with Bob's private key.

    b. A message encrypted with Bob's private key can be decrypted only with Bob's public key.

    c. A message encrypted with Bob's public key can be decrypted with Bob's public key.

    d. Given Bob's public key, it is very difficult or impossible to determine his private key.

27. Which of the following is NOT one of the AES key sizes?

    a. 128 bits

    b. 512 bits

    c. 192 bits

    d. 256 bits

28. A polyalphabetic cipher is also known as:

    a. One-time pad

    b. Vernam cipher

    c. Steganography

    d. Vigenère cipher

29. A method that is used to securely transmit secret messages and that is based on keeping the existence of the messages unknown is called:

    a. Private key encryption

    b. Blind signatures

    c. Steganography

    d. A zero-knowledge proof

30. Which of the following characteristics does NOT apply to a one-time pad, if it is used properly?

    a. The key is truly random with no repeating sequences or patterns.

    b. It can be used, carefully, more than once.

    c. It is unbreakable.

    d. The key must be of the same length as the message to be encrypted.

31. The key length of the DES key is:

    a. 128 bits

    b. 56 bits

    c. 64 bits

    d. 256 bits

32. In generating a digitally signed message using a hash function:

    a. The message is encrypted in the public key of the sender

    b. The message digest is encrypted in the private key of the sender

    c. The message digest is encrypted in the public key of the sender

    d. The message is encrypted in the private key of the sender

33. The theft of a laptop poses a threat to which tenet of the C.I.A. triad?

    a. Confidentiality

    b. Integrity

    c. Availability

    d. All of the above

34. Which choice MOST accurately describes the difference between the role of a data owner versus the role of a data custodian?

  a. The custodian implements the information classification scheme after the initial assignment by the owner.

  b. The data owner implements the information classification scheme after the initial assignment by the custodian.

  c. The custodian makes the initial information classification assignments, and the operations manager implements the scheme.

  d. The custodian implements the information classification scheme after the initial assignment by the operations manager.

35. Which choice is usually the number one-used criterion to determine the classification of an information object?

  a. Value

  b. Useful life

  c. Age

  d. Personal association

36. Which choice BEST describes the type of control that a firewall exerts on a network infrastructure?

  a. Corrective control

  b. Preventive control

  c. Detective control

  d. Application control

37. Which choice is NOT a concern of policy development at the high level?

  a. Identifying the key business resources

  b. Identifying the type of firewalls to be used for perimeter security

  c. Defining roles in the organization

  d. Determining the capability and functionality of each role

38. Which firewall type uses a dynamic state table to inspect the content of packets?

  a. A packet filtering firewall

  b. An application-level firewall

  c. A circuit-level firewall

  d. A stateful inspection firewall

39. Which choice is NOT considered an information classification role?

    a. Data owner

    b. Data custodian

    c. Data alterer

    d. Data user

40. Which PPP authentication method sends passwords in cleartext?

    a. PAP

    b. CHAP

    c. MS-CHAP

    d. MS-CHAP v2

41. Which choice is NOT one of the legal IP address ranges specified by RFC1976 and reserved by the Internet Assigned Numbers Authority (IANA) for nonroutable private addresses?

    a. 10.0.0.0–10.255.255.255

    b. 127.0.0.0–127.0.255.255

    c. 172.16.0.0–172.31.255.255

    d. 192.168.0.0–192.168.255.255

42. Which statement is correct regarding VLANs?

    a. A VLAN restricts flooding to only those ports included in the VLAN.

    b. A VLAN is a network segmented physically, not logically.

    c. A VLAN is less secure when implemented in conjunction with private port switching.

    d. A "closed" VLAN configuration is the least secure VLAN configuration.

# CHAPTER 2

# Risk Management

The goal of this domain is to define those elements that help the information systems security manager identify and manage information security risks. This is accomplished through an examination of risk management principles and practices.

## Risk Management Principles and Practices

Risk management (RM) is the process of identifying, measuring, and controlling events. Most managers today are required to manage their risks, whether they are customer related or information system related. Risks are assumed by connected systems, and enterprise-level systems and their organizations are at risk through the risks of all systems attached to them.

Risk is identified and measured by performing a risk analysis. It is controlled through the application of safeguards and countermeasures, and it is managed by periodically reviewing and taking responsible actions based on the risk. RM's main function is to mitigate risk. Mitigating risk means to reduce the risk until it reaches a level that is acceptable to an organization. We can define RM as the identification, analysis, control, and minimization of loss that is associated with events.

The identification of risk to an organization entails defining the following:

- The actual threat
- The possible consequences of the realized threat
- The probable frequency of the occurrence of a threat
- The extent of how confident we are that the threat will happen

Many formulas and processes are designed to help provide some certainty when answering these questions. We should point out, however, that because life and nature are constantly evolving and changing, we cannot consider every possibility. RM tries as much as possible to see the future and to lower the possibility of threats affecting a company.

## Principles of Risk Management

The RM task process has several elements, including the following:

- Performing a risk analysis, including the cost/benefit analysis of protections
- Implementing, reviewing, and maintaining protections

To enable this process, you will need to determine some properties of the various elements, such as the value of assets, threats, and vulnerabilities and the likelihood of events. A primary part of the RM process is assigning values to threats and estimating how often (or how likely) that threat will occur. To perform this task, several formulas and terms have been developed, and the CISSP candidate must fully understand them. The terms and definitions listed in the following section are ranked in the order that they are defined during the *risk analysis* (RA).

### The Purpose of Risk Analysis

The main purpose of performing a risk analysis is to quantify the impact of potential threats—to put a price or value on the cost of a lost business functionality. The two main results of an RA—the identification of risks and the cost/benefit justification of the countermeasures—are vitally important to the creation of a risk mitigation strategy.

There are several benefits to performing an RA. It creates a clear cost-to-value ratio for security protections. It also influences the decision-making process dealing with hardware configuration and software systems design. In addition, it also helps a company focus its security resources where they are needed most. Furthermore, it can influence planning and construction decisions, such as site selection and building design.

The identification of risk is important to the proper selection of security controls and safeguards. Risk is a function of the probability of a given threat agent exercising a particular vulnerability and the resulting impact of that adverse event on the organization. It entails the potential for the realization of unwanted, adverse consequences to human life, health, property, or the environment.

## *Terms and Definitions*

**Risk.** Risk is a function of the probability of a given threat agent exercising a particular vulnerability and the resulting impact of that adverse event on the organization.

**Asset.** An asset is a resource, process, product, computing infrastructure, and so forth that an organization has determined must be protected. The loss of the asset could affect C.I.A.—confidentiality, integrity, or availability—or have an overall effect, or it could have a discrete dollar value, tangible or intangible. It could also affect the full ability of an organization to continue in business. The value of an asset is composed of all of the elements that are related to that asset—its creation, development, support, replacement, public credibility, considered costs, and ownership values.

**Threat.** The potential for a threat source to exploit (intentionally or accidentally) a specific vulnerability. The presence of any potential event that causes an undesirable impact on the organization is called a threat. A threat could be man-made or natural, be intentional or accidental, and have a small or large effect on a company's security.

**Vulnerability.** Any weakness in an information system, system security procedures, internal controls, or implementation that could be exploited by a threat or threat agent. A minor threat has the potential to become a greater threat, or a more frequent threat, because of a vulnerability. The absence or weakness of a safeguard constitutes a vulnerability.

**Safeguard.** A safeguard is the control or countermeasure employed to reduce the risk associated with a specific threat or group of threats. Safeguards are those controls in place that provide some amount of protection to the asset. Controls can be operational, technical, or administrative. Multiple-layered controls that utilize all three control areas are the best defense against a threat.

**Countermeasures.** Those controls put in place as a result of an analysis of a system's security posture. They are implemented to reduce a specific identified and measured risk.

**Threat agent.** Any circumstance or event with the potential to harm an information system through unauthorized access, destruction, disclosure, modification of data, and/or denial of service.

**Risk reduction.** Taking measures to alter or improve the risk position of an asset throughout the company.

**Risk transference.**   Assigning or transferring the potential cost of a loss to another party (like an insurance company).

**Risk acceptance.**   Accepting the level of loss that will occur and absorbing that loss.

**Exposure factor (EF).**   The EF represents the percentage of loss that a realized threat event would have on a specific asset. This value is necessary to compute the Single Loss Expectancy (SLE), which in turn is necessary to compute the Annualized Loss Expectancy (ALE). The EF can be a small percentage, such as the effect of a loss of some hardware, or a very large percentage, such as the catastrophic loss of all computing resources.

**Single Loss Expectancy (SLE).**   A SLE is the dollar figure that is assigned to a single event. It represents an organization's loss from a single threat and is derived from the following formula:

Asset Value ($) × Exposure Factor (EF) = SLE

For example, an asset valued at $100,000 that is subjected to an exposure factor of 30 percent would yield an SLE of $30,000. While this figure is primarily defined in order to create the Annualized Loss Expectancy (ALE), it is occasionally used by itself to describe a disastrous event for a Business Impact Assessment (BIA).

**Annualized Rate of Occurrence (ARO).**   The ARO is a number that represents the estimated frequency in which a threat is expected to occur. The range for this value can be from 0.0 (never) to a large number (for minor threats, such as misspellings of names in data entry). How this number is derived can be very complicated. It is usually created based on the likelihood of the event and the number of employees who could make that error occur. The loss incurred by this event is not a concern here, only how often it does occur.

For example, a meteorite damaging the data center could be estimated to occur only once every 100,000 years and will have an ARO of .00001. In contrast, 100 data entry operators attempting an unauthorized access attempt could be estimated at six times a year per operator and will have an ARO of 600.

**Annualized Loss Expectancy (ALE).**   The ALE, a dollar value, is derived from the following formula:

Single Loss Expectancy (SLE) × Annualized Rate of Occurrence (ARO) = ALE

In other words, an ALE is the annually expected financial loss to an organization from a threat. For example, a threat with a dollar value of $100,000 (SLE) that is expected to happen only once in 1000 years (ARO of .001) will result in an ALE of $100. This example helps to provide a more reliable cost/benefit analysis. Remember that the SLE is derived from the asset value and the Exposure Factor (EF). Table 2.1 shows these formulas.

**Table 2.1** Risk Analysis Formulas

| CONCEPT | DERIVATION FORMULA |
|---------|--------------------|
| Exposure Factor (EF) | Percentage of asset loss caused by threat |
| Single Loss Expectancy (SLE) | Asset Value × Exposure Factor (EF) |
| Annualized Rate of Occurrence (ARO) | Frequency of threat occurrence per year |
| Annualized Loss Expectancy (ALE) | Single Loss Expectancy (SLE) × Annualized Rate of Occurrence (ARO) |

# Risk Assessment

Risk assessment is the first process in the risk management methodology. The risk assessment process helps organizations identify appropriate controls for reducing or eliminating risk during the risk mitigation process. The main purpose of performing a risk assessment is to quantify the impact of potential threats—that is, to put a price on the cost of a lost business functionality. The two main results of an RA are the identification of risks and the cost/benefit justification of the countermeasures.

There are several benefits to performing an RA:

- It creates a clear cost-to-value ratio for security protections.
- It influences the decision-making process dealing with hardware configuration and software systems design.
- It helps a company focus its security resources where they are needed most.
- It influences planning and construction decisions, such as site selection and building design.

To determine the likelihood of a future adverse event, threats to an IT system must be analyzed in conjunction with the potential vulnerabilities and the controls in place for the IT system. The likelihood that a potential vulnerability could be exercised by a given threat-source can be described as high, medium, or low.

Any combination of the following techniques can be used in gathering information relevant to the IT system within its operational boundary:

**Questionnaire.** The questionnaire should be distributed to the applicable technical and nontechnical management personnel who are designing or supporting the IT system.

**On-site interviews.**   On-site visits also allow risk assessment personnel to observe and gather information about the physical, environmental, and operational security of the IT system.

**Document review.**   Policy documents, system documentation, and security-related documentation can provide good information about the security controls used by and planned for the IT system.

**Use of automated scanning tools.**   Proactive technical methods can be used to collect system information efficiently.

The three primary steps in performing a risk analysis are as follows:

- Estimate the potential losses to assets by determining their value
- Analyze potential threats to the assets
- Determine the threats' likelihood and regularity

After performing the risk analysis, the final results should contain the following:

- Valuations of the critical assets in hard costs
- A detailed listing of significant threats
- Each threat's likelihood and possible occurrence rate
- Loss potential of a threat, which is the dollar impact that the threat will have on an asset
- Recommended remedial measures and safeguards or countermeasures

Let's discuss the four basic elements of the risk analysis process:

- Quantitative risk analysis
- Qualitative risk analysis
- Asset identification and valuation
- Safeguard selection

Quantitative and qualitative risk analysis are two general methodologies used to determine the value of an asset and to analyze risk.

## Quantitative Risk Analysis

Quantitative RA attempts to assign independently objective numeric values (hard dollars, for example) to the components of the risk assessment and to the assessment of potential losses. When all elements (asset value, impact, threat frequency, safeguard effectiveness, safeguard costs, uncertainty, and probability) are measured, rated, and assigned values, the process is considered to be fully quantitative.

Typically the results (quantity) are addressed in terms of dollars. Fully quantitative risk analysis is not possible, however, because qualitative determinations must be made in the process.

The difference between quantitative and qualitative RA is fairly simple: Quantitative RA attempts to assign independently objective numeric values (hard dollars, for example) to the components of the risk assessment and to the assessment of potential losses. Qualitative RA addresses more intangible values of a data loss and focuses on the other issues, rather than on the pure, hard costs.

When all elements (asset value, impact, threat frequency, safeguard effectiveness, safeguard costs, uncertainty, and probability) are measured, rated, and assigned values, the process is considered to be fully quantitative. Fully quantitative risk analysis is not possible, however, because you must apply qualitative measures. Thus, the reader should be aware that even though the figures look hard on paper that does not mean it is possible to foretell the future with any certainty.

A quantitative risk analysis process is a major project, and as such it requires a project or program manager to manage the main elements of the analysis. A major part of the initial planning for the quantitative RA is the estimate of the time required to perform the analysis. In addition, you must also create a detailed process plan and assign roles to the RA team.

### Preliminary Security Examination (PSE)

A Preliminary Security Examination (PSE) is often conducted before the actual quantitative RA. The PSE helps to gather the elements that you will need when the actual RA takes place. A PSE also helps to focus an RA. Elements that are defined during this phase include asset costs and values, a listing of various threats to an organization (in terms of threats to both the personnel and the environment), and documentation of the existing security measures. The PSE is normally then subject to a review by an organization's management before the RA begins.

A risk analysis is commonly much more comprehensive, however, and is designed to be used to quantify complicated, multiple-risk scenarios.

The three primary steps are as follows:

1. Estimate the potential losses to assets by determining their value.

2. Analyze potential threats to the assets.

3. Define the Annualized Loss Expectancy (ALE).

### Estimate Potential Losses

To estimate the potential losses incurred during the realization of a threat, you must value the assets by commonly using some sort of standard asset valuation process (we describe this task in more detail later). This process results in an assignment of an asset's financial value by performing the EF and the SLE calculations.

### Analyze Potential Threats

Here, we determine what the threats are and how likely and often they are to occur. To define the threats, we must also understand the asset's vulnerabilities and perform an ARO calculation for the threat and vulnerabilities.

We should consider all types of threats in this section, no matter whether they seem likely or not. It might be helpful to organize the threat listing into the types of threats by source or by their expected magnitude. In fact, some organizations can provide statistics on the frequency of various threats that occur in your area. In addition, the other domains of InfoSec discussed in this book have several varied listings of the categories of threats.

We could include some of the following categories of threats in this section:

**Data classification.**   Data aggregation or concentration that results in data inference, covert channel manipulation, a malicious code/virus/Trojan horse/worm/logic bomb, or a concentration of responsibilities (lack of separation of duties).

**Information warfare.**   Technology-oriented terrorism, malicious code or logic, or emanation interception for military or economic espionage.

**Personnel.**   Unauthorized or uncontrolled system access, the misuse of technology by authorized users, tampering by disgruntled employees, or falsified data input.

**Application/operational.**   An ineffective security application that results in procedural errors or incorrect data entry.

**Criminal.**   Physical destruction or vandalism, the theft of assets or information, organized insider theft, armed robbery, or physical harm to personnel.

**Environmental.**   Utility failure, service outage, natural disasters, or neighboring hazards.

**Computer infrastructure.**   Hardware/equipment failure, program errors, operating system flaws, or a communications system failure.

**Delayed processing.**   Reduced productivity or a delayed funds collection that results in reduced income, increased expenses, or late charges.

### Define the Annualized Loss Expectancy (ALE)

Once we have determined the SLE and ARO, we can estimate the ALE by using the formula that we previously described.

After performing the risk analysis, the final results should contain the following:

- Valuations of the critical assets in hard costs
- A detailed listing of significant threats
- Each threat's likelihood and possible occurrence rate
- Loss potential by a threat—the dollar impact that the threat will have on an asset
- Recommended remedial measures and safeguards or countermeasures

## Qualitative Risk Analysis

Qualitative RA addresses more intangible values of a data loss and focuses on the other issues, rather than on the pure, hard costs. In a qualitative risk assessment, the seriousness of threats and the relative sensitivity of the assets are given a ranking, or qualitative grading, by using a scenario approach and creating an exposure rating scale for each scenario. This results in a subjective quality rating, such as high, medium, or low, or a scale from 0 to 5.

During a qualitative risk assessment scenario description, threats are matched to assets. This scenario describes the type of threat and the potential loss to each asset and selects the safeguards to mitigate risk. After creating the threat listing, defining the assets for protection, and assigning an exposure level rating, the qualitative risk assessment scenario begins.

As we mentioned previously, a qualitative RA does not attempt to assign hard and fast costs to the elements of the loss. It is more scenario-oriented, and unlike a quantitative RA, a purely qualitative risk analysis is possible. Threat frequency and impact data are required to do a qualitative RA, however.

In a qualitative risk assessment, the seriousness of threats and the relative sensitivity of the assets are given a ranking, or qualitative grading, by using a scenario approach and creating an exposure rating scale for each scenario.

During a scenario description, we match various threats to identified assets. A scenario describes the type of threat and the potential loss to which assets and selects the safeguards to mitigate the risk.

After we have created the threat listing, defined the assets for protection, and assigned an exposure level rating, the qualitative risk assessment scenario begins. See Table 2.2 for a simple exposure rating scale.

**Table 2.2**   Simple Exposure Rating Level Scale

| RATING LEVEL | EXPOSURE PERCENTAGE |
|---|---|
| 0 | No measurable loss |
| 1 | 20% loss |
| 2 | 40% loss |
| 3 | 60% loss |
| 4 | 80% loss |
| 5 | 100% loss |

The procedures in performing the scenario are as follows:

■ A scenario is written that addresses each major threat.

■ The scenario is reviewed by business unit managers for a reality check.

■ The RA team recommends and evaluates the various safeguards for each threat.

■ The RA team works through each finalized scenario by using a threat, asset, and safeguard.

■ The team prepares its findings and submits them to management.

After the scenarios have all been played out and the findings are published, management must implement the safeguards that were selected as being acceptable and begin to seek alternatives for the safeguards that did not work.

## Asset Identification and Valuation

One of the most overlooked elements of a security strategy is the proper identification and valuation of the organization's assets. The proper and cost-effective implementation of security controls requires that the organization conduct a thorough asset identification. A common mistake made by organizations is not accurately identifying the information's value before implementing the security controls. Some of the components that determine an information asset's value are the following:

■ The initial and ongoing cost (to an organization) of purchasing, licensing, developing, and supporting the information asset

■ The asset's value to the organization's production operations, research and development, and business model viability

■ The asset's value established in the external marketplace and the estimated value of the intellectual property (trade secrets, patents, copyrights, and so forth)

Several elements of a process determine the value of an asset. Both quantitative and qualitative RA (and business impact assessment) procedures
require a valuation made of the asset's worth to the organization. This valuation is a fundamental step in all security auditing methodologies. A common
universal mistake made by organizations is not accurately identifying the
information's value before implementing the security controls. This situation
often results in a control that is ill suited for asset protection, not financially
effective, or protective of the wrong asset.

Here are some additional reasons to define the cost or value that we previously described:

■ The asset valuation is necessary to perform the cost/benefit analysis.

■ The asset's value might be necessary for insurance reasons.

■ The asset's value supports safeguard selection decisions.

■ The asset valuation might be necessary to satisfy "due care" and prevent negligence and legal liability.


## Threat Identification

After the identification and valuation of the assets, the identification of the
threats must occur as part of the risk assessment. Threats are often categorized
for this process. Some examples of threat categories might be the following:

**Criminal.**   Physical destruction or vandalism, the theft of assets or information, organized insider theft, armed robbery, or physical harm to
personnel.

**Personnel.**   Unauthorized or uncontrolled system access, the misuse of
technology by authorized users, tampering by disgruntled employees,
or falsified data input.

**Environmental.**   Utility failure, service outage, natural disasters, or neighboring hazards.

**Information warfare.**   Technology-oriented terrorism, malicious code or
logic, or emanation interception for military or economic espionage.

**Application/operational.**   An ineffective security application that results
in procedural errors or incorrect data entry.

**Computer infrastructure.**   Hardware/equipment failure, program errors, operating system flaws, or a communications system failure.

**Data classification.**   Data aggregation or concentration that results in data inference, covert channel manipulation, a malicious code/virus/Trojan horse/worm/logic bomb, or a concentration of responsibilities (lack of separation of duties).

**Delayed processing.**   Reduced productivity or a delayed funds collection that results in reduced income, increased expenses, or late charges.

## Vulnerability Definition

After identifying the threats, the vulnerabilities that those threats could impact are defined. A vulnerability assessment is a common method of matching potential threats to existing vulnerabilities in the organization.

Common steps to performing a vulnerability assessment could be the following:

- Listing potential emergencies, both internally to the facility and externally to the community. Natural, man-made, technological, and human error are all categories of potential emergencies and errors.

- Estimating the likelihood that each emergency could occur.

- Assessing the potential impact of the emergency on the organization in the areas of human impact, property impact, and business asset impact.

- Assessing external and internal resources required to deal with the emergency and determining if they are located internally or if external resources are required.

## Risk Mitigation Strategies

To mitigate risk, the organization needs to know the threat, consequences of the realized threat, the frequency of the occurrence of a threat, and how likely this threat will occur. There are three strategic remedies to risk:

**Risk reduction.**   Taking measures to alter or improve the risk position of an asset throughout the company.

**Risk transference.**   Assigning or transferring the potential cost of a loss to another party (like an insurance company).

**Risk acceptance.**   Accepting the level of loss that will occur and absorbing that loss.

Either one or a combination of all three strategies may be adopted. The remedy chosen will usually be the one that results in the greatest risk reduction while retaining the lowest annual cost necessary to maintain a company.

Once the risk analysis has been completed, safeguards and countermeasures must be researched and recommended. Several standard principles are used in the selection of safeguards to ensure that a safeguard is properly matched to a threat and to ensure that a safeguard most efficiently implements the necessary controls. You must examine important criteria before selecting an effective countermeasure.

## Cost/Benefit Analysis

The number one safeguard selection criteria is the cost effectiveness of the control to be implemented, which is derived through the process of the cost/benefit analysis. To determine the total cost of the safeguard, you need to consider many elements (including the following):

- The purchase, development, and/or licensing costs of the safeguard
- The physical installation costs and the disruption to normal production during the installation and testing of the safeguard
- Normal operating costs, resource allocation, and maintenance/repair costs

The simplest calculation to compute a cost/benefit for a given safeguard is as follows:

(ALE before safeguard implementation) – (ALE after safeguard implementation) – (annual safeguard cost) = value of safeguard to the organization

For example, if you have determined an ALE of a threat to be $10,000, the ALE after the safeguard implementation to be $1,000, and the annual cost to operate the safeguard to be $500, then the value of a given safeguard is thought to be $8,500 annually. This amount is then compared against the startup costs, and the benefit or lack of benefit is determined.

This value can be derived for a single safeguard or for a collection of safeguards through a series of complex calculations. In addition to the financial cost/benefit ratio, other factors can influence the decision of whether to implement a specific security safeguard. For example, an organization is exposed to legal liability if the cost to implement a safeguard is less than the cost resulting from the threat realized and the organization does not implement the safeguard.

## Level of Manual Operations

The amount of manual intervention required to operate the safeguard is also a factor in the choice of a safeguard. In case after case, vulnerabilities are created due to human error or an inconsistency in application. In fact, automated systems require fail-safe defaults to allow for manual shutdown capability in case a vulnerability occurs. The more automated a process, the more sustainable and reliable that process will be.

In addition, a safeguard should not be too difficult to operate, and it should not unreasonably interfere with the normal operations of production. These characteristics are vital for the acceptance of the control by operating personnel and for acquiring the all-important management support required for the safeguard to succeed.

## Auditability and Accountability Features

The safeguard must allow for the inclusion of auditing and accounting functions. The safeguard must also give auditors the ability to audit and test it, as well as accountability to effectively track each individual who accesses the countermeasure or its features.

## Recovery Ability

You should evaluate the safeguard's countermeasure with regard to its functioning state after activation or reset. During and after a reset condition, the safeguard must provide the following:

- No asset destruction during activation or reset
- No covert channel access to or through the control during reset
- No security loss or increase in exposure after activation or reset
- Defaults to a state that does not give any operator access or rights until the controls are fully operational

## Vendor Relations

You must examine the credibility, reliability, and past performance of the safeguard vendor. In addition, the openness (open source) of the application programming should also be known in order to avoid any design secrecy that prevents later modifications or that enables an unknown application to have a back door into the system. You should also consider vendor support and documentation.

# NIST RA Process

The National Institute of Standards and Technology (NIST) defines nine steps in the risk assessment process. These steps are as follows:

1. System characterization
2. Threat identification
3. Vulnerability identification
4. Control analysis
5. Likelihood determination
6. Impact analysis
7. Risk determination
8. Control recommendations
9. Results documentation

Let's examine these steps in more detail.

## Step 1: System Characterization

In assessing risks for an IT system, the first step is to define the scope of the effort. In this step, the boundaries of the IT system are identified, along with the resources and the information that constitute the system. Characterizing an IT system establishes the scope of the risk assessment effort, delineates the operational authorization (or accreditation) boundaries, and provides information (for example, hardware, software, system connectivity, and responsible division or support personnel) essential to defining the risk.

### Information-Gathering Techniques

Any, or a combination, of the following techniques can be used in gathering information relevant to the IT system within its operational boundary:

**Questionnaire.**  To collect relevant information, risk assessment personnel can develop a questionnaire concerning the management and operational controls planned for or used in the IT system. This questionnaire should be distributed to the applicable technical and nontechnical management personnel who are designing or supporting the IT system. The questionnaire could also be used during on-site visits and interviews.

**On-site interviews.**  Interviews with IT system support and management personnel can enable risk assessment personnel to collect useful information about the IT system (for example, how the system is operated and managed). On-site visits also allow risk assessment personnel to observe and gather information about the physical, environmental, and operational security of the IT system. For systems still in the design phase, the on-site visit would be a face-to-face data gathering exercise and could provide the opportunity to evaluate the physical environment in which the IT system will operate.

**Document review.** Policy documents (for example, legislative documentation, directives), system documentation (for example, system user guide, system administrative manual, system design and requirement document, acquisition document), and security-related documentation (for example, previous audit report, risk assessment report, system test results, system security plan, security policies) can provide good information about the security controls used by and planned for the IT system. An organization's mission impact analysis or asset criticality assessment provides information regarding system and data criticality and sensitivity.

**Use of automated scanning tools.** Proactive technical methods can be used to collect system information efficiently. For example, a network mapping tool can identify the services that run on a large group of hosts and provide a quick way of building individual profiles of the target IT systems.

The completion of Step 1 should result in the following:

- Characterization of the IT system assessed
- A good picture of the IT system environment
- Delineation of system boundary

## Step 2: Threat Identification

The goal of this step is to identify the potential threat-sources and compile a threat statement listing potential threat-sources that are applicable to the IT system being evaluated. In assessing threat-sources, it is important to consider all potential threat-sources that could cause harm to an IT system and its processing environment. For example, although the threat statement for an IT system located on a hill may not include natural flooding because of the low likelihood of such an event occurring, environmental threats such as a bursting pipe can quickly flood a computer room and cause damage to an organization's IT assets and resources.

Humans can be threat-sources through intentional acts, such as deliberate attacks by malicious persons or disgruntled employees, or unintentional acts, such as negligence and errors. A deliberate attack can be either (1) a malicious attempt to gain unauthorized access to an IT system (for example, via password guessing) in order to compromise system and data integrity, availability, or confidentiality or (2) a benign, but nonetheless purposeful, attempt to circumvent system security. One example of the latter type of deliberate attack is a programmer writing a Trojan horse program to bypass system security in order for the (Trojan) attack to succeed.

Common threat sources are the following:

**Natural threats.**   Floods, earthquakes, tornadoes, landslides, avalanches, electrical storms, and other such events.

**Human threats.**   Events that are either enabled by or caused by human beings, such as unintentional acts (inadvertent data entry or operational mistake) or deliberate actions (network-based attacks, malicious software upload, unauthorized access to confidential information).

**Environmental threats.**   Long-term power failure, pollution, chemicals, liquid leakage.

A threat statement containing a list of threat-sources that could exploit system vulnerabilities is the result of this step.

## Step 3: Vulnerability Identification

The analysis of the threat to an IT system must include an analysis of the vulnerabilities associated with the system environment. The goal of this step is to develop a list of system vulnerabilities (flaws or weaknesses) that could be exploited by the potential threat-sources.

Recommended methods for identifying system vulnerabilities are through the use of vulnerability sources, the performance of system security testing, and the development of a security requirements checklist.

### System Security Testing

Proactive methods, employing system testing, can be used to identify system vulnerabilities efficiently, and they can be done on a recurring basis, the frequency of which depends on the criticality of the IT system and available resources (for example, allocated funds, available technology, persons with the expertise to conduct the test). Test methods include the following:

**Automated vulnerability scanning tool.**   The automated vulnerability scanning tool is typically used to scan a group of hosts or a network for known vulnerable services (for example, the system allows anonymous File Transfer Protocol [FTP], sendmail relaying). It should be noted, though, that some of the potential vulnerabilities identified by the automated scanning tool may not represent real vulnerabilities in the context of the system environment. For example, some of these scanning tools rate potential vulnerabilities without considering the site's environment and requirements. Some of the vulnerabilities flagged by the automated scanning software may actually not be vulnerable for a particular site but may be configured that way because their environment requires it. Thus, this test method may produce false positives.

**Security Test and Evaluation (ST&E).**   ST&E is another technique that can be used in identifying IT system vulnerabilities during the risk assessment process. It includes the development and execution of a test plan (for example, test script, test procedures, and expected test results). The purpose of system security testing is to test the effectiveness of the security controls of an IT system as they have been applied in an operational environment. The objective is to ensure that the applied controls meet the approved security specification for the software and hardware and implement the organization's security policy or meet industry standards.

**Penetration testing.**   Penetration testing can be used to complement the review of security controls and ensure that external-facing facets of the IT system are secure. Penetration testing, when employed in the risk assessment process, can be used to assess an IT system's ability to withstand intentional attempts to circumvent system security. Its objective is to test the IT system from the viewpoint of a threat-source and to identify potential failures in the IT system protection schemes.

### Development of a Security Requirements Checklist

A security requirements checklist contains the basic security standards that can be used to systematically evaluate and identify the vulnerabilities of the assets (personnel, hardware, software, information), manual procedures, processes, and information transfers associated with a given IT system in the following security areas:

- Management
- Operations
- Technical areas

During this step, the risk assessment personnel determine whether the security requirements stipulated for the IT system, and collected during system characterization, are being met by existing or planned security controls. Typically, the system security requirements can be presented in table form, with each requirement accompanied by an explanation of how the system's design or implementation does or does not satisfy that security control requirement.

A list of the system vulnerabilities that could be exercised by the potential threat-sources is the output from this step.

# Step 4: Control Analysis

The goal of this step is to analyze the controls that have been implemented, or are planned for implementation, by the organization to minimize or eliminate the likelihood (or probability) of a threat's acting on a system vulnerability.

To derive an overall likelihood rating that indicates the probability that a potential vulnerability may be exercised within the construct of the associated threat environment (see Step 5), the implementation of current or planned controls must be considered. For example, a vulnerability (for example, a system or procedural weakness) is not likely to be exercised or the likelihood is low if there is a low level of threat-source interest or capability or if there are effective security controls that can eliminate, or reduce the magnitude of, harm.

**Control methods.**   Security controls encompass the use of technical and nontechnical methods. Technical controls are safeguards that are incorporated into computer hardware, software, or firmware (for example, access control mechanisms, identification and authentication mechanisms, encryption methods, intrusion detection software). Nontechnical controls are management and operational controls, such as security policies; operational procedures; and personnel, physical, and environmental security.

**Control categories.**   The control categories for both technical and nontechnical control methods can be further classified as either preventive or detective. These two subcategories are explained as follows:

- *Preventive controls.* These inhibit attempts to violate security policy and include such controls as access control enforcement, encryption, and authentication.

- *Detective controls.* These warn of violations or attempted violations of security policy and include such controls as audit trails, intrusion detection methods, and checksums.

The implementation of such controls during the risk mitigation process is the direct result of the identification of deficiencies in current or planned controls during the risk assessment process (for example, controls are not in place or controls are not implemented properly).

The development of a security requirements checklist or the use of an available checklist will be helpful in analyzing controls in an efficient and systematic manner. The security requirements checklist can be used to validate security noncompliance as well as compliance. Therefore, it is essential to update such checklists to reflect changes in an organization's control environment (for example, changes in security policies, methods, and requirements) to ensure the validity of the checklist.

The completion of this step should result in a list of current or planned controls used for the IT system to mitigate the likelihood of a vulnerability that is being exercised and reduce the impact of such an adverse event.

## Step 5: Likelihood Determination

To derive an overall likelihood rating that indicates the probability that a potential vulnerability may be exercised within the construct of the associated threat environment; the following governing factors must be considered:

- Threat-source motivation and capability
- Nature of the vulnerability
- Existence and effectiveness of current controls

The likelihood that a potential vulnerability could be exercised by a given threat-source can be qualitatively described as high, medium, or low.

## Step 6: Impact Analysis

The next major step in measuring level of risk is to determine the adverse impact resulting from a successful threat-source acting on a vulnerability. To create the impact analysis it is necessary to obtain the following:

- System mission (for example, the processes performed by the IT system)
- System and data criticality (for example, the system's value or importance to an organization)

## Step 7: Risk Determination

The purpose of this step is to assess the level of risk to the IT system. The determination of risk for a particular threat/vulnerability pair can be expressed as a function of the following factors:

- The likelihood of a given threat-source attempting to act on a given vulnerability
- The magnitude of the impact should a threat-source successfully act on the vulnerability
- The adequacy of planned or existing security controls for reducing or eliminating risk

To measure risk, a risk scale and a risk-level matrix must be developed. The following sections present a standard risk-level matrix and the resulting risk levels.

The final determination of mission risk is derived by multiplying the ratings that are assigned for threat likelihood (for example, probability) and threat impact (or loss).

## Step 8: Control Recommendations

During this step of the process, controls that could mitigate or eliminate the identified risks, as appropriate to the organization's operations, are provided. The goal of the recommended controls is to reduce the level of risk to the IT system and its data to an acceptable level. The following factors should be considered in recommending controls and alternative solutions to minimize or eliminate identified risks:

- Effectiveness of recommended options (for example, system compatibility)
- Legislation and regulation
- Organizational policy
- Operational impact
- Safety and reliability

The control recommendations are the results of the risk assessment process and provide input to the risk mitigation process, during which the recommended procedural and technical security controls are evaluated, prioritized, and implemented.

Note that not all possible recommended controls can be implemented to reduce loss. To determine which ones are required and appropriate for a specific organization, a cost/benefit analysis should be conducted for the proposed recommended controls, to demonstrate whether the costs of implementing the controls can be justified by the reduction in the level of risk. In addition, the operational impact (for example, the effect on system performance) and feasibility (for example, the technical requirements, user acceptance) of introducing the recommended option should be evaluated carefully during the risk mitigation process.

A recommendation of control(s) and alternative solutions to mitigate risk should be the result of this step.

## Step 9: Results Documentation

Once the risk assessment has been completed (threat sources and vulnerabilities identified, risks assessed, and recommended controls provided), the results should be documented in an official report or briefing.

A risk assessment report is a management report that helps senior management, the mission owners, make decisions on policy, procedural, budget, and system operational and management changes. Unlike an audit or investigation report, which looks for wrongdoing, a risk assessment report should not be presented in an accusatory manner but as a systematic and analytical approach to assessing risk so that senior management will understand the risks and allocate resources to reduce and correct potential losses. For this reason, some people prefer to address the threat/vulnerability pairs as observations instead of findings in the risk assessment report.

The step should result in a risk assessment report that describes the threats and vulnerabilities, measures the risk, and provides recommendations for control implementation.

# Sample Questions

Answers to the Sample Questions for this and the other chapters are found in Appendix C.

1. What is the prime directive of Risk Management?
   a. Reduce the risk to a tolerable level
   b. Reduce all risk regardless of cost
   c. Transfer any risk to external third parties
   d. Prosecute any employees that are violating published security policies

2. Which choice MOST closely depicts the difference between qualitative and quantitative risk analysis?
   a. A quantitative RA does not use the hard costs of losses, and a qualitative RA does.
   b. A quantitative RA uses less guesswork than a qualitative RA.
   c. A qualitative RA uses many complex calculations.
   d. A quantitative RA cannot be automated.

3. What is the BEST description of risk reduction?
   a. Altering elements of the enterprise in response to a risk analysis
   b. Removing all risk to the enterprise at any cost
   c. Assigning any costs associated with risk to a third party
   d. Assuming all costs associated with the risk internally

4. How is an SLE derived?
   a. (Cost – Benefit) × (% of Asset Value)
   b. AV × EF
   c. ARO × EF
   d. % of AV – Implementation Cost

5. What is an ARO?
   a. A dollar figure assigned to a single event
   b. The annual expected financial loss to an organization from a threat
   c. A number that represents the estimated frequency of an occurrence of an expected threat
   d. The percentage of loss that a realized threat event would have on a specific asset

6. What does an Exposure Factor (EF) describe?

    a. A dollar figure that is assigned to a single event

    b. A number that represents the estimated frequency of the occurrence of an expected threat

    c. The percentage of loss that a realized threat event would have on a specific asset

    d. The annual expected financial loss to an organization from a threat

7. Which choice is the BEST description of a vulnerability?

    a. A weakness in a system that could be exploited

    b. A company resource that could be lost due to an incident

    c. The minimization of loss associated with an incident

    d. A potential incident that could cause harm

8. Which choice is NOT a common result of a risk analysis?

    a. A detailed listing of relevant threats

    b. Valuations of critical assets

    c. Likelihood of a potential threat

    d. Definition of business recovery roles

9. Which statement BEST describes the primary purpose of risk analysis?

    a. To create a clear cost-to-value ratio for implementing security controls

    b. To influence the system design process

    c. To influence site selection decisions

    d. To quantify the impact of potential threats

10. Put the following steps in the qualitative scenario procedure in order:

    a. The team prepares its findings and presents them to management.

    b. A scenario is written to address each identified threat.

    c. Business unit managers review the scenario for a reality check.

    d. The team works through each scenario by using a threat, asset, and safeguard.

11. Which statement is NOT correct about safeguard selection in the risk analysis process?

    a. Maintenance costs need to be included in determining the total cost of the safeguard.

    b. The best possible safeguard should always be implemented, regardless of cost.

c. The most commonly considered criteria is the cost effectiveness of the safeguard.

d. Many elements need to be considered in determining the total cost of the safeguard.

12. Which choice most accurately reflects the goals of risk mitigation?

a. Defining the acceptable level of risk the organization can tolerate and reducing risk to that level

b. Analyzing and removing all vulnerabilities and threats to security within the organization

c. Defining the acceptable level of risk the organization can tolerate and assigning any costs associated with loss or disruption to a third party, such as an insurance carrier

d. Analyzing the effects of a business disruption and preparing the company's response

13. Which answer is the BEST description of a Single Loss Expectancy (SLE)?

a. An algorithm that represents the magnitude of a loss to an asset from a threat

b. An algorithm that expresses the annual frequency with which a threat is expected to occur

c. An algorithm used to determine the monetary impact of each occurrence of a threat

d. An algorithm that determines the expected annual loss to an organization from a threat

14. Which choice is the BEST description of an Annualized Loss Expectancy?

a. The expected risk factor of an annual threat event, derived by multiplying the SLE by its ARO

b. An estimate of how often a given threat event may occur annually

c. The percentile of the value of the asset expected to be lost, used to calculate the SLE

d. A value determined by multiplying the value of the asset by its exposure factor

15. Which choice is NOT a common information-gathering technique when performing a risk analysis?

   a. Distributing a questionnaire

   b. Employing automated risk assessment tools

   c. Reviewing existing policy documents

   d. Interviewing terminated employees

16. Which statement is NOT accurate regarding the process of risk assessment?

   a. The likelihood of a threat must be determined as an element of the risk assessment.

   b. The level of impact of a threat must be determined as an element of the risk assessment.

   c. Risk assessment is the first process in the risk management methodology.

   d. Risk assessment is the final result of the risk management methodology.

17. Which formula accurately represents an Annualized Loss Expectancy (ALE) calculation?

   a. $SLE \times ARO$

   b. Asset Value $(AV) \times EF$

   c. $ARO \times EF - SLE$

   d. % of $ARO \times AV$

18. What is the MOST accurate definition of a safeguard?

   a. A guideline for policy recommendations

   b. A step-by-step instructional procedure

   c. A control designed to counteract a threat

   d. A control designed to counteract an asset

19. Three things that must be considered for the planning and implementation of access control mechanisms are:

   a. Threats, assets, and objectives

   b. Threats, vulnerabilities, and risks

   c. Vulnerabilities, secret keys, and exposures

   d. Exposures, threats, and countermeasures

20. Which choice BEST describes a threat?

    a. A potential incident that could cause harm

    b. A weakness in a system that could be exploited

    c. A company resource that could be lost due to an incident

    d. The minimization of loss associated with an incident

21. Which choice is an incorrect description of a control?

    a. Detective controls discover attacks and trigger preventive or corrective controls.

    b. Corrective controls reduce the likelihood of a deliberate attack.

    c. Corrective controls reduce the effect of an attack.

    d. Controls are the countermeasures for vulnerabilities.

22. Which of the following would NOT be a component of a general enterprise security architecture model for an organization?

    a. Information and resources to ensure the appropriate level of risk management

    b. Consideration of all the items that make up information security, including distributed systems, software, hardware, communications systems, and networks

    c. A systematic and unified approach for evaluating the organization's information systems security infrastructure and defining approaches to implementation and deployment of information security controls

    d. IT system auditing

23. Access control must consider which of the following?

    a. Vulnerabilities, biometrics, and exposures

    b. Threats, assets, and safeguards

    c. Exposures, threats, and countermeasures

    d. Threats, vulnerabilities, and risks

24. What are high-level policies?

    a. They are recommendations for procedural controls.

    b. They are the instructions on how to perform a quantitative risk analysis.

    c. They are statements that indicate a senior management's intention to support InfoSec.

    d. They are step-by-step procedures to implement a safeguard.

25. Which choice is NOT a good criterion for selecting a safeguard?

    a. The ability to recover from a reset with the permissions set to "allow all"

    b. Comparing the potential dollar loss of an asset to the cost of a safeguard

    c. The ability to recover from a reset without damaging the asset

    d. Accountability features for tracking and identifying operators

26. Which statement is accurate about the reasons to implement a layered security architecture?

    a. A layered security approach is not necessary when using COTS products.

    b. A good packet-filtering router will eliminate the need to implement a layered security architecture.

    c. A layered security approach is intended to increase the work factor for an attacker.

    d. A layered approach doesn't really improve the security posture of the organization.

27. Which choice describes a control?

    a. Competitive advantage, credibility, or good will

    b. Events or situations that could cause a financial or operational impact to the organization

    c. Personnel compensation and retirement programs

    d. Protection devices or procedures in place that reduce the effects of threats

28. According to NIST, which choice is not an accepted security self-testing technique?

    a. War dialing

    b. Virus distribution

    c. Password cracking

    d. Virus detection

29. What is the BEST reason for the security administrator to initiate internal vulnerability scanning?

    a. Vulnerability scanning can replicate a system crash.

    b. Vulnerability scanning can identify exposed ports.

    c. Vulnerability scanning can return false positives.

    d. Vulnerability scanning can return false negatives.

30. What are the detailed instructions on how to perform or implement a control called?

    a. Procedures

    b. Policies

    c. Guidelines

    d. Standards

31. Which of the following is a reason to institute output controls?

    a. To preserve the integrity of the data in the system while changes are being made to the configuration

    b. To protect the output's confidentiality

    c. To detect irregularities in the software's operation

    d. To recover damage after an identified system failure

32. Why are maintenance accounts a threat to operations controls?

    a. Maintenance personnel could slip and fall and sue the organization.

    b. Maintenance accounts are commonly used by hackers to access network devices.

    c. Maintenance account information could be compromised if printed reports are left out in the open.

    d. Maintenance might require physical access to the system by vendors or service providers.

33. Who has the final responsibility for the preservation of the organization's information?

    a. Technology providers

    b. Senior management

    c. Users

    d. Application owners

34. Which choice represents an application or system demonstrating a need for a high level of confidentiality protection and controls?

    a. Unavailability of the system could result in inability to meet payroll obligations and could cause work stoppage and failure of user organizations to meet mission-critical requirements. The system requires 24-hour access.

    b. The application contains proprietary business information and other financial information, which, if disclosed to unauthorized sources, could cause unfair advantage for vendors, contractors, or individuals and could result in financial loss or adverse legal action to user organizations.

    c. Destruction of the information would require significant expenditures of time and effort to replace. Although corrupted information would present an inconvenience to the staff, most information, and all vital information, is backed up either by paper documentation or on disk.

    d. The mission of this system is to produce local weather forecast information that is made available to the news media forecasters and the general public at all times. None of the information requires protection against disclosure.

35. Using prenumbered forms to initiate a transaction is an example of what type of control?

    a. Deterrent control

    b. Preventive control

    c. Detective control

    d. Application control

# CHAPTER 3

# Information Security Program Management

As defined by ISACA, this domain relates to the "design, development, and management of an information security program to implement the information security governance framework."

## Control and Safeguard Selection

As a prelude to discussing the selection of controls and safeguards, a review of these and related terms is useful in understanding the rationale behind protection mechanisms. A *threat* is a situation or incident that could cause harm through violation of the security of an information system. A *vulnerability* is a weakness in an information system that could be exploited by a threat. A *safeguard* or *countermeasure* is a procedure, mechanism, technique, or method that reduces the vulnerability of system to a threat. *Controls* are management safeguards.

International standards organizations, governments, professional societies, laws, and regulations promulgate safeguards. In order to implement safeguards, administrative and technical means are employed.

## Control and Safeguard Implementation Methods

Because threats exist in a variety of forms, safeguards and their implementation range from administrative controls to technical approaches through hardware and software mechanisms. Administrative or management safeguards include policies, procedures, guidelines, training, and physical security. Technical safeguards include access control mechanisms, intrusion detection devices, encryption, software development and coding practices, and biometrics for authentication.

Safeguards are used for the following:

- Avoidance by reducing the exposure of sensitive resources to threats
- Prevention through management controls and hardware and software protection devices
- Detection of an incident of an information security policy violation and mitigation of the resulting harm done to the information system
- Recovery by restoring the information system to the state that existed before an incident occurred and addressing the vulnerability that allowed the incident to occur

Implementation of safeguards can be a function of a cost/benefit analysis, as discussed later in this section, or can be driven by a set of minimum or *baseline* protections that must be in place. For example, in military systems, classified information must be protected from confidentiality or integrity violations, regardless of the cost. The *Common Criteria* are an example of evaluation criteria used to evaluate the assurance levels of an information system. *Assurance* is the degree of confidence in the satisfaction of security needs. The Common Criteria evolved from a number of evaluation criteria that were developed in the United States and internationally.

### Evaluation Criteria

In 1985, the *Trusted Computer System Evaluation Criteria* (TCSEC) was developed by the *National Computer Security Center* (NCSC) to provide guidelines for evaluating vendors' products for the specified security criteria. TCSEC provides the following:

- A basis for establishing security requirements in the acquisition specifications
- A standard of the security services that should be provided by vendors for the different classes of security requirements
- A means to measure the trustworthiness of an information system

The TCSEC document, called the Orange Book because of its color, is part of a series of guidelines with covers of different colors called the Rainbow Series. In the Orange Book, the basic control objectives are security policy, assurance, and accountability. TCSEC addresses confidentiality but does not cover integrity. Also, functionality (security controls applied) and assurance (confidence that security controls are functioning as expected) are not separated in TCSEC as they are in other evaluation criteria developed later. The Orange Book defines the major hierarchical classes of security by the letters D through A as follows:

D. Minimal protection

C. Discretionary protection (C1 and C2)

B. Mandatory protection (B1, B2, and B3)

A. Verified protection; formal methods (A1)

The DoD *Trusted Network Interpretation* (TNI) is analogous to the Orange Book. It addresses confidentiality and integrity in trusted computer/communications network systems and is called the Red Book. The Trusted Database Management System Interpretation (TDI) addresses trusted database management systems.

The European Information Technology Security Evaluation Criteria (ITSEC) address confidentiality, integrity, and availability (CIA) issues. The product or system to be evaluated by ITSEC is defined as the Target of Evaluation (TOE). The TOE must have a security target, which includes the security enforcing mechanisms and the system's security policy.

ITSEC separately evaluates functionality and assurance, and it includes 10 functionality classes (F), 8 assurance levels (Q), 7 levels of correctness (E), and 8 basic security functions in its criteria. It also defines two kinds of assurance. One assurance measure is of the correctness of the security functions' implementation, and the other is the effectiveness of the TOE while in operation.

The ITSEC ratings are in the form F-X,E, where functionality and assurance are listed. The ITSEC ratings that are equivalent to TCSEC ratings are as follows:

F-C1, E1 = C1

F-C2, E2 = C2

F-B1, E3 = B1

F-B2, E4 = B2

F-B3, E5 = B3

F-B3, E6 = A1

The other classes of the ITSEC address high integrity and high availability.

TCSEC, ITSEC, and the *Canadian Trusted Computer Product Evaluation Criteria* (CTCPEC) evolved into the Common Criteria. The Common Criteria define a *Protection Profile* (PP), which is an implementation-independent specification of the security requirements and protections of a product that could be built. The Common Criteria terminology for the degree of examination of the product to be tested is the *Evaluation Assurance Level* (EAL). EALs range from EA1 (functional testing) to EA7 (detailed testing and formal design verification). The Common Criteria *TOE* refers to the product to be tested. A *Security Target* (ST) is a listing of the security claims for a particular IT security product. Also, the Common Criteria describe an intermediate grouping of security requirement components as a *package*. *Functionality* in the Common Criteria refers to standard and well-understood functional security requirements for IT systems. These functional requirements are organized around Trusted Computing Base (TCB) entities that include physical and logical controls, startup and recovery, reference mediation, and privileged states.

## Cost versus Benefits of Physical, Administrative, and Technical Controls

To evaluate the cost versus benefits of implementing safeguards, an analysis of the vulnerabilities and threats to an information system has to be performed. This activity is termed a *risk analysis* and is used to determine the potential for harm or loss as a result of a threat materializing. The results of the risk analysis are used to identify cost-effective safeguards.

The *Annualized Loss Expectancy* (ALE) is used in risk analysis to estimate the potential losses to an information system as a result of the exploitation of a vulnerability. The formula for the ALE in dollars is as follows:

ALE = Single Loss Expectancy (SLE) × Annualized Rate of Occurrence (ARO)

where the SLE is the dollar figure that represents an organization's loss from the occurrence of a single threat and the ARO is a number that represents the estimated annual frequency with which a threat is expected to occur.

The SLE, in turn, is derived from the following formula:

Asset Value ($) × Exposure Factor (EF) = SLE

where the EF represents the percentage of loss that a realized threat event would have on a specific asset. For example, if an asset valued at $1 million would have an exposure of 30 percent as a result of a threat realized, SLE would be $1 million × .30 or $300,000.

To incorporate all the components of the ALE formula, the ALE for the SLE asset example that is exposed to an earthquake threat that is estimated to occur once every 100 years is calculated as follows:

SLE = $300,000

ARO = 1/100 = .01

ALE = $ 300,000 × .01 = $ 3000

Thus, the risk to the asset from an earthquake is $ 3000. From this result, safeguards can be identified, and the ALE can be recalculated to reflect the reduction of the risk achieved by incorporating the different safeguards. From this exercise, the cost effectiveness of the safeguards can be determined.

This simple example does not take into account difficult-to-estimate losses that can occur from an incident. For example, the reputation of a company may be affected, business may be lost, or a particular type of safeguard may have an adverse impact on another critical resource. In selecting and evaluating safeguards, the information security manager should also take into account the maintenance costs as well as the acquisition costs.

# Information Security Process Improvement

Process improvement modeling traces its roots back to the Software Capability Maturity Model (CMM). The Software CMM was first developed at the Carnegie Mellon University Software Engineering Institute (SEI) in 1986 with support from the Mitre Corporation. The Software CMM is based on the premise that the quality of a software product is a direct function of the quality of its associated software development and maintenance processes.

## Information Security Process Improvement Model

The Systems Security Engineering Capability Maturity Model (SSE-CMM) is a formal security process improvement model based on derivatives of the Software CMM. Therefore, it is useful to review the Software CMM prior to discussing the SSE-CMM.

### The Software Capability Maturity Model (CMM)

A process is defined by the SEI as "a set of activities, methods, practices, and transformations that people use to develop and maintain systems and associated products" (SEI, *The Capability Maturity Model: Guidelines for Improving the Software Process*, Reading, MA: Addison Wesley, 1995).

The SEI defines five maturity levels that serve as a foundation for conducting continuous process improvement and as an ordinal scale for measuring the maturity of the organization involved in the software processes. The following are the five maturity levels and their corresponding focuses and characteristics:

- Level 1—Initiating: Competent people and heroics; processes are informal and ad hoc.

- Level 2—Repeatable: Project management processes; project management practices are institutionalized.

- Level 3—Defined: Engineering processes and organizational support; technical practices are integrated with management practices institutionalized.

- Level 4—Managed: Product and process improvement; product and process are quantitatively controlled.

- Level 5—Optimizing: Continuous process improvement; process improvement is institutionalized.

In the CMM for software, *software process capability* "describes the range of expected results that can be achieved by following a software process." Software process capability is a means of predicting the outcome of the next software project conducted by an organization. *Software process performance* is the result achieved by following a software process. Thus, software capability is aimed at expected results while software performance is focused on results that have been achieved.

Software process maturity, then, provides for the potential for growth in capability of an organization. An immature organization develops software in a crisis mode and usually exceeds budgets and time schedules; software processes are developed in an ad hoc fashion during the project. In a mature organization, the software process is effectively communicated to staff, the required processes are documented and consistent, software quality is evaluated, and roles and responsibilities for the project are understood.

The Software CMM is a component that supports the concept of continuous process improvement. This concept is embodied in the SEI Process Improvement IDEAL® Model and is shown in Figure 3.1.

- Phase 1 of the IDEAL Model is the initiation phase in which management support is obtained for process improvement, the objectives and constraints of the process improvement effort are defined, and the resources and plans for the next phase are obtained.

- Phase 2 identifies the appropriate appraisal method (such as CMM-based), identifies the project(s) to be appraised, trains the appraisal team, conducts the appraisal, and briefs management and the organization on the appraisal results.

- In Phase 3, an action plan is developed based on the results of Phase 2, management is briefed on the action plan, and the resources and group(s) are coordinated to implement the action plan.

**Process Improvement's IDEAL Model**

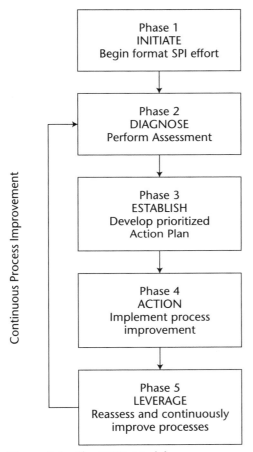

**Figure 3.1**   The IDEAL Model.

- Phase 4 is the action phase where resources are recruited for implementation of the action plan, the action plan is implemented, the improvement effort is measured, and the plan and implementation are modified based on measurements and feedback.

- Phase 5 is the review phase, which ensures that all success criteria have been achieved, all feedback is evaluated, the lessons learned are analyzed, the business plan and process improvement are compared for the desired outcome, and the next stage of the process improvement effort is planned.

The benefits of a long-term, formal software process improvement plan are as follows:

- Improved software quality
- Reduced life cycle time
- More accurate scheduling and meeting of milestones
- Management visibility
- Proactive planning and tracking

With this background of the Software CMM, the SSE-CMM information security process improvement model can now be covered.

## The Systems Security Engineering Capability Maturity Model (SSE-CMM)

The Systems Security Engineering Capability Maturity Model (SSE-CMM), copyright 1999 by the SSE-CMM Project, is based on the Systems Engineering CMM (SE-CMM) that applied the principles of the Software CMM to systems engineering. The SSE-CMM was developed by a consortium of government and industry experts and is now under the auspices of the International Systems Security Engineering Association (ISSEA) at www.issea.org. Version 2 of the SSE-CMM has been accepted by the International Organization for Standardization (ISO)/International Electrotechnical Commission (IEC) as Document ISO/IEC DIS 21827.

The SSE-CMM has the following salient points:

- It describes those characteristics of security engineering processes essential to ensure good security engineering.
- It captures industry's best practices.
- It is the accepted way of defining practices and improving capability.
- It provides measures of growth in capability of applying processes.

The SSE-CMM addresses the following areas of security:

- Operations security
- Information security
- Network security
- Physical security
- Personnel security
- Administrative security
- Communications security
- Emanations security
- Computer security

The SSE-CMM methodology and metrics provide a reference for comparing existing systems security engineering best practices against the essential systems security engineering elements described in the model. It defines two dimensions that are used to measure the capability of an organization to perform specific activities. These dimensions are *domain* and *capability*. The domain dimension consists of all the practices that collectively define security engineering. These practices are called Base Practices (BPs). Related BPs are grouped into Process Areas (PAs). The capability dimension represents practices that indicate process management and institutionalization capability. These practices are called Generic Practices (GPs) because they apply across a wide range of domains. The GPs represent activities that should be performed as part of performing BPs.

For the domain dimension, the SSE-CMM specifies 11 security engineering PAs and 11 organizational and project-related PAs, each consisting of BPs. BPs are mandatory characteristics that must exist within an implemented security engineering process before an organization can claim satisfaction in a given PA. The 22 PAs and their corresponding BPs incorporate the best practices of systems security engineering, as described in the sections that follow.

## *Security Engineering*

- PA01 Administer Security Controls
- PA02 Assess Impact
- PA03 Assess Security Risk
- PA04 Assess Threat
- PA05 Assess Vulnerability
- PA06 Build Assurance Argument
- PA07 Coordinate Security
- PA08 Monitor Security Posture
- PA09 Provide Security Input
- PA10 Specify Security Needs
- PA11 Verify and Validate Security

## *Project and Organizational Practices*

- PA12 Ensure Quality
- PA13 Manage Configuration

- PA14 Manage Project Risk
- PA15 Monitor and Control Technical Effort
- PA16 Plan Technical Effort
- PA17 Define Organization's Systems Engineering Process
- PA18 Improve Organization's Systems Engineering Process
- PA19 Manage Product Line Evolution
- PA20 Manage Systems Engineering Support Environment
- PA21 Provide Ongoing Skills and Knowledge
- PA22 Coordinate with Suppliers

The GPs are ordered in degrees of maturity and are grouped to form and distinguish among five levels of security engineering maturity. The attributes of these five levels are as follows:

- Level 1
  - 1.1 BPs Are Performed
- Level 2
  - 2.1 Planning Performance
  - 2.2 Disciplined Performance
  - 2.3 Verifying Performance
  - 2.4 Tracking Performance
- Level 3
  - 3.1 Defining a Standard Process
  - 3.2 Perform the Defined Process
  - 3.3 Coordinate the Process
- Level 4
  - 4.1 Establishing Measurable Quality Goals
  - 4.2 Objectively Managing Performance
- Level 5
  - 5.1 Improving Organizational Capability
  - 5.2 Improving Process Effectiveness

The corresponding descriptions of the five levels are given as follows ("The Systems Security Engineering Capability Maturity Model v2.0," 1999):

- Level 1, "Performed Informally," focuses on whether an organization or project performs a process that incorporates the BPs. A statement characterizing this level would be, "You have to do it before you can manage it."

- Level 2, "Planned and Tracked," focuses on project-level definition, planning, and performance issues. A statement characterizing this level would be, "Understand what's happening on the project before defining organization-wide processes."

- Level 3, "Well Defined," focuses on disciplined tailoring from defined processes at the organization level. A statement characterizing this level would be, "Use the best of what you've learned from your projects to create organization-wide processes."

- Level 4, "Quantitatively Controlled," focuses on measurements being tied to the business goals of the organization. Although it is essential to begin collecting and using basic project measures early, measurement and use of data are not expected organization-wide until the higher levels have been achieved. Statements characterizing this level would be, "You can't measure it until you know what 'it' is," and "Managing with measurement is meaningful only when you're measuring the right things."

- Level 5, "Continuously Improving," gains leverage from all the management practice improvements seen in the earlier levels, then emphasizes the cultural shifts that will sustain the gains made. A statement characterizing this level would be, "A culture of continuous improvement requires a foundation of sound management practice, defined processes, and measurable goals."

## Security Architecture Development and Modeling

A *security architecture* is a description of a system's composition for meeting the information security requirements. It is a high-level definition of all the components of the system that are related to information security. The concept of information security architecture is illustrated in Figure 3.2.

The architecture follows from the information security requirements and is the highest level of design of information security elements. Then, the design proceeds through successive levels of refinement and detail to implement the architectural approach. In formal methods, the security requirements are given as an information security model in mathematical terms. These requirements then drive the formal specifications. The specifications have to be verified to ensure that they correspond to the requirements as they proceed through steps of successive refinement to the implementation level.

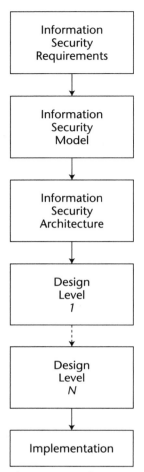

**Figure 3.2**   Information security architecture.

Another important aspect of a security architecture is a *protection mechanism* designed to prevent different users on multiprocessing systems from accessing information that they are not authorized to view. In a multiprocessor system, each process has the ability to access certain memory locations and to execute a subset of the computer's instruction set. The execution and memory space assigned to each process is called a *protection domain*. This domain can be extended to virtual memory, which increases the apparent size of real memory by using disk storage. The purpose of establishing a protection domain is to protect programs from all unauthorized modification or executional interference.

### The Trusted Computing Base

One type of architectural component that is used to implement protection is the *Trusted Computing Base* (TCB). The TCB is the total combination of protection mechanisms within a computer system, which includes the hardware, software, and firmware that are trusted to enforce a security policy. The *security perimeter* is the boundary that separates the TCB from the remainder of the system. A *trusted path* must also exist so that a user can access the TCB without being compromised by other processes or users. A *trusted computer system* is one that employs the necessary hardware and software assurance measures to enable its use in processing multiple levels of classified or sensitive information. This system meets the specified requirements for reliability and security.

Resources can also be protected through the principle of abstraction. *Abstraction* involves viewing system components at a high level and ignoring or segregating its specific details. This approach enhances the system's ability to understand complex systems and to focus on critical, high-level issues. In object-oriented programming, for example, methods (programs) and data are encapsulated in an object that can be viewed as an abstraction. This concept is called *information hiding* because the object's functioning details are hidden. Communication with this object takes place through messages to which the object responds as defined by its internal method.

### Rings

One scheme that supports multiple protection domains is the use of *protection rings*. These rings are organized with the most privileged domain located in the center of the ring and the least privileged domain in the outermost ring.

The operating system security kernel is usually located at Ring 0 and has access rights to all domains in that system. A *security kernel* is defined as the hardware, firmware, and software elements of a trusted computing base that implement the reference monitor concept. A *reference monitor* is a system component that enforces access controls on an object. Therefore, the reference monitor concept is an abstract machine that mediates all access of subjects to objects. The security kernel must do the following:

- Mediate all accesses
- Be protected from modification
- Be verified as correct

In the ring concept, access rights decrease as the ring number increases. Thus, the most trusted processes reside in the center rings. System components are placed in the appropriate ring according to the principle of least privilege. Therefore, the processes have only the minimum privileges necessary to perform their functions.

The ring protection mechanism was implemented in MIT's MULTICS time-shared operating system that was enhanced for secure applications by the Honeywell Corporation. MULTICS was initially targeted for use on specific hardware platforms because some of its functions could be implemented through the hardware's customization. It was designed to support 64 rings, but, in practice, only 8 rings were defined.

There are also other related kernel-based approaches to protection:

- Using a separate hardware device that validates all references in a system.

- Implementing a virtual machine monitor, which establishes a number of virtual machines isolated from each other that are running on the actual computer. The virtual machines mimic the architecture of a real machine, in addition to establishing a multilevel security environment—each virtual machine can run at a different security level.

- Using a software security kernel that operates in its own hardware protection domain.

## Security Labels

A security label is assigned to a resource to denote a type of classification or designation. This label can then indicate special security handling, or it can be used for access control. Once labels are assigned they usually cannot be altered and are an effective access control mechanism. Because labels must be compared and evaluated in accordance with the security policy, they incur additional processing overhead when used.

## Security Modes

An information system operates in different security modes that are determined by an information's classification level and the clearance of the users. A major distinction in its operation is between the system high mode and the multilevel security mode. In the *system high mode* of operation, a system operates at the highest level of information classification where all users must have clearances for the highest level. Not all users, however, may have a need to know for all the data. The *multilevel mode* of operation supports users with different clearances and data at multiple classification levels. Additional modes of operation are defined as follows:

**Dedicated.**   All users have a clearance or an authorization and a need-to-know for all information that is processed by an information system; a system may handle multiple classification levels.

**Compartmented.** All users have a clearance for the highest level of information classification, but they do not necessarily have the authorization and a need-to-know for all the data handled by the computer system.

**Controlled.** It is a type of multilevel security where a limited amount of trust is placed in the system's hardware/software base along with the corresponding restrictions on the classification of the information levels that can be processed.

**Limited access.** It is a type of system access where the minimum user clearance is not cleared and the maximum data classification is unclassified but sensitive.

## Security Architecture Vulnerabilities

Vulnerabilities in the system security architecture can lead to violations of the system's security policy. Typical architecturally related vulnerabilities include the following:

**Covert channel.** An unintended communication path between two or more subjects sharing a common resource, which supports the transfer of information in such a manner that violates the system's security policy. The transfer usually takes place through common storage areas or through access to a common path that can use a timing channel for the unintended communication.

**Lack of parameter checking.** The failure to check the size of input streams specified by parameters. Buffer overflow attacks exploit this vulnerability in certain operating systems and programs.

**Maintenance hook.** A hardware or software mechanism that was installed to permit system maintenance and to bypass the system's security protections. This vulnerability is sometimes referred to as a trapdoor.

**Time of Check to Time of Use (TOC/TOU) attack.** An attack that exploits the difference in the time that security controls were applied and the time the authorized service was used.

## System Failure Architectural Considerations

Whenever a hardware or software component of a trusted system fails, it is important that the failure does not compromise the security policy requirements of that system. In addition, the recovery procedures should not also provide an opportunity for violation of the system's security policy. If a system restart is required, the system must restart in a secure state. Startup should occur in the *maintenance mode* that permits access only by privileged users from privileged terminals. This mode supports the restoring of the system state and the security state.

When a computer or network component fails and the computer or the network continues to function, it is called a fault-tolerant system. For *fault tolerance* to operate, the system must be capable of detecting that a fault has occurred, and the system must then have the ability to correct the fault or operate around it. In a *fail-safe* system, program execution is terminated, and the system is protected from being compromised when a hardware or software failure occurs and is detected. In a system that is *fail soft or resilient*, selected, noncritical processing is terminated when a hardware or software failure occurs and is detected. The computer or network then continues to function in a degraded mode. The term *failover* refers to switching to a duplicate "hot" backup component in real time when a hardware or software failure occurs, which enables the system to continue processing.

A *cold start* occurs in a system when there is a TCB or media failure and the recovery procedures cannot return the system to a known, reliable, secure state. In this case, the TCB and portions of the software and data may be inconsistent and require external intervention. At that time, the maintenance mode of the system usually has to be employed.

## Modeling

Models are used in information security to formalize security policies. These models might be abstract or intuitive and provide a framework for the understanding of fundamental information security architectural concepts. Access control models, integrity models, and information flow models will be discussed to illustrate the different model types.

## Access Control Models

Access control philosophies can be organized into models that define the major and different approaches to this issue. These models are the access matrix, the Take-Grant model, the Bell-LaPadula confidentiality model, and the state machine model.

### The Access Matrix

The access matrix is a straightforward approach that provides access rights to subjects for objects. Access rights are of the type read, write, and execute. A subject is an active entity that is seeking rights to a resource or object. A subject can be a person, a program, or a process. An object is a passive entity such as a file or a storage resource. In some cases, an item can be a subject in one context and an object in another. A typical access control matrix is shown in Figure 3.3.

| Subject＼Object | File Gross Sales | File Expenses | Process Income | Print Server B |
|---|---|---|---|---|
| Patrick | Read | Read/Write | Execute | Write |
| Aaron | Read | Read | None | Write |
| Process Salaries | Read/Write | Read | Execute | None |
| Program Tax | Read/Write | Read/Write | Call | Write |

**Figure 3.3**   Example access matrix.

The columns of the access matrix are called *Access Control Lists* (ACLs), and the rows are called *capability lists*. The access matrix model supports discretionary access control because the entries in the matrix are at the discretion of the individual(s) who have the authorization authority over the table. In the access control matrix, a subject's capability can be defined by the triple (object, rights, random #.) Thus, the triple defines the rights a subject has to an object along with a random number used to prevent a replay or spoofing of the triple's source.

### Take-Grant Model

The Take-Grant model uses a directed graph to specify the rights that a subject can transfer to an object or that a subject can take from another subject. For example, assume that Subject A has a set of rights (S) that includes Grant rights to Object B. This capability is represented in Figure 3.4a. Then, assume that Subject A can transfer Grant rights for Object B to Subject C, and that Subject A has another set of rights (Y) to Object D. In some cases, Object D acts as an object, and in other cases, it acts as a subject. Then, as shown by the heavy arrow in Figure 3.4b, Subject C can grant a subset of the Y rights to Subject/Object D because Subject A passed the Grant rights to Subject C.

The Take capability operates in an identical fashion as the Grant illustration.

### Bell-LaPadula Model

The Bell-LaPadula model was developed to formalize the U.S. Department of Defense (DoD) multilevel security policy. The DoD labels materials at different levels of security classification. As previously discussed, these levels are Unclassified, Confidential, Secret, and Top Secret—from least sensitive to most sensitive. An individual who receives a clearance of Confidential, Secret, or Top Secret can access materials at that level of classification or below. An additional stipulation, however, is that the individual must have a *need-to-know* for that material. Thus, an individual cleared for Secret can access only the Secret-labeled documents that are necessary for that individual to perform an assigned job function. The Bell-LaPadula model deals only with the confidentiality of classified material. It does not address integrity or availability.

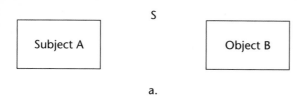

a.

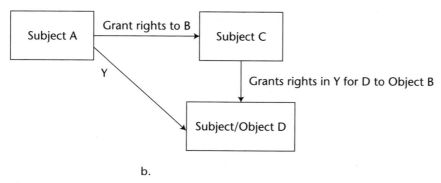

b.

**Figure 3.4**  Take-Grant model illustration.

The Bell-LaPadula model is built on the state machine concept. This concept defines a set of allowable states ($A_i$) in a system. The transition from one state to another on receipt of an input(s) ($X_i$) is defined by transition functions ($f_k$). The objective of this model is to ensure that the initial state is secure and that the transitions always result in a secure state. The transitions between two states are illustrated in Figure 3.5.

The Bell-LaPadula model defines a secure state through three multilevel properties. The first two properties implement mandatory access control, and the third one permits discretionary access control. These properties are defined as follows:

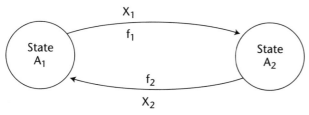

**Figure 3.5**  State transitions defined by function f with inputs X.

**The Simple Security Property (ss Property).**    States that reading of information by a subject at a lower sensitivity level from an object at a higher sensitivity level is not permitted (no read up).

**The * (star) Security Property.**    States that writing of information by a subject at a higher level of sensitivity to an object at a lower level of sensitivity is not permitted (no write down).

**The Discretionary Security Property.**    Uses an access matrix to specify discretionary access control.

There are instances where the * (star) property is too restrictive, and it interferes with required document changes. For instance, it may be desirable to move a low sensitivity paragraph in a higher sensitivity document to a lower sensitivity document. This transfer of information is permitted by the Bell-LaPadula model through a Trusted Subject. A Trusted Subject can violate the * property, yet it cannot violate its intent. These concepts are illustrated in Figure 3.6.

In some instances, a property called the *Strong * Property* is cited. This property states that reading or writing is permitted at a particular level of sensitivity, but not to either higher or lower levels of sensitivity.

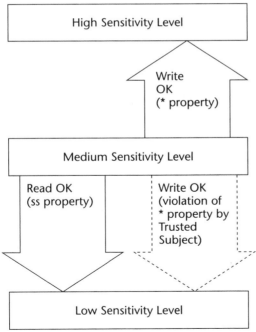

**Figure 3.6**    Illustration of Bell-LaPadula Simple Security and star Properties.

This model defines requests (R) to the system. A request is made while the system is in the state v1; a decision (d) is made upon the request, and the system changes to the state v2. (R, d, v1, v2) represents this tuple in the model. Again, the intent of this model is to ensure that there is a transition from one secure state to another secure state.

The discretionary portion of the Bell-LaPadula model is based on the access matrix. The system security policy defines who is authorized to have certain privileges to the system resources. Authorization is concerned with how access rights are defined and how they are evaluated. Some discretionary approaches are based on context-dependent and content-dependent access control. *Content-dependent control* makes access decisions based on the data contained in the object, whereas *context-dependent control* uses subject or object attributes or environmental characteristics to make these decisions. Examples of such characteristics include a job role, earlier accesses, and file creation dates and times.

As with any model, the Bell-LaPadula model has some weaknesses. These are the major ones:

- The model considers normal channels of the information exchange and does not address covert channels.

- The model does not deal with modern systems that use file sharing and servers.

- The model does not explicitly define what it means by a secure state transition.

- The model is based on multilevel security policy and does not address other policy types that may be used by an organization.

## Integrity Models

In many organizations, both governmental and commercial, integrity of the data is as important as or more important than confidentiality for certain applications. Thus, formal integrity models evolved. Initially, the integrity model was developed as an analog to the Bell-LaPadula confidentiality model and then became more sophisticated to address additional integrity requirements.

### The Biba Integrity Model

Integrity is usually characterized by the three following goals:

- The data is protected from modification by unauthorized users.

- The data is protected from unauthorized modification by authorized users.

- The data is internally and externally consistent—the data held in a database must balance internally and must correspond to the external, real-world situation.

To address the first integrity goal, the Biba model was developed in 1977 as an integrity analog to the Bell-LaPadula confidentiality model. The Biba model is lattice based and uses the less-than or equal-to relation. A lattice structure is defined as a partially ordered set with a least upper bound (LUB) and a greatest lower bound (GLB). The lattice represents a set of integrity classes (ICs) and an ordered relationship among those classes. A lattice can be represented as (IC, #, LUB, GUB).

Similar to the Bell-LaPadula model's classification of different sensitivity levels, the Biba model classifies objects into different levels of integrity. The model specifies the three following integrity axioms:

**The Simple Integrity Axiom.** States that a subject at one level of integrity is not permitted to observe (read) an object of a lower integrity (no read down).

**The * (star) Integrity Axiom.** States that an object at one level of integrity is not permitted to modify (write to) an object of a higher level of integrity (no write up).

**Axiom 3.** States that a subject at one level of integrity cannot invoke a subject at a higher level of integrity.

These axioms and their relationships are illustrated in Figure 3.7.

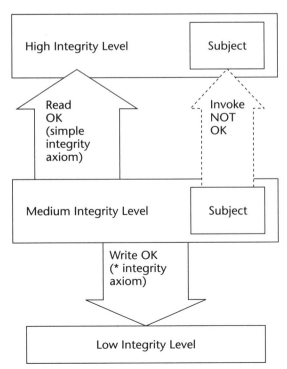

**Figure 3.7**   Biba model axioms.

### The Clark-Wilson Integrity Model

The approach of the Clark-Wilson model (1987) was to develop a framework for use in the real-world, commercial environment. This model addresses the three integrity goals and defines the following terms:

**Constrained data item (CDI).**   A data item whose integrity is to be preserved.

**Integrity verification procedure (IVP).**   Confirms that all CDIs are in valid states of integrity.

**Transformation procedure (TP).**   Manipulates the CDIs through a well-formed transaction, which transforms a CDI from one valid integrity state to another valid integrity state.

**Unconstrained data item (UDI).**   Data items outside of the control area of the modeled environment such as input information.

The Clark-Wilson model requires integrity labels to determine the integrity level of a data item and to verify that this integrity was maintained after an application of a TP. This model incorporates mechanisms to enforce internal and external consistency, a separation of duty, and a mandatory integrity policy.

### Information Flow Models

An information flow model is based on a state machine, and it consists of objects, state transitions, and lattice (flow policy) states. In this context, objects can also represent users. Each object is assigned a security class and value, and information is constrained to flow in the directions that are permitted by the security policy. An example is shown in Figure 3.8.

In Figure 3.8, information flows from Unclassified to Confidential in tasks in Project X and to the combined tasks in Project X. This information can flow in only one direction.

### Noninterference Model

This model is related to the information flow model with restrictions on the information flow. The basic principle of this model is that a group of users (A), who are using the commands (C), do not interfere with the user group (B), who are using commands (D). This concept is written as A, C: | B, D. Restating this rule, the actions of Group A who are using commands C are not seen by users in Group B using commands D.

### Composition Theories

In most applications, systems are built by combining smaller systems. An interesting situation to consider is whether the security properties of component systems are maintained when they are combined to form a larger entity.

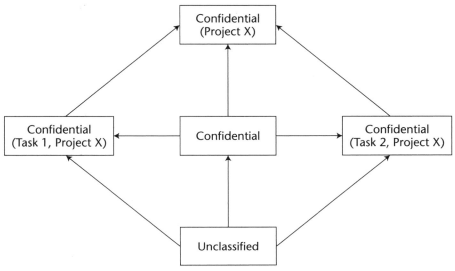

**Figure 3.8** Information flow model example.

John McLean studied this issue in 1994 (McLean, J. "A General Theory of Composition for Trace Sets Closed under Selective Interleaving Functions," *Proceedings of 1994 IEEE Symposium on Research in Security and Privacy*, Piscataway, New Jersey: IEEE Press, 1994).

He defined two compositional constructions—external and internal. The following are the types of external constructs:

**Cascading.** One system's input is obtained from the output of another system.

**Feedback.** One system provides the input to a second system, which, in turn, feeds back to the input of the first system.

**Hookup.** A system that communicates with another system as well as with external entities.

The internal composition constructs are intersection, union, and difference.

The general conclusion of this study was that the security properties of the small systems were maintained under composition (in most instances) in the cascading construct, yet are also subject to other system variables for the other constructs.

## Project Management Methods and Techniques

The success of a project is evaluated through a number of metrics such as meeting the schedule, remaining within budget and resource estimates, the quality of the product or service delivered, and satisfying the overall goals of the organization. Successful projects are usually the result of good project management. *Project management* can be defined as a set of procedures, rules, technology, and knowledge that a project manager uses to plan, staff, coordinate, direct, and control a project to accomplish a successful outcome.

Some key items to be considered in developing a project management plan are the following:

- Establishing the project start and completion dates
- Determining the development life cycle or prototyping model to be used
- Determining the tasks in each phase of the development
- Establishing critical points and milestones in the development process and associated promised or expected completion dates
- Estimating the resources required to complete the project successfully
- Matching the available personnel and their skill levels to the estimated project personnel resource requirements
- Determining the flow of the tasks—that is, what tasks are required to be done serially and what tasks can be done in parallel with other tasks
- Estimating project costs and break-even points
- Establishing project review criteria

## Work Breakdown Structure

In order to develop the list of tasks to be accomplished in the project, a work breakdown structure (WBS) can be used. A WBS is a hierarchical breakdown of a project's activities into increasingly finer detail. A WBS can be thought of as a document outline with each section numbered into multiple subsections. Using the systems development life cycle approach, the highest level in the WBS would be the life cycle phases (see the discussion on the systems development life cycle later in this chapter). Then, the next level would be a breakdown of tasks in each of the life cycle phases. The following, more detailed level of the WBS would be subtasks of the tasks in each phase and so on. The goal is to break down the overall project until manageable subtasks are obtained.

## Gantt Chart

One useful tool for visualizing the project tasks with respect to time is the Gantt chart. In the Gantt chart, all the project tasks are listed on the vertical axis with units of time listed on the horizontal axis. Markers are used to note the estimated and actual start and end times. The personnel assigned to each

task may also be indicated on a separate line. The Gantt chart does not emphasize relationships among tasks, but focuses on task durations.

An example Gantt chart is shown in Figure 3.9.

## PERT Chart

A PERT chart is another project management tool; however, it emphasizes the
relationships and dependencies among tasks. The letters PERT stand for the
Program Evaluation Review Technique, which was developed in the 1950s by
the U.S. Navy to use in managing the Polaris submarine missile program. Near
the same time, a similar methodology, the Critical Path Method (CPM), was
developed in the private sector. CPM and PERT are sometimes used interchangeably and refer to the same type of methodology.

A PERT chart is, essentially, a network diagram that uses labeled nodes to
represent milestones or significant events in the project development cycle.
The starting point is an initiation node from which the first task, or tasks, orig-
inates. If a number of tasks begin at the same time, they begin from the same
node and branch out in different directions. A task is represented by a line that
indicates its name, its duration, and the number of people assigned to the task.
The opposite end of the task line ends on another node, which is the beginning
of another task, or the beginning of any slack time. Slack time is the "waiting"
time between tasks. The critical path is the longest path, in terms of duration,
of dependent tasks through the PERT chart.

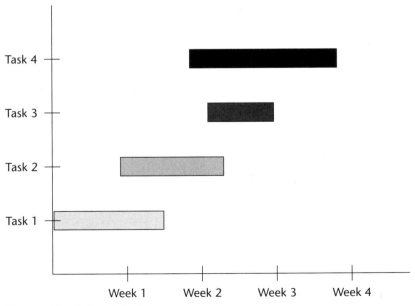

**Figure 3.9**   A Gantt chart.

The nodes are interconnected by directional lines or vectors that show the sequencing of the tasks and any dependencies among the tasks.

It is important to emphasize that the tasks in a PERT chart are the vectors connecting the nodes and not the nodes themselves. An example of a PERT chart is given in Figure 3.10.

In Figure 3.10, the vectors are labeled as tasks and the number following the task number is the duration of the task. Thus, Task A.2 represents Task A and the 2 indicates that Task A will take 2 days to complete. If the tasks are traced through on the PERT chart, the path A,D,E,I,H is the critical path because the total time to complete the tasks in this path is 15 days. Any other path taken is less than 15 days. The path E to I and the parallel path of F to G provide an example of slack time. The slack time of Task F is 2 days because the total time to complete tasks E and I is 6 days while the total time to complete tasks F and G is 4 days. Thus, Task F can take an additional 2 days to complete because Task H cannot begin until Tasks E and I are completed.

As mentioned earlier, the Critical Path Method (CPM) chart is very similar to a PERT chart. The critical path in a CPM chart is highlighted and depicts the path through a set of dependent tasks that takes the greatest amount of time to complete. This special notation of the critical path allows the project manager to pay special attention to the tasks on the critical path to ensure the timely and successful completion of the project.

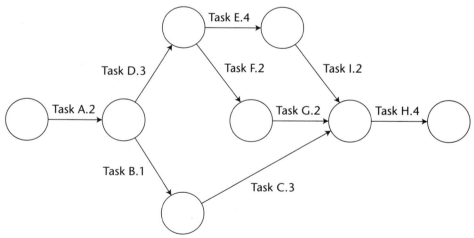

**Figure 3.10**   A PERT chart example.

## The Management Approach

In addition to support tools, project management has to address the individuals involved in the project. The organization of the project team and the experience, motivation, personalities, and responsibilities of the team members are critical to the success of a project. A key consideration is the style of the project manager. There are many ways to label and categorize management styles. One example is given in the following list:

**The coaching style.**   The manager supervises, but also interacts with the subordinates, explains decisions, asks for their input, and so on.

**The supporting style.**   The manager shares responsibility for making decisions and generally provides support to subordinates.

**The directing style.**   The manager supervises subordinates very closely and gives detailed directions.

**The delegating style.**   Responsibilities and decision-making authority are given to a subordinate.

Table 3.1 provides general guidance on what styles work well with the different types of individuals who are usually involved in a project.

A good manager must also be able to handle conflicts among his or her subordinates and/or team members. Conflicts usually are the result of poor definition of objectives or responsibilities, responsibility without the corresponding authority, overlap of duties, overload of work assignments, and competing work assignments. The usual ways to handle conflicts are through reassignment, having the conflicting individuals meet and work things out, arbitration, or coming to a mutual agreement on objectives, responsibilities, and assignments.

**Table 3.1**   Management Styles for Different Types of Individuals

| MANAGEMENT STYLE | SUBORDINATES' PERSONAL CHARACTERISTICS |
| --- | --- |
| Coaching | Moderate competence, low motivation, low level of commitment |
| Supporting | High competence, different levels of commitment |
| Directing | Low competence, high level of commitment |
| Delegating | High competence, high level of motivation, high level of commitment |

# Systems Development Life Cycle (SDLC) Methodologies

Life cycle models provide an insight into the development process and highlight the relationships among the different activities in this process. These models describe a structured approach to the development and adjustment processes involved in producing and maintaining systems. Life cycle models address specifications, requirements, design, verification and validation, and maintenance activities.

As a prelude to discussions on the security systems development life cycle, it is useful to review the traditional development life cycle evolution using system software as an example.

## Traditional SDLC

Software can be defined programs, documentation, and operating procedures by which computers can be made useful to man.

In systems software development, the term *verification* is defined as the process of establishing the truth of correspondence between a software product and its specification. *Validation* establishes the fitness or worth of a software product for its operational mission. *Requirements*, as defined in the Waterfall model (W.W. Royce, "Managing the Development of Large Software Systems: Concepts and Techniques," *Proceedings* WESCON, Manhattan Beach, CA: August 1970), are a complete, validated specification of the required functions, interfaces, and performance for the software product. *System design* is a complete, verified specification of the overall hardware-software architecture, control structure, and data structure for the product.

Quality software is difficult to obtain without a development process. As with any project, two principal goals of software development are to produce a quality product that meets the customer's requirements and to stay within the budget and time schedule. A succession of models has emerged over time incorporating improvements in the development process. An early model defined succeeding stages, taking into account the different staffing and planning that were required for each stage. The model was simplistic in that it assumed that each step could be completed and finalized without any effect from the later stages that might require rework. This model is shown in Figure 3.11.

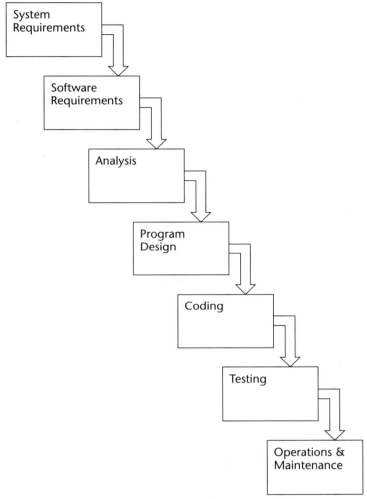

**Figure 3.11**    Simplistic software development model.

## The Waterfall Model

Because subsequent stages such as design, coding, and testing in the development process might require modifying earlier stages in the model, the Waterfall model emerged. Under this model, software development can be managed if the developers are limited to going back only one stage to rework. If this limitation is not imposed (particularly on a large project with several team members), then any developer can be working on any phase at any time, and the required rework might be accomplished several times. Obviously, this approach results in a lack of project control, and it is difficult to manage. The Waterfall model is shown in Figure 3.12.

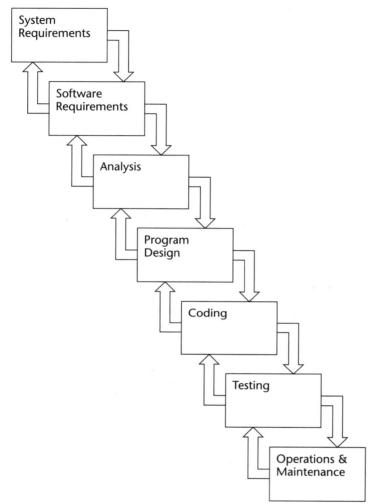

**Figure 3.12** The Waterfall model.

One fundamental problem with these models is that they assume that a phase or stage ends at a specific time; however, this is not usually the case in real-world applications. If an ending phase is forcibly tied to a project milestone, the situation can be improved. If rework is required in this mode, the phase is not officially pronounced as ending. The rework must then be accomplished and the project milestone met before the phase is officially recognized as completed.

In 1976, Barry Boehm reinterpreted the Waterfall model to have phases end at project milestones and to have the backward arrows represent back references for verification and validation (V&V) against defined baselines. Verification evaluates the product during development against the specification, and validation refers to the work product satisfying the real-world requirements and concepts. In simpler terms, Barry Boehm states, "Verification is doing the job right, and validation is doing the right job." These concepts are illustrated in Figure 3.13. In summary, the steps of the modified Waterfall model are as follows:

- System feasibility
- Software plans and requirements
- Product design
- Detailed design
- Code
- Integration
- Implementation
- Operations and maintenance

In this modified version of the Waterfall model, the end of each phase is a point in time for which no iteration of phases is provided. Rework can be accomplished within a phase when the phase end review shows that it is required.

## The Spiral Model

In 1988, Barry Boehm developed the Spiral model, which is actually a meta-model that incorporates a number of the software development models. This model depicts a spiral that incorporates the various phases of software development. As shown in Figure 3.14, the angular dimension represents the progress made in completing the phases, and the radial dimension represents the cumulative project cost. The model states that each cycle of the spiral involves the same series of steps for each part of the project.

The lower-left quadrant focuses on developing plans that will be reviewed in the upper quadrants of the diagram prior to finalization of the plans. Then, after a decision to proceed with the project is made, the spiral is initiated in the upper-left quadrant. This particular quadrant defines the objectives of the part of the project being addressed, alternative means of accomplishing this part of the project, and the constraints associated with these alternatives.

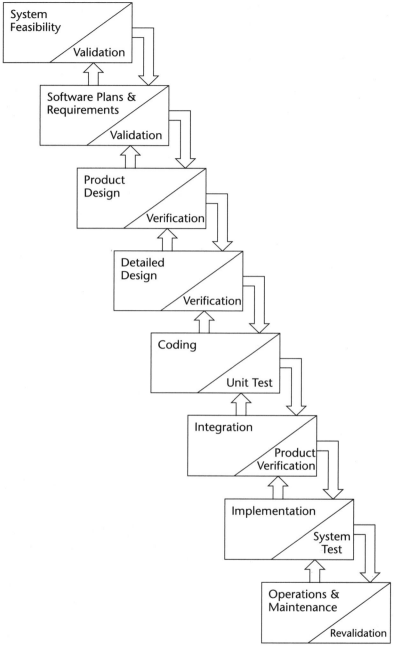

**Figure 3.13**   A modified Waterfall model.

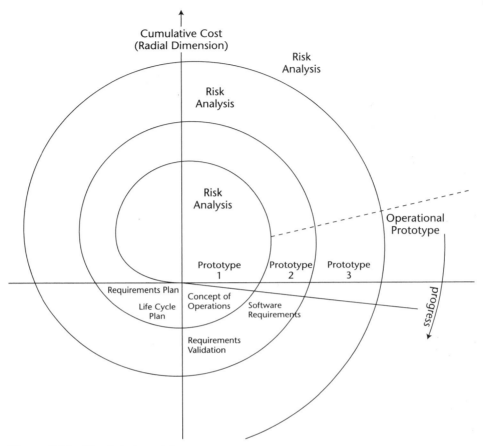

**Figure 3.14**   The Spiral model.

The next step involves assessing the alternatives in regard to the project objectives and constraints. This assessment can include prototyping, modeling, and simulation. The purpose of this step is to identify and evaluate the risks involved, and it is shown in the upper-right quadrant of the model. Once these issues are resolved, the next step in this procedure follows the traditional life cycle model approach. The lower-right quadrant of the spiral depicts the final developmental phase for each part of the product. An important concept of the Spiral model is that the left horizontal axis depicts the major review that is required to complete each full cycle.

## *Change Control and Software Maintenance*

In the life cycle models we have presented, the maintenance phase is listed at the end of the cycle with operations. One way of looking at the maintenance phase is to divide it into the following three subphases:

- Request control
- Change control
- Release control

The request control activity manages the users' requests for changes to the software product and gathers information that can be used for managing this activity. The following steps are included in this activity:

- Establishing the priorities of requests
- Estimating the cost of the changes requested
- Determining the interface that is presented to the user

The change control process is the principal step in the maintenance phase. Issues that are addressed by change control include the following:

- Recreating and analyzing the problem
- Developing the changes and corresponding tests
- Performing quality control

In addition, there are also other considerations such as the following:

- The tool types to be used in implementing the changes
- The documentation of the changes
- The restriction of the changes' effects on other parts of the code
- Recertification and accreditation, if necessary

Release control is associated with issuing the latest release of the software. This step involves deciding which requests will be included in the new release, archiving of the release, configuration management, quality control, distribution, and acceptance testing.

## *Configuration Management*

In order to manage evolving changes to software products and to formally track and issue new versions of software products, configuration management is employed. According to the British Standards Institution (British Standards Institute, U.K., "Information Security Management, British Standard 7799," 1998), configuration management is "the discipline of identifying the components of a continually evolving system for the purposes of controlling changes to those components and maintaining integrity and traceability throughout the life cycle." The following definitions are associated with configuration management:

**Configuration Item.**   A component whose state is to be recorded and against which changes are to be progressed.

**Version.**   A recorded state of the configuration item.

**Configuration.**   A collection of component configuration items that comprise a configuration item in some stage of its evolution (recursive).

**Building.**   The process of assembling a version of a configuration item from versions of its component configuration items.

**Build List.**   The set of the versions of the component configuration items that is used to build a version of a configuration item.

**Software Library.**   A controlled area that is accessible only to approved users who are restricted to the use of approved procedures.

The following procedures are associated with configuration management:

- Identify and document the functional and physical characteristics of each configuration item (configuration identification).
- Control changes to the configuration items, and issue versions of configuration items from the software library (configuration control).
- Record the processing of changes (configuration status accounting).
- Control the quality of the configuration management procedures (configuration audit).

### Cost Estimation Models

An early model for estimating the cost of software development projects was the Basic Construction Cost Model, COCOMO, proposed by Barry Boehm (B.W. Boehm, *Software Engineering Economics*, Englewood Cliffs, NJ: Prentice-Hall, 1981). This model estimates software development effort and cost as a function of the size of the software product in source instructions. It develops the following equations:

- The number of man-months (MM) required to develop the most common type of software product, in terms of the number of thousands of delivered source instructions (KDSI) in the software product:

  $$MM = 2.4 \, (KDSI)^{1.05}$$

- The development schedule (TDEV) in months:

  $$TDEV = 2.5(MM)^{0.38}$$

In addition, Boehm developed an Intermediate COCOMO Model that also takes into account hardware constraints, personnel quality, use of modern tools, and other attributes and their aggregate impact on overall project costs. A Detailed COCOMO Model, by Boehm, accounts for the effects of the additional factors used in the intermediate model on the costs of individual project phases. These models are now referred to as COCOMO 81 because Boehm has developed a newer model, COCOMO II (Barry Boehm, et al., "The COCOMO 2.0 Software Cost Estimation Model," *International Society of Parametric Analysts*, May 1995).

COCOMO II is made up of submodels that increase in fidelity as the development process progresses. In increasing order of fidelity, these models are Applications Composition, Early Design, and Post-architecture. The COCOMO II model supports the estimation of effort, costs, and schedule for a software development project. COCOMO II was developed to incorporate the changes in software development away from the batch environment to distributed processing, process improvement, and software reuse.

Another model, the function point measurement model, does not require the user to estimate the number of delivered source instructions. The software development effort is determined by using the following five user functions:

- External input types
- External output types
- Logical internal file types
- External interface file types
- External inquiry types

These functions are tallied and weighted according to complexity and used to determine the software development effort.

A third type of model applies the Rayleigh curve to software development cost and effort estimation. A prominent model using this approach is the Software Life Cycle Model (SLIM) estimating method. In this method, estimates based on the number of lines of source code are modified by the following two factors:

- The manpower buildup index (MBI), which estimates the rate of buildup of staff on the project
- A productivity factor (PF), which is based on the technology used

# Information Security and the Systems Development Life Cycle

As is the case with most engineering and software development practices, the earlier in the process a component is introduced, the better chance there is for success, lower development costs, and reduced rework. Information security is no exception. Information security controls' conception, development, implementation, testing, and maintenance should be conducted concurrently with the system software life cycle phases. One approach is shown conceptually in Figure 3.15.

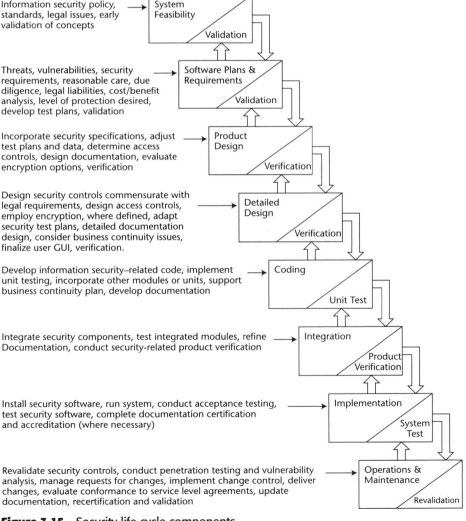

**Figure 3.15** Security life cycle components.

Testing of the software modules or unit testing should be addressed when the modules are being designed. Personnel other than the programmers should conduct this testing. The test data is part of the specifications. Testing should not only check the modules using normal and valid input data, but also check for incorrect types, out-of-range values, and other bounds and/or conditions. Live or actual field data is not recommended for use in the testing procedures because both data types might not cover out-of-range situations and the correct outputs of the test are unknown. Special test suites of data that exercise all paths of the software to the fullest extent possible and whose correct resulting outputs are known beforehand should be used.

## The Systems Development Life Cycle

In order to address the development of controlled and auditable large information systems, the U.S. government commissioned a task force study (Ruthberry, Zella, et. al., "Guide to Auditing for Controls and Security: A System Development Life Cycle Approach," *NBS Special Publication 500-153*, Gaithersburg, MD: National Bureau of Standards, 1988). A few of the salient points of the publication are that auditors should ensure the following:

- The system is capable of being audited.
- The new system meets a need.
- The cost of a new system is justified.
- Risk analyses and security controls are components of the system requirements.
- Financial controls are included in the system.
- Critical assets and data are noted and labeled properly.
- Adequate business continuity planning and disaster recovery modes are part of the implementation.
- The audit trail is protected, and the associated information is protected from destruction or modification.
- The principle of separation of duties and least privilege are practiced.

A summary of the audit objectives associated with each phase of an SDLC as contained in NIST Publication 500-153 is given in Table 3.2.

A later document, NIST Special Publication 800-18, *Guide for Developing Security Plans for Information Technology Systems,* was published in December 1998 and provides further guidance on the incorporation of information security into the SDLC. This publication addresses the basic SDLC phases of initiation, development/acquisition, implementation, operation, and disposal. An excerpt from NIST Special Publication 800-18 defines the security aspects of these phases as follows.

**Table 3.2**   SDLC Phases and Audit Objectives

| SDLC PHASE | AUDIT OBJECTIVE |
| --- | --- |
| Initiation | System need is established.<br>Cost of system is justified. |
| Definition | Users' needs are defined.<br>Users' needs translate into requirements statements that incorporate appropriate controls. |
| Design | Systems requirements are incorporated into design specifics to include controls that support the auditing of the system. |
| Programming and training | The software and other components of the system faithfully incorporate the design specifications.<br>Proper documentation and training are provided. |
| Evaluation and acceptance | System and data are validated.<br>System meets all user requirements.<br>System meets all control requirements. |

### 4.4.1 Initiation Phase

During the initiation phase, the need for a system is expressed and the purpose of the system is documented. A sensitivity assessment can be performed that looks at the sensitivity of the information to be processed and the system itself.

### 4.4.2 Development/Acquisition Phase

During this phase, the system is designed, purchased, programmed, developed, or otherwise constructed. This phase often consists of other defined cycles, such as the system development cycle or the acquisition cycle.

During the first part of the development/acquisition phase, security requirements should be developed at the same time system planners define the requirements of the system. These requirements can be expressed as technical features (for example, access controls), assurances (for example, background checks for system developers), or operational practices (for example, awareness and training). If the system or part of the system is in this phase, include a general description of any specifications that were used and whether they are being maintained. Among the questions that should be addressed are the following:

- During the system design, were security requirements identified?
- Were the appropriate security controls with associated evaluation and test procedures developed before the procurement action?
- Did the solicitation documents (for example, Request for Proposals) include security requirements and evaluation/test procedures?

- Did the requirements permit updating security requirements as new threats/vulnerabilities are identified and as new technologies are implemented?

- If this is a purchased commercial application or if the application contains commercial, off-the-shelf components, were security requirements identified and included in the acquisition specifications?

### 4.4.3 Implementation Phase

In the implementation phase, the system's security features should be configured and enabled, the system should be tested and installed or fielded, and the system should be authorized for processing. A design review and systems test should be performed prior to placing the system into operation to ensure that it meets security specifications. In addition, if new controls are added to the application or the support system, additional acceptance tests of those new controls must be performed. This ensures that new controls meet security specifications and do not conflict with or invalidate existing controls. The results of the design reviews and system tests should be fully documented, updated as new reviews or tests are performed, and maintained in the official organization records.

If the system or parts of the system are in the implementation phase, describe who conducted the design reviews and systems tests and when. Include information about additional design reviews and systems tests for any new controls added after the initial acceptance tests were completed. Discuss whether the documentation of these reviews and tests has been kept up-to-date and maintained in the organization records.

### 4.4.4 Operation/Maintenance Phase

During this phase, the system performs its work. The system is almost always being continuously modified by the addition of hardware and software and by numerous other events. If the system is undergoing modifications, determine which phase of the life cycle the system modifications are in, and describe the security activities conducted or planned for in that part of the system. For the system in the operation/maintenance phase, the security plan documents the security activities. In appropriate sections of this security plan, the following high-level items should be described:

**Security operations and administration.**   Operation of a system involves many security activities. Performing backups, holding training classes, managing cryptographic keys, keeping up with user administration and access privileges, and updating security software are some examples.

**Operational assurance.**   Operational assurance examines whether a system is operated according to its current security requirements. This includes both the actions of people who operate or use the system and the functioning of technical controls. A management official must authorize in writing the use of the system based on the implementation of its security plan.

**Audits and monitoring.**    To maintain operational assurance, organizations use two basic methods: system audits and monitoring. These terms are used loosely in the computer security community and often overlap. A system *audit* is a one-time or periodic event to evaluate security. *Monitoring* refers to an ongoing activity that examines either the system or the users. In general, the more "real time" an activity is, the more it falls into the category of monitoring.

### 4.4.5 Disposal Phase

The disposal phase of the IT system life cycle involves the disposition of information, hardware, and software. If the system or part of the system is at the end of the life cycle, briefly describe in this section how the following items are disposed:

**Information.**    Information may be moved to another system, archived, discarded, or destroyed. When archiving information, consider the method for retrieving the information in the future. While electronic information is generally easier to retrieve and store, the technology used to create the records may not be readily available in the future. Measures may also have to be taken for the future use of data that has been encrypted, such as taking appropriate steps to ensure the secure long-term storage of cryptographic keys. It is important to consider legal requirements for records retention when disposing of IT systems. For federal systems, system management officials should consult with the office responsible for retaining and archiving federal records.

**Media sanitization.**    The removal of information from a storage medium (such as a hard disk or tape) is called sanitization. Different kinds of sanitization provide different levels of protection. A distinction can be made between clearing information (rendering it unrecoverable by keyboard attack) and purging (rendering information unrecoverable against laboratory attack). There are three general methods of purging media: overwriting, degaussing (for magnetic media only), and destruction.

## Prototyping

In the traditional systems development process, numerous specification and requirements documents are generated. These documents are usually large and might contain ambiguities. Furthermore, errors in the documents or different interpretations of the document may not surface until significant expenditures of time and money have occurred. One alternative to the traditional process is prototyping. In *prototyping,* a scaled-down, limited version of a system or portion of a system to be developed is produced and evaluated by the customer to uncover problems early in the development cycle. Prototyping can also be used to explore design alternatives, train the system users, and as a tool for testing. In order to develop a prototype in a reasonable time, some of the requirements of the proposed system must be relaxed for the prototype. Examples include implementing a subset of the required functions, relaxing response time characteristics, and simplifying the graphical user interface.

The following list summarizes the three general types of prototypes:

**Incremental prototyping.**   This type of prototyping involves breaking the project into subunits or subfunctions and delivering successive versions of subsystems incorporating more detailed requirements. This process continues until the full, final system is delivered.

**Evolutionary prototyping.**   In evolutionary prototyping, a prototype of a system is built and then evolves into the final system. This evolution incorporates corrective and adaptive changes that might have occurred in the maintenance phase of the traditional life cycle development process.

**Throw-away prototyping.**   In this prototyping, a version of the system is built to check the requirements and is then discarded.

Management of prototyping projects differs from that of conventional development projects. In the prototyping project, the prototyping objectives should be defined and stated as early as possible. The objectives should spell out which one of the three types of prototypes is to be developed. Also, criteria for evaluation of the prototype have to be generated and agreed on. Because change is inherent in a prototype project, configuration management techniques should be used and all changes documented.

# Certification and Accreditation

In many environments, formal methods must be applied to ensure that the appropriate information system security safeguards are in place and that they are functioning per the specifications. In addition, an authority must take responsibility for putting the system into operation. These actions are known as *certification* and *accreditation*, respectively. Specifically, certification is the comprehensive evaluation of the technical and nontechnical security features of an information system and the other safeguards, which are created in support of the accreditation process to establish the extent to which a particular design and implementation meet the set of specified security requirements. Accreditation is the formal declaration by a *Designated Approving Authority* (DAA) where an information system is approved to operate in a particular security mode by using a prescribed set of safeguards at an acceptable level of risk.

The certification and accreditation of a system must be checked after a defined period of time or when changes occur in the system and/or its environment. Then, *recertification* and *re-accreditation* are required.

Two U.S. defense and government certification and accreditation standards have been developed for the evaluation of critical information systems. These standards are the *Defense Information Technology Security Certification and Accreditation Process* (DITSCAP) and the *National Information Assurance Certification and Accreditation Process* (NIACAP).

## DITSCAP

DITSCAP establishes a standard process, a set of activities, general task descriptions, and a management structure to certify and accredit the IT systems that will maintain the required security posture. This process is designed to certify that the IT system meets the accreditation requirements and that the system will maintain the accredited security posture throughout its life cycle. DITSCAP comprises the following four phases:

**Phase 1, Definition.**   Phase 1 focuses on understanding the mission, the environment, and the architecture in order to determine the security requirements and level of effort necessary to achieve accreditation.

**Phase 2, Verification.**   Phase 2 verifies the evolving or modified system's compliance with the information agreed on in the System Security Authorization Agreement (SSAA). The objective is to use the SSAA to establish an evolving yet binding agreement on the level of security required before system development begins or changes to a system are made. After accreditation, the SSAA becomes the baseline security configuration document.

**Phase 3, Validation.**   Phase 3 validates the compliance of a fully integrated system with the information stated in the SSAA.

**Phase 4, Post Accreditation.**   Phase 4 includes the activities that are necessary for the continuing operation of an accredited IT system in its computing environment and for addressing the changing threats that a system faces throughout its life cycle.

## NIACAP

The NIACAP establishes the minimum national standards for certifying and accrediting national security systems. This process provides a standard set of activities, general tasks, and a management structure to certify and accredit systems that maintain the information assurance and the security posture of a system or site. The NIACAP is designed to certify that the information system meets the documented accreditation requirements and will continue to maintain the accredited security posture throughout the system's life cycle. There are three types of NIACAP accreditation:

**A site accreditation.**   Evaluates the applications and systems at a specific, self-contained location.

**A type accreditation.**   Evaluates an application or system that is distributed to a number of different locations.

**A system accreditation.**   Evaluates a major application or general support system.

The NIACAP is composed of four phases: Definition, Verification, Validation, and Post Accreditation. These are essentially identical to those of the DITSCAP.

# Security Metrics Implementation

A number of different methodologies can be applied to implement security metrics. One approach is to use the SSE-CMM described earlier in this chapter as a tool to measure the effectiveness of information security controls. Another method is National Security Agency INFOSEC Assessment Methodology (NSA-IAM).

## NSA-IAM

Information on the IAM can be found at www.nsa.gov/isso/iam/index.htm. The IAM evaluates information systems at a high level and uses a subset of the SSE-CMM process areas to measure the implementation of information security on these systems. The IAM is defined as a Level 1 assessment—that is, it performs a nonintrusive, standardized baseline analysis of the information security characteristics of an information system. The outcome of an IAM assessment is the means of eliminating or mitigating vulnerabilities that could be exploited by threats. The results of the assessment are qualitative rather than quantitative. An IAM assessment is conducted in three phases, as described in Table 3.3.

**Table 3.3**   IAM Assessment Phases

| IAM PHASES | ACTIVITY | DURATION |
|---|---|---|
| 1. Pre-assessment | Define customer needs<br>Identify the system and boundaries<br>Identify the criticality of the information<br>Begin to write assessment plan | Two to four weeks |
| 2. On-site | Explore and confirm conclusions made during phase 1<br>Gather data and documentation<br>Conduct interviews<br>Provide an initial analysis | One to two weeks |
| 3. Post-assessment | Finalize the analysis<br>Prepare the report<br>Distribute the report and recommendations | Two to eight weeks |

The IAM is based on the Organizational Criticality Matrix. The characteristics of this matrix are the following:

- Qualitative impact attributes (high, medium, or low) are assigned to relevant automated information systems.

- Attributes are assigned based on their impact on the confidentiality, integrity, and availability of the information system.

- Additional attributes such as authentication and non-repudiation can be added, if desired.

## The Automated Security Self-Evaluation Tool (ASSET)

ASSET is a tool developed by NIST to automate the process of self-assessment through the use of the questionnaire in NIST Special Publication 800-26 (Marianne Swanson, "Security Self-Assessment Guide for Information Technology Systems," *NIST Special Publication 800-26*, Gaithersburg, MD: National Institute for Standards and Technology, November 2001). The Web site for viewing the document is http://csrc.nist.gov.

The assessment described in Special Publication 800-26 uses an extensive questionnaire "containing specific control objectives and techniques against which an unclassified system or group of interconnected systems can be tested and measured." Special Publication 800-26 builds on the Federal IT Security Assessment Framework developed by NIST for the Federal Chief Information

Officer (CIO) Council. This framework defines five levels of information security that can be used to determine whether the level is adequately implemented. In addition, the framework addresses 17 control areas that can be evaluated.

The steps in the assessment process are as follows:

1. *Data collection*. The process of gathering and entering system data.

2. *Reporting*. Creating aggregate data so that it can be analyzed.

3. *Analysis*. The process of understanding, evaluating, and making judgments on a set of system data.

The ASSET tool supports self-assessment by facilitating data collection and reporting.

The self-assessment process defines the following roles:

**Manager.**   Individual responsible for the assessment and responsible for analysis of the results.

**Reporter.**   Individual responsible for importing multiple system data into ASSET, making sure that all questions are answered for all systems, aggregating results from all systems with the enterprise, and generating reports.

**Collector.**   Individual who ensures that all questions are answered for each system under the collector's review, interacts with the subject matter expert to gather system information, and enters individual system data into ASSET.

**Subject matter expert.**   Individual who is knowledgeable about the system or topic areas being assessed, provides specific responses to assessment questions, and interacts with the collector on an as-needed basis.

A typical ASSET assessment will have a number of collectors and one reporter. ASSET comprises two separate host-based applications, the ASSET Manager and the ASSET System. The ASSET Manager houses the recorder role, and the ASSET System incorporates the collector role. The questionnaire is presented in the ASSET System. The ASSET System performs the following additional functions:

- Tracks all collectors and subject matter experts who provide answers to ASSET questions

- Provides for entry and storage of individual system data

- Generates single system summary reports intended for the user who completes the questionnaire

The ASSET Manager supports the sorting of questionnaire results and aggregating data from multiple systems agency-wide for the purpose of generating enterprise-wide reports. It also tracks all collectors and subject matter experts who answer the questions in the questionnaire. Reports generated by the ASSET Manager include the following:

- Summary of all systems
- Summary of system types
- Summary by system sensitivities
- Summary by organization

## Defense-Wide Information Assurance Program (DIAP)

Another information system security metric approach is the Information Assurance Readiness Assessment developed under the U.S. Department of Defense DIAP. The objectives of the Readiness Assessment program are to do the following:

- Define IA readiness in an operational context
- Establish metrics for measuring IA readiness
- Establish standard criteria for applying IA readiness metrics
- Establish an IA readiness assessment process
- Integrate IA readiness assessments into existing DOD processes

The DIAP Information Readiness Assessment function has the following characteristics:

- Provides data needed to accurately assess IA readiness
- Identifies and generates IA requirements
- Performs vulnerability/threat analysis assessment

An example of an assessment framework metrics map is given in Table 3.4. In summary, the DIAP assessment framework concept is designed to incorporate the following principles:

**Consistency.**  Standard metrics should be composites to adequately measure different areas of interest; metrics should be unchanging for incorporation into permanent processes.

**Flexibility.**  Criteria will apply standard metrics across diverse environments; means are provided to change the content of metrics.

**Relevance.**  The framework should provide for analysis to forecast capabilities and effectiveness.

**Table 3.4**   Assessment Framework Metrics Map

| CATEGORY | METRIC | AVAILABILITY | INTEGRITY | CONFIDENTIALITY | AUTHENTICATION | NON-REPUDIATION |
|---|---|---|---|---|---|---|
| People | Adequacy of critical IT/IA staff manning levels | X | X | X | | |
| | Adequacy of critical IT/IA staff proficiency | X | X | X | X | X |
| | Adequacy of security clearances for privileged users | X | X | X | | |
| | Effectiveness of information systems security program | X | X | X | X | |
| Operations and Training | Adequacy of failover testing for mission-critical systems | X | X | X | | |
| | Adequacy of performance measurement for network infrastructure and mission-critical systems | X | X | | | |
| | Effectiveness of network penetration detection and defense capabilities | X | X | X | X | |
| | Effectiveness of network management auditing program | X | X | X | X | X |

**Table 3.4**   (continued)

| CATEGORY | METRIC | AVAIL-ABILITY | INTEGRITY | CONFIDEN-TIALITY | AUTHEN-TICATION | NON-REPUDIATION |
|---|---|---|---|---|---|---|
| | Effectiveness of firewall administration practices, procedures, and compliance | X | X | X | X | X |
| | Adequacy of requirements for IT contractor support | X | X | X | X | |
| | Effectiveness of IA vulnerability alert procedures | X | X | X | X | |
| Equipment and Infrastructure | Adequacy of technology to support assigned missions | X | X | X | X | |
| | Adequacy of bandwidth to support mission-critical systems | X | X | | | |
| | Adequacy of connectivity robustness for mission-critical systems | X | X | X | | |
| | Adequacy and effectiveness of survivable power | X | X | X | | |
| | Adequacy and effectiveness of facility security systems, practices, and procedures | X | X | X | X | |
| | Adequacy and effectiveness of entry control systems for mission-critical and infrastructure facilities | X | X | X | | |

# Sample Questions

Answers to the Sample Questions for this and the other chapters are found in Appendix C.

1. The simplistic model of software life cycle development assumes that:
   a. Iteration will be required among the steps in the process.
   b. Each step can be completed and finalized without any effect from the later stages that may require rework.
   c. Each phase is identical to a completed milestone.
   d. Software development requires reworking and repeating some of the phases.

2. What does the Spiral model depict?
   a. A spiral that incorporates various phases of software development
   b. A spiral that models the behavior of biological neurons
   c. The operation of expert systems
   d. Information security checklists

3. In the software life cycle, verification:
   a. Evaluates the product in development against real-world requirements
   b. Evaluates the product in development against similar products
   c. Evaluates the product in development against general baselines
   d. Evaluates the product in development against the specification

4. In the modified Waterfall model:
   a. Unlimited backward iteration is permitted.
   b. The model was reinterpreted to have phases end at project milestones.
   c. The model was reinterpreted to have phases begin at project milestones.
   d. Product verification and validation are not included.

5. In a system life cycle, information security controls should be:
   a. Designed during the product implementation phase
   b. Implemented prior to validation
   c. Part of the feasibility phase
   d. Specified after the coding phase

6. In configuration management, what is a software library?

    a. A set of versions of the component configuration items

    b. A controlled area accessible only to approved users who are restricted to the use of an approved procedure

    c. A repository of backup tapes

    d. A collection of software build lists

7. What is configuration control?

    a. Identifying and documenting the functional and physical characteristics of each configuration item

    b. Controlling changes to the configuration items and issuing versions of configuration items from the software library

    c. Recording the processing of changes

    d. Controlling the quality of the configuration management procedures

8. Which one of the following is NOT one of the maturity levels of the Software Capability Maturity Model (CMM)?

    a. Fundamental

    b. Repeatable

    c. Defined

    d. Managed

9. What does the Bell-LaPadula model NOT allow?

    a. Subjects to read from a higher level of security relative to their level of security

    b. Subjects to read from a lower level of security relative to their level of security

    c. Subjects to write to a higher level of security relative to their level of security

    d. Subjects to read at their same level of security

10. In the * (star) property of the Bell-LaPadula model:

    a. Subjects cannot read from a higher level of security relative to their level of security

    b. Subjects cannot read from a lower level of security relative to their level of security

    c. Subjects cannot write to a lower level of security relative to their level of security

    d. Subjects cannot read from their same level of security

11.  The Clark-Wilson model focuses on data's:

a.  Integrity

b.  Confidentiality

c.  Availability

d.  Format

12.  The * (star) property of the Biba model states:

a.  Subjects cannot write to a lower level of integrity relative to their level of integrity.

b.  Subjects cannot write to a higher level of integrity relative to their level of integrity.

c.  Subjects cannot read from a lower level of integrity relative to their level of integrity.

d.  Subjects cannot read from a higher level of integrity relative to their level of integrity.

13.  Which of the following does the Clark-Wilson model NOT involve?

a.  Constrained data items

b.  Transformational procedures

c.  Confidentiality items

d.  Well-formed transactions

14.  Which one of the following is NOT a type of prototyping?

a.  Incremental

b.  Architectural

c.  Evolutionary

d.  Throw-away

15.  The basic version of the Construction Cost Model (COCOMO), which proposes quantitative, life-cycle relationships, performs what function?

a.  Estimates software development effort based on user function categories

b.  Estimates software development effort and cost as a function of the size of the software product in source instructions

c.  Estimates software development effort and cost as a function of the size of the software product in source instructions modified by manpower buildup and productivity factors

d.  Estimates software development effort and cost as a function of the size of the software product in source instructions modified by hardware and input functions

16. A refinement to the basic Waterfall model that states that software should be developed in increments of functional capability is called:

    a. Functional refinement

    b. Functional development

    c. Incremental refinement

    d. Incremental development

17. The Spiral model of the software development process (B.W. Boehm, "A Spiral Model of Software Development and Enhancement," *IEEE Computer*, May 1988) uses the following metric relative to the spiral:

    a. The radial dimension represents the cost of each phase

    b. The radial dimension represents progress made in completing each cycle

    c. The angular dimension represents cumulative cost

    d. The radial dimension represents cumulative cost

18. In the Capability Maturity Model (CMM) for software, the definition "describes the range of expected results that can be achieved by following a software process" is that of:

    a. Structured analysis/structured design (SA/SD)

    b. Software process capability

    c. Software process performance

    d. Software process maturity

19. Which of the following composes the four phases of the National Information Assurance Certification and Accreditation Process (NIACAP)?

    a. Definition, Verification, Validation, and Confirmation

    b. Definition, Verification, Validation, and Post Accreditation

    c. Verification, Validation, Authentication, and Post Accreditation

    d. Definition, Authentication, Verification, and Post Accreditation

20. Which of the following are the three types of NIACAP accreditation?

    a. Site, type, and location

    b. Site, type, and system

    c. Type, system, and location

    d. Site, type, and general

21. In the Common Criteria, a Protection Profile:

    a. Specifies the mandatory protection in the product to be evaluated

    b. Is also known as the Target of Evaluation (TOE)

    c. Is also known as the Orange Book

    d. Specifies the security requirements and protections of the products to be evaluated

22. In a ring protection system, where is the security kernel usually located?

    a. Highest ring number

    b. Arbitrarily placed

    c. Lowest ring number

    d. Middle ring number

23. What are the hardware, firmware, and software elements of a Trusted Computing Base (TCB) that implement the reference monitor concept called?

    a. The trusted path

    b. A security kernel

    c. An operating system (OS)

    d. A trusted computing system

24. The standard process to certify and accredit U.S. defense critical information systems is called:

    a. DITSCAP

    b. NIACAP

    c. CIAP

    d. DIACAP

25. What information security model formalizes the U.S. Department of Defense multilevel security policy?

    a. Clark-Wilson

    b. Stark-Wilson

    c. Biba

    d. Bell-LaPadula

26. The Biba model axiom "an object at one level of integrity is not permitted to modify (write to) an object of a higher level of integrity (no write up)" is called:

    a. The Constrained Integrity Axiom

    b. The * (star) Integrity Axiom

    c. The Simple Integrity Axiom

    d. The Discretionary Integrity Axiom

27. The property that states "reading or writing is permitted at a particular level of sensitivity, but not to either higher or lower levels of sensitivity" is called the:

    a. Strong * (star) Property

    b. Discretionary Security Property

    c. Simple * (star) Property

    d. * (star) Security Property

28. Which one the following is NOT one of the three major parts of the Common Criteria (CC)?

    a. Introduction and General Model

    b. Security Evaluation Requirements

    c. Security Functional Requirements

    d. Security Assurance Requirements

29. Configuration management control best refers to:

    a. The concept of "least control" in operations

    b. Ensuring that changes to the system do not unintentionally diminish security

    c. The use of privileged-entity controls for system administrator functions

    d. Implementing resource protection schemes for hardware control

30. The SEI Software Capability Maturity Model is based on the premise that:

    a. Good software development is a function of the number of expert programmers in the organization

    b. The maturity of an organization's software processes cannot be measured

    c. The quality of a software product is a direct function of the quality of its associated software development and maintenance processes

    d. Software development is an art that cannot be measured by conventional means

31. In configuration management, a configuration item is:

    a. The version of the operating system, which is operating on the workstation, that provides information security services

    b. A component whose state is to be recorded and against which changes are to be progressed

    c. The network architecture used by the organization

    d. A series of files that contain sensitive information

32. What is the formula for the Annualized Loss Expectancy or ALE that is used in risk analysis to estimate the potential losses to an information system as a result of the exploitation of a vulnerability?

    a. ALE = Single Loss Expectancy (SLE) × Annualized Rate of Occurrence (ARO)

    b. ALE = Multiple Loss Expectancy (MLE) × Annualized Rate of Occurrence (ARO)

    c. ALE = Single Loss Expectancy (SLE) × Modified Annualized Rate of Occurrence (MARO)

    d. ALE = Multiple Loss Expectancy (MLE) × Modified Annualized Rate of Occurrence (ARO)

33. Which one of the following items is NOT one of the System Development Life Cycle (SDLC) phases discussed in NIST Special Publication 800-18, *Guide for Developing Security Plans for Information Technology Systems*?

    a. Initiation Phase

    b. Development/Acquisition Phase

    c. Organizing Phase

    d. Disposal Phase

34. Management techniques for prototyping projects differ from those used in conventional development projects. Which one of the following statements is NOT true with respect to prototyping project management techniques?

    a. One of the three types of prototypes should be decided on at the beginning of the project.

    b. Evaluation criteria should be defined up front.

    c. Configuration management is not required.

    d. Prototyping objectives should be stated and agreed on early in the project.

35. The comprehensive evaluation of the technical and nontechnical security features of an information system and the other safeguards to establish the extent to which a particular design and implementation meet the set of specified security requirements is called:

    a. Accreditation

    b. Validation

    c. Verification

    d. Certification

36. Which one of the following is NOT a phase of the National Security Agency INFOSEC Assessment Methodology (NSA-IAM)?

    a. Post-assessment

    b. Operational

    c. Pre-assessment

    d. On-site

37. Which self-assessment methodology defines the terms "managers," "reporters," "subject matter experts," and "collectors"?

    a. The National Security Agency INFOSEC Assessment Methodology (NSA-IAM)

    b. The Systems Security Engineering Capability Maturity Model (SSE-CMM)

    c. The Defense-Wide Information Assurance Program (DIAP) Information Assurance Readiness Assessment

    d. The NIST Automated Security Self Evaluation Tool (ASSET)

38. Which information security assessment method includes Manager and System Applications?

    a. The NIST Automated Security Self Evaluation Tool (ASSET)

    b. The National Security Agency INFOSEC Assessment Methodology (NSA-IAM)

    c. The Systems Security Engineering Capability Maturity Model (SSE-CMM)

    d. The Defense-Wide Information Assurance Program (DIAP) Information Assurance Readiness Assessment

39. When a computer or network component fails and the computer or the network continues to function, it is called a:

    a. Fail-safe system

    b. Fail-soft system

    c. Fault-tolerant system

    d. Resilient system

40. In a PERT chart, the critical path is:

    a. The path along dependent project tasks that takes the shortest time to complete

    b. The path along dependent project tasks that has the most slack time

    c. The path along dependent project tasks that takes the longest time to complete

    d. The path along dependent project tasks that is the average of all the completion times

# Information Security Management

As defined by ISACA, the goal of this domain is to "oversee and direct information security activities to execute the information security program."

## Administration Processes and Procedures

The administration and management of information security activities are complex and, sometimes, abstract endeavors. The responsibilities for requesting, evaluating, acquiring, and managing outside services are demanding. The information security activities have to be coordinated with the IT operation to ensure a comprehensive, effective information security enterprise. This section will explore acquisition management, service level agreements, contracts, problem management, and third-party service providers.

### Acquisition Management Methods and Techniques

A number of formal methods have been developed to manage the acquisition process. Two such methods are the National Security Agency/Central Security Service (NSA/CSS) Circular No. 500R and The Software Acquisition Capability Maturity Model® (SA-CMM®). These documents capture the fundamental principles of acquisition management.

## The National Security Agency/Central Security Service (NSA/CSS) Circular No. 500R

The NSA/CSS Circular No. 500R was published on January 9, 2001, and its purpose is to "promote management of acquisition programs to optimize total system performance and minimize life-cycle costs."

The objective is to manage the project based on risk, cost, performance, and schedule by applying functional analysis, design synthesis, verification, and system analysis and control. It also states that requirements shall be reviewed at key decision points and, if necessary, refined to meet cost, schedule, and performance objectives. The circular recognizes that there might have to be trade-offs between the cost, schedule, and performance objectives.

The circular also specifically addresses software engineering and lists the following points relative to the acquisition management of software engineering projects:

- Apply best practices and processes to reduce costs, maintain schedule, manage risks, and meet performance requirements
- Employ systems architectures that support open system concepts
- Where possible, use commercial off-the-shelf (COTS) products
- Employ software reuse
- Select programming languages based on the systems engineering and interoperability requirements
- Choose contractors who have proven, mature software development capabilities and who have had success in performing similar projects
- Apply software metrics
- Assess and mitigate information assurance risks

Relative to information assurance, the circular emphasizes the following practices:

- The requirements for information assurance shall be developed and applied throughout the acquisition cycle.
- Information assurance management shall employ the best practices known to reduce risks.
- Systems design activities shall employ information assurance practices to ensure confidentiality, availability, integrity, authentication, and non-repudiation of critical project information.
- Intrusion protection, detection, and reaction capabilities shall be applied.

Circular 500R defines the acquisition management process as shown in Figure 4.1.

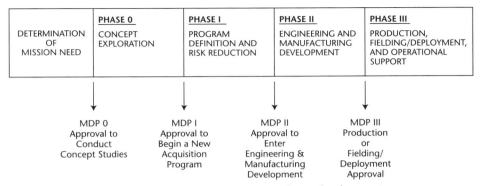

**Figure 4.1**  Acquisition Management Process—NSA/CSS Circular 500R.

## The Software Acquisition Capability Maturity Model

The SA-CMM embodies the same CMM principles that are applied in the software and systems engineering capability maturity models and focuses on the software acquisition management processes. The SA-CMM was developed as a cooperative project among the Carnegie Mellon Software Engineering Institute, federal agencies, the U.S. DoD, and various acquisition experts. Version 1.03 of the SA-CMM was published in March of 2002.

Key Process Areas (KPAs) are associated with each maturity level that indicates an acquisition process capability in the model. Common practices are institutionalized through the goals and common features of the KPAs.

A summary of the SA-CMM KPAs is given in Table 4.1.

**Table 4.1**  SA-CMM Key Process Areas

| LEVEL | FOCUS | KEY PROCESS AREAS |
|---|---|---|
| 1 Initial | Competent people and heroics | N/A |
| 2 Repeatable management | Basic project | Transition to support<br>Evaluation<br>Contract tracking and oversight<br>Project management<br>Requirements development and management<br>Solicitation<br>Software acquisition planning |

*(continued)*

**Table 4.1** *(continued)*

| LEVEL | FOCUS | KEY PROCESS AREAS |
|---|---|---|
| 3 Defined | Process standardization | Training program<br>Acquisition risk management<br>Contract performance management<br>Project performance management<br>User requirements<br>Process definition and maintenance |
| 4 Quantitative | Quantitative management | Quantitative acquisition management<br>Quantitative process management |
| 5 Optimizing | Continuous process improvement | Acquisition innovation management<br>Continuous process improvement |

## The U.S. Office of the Secretary of Defense (OSD) Acquisition Reform

On February 9th, 1994, the U.S. OSD published 10 Principles of Acquisition Reform in order to clarify and define acquisition management in the DoD. These principles were the result of the initiatives of former Secretary of Defense William Perry and are aimed at making the DoD acquisition practices more practical, less cumbersome, more cost-effective, and able to take advantage of technological developments in the commercial arena. These principles are as follows:

**Empower People to Manage—Not Avoid Risk:**

1. Delegate authority and reward results.
2. Encourage innovation by issuing guidance, not rules.
3. Train in a multifunctional environment.
4. Commit to quality through customer focus and continuous improvement.

**Operate in Integrated Product Teams:**

1. Replace functional stove pipes with integrated program teams.
2. Manage with early insight on program issues, rather than after-the-fact oversight.
3. Resolve issues at the lowest possible management level.
4. Use concurrent engineering to integrate process and product development.
5. Partner and team with industry.

### Reduce Cycle Time by 50 Percent:

1. Establish a zero base for functional requirements.
2. Tailor the process to the specific acquisition.
3. Waive or seek relief from low value-added directives.
4. Structure so that fewer people are involved and the need for coordination is reduced.
5. Reduce cost of ownership.
6. Manage overall life cycle cost, not just initial acquisition cost.
7. Treat total cost as an independent variable relative to user requirements.
8. Make cost performance trade-offs early in the acquisition process.
9. Put a high priority on logistics, and support cost visibility.

### Expand Use of Commercial Products and Processes:

1. Research the global commercial market before establishing new requirements.
2. Begin dialogue with industry early in the requirements development process.
3. State requirements in terms of essential performance specifications.
4. Give priority to customary commercial practices.

### Use Performance Specifications and Nongovernment Standards:

1. Minimize government-unique terms and conditions.
2. Use performance specifications as the preferred choice for all programs.
3. Use nongovernment standards when performance specifications are not practicable.
4. Use MIL specifications/standards only as a last resort with an appropriate waiver.

### Issue Solicitations That Reflect the Quality of a World Class Buyer:

1. Write cohesive statements of work that specify "what," not "how."
2. Minimize data requirements to emphasize electronic commerce and product over paper.
3. Integrate oversight requirements with a contractor program management scheme.
4. Coordinate in advance to gain mutual understanding of requirements and capabilities.
5. Maximize the use of simplified acquisition procedures.

### Procure Goods and Services with "Best Value" Techniques:

1. Evaluate bids and proposals on a total-cost-of-ownership basis to seek out qualities other than lowest price.
2. Use past performance as a key factor.
3. Reduce the time and cost of making the award.
4. Debrief offerors promptly and openly to avoid misunderstanding and protest.

### Test and Inspect in the Least Obtrusive Manner to Add Value to the Process or Product:

1. Make testers/evaluators value-added team participants from the start, not inspectors after-the-fact.
2. Take advantage of contractor testing.
3. Use modeling and advanced simulation to save time and reduce cost.
4. Achieve quality with statistical process control rather than with end item inspection.

### Manage Contracts for End Results:

1. Focus on the customer and the product or service required.
2. Control only the performance specification, giving contractors freedom for design innovation.
3. Acquire technical data rights only to extent necessary for breakout and spares procurement.
4. Aggregate contracts and acquisition phases to benefit from stable contractor operations.
5. Operate on the basis of trust and tailor oversight to estimated performance risk.

## Evolutionary Acquisition

On October 30, 2002, the OSD issued the *Interim Defense Acquisition Guidebook*. The guidebook references the former DoD 5000.2-R regulation, which will be used until the Defense Acquisition Policy Working Group creates a newer, streamlined guidebook. The *Interim Defense Acquisition Guidebook* states that: "Every acquisition program shall establish program goals—thresholds and objectives—for the minimum number of cost, schedule, and performance parameters that describe the program over its life cycle. The Department shall link program goals to the DoD Strategic Plan and other appropriate subordinate strategic plans."

Regulation 5000.2-R promotes an evolutionary acquisition strategy that "defines, develops, produces or acquires, and fields an initial hardware or software increment (or block) of operational capability." The idea is to provide incremental capabilities in shorter periods of time. Then, the following iterations can take advantage of new technological developments and adapt to the changing environment. The regulation defines the following two types of evolutionary acquisition:

1. The required final functionality of the target deliverable is defined at the start of the program, and each increment takes advantage of developments in technology.

2. The required functionality is not definable up front, but evolves in each increment with the changing needs of the user and maturing technology.

### Service Level Agreements (SLAs)

A service level agreement (SLA) is a contract between a customer and provider that specifies a minimum level of service that will be supplied by the provider. The contract also guarantees a mutually agreed-upon quality of service that will be delivered by the provider. Metrics should be defined for the levels of service in order to identify and correct problems later.

An information system-related SLA usually has to address the following items:

- Average CPU usage
- Minimum required system up time
- Average response times
- Turnaround times
- Baseline performance levels to which actual performance levels can be compared
- Maximum response times for help desk inquiries
- Dial-in access capabilities
- Schedule for advance notification of any system changes that will impact service to the users
- Transaction volumes
- Usage rates
- Number of users

SLAs may also used within an organization to define services that one department provides to another and for comparison to services that are available from outside providers.

As another example, an SLA between a customer and a provider of telecommunications services might address the following topics:

- Help desks
- Bandwidth to be provided
- Up time
- Burst bandwidth that can be used by the customer and the threshold over which the customer will be charged for use of burst transmissions
- Quality of service for different types of services
- On-site customer support that will be provided
- Penalties that will have to paid by the provider if agreed-upon service levels are not met

Because SLAs normally involve a contract between two parties, it is useful to review the basics of contracts and contract law.

## Contracts

Fundamentally, a contract is an agreement to do or not to do a specific thing. Agreement means that the parties entering into the contract have mutual assent and understanding of the same terms in the contract. This agreement on the terms must be mutual, free, and communicated to each other. In evaluating the mutual assent and intent of the agreement, the usual criterion is to evaluate what a reasonable person in the position of the other party would conclude that terms in the contract mean.

A contract may be totally in writing, partially in writing, or oral. All three types are considered valid contracts. Contracts can also be implied or express. An *implied contract* is inferred from the conduct of the parties involved. In an *express contract*, the contract exists in writing. The basic principle underlying both types of contracts is that the parties entering into the agreement have the same intentions.

If, on the other hand, the parties of the contract have different understandings of the meanings of a term or terms in the contract, then the parties are not bound by the contract. An exception to this case occurs if one of the parties knew the different meaning that was assumed by the other party of the contract.

If the parties to the contract should happen to omit a critical term in the contract that affects their rights, the court will provide a term that it deems reasonable.

## Entering into a Contract

Another important issue pertaining to contacts is whether an individual has the capacity and ability to enter into a contract. Examples of such individuals are those who are mentally infirm and minors. Minors can void contracts based on the fact that they may have entered into a contract contrary to their own best interests because they were not capable of making mature judgments. Similarly, a person with a mental illness can also void a contract if it can be shown that he or she was unable to act in a reasonable manner on his or her own behalf.

Contracts may also be unenforceable in court if they are unreasonably favorable to another party or excessively harsh. Similarly, a contract can be deemed voidable if it was entered into under extreme duress or if it is illegal. Illegal contracts are those that are contrary to express statutes, those that are contrary to the policy of express statutes, and those that are contrary to accepted moral standards.

## Damages

Generally, contract damages are aimed at making sure that the injured party receives what they expected from the agreement. In addition, the injured party may recover an amount to compensate for any damage caused by the breach of the contract, which would result from the breach, and if applicable, any loss of profits that were reasonably certain and were a direct consequence of the breach. There are certain limitations to damages that can be awarded to the injured party. These limitations include losses that were foreseeable, losses that could have been avoided, and damages for mental or emotional distress. In general, punitive damages are not recoverable for a breach of contract.

## Contract Performance

The following points address issues related to contract performance:

- A defaulting party who has not substantially performed may nevertheless be entitled to payment less any damages suffered by the other party. Generally, payment should be made for services actually rendered.

- A contract obligation may be conditional in that it depends on an event that has not occurred or it has been voided because an event has occurred.

- The performance by one party in the contract may be dependent on performance by the other party in the contract.

- The performance of one party may not be obstructed by the other party.

- An unwarranted failure to perform a contract at the time performance is due is called an *actual breach*.

- A repudiation of a contract that occurs before the time when performance is due is called an *anticipatory breach*.

## Problem Management

The topic of Administration Processes and Procedures would not be complete without addressing the handling and resolving problems and conflicts in an IT and information security environment. Problem management can be defined as a set of policies, procedures, and tools to manage and resolve problems. Problems in the information security arena can be categorized as unusual or unexpected events; compromise of confidentiality, integrity, and availability; divergence from best practices or standards; and any abnormal situations.

Good problem management identifies, tracks, and resolves problems using a variety of methods and tools. The objectives of problem management are to prevent problems from occurring in the first place, reducing the occurrence of problems that cannot be prevented, and minimizing the effect of problems on information systems. Effective problem management requires the participation of all levels of management as well as team leaders and team members.

### Tools

A project management effort can be aided significantly by the use of automated tools that support the identification and remediation of problems. Some of the functions provided by such tools are the following:

- Incorporating standards, policies, and procedures
- Tracking problems
- Providing mechanisms for reporting problems, including information on the initiator of the problem report and the initiator's comments
- Identifying the individual responsible for handling the problem report
- Identifying the other individuals involved
- Displaying the status of the problem
- Recording the time required to resolve the problem
- Prioritizing problem resolution assignments
- Supporting the determination of the impact of the problem on the organization or project

In managing problems involving individuals, the problems are usually the result of an argument, competition, or conflict. An argument can be viewed as either a positive or negative situation, whereas competition can be seen as a positive activity. Conflict, on the other hand, usually is a negative occurrence.

Competition can be used to motivate personnel positively, distinguish among different levels of performance, and promote higher standards in the conduct of the project. In order to use argument in a positive fashion, the problem manager has to get to the root of the problem and identify the fundamental differences or lack of information that caused the argument. Conflict has to be turned into either competition or argument to have a chance of resolution.

## Third-Party Service Providers

A good example of a third-party service provider is an Internet Service Provider (ISP). One issue of concern to managers involved with a third-party service provider is that of vicarious liability. *Vicarious liability* imposes legal responsibility on an entity or individual for causing an injury to someone or something when, in reality, the entity or individual had nothing whatsoever to do with actually causing the injury. Vicarious liability is commonly applied through the doctrine of the *respondeat superior*, where a superior is legally responsible for the acts of a subordinate.

Relative to the third-party service provider, vicarious liability may be incurred if the service provider serves as a conduit for a mechanism originated by one party that causes harm to another party. The rulings on this issue are not clear at this time, but the trend seems to be that the third-party provider may eventually have to police material that it is passing through or get out of the business. A hot issue at this time is that of illegal use of copyrighted material. In some instances, vicarious liability may found even if the third party lacks actual knowledge of the copyright infringement activity.

In the situation where an independent contractor working on behalf of a client causes harm to another party without the knowledge of the client, the client would not usually be vicariously liable.

In contrast to vicarious liability, the U.S. Supreme Court has characterized a *contributory infringer* as one "who was in a position to control the use of copyrighted works by others and had authorized the use without permission from the copyright owner." [Sony Corp. v. Universal City Studios, Inc., 464 U.S. 417, 437 (1984)]. The difference between contributory infringement and vicarious liability is that contributory infringement involves knowledge and participation while vicarious liability is distinguished by benefit and control.

When a manager engages a service provider, the key liability issue is whether or not the provider is considered an employee or an independent contractor. The guidance given by the U.S. Supreme Court is to ask if the person who is engaged in the services is performing them in business on his or her own account. An answer of yes usually defines that person as an independent contractor. Thus the client who contracted for the service should not be vicariously liable for the activities of the service provider. Another critical issue is the degree of control that the client has over the service provider's activities.

Some guidance on the selection of a service provider relative to liability is to determine the degree to which the service provider does the following:

- Provides its own equipment
- Hires its own assistants
- Takes a financial risk
- Makes a profit in executing its tasks
- Takes responsibility for investment
- Takes responsibility for management

# Monitoring and Auditing

System audits and monitoring are the two methods organizations use to maintain operational assurance. Although the terms are used loosely within the computer security community, a system audit is a one-time or periodic event to evaluate security, whereas monitoring refers to an ongoing activity that examines either the system or the users. In general, the more "real-time" an activity is, the more it falls into the category of monitoring.

It is necessary to regularly review user accounts on a system. Such reviews may examine the levels of access each individual has, conformity with the concept of least privilege, whether all accounts are still active, whether management authorizations are up-to-date, or whether required training has been completed, for example. These reviews can be conducted on at least two levels: on an application-by-application basis or on a system-wide basis. Both kinds of reviews can be conducted by, among others, in-house systems personnel (a self-audit), the organization's internal audit staff, or external auditors.

## Monitoring

Problem identification and problem resolution are the primary goals of monitoring. The concept of monitoring contains the mechanisms, tools, and techniques that permit the identification of security events that could impact the operation of a computer facility. It also includes the actions to identify the important elements of an event and to report that information appropriately.

The concept of monitoring includes monitoring for illegal software installation, monitoring the hardware for faults and error states, and monitoring operational events for anomalies.

### Intrusion Detection

Intrusion detection is a useful tool that can assist in the detective analysis of intrusion attempts. ID can be used not only to identify intruders, but also to create a sampling of traffic patterns. By analyzing the activities occurring outside of normal clipping levels, a security practitioner can find evidence of events such as in-band signaling or other system abuses.

### Violation Analysis

One of the most used techniques to track anomalies in user activity is violation tracking, processing, and analysis. To make violation tracking effective, clipping levels must be established. A clipping level is a baseline of user activity that is considered a routine level of user errors. A clipping level is used to enable a system to ignore normal user errors. When the clipping level is exceeded, a violation record is then produced. Clipping levels are also used for variance detection.

Using clipping levels and profile-based anomaly detection, the following are common types of violations that should be tracked, processed, and analyzed:

- Repetitive mistakes that exceed the clipping level number
- Individuals who exceed their authority
- Too many people with unrestricted access
- Patterns indicating serious intrusion attempts

Profile-based anomaly detection uses profiles to look for abnormalities in user behavior. A profile is a pattern that characterizes the behavior of users. Patterns of use are established according to the various types of activities the users engage in, such as processing exceptions, resource utilization, and patterns in actions performed, for example. The ways in which the various types of activity are recorded in the profile are referred to as profile metrics.

## Auditing

The purpose of auditing is to provide information to management so that they are informed about the operation of the target systems. The audit function provides the ability to determine if the system is being operated in accordance with accepted industry practices and standards.

Auditing cannot provide information to completely eliminate risks. Risks can never be completely eliminated, but they can be mitigated and understood. Management has to determine the level of risk it is willing to tolerate. This type of decision is based on the cost of addressing a specific risk versus the potential cost of the harm to the system if the risk is exploited.

There are three types of risk associated with an information system security audit:

- *Control risk* is the risk that controls put in place will not prevent, correct, or detect errors on a timely basis.

- *Detection risk* is the risk that the procedures conducted by the audit team will not detect a material problem.

- *Inherent risk* is the susceptibility of a business or process to commit relevant errors, assuming there were no internal controls in place.

Relative to information system security, the audit is accomplished by collecting, storing, and reviewing system logs in order to determine what material events have occurred. This activity also entails a review of the system security and identifying potential breaches in security. If a breach is discovered, the audit attempts to reconstruct the events that led to a security breach and reconstitute the activities performed during the breach. Information security auditing occurs at the network protection layer, at subnet gateways, at the servers (email, file, apps), and at the users' workstations.

Events that should be logged include logon, logout, permission changes, sending information to removable media, invoking privileged commands, application initiation, repeated attempts to access sensitive files, and system startup and shutdown. Audit files should be protected at the highest level of security in an information system to prevent unauthorized access and modification or destruction of the files.

Access control auditing is used to identify where access was attempted and who attempted it. Facility or entrance access audit trails should log the following information:

- Date and time of the access attempt
- At which entrance the access was attempted
- Whether the attempt was successful
- Who attempted the access

The implementation of regular system audits is the foundation of operational security controls monitoring. In addition to enabling internal and external compliance checking, regular auditing of audit trails and logs can assist the monitoring function by helping to recognize patterns of abnormal user behavior.

### Security Auditing

Information technology (IT) auditors are often divided into two types: internal and external. Internal auditors typically work for a given organization while external auditors do not. External auditors are often Certified Public Accountants (CPAs) or other audit professionals who are hired to perform an independent audit of an organization's financial statements. Internal auditors, on the other hand, usually have a much broader mandate—checking for compliance and standards of due care, auditing operational cost efficiencies, and recommending the appropriate controls.

IT auditors typically audit the following:

- Backup controls
- System and transaction controls
- Data library procedures
- Systems development standards
- Data center security
- Contingency plans

In addition, IT auditors might also recommend improvement to controls, and they often participate in a system's development process to help an organization avoid costly re-engineering after the system's implementation.

### Audit Trails

Audit trails help an administrator reconstruct the details of a physical facility intrusion for forensic analysis. An audit (or transaction) trail enables a security practitioner to trace a transaction's history. This transaction trail provides information about additions, deletions, or modifications to the data within a system. Audit trails enable the enforcement of individual accountability by creating a reconstruction of events. Like monitoring, one purpose of an audit trail is to assist in a problem's identification that leads to a problem's resolution. An effectively implemented audit trail also enables the data to be retrieved and easily certified by an auditor. Any unusual activity and variations from the established procedures should be identified and investigated.

The audit logs should record the following:

- The transaction's date and time
- Who processed the transaction
- At which terminal the transaction was processed
- Various security events relating to the transaction

In addition, an auditor should also examine the audit logs for the following:

- Amendments to production jobs
- Production job reruns
- Computer operator practices

Maintaining a proper audit trail is more difficult now because more transactions are not recorded to paper media, and thus they will always stay in an electronic form. In the old paper system, a physical purchase order might be prepared with multiple copies, initiating a physical, permanent paper trail. An auditor's job is now more complicated because digital media is more transient and a paper trail might not exist.

Some examples of abnormal events that could be discovered during an audit are these:

- Degraded hardware or software resource availability
- Deviations from the standard transaction procedures
- Unexplained occurrences in a processing chain

Important security issues regarding the use of audit logs are the retention and protection of the audit media and reports when stored off-site, protection against the alteration of the audit logs, and protection against the unavailability of an audit media during an event.

### Problem Management and Auditing

The concepts of problem management that were described previously share the same concerns of auditing. An auditor might use problem management to resolve the issues arising from an IT security audit, for example.

The goal of problem management is threefold:

1. To reduce failures to a manageable level
2. To prevent the occurrence or reoccurrence of a problem
3. To mitigate the negative effect of problems on computing services and resources

The first step in implementing problem management is to define the potential problem areas and the abnormal events that should be investigated. Some examples of potential problem areas are the following:

- The performance and availability of computing resources and services
- The system and networking infrastructure
- Procedures and transactions
- The safety and security of personnel

# Configuration Management

Configuration management is the process of tracking and approving changes to a system. It involves identifying, controlling, and auditing all changes made to the system. It can address hardware and software changes, networking changes, or any other change affecting security. Configuration management can also be used to protect a trusted system while it is being designed and developed.

The primary security goal of configuration management is to ensure that changes to the system do not unintentionally diminish security. For example, configuration management might prevent an older version of a system from being activated as the production system. Configuration management also makes it possible to roll back accurately to a previous version of a system in case a new system is found to be faulty. Another goal of configuration management is to ensure that system changes are reflected in current documentation to help mitigate the impact that a change might have on the security of other systems, while in the production or planning stages.

Configuration management is a discipline applying technical and administrative direction to do the following:

- Identify and document the functional and physical characteristics of each configuration item for the system
- Manage all changes to these characteristics
- Record and report the status of change processing and implementation

Configuration management involves process monitoring, version control, information capture, quality control, bookkeeping, and an organizational framework to support these activities. The configuration being managed is the verification system plus all tools and documentation related to the configuration process. In applications development, change control involves the analysis and understanding of the existing code and the design of changes and corresponding test procedures.

The primary functions of configuration management or change control are these:

- To ensure that the change is implemented in an orderly manner through formalized testing
- To ensure that the user base is informed of the impending change
- To analyze the effect of the change on the system after implementation
- To reduce the negative impact that the change might have had on the computing services and resources

Five generally accepted procedures exist to implement and support the change control process:

- Applying to introduce a change
- Cataloging the intended change
- Scheduling the change
- Implementing the change
- Reporting the change to the appropriate parties

The four major aspects of configuration management are as follows:

- Configuration identification
- Configuration control
- Configuration status accounting
- Configuration auditing

## Configuration Identification

Configuration management entails decomposing the verification system into identifiable, understandable, manageable, trackable units known as Configuration Items (CIs). The decomposition process of a verification system into Configuration Items is called configuration identification. A CI is a uniquely identifiable subset of the system that represents the smallest portion to be subject to independent configuration control procedures.

A CI is a uniquely identifiable subset of the system that represents the smallest portion to be subject to independent configuration control procedures. The decomposition process of a verification system into CIs is called configuration identification. CIs can vary widely in size, type, and complexity. Although there are no hard-and-fast rules for decomposition, the granularity of CIs can have great practical importance. A favorable strategy is to designate relatively large CIs for elements that are not expected to change over the life of the system and small CIs for elements likely to change more frequently.

## Configuration Control

Configuration control is a means of ensuring that system changes are approved before being implemented, only the proposed and approved changes are implemented, and the implementation is complete and accurate. This involves strict procedures for proposing, monitoring, and approving system changes and their implementation. Configuration control entails central direction of the change process by personnel who coordinate analytical tasks, approve system changes, review the implementation of changes, and supervise other tasks such as documentation.

All analytical and design tasks are conducted under the direction of the vendor's corporate entity called the Configuration Control Board (CCB). The CCB is headed by a chairperson who is responsible for ensuring that changes made do not jeopardize the soundness of the verification system and that the changes made are approved, tested, documented, and implemented correctly.

The members of the CCB should interact periodically, either through formal meetings or other available means, to discuss configuration management topics such as proposed changes, configuration status accounting reports, and other topics that may be of interest to the different areas of the system development. These interactions should be held to keep the entire system team updated on all advances to or alterations in the verification system.

## Configuration Status Accounting

Configuration accounting documents the status of configuration control activities and, in general, provides the information needed to manage a configuration effectively. It allows managers to trace system changes and establish the history of any developmental problems and associated fixes. Configuration accounting also tracks the status of current changes as they move through the configuration control process. Configuration accounting establishes the granularity of recorded information and thus shapes the accuracy and usefulness of the audit function. The configuration accounting reports are reviewed by the CCB.

## Configuration Auditing

Configuration auditing is the quality assurance component of configuration management. It involves periodic checks to determine the consistency and completeness of accounting information and to verify that all configuration management policies are being followed. A vendor's configuration management program must be able to sustain a complete configuration audit by a review team.

## Documentation Change Control

It's important to update all relevant documentation when system changes occur. Such changes could include the following:

- Changes to the system infrastructure
- Changes to security policies or procedures
- Changes to the disaster recovery or business continuity plans
- Facility environment changes, such as office moves or HVAC and electrical changes

Documentation control is a cornerstone of configuration management. Configuration management specifies strict adherence to documenting system changes and the process of the documentation itself.

Configuration management applies technical and administrative direction to the following:

- Identifying and documenting the functional and physical characteristics of each configuration item for the system

- Managing all changes to these characteristics

- Recording and reporting the status of change processing and implementation

Configuration management involves process monitoring, version control, information capture, quality control, bookkeeping, and an organizational framework to support these activities, plus all documentation related to the configuration process.

Documentation control is a means of ensuring that system changes are approved before being implemented, only the proposed and approved changes are implemented, and the implementation is complete and accurate. This involves strict procedures for proposing, monitoring, and approving system changes and their implementation. Documentation control assists the change process by supporting the personnel who coordinate analytical tasks, approve system changes, review the implementation of changes, and supervise other tasks such as documenting the controls.

## Security Review and Testing

An active, ongoing security audit, review, and test process is vital to preserving an organization's security posture. Major elements of this review process include the following:

- Incident, threat, and vulnerability data collection and review
- Testing of the infrastructure, both externally and internally
- Establishing baselines for future review

Common steps in performing a security review are the following:

1. Review policies
2. Develop security matrix
3. Review security documentation
4. Review audit capability and use
5. Review security patches and updates releases for all components

6. Run analysis tools

7. Correlate all information

8. Develop report

9. Make recommendations to correct problems

## System Scanning

System scanning is a process used to collect information about a device or network to facilitate an attack on the system. It is used by attackers to discover what ports are open, determine what services are running, and identify system software. Scanning enables an attacker to detect and exploit known vulnerabilities more easily within a target machine. Rather than an end in its own right, scanning is often one element of a network attack plan, consisting of the following:

**Network reconnaissance.**   Through scanning, an intruder can find out valuable information about the target network such as the following items:

■ Domain names and IP blocks

■ Intrusion detection systems

■ Running services

■ Platforms and protocols

■ Firewalls and perimeter devices

■ General network infrastructure

**Gaining system access.**   Gaining access to a system can be achieved many ways, such as by doing the following:

■ Session hijacking

■ Password cracking

■ Sniffing

■ Directly accessing an uncontrolled machine

■ Exploiting default accounts

■ Doing social engineering

**Removing evidence of the attack.**   After the attack, traces of the attack can be eliminated by doing the following:

■ Editing and clearing security logs

■ Compromising the syslog server

■ Replacing system files by using rootkit tools

- Creating legitimate accounts
- Leaving back-door Trojan viruses, like SubSeven or NetBus

Security administrators should also scan to determine any evidence of compromise and to identify vulnerabilities. Because scanning activity is often a prelude to a system attack, detecting malicious scans should be accompanied by monitoring and analyzing the logs and blocking unused and exposed ports.

## Vulnerability Scanning

Vulnerability scanning should be implemented by the security professional to help identify weaknesses in a system. It should be conducted on a regular periodic basis to identify compromised or vulnerable systems. The scans directed at a target system can either be internal, originating from within the system, or external, originating from outside the target system.

Conducting scans inside the enterprise on a regular basis is one way to identify and track several types of potential problems, such as unused ports that respond to network requests. Also, uncontrolled or unauthorized software may be located using these scanning techniques.

A common vulnerability scanning methodology may employ several steps, including an IP device discovery scan, workstation vulnerability scan, and server vulnerability scan.

### Discovery Scanning

The intent of a discovery scan is to collect enough information about each network device to identify what type of device it is (workstation, server, router, firewall, etc.), its operating system, and if it is running any externally vulnerable services, like Web services, FTP, or email. The discovery scan contains two elements, inventory and classification. The inventory scan provides information about the target system's operating system and its available ports. The classification process identifies applications running on the target system, which aids in determining the device's function.

### Workstation Scanning

A full workstation vulnerability scan of the standard corporate desktop configuration should be implemented regularly. This scan helps ensure that the standard software configuration is current with the latest security patches and software and helps locate uncontrolled or unauthorized software.

### Server Scanning

A full server vulnerability scan will determine if the server OS has been configured to the corporate standards and identify if applications have been updated with the latest security patches and software versions. All services must be inspected for elements that may compromise security, such as default accounts and weak passwords. Also, unauthorized programs like Trojan horses may be identified.

## Port Scanning

Port scanning describes the process of sending a data packet to a port to gather information about the state of the port. This is also called a "probe." Port scanning makes it possible to find what TCP and UDP ports are in use. For example, if ports 25, 80, and 110 are open, the device is running the SMTP, HTTP, and POP3 services.

A cracker can use port-scanning software to determine which hosts are active and which are inactive (down) in order to avoid wasting time on inactive hosts. A port scan can gather data about a single host or hosts within a subnet (256 adjacent network addresses).

A scan may first be implemented using the ping utility; then, after determining which hosts and associated ports are active, the cracker can initiate different types of probes on the active ports.

Examples of probe processes are the following:

- Gathering information from the Domain Name System (DNS)
- Determining the network services that are available, such as email, FTP, and remote logon
- Determining the type and release of the operating system

## TCP/UDP Scanning Types

Many types of TCP/UDP scanning techniques exist. Some are simple and easily detectable by firewalls and intrusion detection systems; some are more complicated and hard to detect.

### Stealth Scans

Certain types of scans are called "stealth" scans because they try to evade or minimize their chances of detection. Several of the scans outlined in the text that follows, such as the TCP SYN or TCP FIN, scan be described as stealth scans.

Another example of a stealth scan is implemented by fragmenting the IP datagram within the TCP header. This will bypass some packet filtering firewalls because they don't get a complete TCP header to match the filter rules.

### Spoofed Scans

While the term "spoofing" comes up often in any discussion of security, it can also be applied here to conceal the true identity of an attacker. Spoofing allows an attacker to probe the target's ports without revealing the attacker's own IP address. The FTP proxy bounce attack that is described in the following section is an example of a spoofed scan that compromises a third-party FTP server.

The HPing network analysis tool also described in the text that follows hides the source of its scans by using another host through which to probe the target site. Also, NMap provides spoofing capability by allowing the operator to enter an optional "source" address of the scanning packet.

## Scanning Tools

While crackers and intruders use many scanning tools, these same tools also help the security administrator to detect and stop malicious scans. Used with intrusion detection systems, these tools can provide some level of protection by identifying vulnerable systems, and they can provide data about the level of activity directed against a machine or network. Because scanning is a continuous activity—that is, all networked systems are being scanned all of the time—it's very important that the security professional know what can be compromised. Some common scanning tools are these:

**Computer Oracle and Password System (COPS).**  Examines a system for a number of known weaknesses and alerts the administrator.

**HPing.**  A network analysis tool that sends packets with nontraditional IP stack parameters. It allows the scanner to gather information from the response packets generated.

**Legion.**  Scans for and identifies shared folders on scanned systems, allowing the scanner to map drives directly.

**Nessus.**  A free security-auditing tool for Linux, BSD, and a few other platforms. It requires a back-end server that has to run on a Unix-like platform.

**NMap.**  A very common port-scanning package. NMap scans for most ports from 1 to 1024, as well as a number of others in the registered and undefined ranges. NMap allows scanning of both TCP and UDP ports, with root privilege required for UDP.

**Remote Access Perimeter Scanner (RAPS).**  Part of the corporate edition of PCAnywhere by Symantec. RAPS will detect most commercial remote-control and back-door packages like NetBus, and it can help lock down PCAnywhere.

**Security Administrator's Integrated Network Tool (SAINT).** Examines network services, such as finger, NFS, NIS, FTP and TFTP, rexd, statd, and others, to report on potential security flaws.

**System Administrator Tool for Analyzing Networks (SATAN).** One of the oldest network security analyzers. SATAN scans network systems for well-known and often exploited vulnerabilities.

**Tcpview.** Allows identification of what application opened which port on Windows platforms.

### Issues with Vulnerability Scanning

Some precautions need to be taken when the security administrator begins a program of vulnerability scanning his or her own network. Some of the issues could cause a system crash or create unreliable scan data:

**False positives.** Some legitimate software uses port numbers registered to other software, which can cause false alarms when port scanning. This can lead to blocking legitimate software that appear to be intrusions.

**Heavy traffic.** Port scanning can have an adverse effect on WAN links and even effectively disable slow links. Because heavy port scanning generates a lot of traffic, it is usually preferable to perform the scanning outside normal business hours.

**False negatives.** Port scanning can sometimes exhaust resources on the scanning machine, creating false negatives and not properly identifying vulnerabilities.

**System crash.** Port scanning has been known to render needed services inoperable or actually crash systems. This may happen when systems have not been currently patched or the scanning process exhausts the targeted system's resources.

**Unregistered port numbers.** Many port numbers in use are not registered, which complicates the act of identifying what software is using them.

## External Vulnerability Testing

External vulnerability testing, or penetration testing, is the process of testing a network's defenses by attempting to access the system from the outside by using the same techniques that an external intruder (for example, a cracker) would use. This testing gives a security professional a better snapshot of the organization's security posture.

Among the techniques used to perform a penetration test are the following:

**Scanning and probing.** Various scanners, like a port scanner, can reveal information about a network's infrastructure and enable an intruder to access the network's unsecured ports.

**Demon dialing.** Demon (or "war") dialers automatically test every phone line in an exchange to try to locate modems that are attached to the network. Information about these modems can then be used to attempt external unauthorized access.

**Sniffing.** A protocol analyzer can be used to capture data packets that are later decoded to collect information such as passwords or infrastructure configurations.

Other techniques that are not solely technology-based can be used to complement the penetration test. The following are examples of such techniques:

**Dumpster diving.** Searching paper disposal areas for unshredded or otherwise improperly disposed-of reports.

**Social engineering.** The most commonly used technique of all, getting information (like passwords) just by asking for them.

# Security Awareness and Education

People are often the weakest link in a security chain because they are not trained or generally aware of what security is all about. Employees must understand how their actions, even seemingly insignificant actions, can greatly affect the overall security position of an organization.

Employees must be aware of the need to secure information and to protect the information assets of an enterprise. Operators need training in the skills that are required to fulfill their job functions securely, and security practitioners need training to implement and maintain the necessary security controls.

All employees need education in the basic concepts of security and its benefits to an organization. The benefits of the three pillars of security awareness training—awareness, training, and education—will manifest themselves through an improvement in the behavior and attitudes of personnel and through a significant improvement in an enterprise's security.

The purpose of computer security awareness and education is to enhance security by doing the following:

- Making computer system users aware of their security responsibilities and teaching them correct practices, which help users change their behavior

- Developing skills and knowledge so that computer users can perform their jobs more securely

- Building in-depth knowledge, as needed, to design, implement, or operate security programs for organizations and systems

An effective computer security awareness and education program requires proper planning, implementation, maintenance, and periodic evaluation. NIST recommends the following steps*:

- Identify program scope, goals, and objectives

- Identify training staff

- Identify target audiences

- Motivate management and employees

- Administer the program

- Maintain the program

- Evaluate the program

Security awareness and education are often overlooked elements of security management because most of a security administrator's time is spent on proactively or reactively administering security. All employees need to be aware of basic security concepts and of security's benefit to an organization. Employees must be aware of the need to secure information and to protect the information assets of the enterprise, and they must understand how their actions affect the overall security posture of the organization.

## Awareness Methods and Techniques

Security awareness refers to the general, collective awareness of an organization's personnel of the importance of security and security controls. Awareness is used to reinforce the fact that security supports the mission of the organization by protecting valuable resources. Security awareness supports individual accountability. Without the knowledge of necessary security measures and to how to use them, users cannot be truly accountable for their actions. Also, management commitment is necessary because of the resources used in developing and implementing the program and because the program affects their staff.

* NIST Special Publication 800-14, "Generally Accepted Principles and Practices for Securing Information Technology Systems."

Security awareness programs also have other benefits. They do the following:

- Make a measurable reduction in the unauthorized actions attempted by personnel
- Significantly increase the effectiveness of the protection controls
- Help to avoid the fraud, waste, and abuse of computing resources

Personnel are considered "security aware" when they clearly understand the need for security, how security affects viability and the bottom line, and the daily risks to computing resources. It's also important to have periodic awareness sessions to orient new employees and refresh senior employees. A common awareness technique is to create a hypothetical security vulnerability scenario and to get the participant's input on the possible solutions or outcomes.

## Integrating Awareness

It is important to have periodic awareness sessions to orient new employees and refresh senior employees. The material should always be direct, simple, and clear. It should be fairly motivational and should not contain a lot of techno-jargon, and it should be conveyed in a style that the audience easily understands. The material should show how the security interests of the organization parallel the interest of the audience and how they are important to the security protections.

Ways that security awareness can be integrated into the corporate culture include the following:

**Live/interactive presentations.**   Lectures, videos, and computer-based training (CBT).

**Publishing/distribution.**   Posters, company newsletters, bulletins, and the intranet.

**Incentives.**   Awards and recognition for security-related achievement.

**Reminders.**   Login banner messages and marketing paraphernalia such as mugs, pens, sticky notes, and mouse pads.

Training is a little different from awareness in that it utilizes specific classroom or one-on-one training. Examples of InfoSec training include the following:

- Security-related job training for operators and specific users
- Awareness training for specific departments or personnel groups with security-sensitive positions
- Technical security training for IT support personnel and system administrators

- Advanced InfoSec training for security practitioners and information systems auditors

- Security training for senior managers, functional managers, and business unit managers

In-depth training and education for systems personnel, auditors, and security professionals are very important and are considered necessary for career development. In addition, specific product training for security software and hardware is also vital to the protection of the enterprise.

A good starting point for defining a security training program could be the topics of policies, standards, guidelines, and procedures that are in use at an organization. A discussion of the possible environmental or natural hazards or a discussion of the recent common security errors or incidents—without blaming anyone publicly—could work. Motivating the students is always the prime directive of any training, and their understanding of the value of security's effect on the bottom line is also vital. A common training technique is to create hypothetical security vulnerability scenarios and to get the students' input on the possible solutions or outcomes.

## Changing Culture and Behavior of Staff

All personnel using a system should have some kind of security training that is either specific to the controls employed or about general security concepts. Training is especially important for those users who are handling sensitive or critical data. The advent of the microcomputer and distributed computing has created an opportunity for serious failures of confidentiality, integrity, and availability.

Education and training are vital to the smooth operation of security controls, and particularly the proper operation and maintenance of these controls by security personnel. Operators need training in the skills required to fulfill their job functions securely, and security practitioners need education to implement and maintain necessary security controls.

In-depth training and education for systems personnel, auditors, and security professionals are very important and are considered necessary for career development. In addition, specific product training for security software and hardware is also vital to the protection of the enterprise.

Examples of security education programs include the following:

- Security-related job training for operators and specific users

- Awareness training for specific departments or personnel groups with security-sensitive positions

- Technical security training for IT support personnel and system administrators

- Advanced InfoSec training for security practitioners and information systems auditors

- Security training for senior managers, functional managers, and business unit managers

A starting point for a security education program could be the topic of policies, standards, guidelines, and procedures that are in use in the organization.

# Sample Questions

Answers to the Sample Questions for this and the other chapters are found in Appendix C.

1. As stated in the National Security Agency/Central Security Service (NSA/CSS) Circular No. 500R, the objective of acquisition management is to manage a project by applying a number of techniques. Which one of the following is NOT one of these techniques?

   a. Functional analysis

   b. Design synthesis

   c. Freezing requirements early in the design cycle

   d. Verification

2. In addressing software engineering projects, the NSA/CSS circular emphasizes good practices to use in acquisition management of these projects. Which one of the following items is NOT one of these recommended practices?

   a. Employ software reuse

   b. Apply software metrics

   c. Assess and mitigate information assurance risks

   d. Avoid the use of commercial off-the-shelf (COTS) products

3. Which one of the following is NOT one of the maturity levels of the Software Acquisition Capability Maturity Model® (SA-CMM®)?

   a. Quantitative

   b. Repeatable

   c. Defined

   d. Standardized

4. The following focus points are associated with what maturity level of the SA-CMM?

   - Evaluation
   - Contract tracking and oversight
   - Project management
   - Requirements development and management
   - Software acquisition planning

   a. Defined

   b. Repeatable

   c. Quantitative

   d. Optimizing

5. The following principles are taken from which one of the following documents?

   ■ Reduce cost of ownership

   ■ Expand the use of commercial products and processes

   ■ Evaluate bids and proposals on a total-cost-of-ownership basis

   ■ Manage contracts for end results

   a. SA-CMM

   b. NSA/CSS Circular No. 500R

   c. Office of the Secretary of Defense (OSD) Principles of Acquisition Reform

   d. DoD Standard Service Level Agreement (DoD-SLA)

6. An acquisition strategy in which the required final functionality of the target deliverable is defined at the start of the program and increments during the program to take advantage of technological developments is called:

   a. Developmental acquisition

   b. Evolutionary acquisition

   c. Conditional acquisition

   d. Relative acquisition

7. A contract between a customer and provider that specifies a minimum level of service that will be supplied by the provider is called a:

   a. Quality of service agreement

   b. Service level agreement

   c. Measured service agreement

   d. Service legal agreement

8. Which one of the following does NOT describe the terms under which a contractual agreement must be made?

   a. Mutual

   b. Free

   c. Communicated to each other

   d. Unilateral

9. Which one of the following best describes an express contract?

   a. Exists in writing

   b. Inferred from the conduct of the involved parties

   c. An oral agreement

   d. A voided contract

10. Which one of the following is NOT a condition under which a contract may be unenforceable in court?

   a. Excessively harsh

   b. Entered into under duress

   c. Contrary to express statutes

   d. Mutual assent

11. Which one of the following statements is NOT true regarding recovery of contractual damages?

   a. Injured parties may normally recover an amount to compensate for any damage caused by breach of contract.

   b. Injured parties may normally recover an amount to compensate for any damage that would result from breach of contract.

   c. Injured parties may recover punitive damages.

   d. Injured parties may recover loss of profits that were a direct result of the breach of contract.

12. A repudiation of a contract that occurs before the time when performance is due is called a(n):

   a. Anticipatory breach

   b. Actual breach

   c. Expected breach

   d. Nonperforming breach

13. A set of policies, procedures, and tools to manage and resolve problems is defined as:

   a. Project management

   b. Problem management

   c. Problem resolution

   d. Problem prevention

14. Which one of the following is NOT usually associated with problems among individuals?

   a. Conflict

   b. Argument

   c. Dissolution

   d. Competition

15. A third-party liability in which an individual may be responsible for an action by another party is called:

   a. Contributory liability

   b. Relational liability

   c. Engaged liability

   d. Vicarious liability

16. Clipping levels are used to:

   a. Limit the number of letters in a password

   b. Set thresholds for voltage variations

   c. Reduce the amount of data to be evaluated in audit logs

   d. Limit errors in callback systems

17. Which of the following is NOT a use of an audit trail?

   a. Provides information about additions, deletions, or modifications to the data

   b. Collects information such as passwords or infrastructure configurations

   c. Assists the monitoring function by helping to recognize patterns of abnormal user behavior

   d. Enables the security practitioner to trace a transaction's history

18. An audit trail is an example of what type of control?

   a. Deterrent control

   b. Preventive control

   c. Detective control

   d. Application control

19. Which of the following would be the BEST description of clipping levels?

    a. A baseline of user errors above which violations will be recorded

    b. A listing of every error made by users to initiate violation processing

    c. Variance detection of too many people with unrestricted access

    d. Changes to a system's stored data characteristics

20. Which choice would NOT be a common element of a transaction trail?

    a. The date and time of the transaction

    b. Who processed the transaction

    c. Why the transaction was processed

    d. At which terminal the transaction was processed

21. Which task would normally be a function of the security administrator, not the system administrator?

    a. Installing system software

    b. Adding and removing system users

    c. Reviewing audit data

    d. Managing print queues

22. What does an audit trail or access log usually NOT record?

    a. How often a diskette was formatted

    b. Who attempted access

    c. The date and time of the access attempt

    d. Whether the attempt was successful

23. Which choice is an accurate statement about the difference between monitoring and auditing?

    a. Monitoring is a one-time event to evaluate security.

    b. A system audit is a ongoing "real-time" activity that examines the system.

    c. A system audit cannot be automated.

    d. Monitoring is an ongoing activity that examines either the system or the users.

24. Which choice is the BEST description of an audit trail?

    a. Audit trails are used to detect penetration of a computer system and to reveal usage that identifies misuse.

    b. An audit trail is a device that permits simultaneous data processing of two or more security levels without risk of compromise.

    c. An audit trail mediates all access to objects within the network by subjects within the network.

    d. Audit trails are used to prevent access to sensitive systems by unauthorized personnel.

25. Which choice is NOT a security goal of an audit mechanism?

    a. Deter perpetrators' attempts to bypass the system protection mechanisms

    b. Review employee production output records

    c. Review patterns of access to individual objects

    d. Discover when a user assumes a functionality with privileges greater than his or her own

26. Which statement is NOT correct about reviewing user accounts?

    a. User account reviews cannot be conducted by outside auditors.

    b. User account reviews can examine conformity with "least privilege."

    c. User account reviews may be conducted on a system-wide basis.

    d. User account reviews may be conducted on an application-by-application basis.

27. During the investigation of a computer crime, audit trails can be very useful. To ensure that the audit information can be used as evidence, certain procedures must be followed. Which of the following is NOT one of these procedures?

    a. The audit trail information must be used during the normal course of business.

    b. There must be a valid organizational security policy in place and in use that defines the use of the audit information.

    c. Mechanisms should be in place to protect the integrity of the audit trail information.

    d. Audit trails should be viewed prior to the image backup.

28. Which one of the following conditions must be met if legal electronic monitoring of employees is conducted by an organization?

    a. Employees must be unaware of the monitoring activity.

    b. All employees must agree with the monitoring policy.

    c. Results of the monitoring cannot be used against the employee.

    d. The organization must have a policy stating that all employees are regularly notified that monitoring is being conducted.

29. Which one of the following is NOT a recommended practice regarding electronic monitoring of employees' email?

    a. Apply monitoring in a consistent fashion

    b. Provide individuals being monitored with a guarantee of email privacy

    c. Inform all that email is being monitored by means of a prominent login banner

    d. Explain who is authorized to read monitored email

30. Configuration management control best refers to:

    a. The concept of "least control" in operations

    b. Ensuring that changes to the system do not unintentionally diminish security

    c. The use of privileged-entity controls for system administrator functions

    d. Implementing resource protection schemes for hardware control

31. In configuration management, a configuration item is:

    a. The version of the operating system that is operating on the workstation that provides information security services

    b. A component whose state is to be recorded and against which changes are to be progressed

    c. The network architecture used by the organization

    d. A series of files that contain sensitive information

32. Which choice does NOT accurately describe a task of the Configuration Control Board?

    a. The CCB should meet periodically to discuss configuration status accounting reports.

    b. The CCB is responsible for documenting the status of configuration control activities.

    c. The CCB is responsible for ensuring that changes made do not jeopardize the soundness of the verification system.

    d. The CCB ensures that the changes made are approved, tested, documented, and implemented correctly.

33. Which element of configuration management involves the use of Configuration Items (CIs)?

    a. Configuration accounting

    b. Configuration audit

    c. Configuration control

    d. Configuration identification

34. The discipline of identifying the components of a continually evolving system for the purposes of controlling changes to those components and maintaining integrity and traceability throughout the life cycle is called:

    a. Change control

    b. Request control

    c. Release control

    d. Configuration management

35. Which choice best describes the function of change control?

    a. To ensure that system changes are implemented in an orderly manner

    b. To guarantee that an operator is given only the privileges needed for the task

    c. To guarantee that transaction records are retained in accordance with compliance requirements

    d. To assign parts of security-sensitive tasks to more than one individual

36. A purpose of a security awareness program is to improve:

    a. The security of vendor relations

    b. The performance of a company's intranet

    c. The possibility for career advancement of the IT staff

    d. The company's attitude about safeguarding data

37. Which choice is an example of a cost-effective way to enhance security awareness in an organization?

    a. Train every employee in advanced InfoSec

    b. Create an award or recognition program for employees

    c. Calculate the cost/benefit ratio of the asset valuations for a risk analysis

    d. Train only managers in implementing InfoSec controls

38. Which choice is not an example of an appropriate security management practice?

    a. Reviewing access logs for unauthorized behavior

    b. Monitoring employee performance in the workplace

    c. Researching information on new intrusion exploits

    d. Promoting and implementing security awareness programs

39. Which statement is NOT true about security awareness, training, and educational programs?

    a. Awareness and training help users become more accountable for their actions.

    b. Security education assists management in determining who should be promoted.

    c. Security improves the users' awareness of the need to protect information resources.

    d. Security education assists management in developing the in-house expertise to manage security programs.

40. Which choice is NOT a generally accepted benefit of security awareness, training, and education?

    a. A security awareness program can help operators understand the value of the information.

    b. A security education program can help system administrators recognize unauthorized intrusion attempts.

    c. A security awareness and training program will help prevent natural disasters from occurring.

    d. A security awareness and training program can help an organization reduce the number and severity of errors and omissions.

41. Which statement most accurately describes the difference between security awareness, security training, and security education?

    a. Security training teaches the skills that will help employees to perform their jobs more securely.

    b. Security education is required for all system operators.

    c. Security awareness is not necessary for high-level senior executives.

    d. Security training is more in-depth than security education.

42. Which statement is true about security awareness and educational programs?

    a. Awareness and training help users become more accountable for their actions.

    b. Security education assists management in determining who should be promoted.

    c. A security awareness and training program helps prevent the occurrence of natural disasters.

    d. Security awareness is not necessary for high-level senior executives.

43. Which choice would NOT be considered a benefit of employing incident-handling capability?

    a. An individual acting alone would not be able to subvert a security process or control.

    b. It enhances internal communications and the readiness of the organization to respond to incidents.

    c. It assists an organization in preventing damage from future incidents.

    d. Security training personnel would have a better understanding of users' knowledge of security issues.

# CHAPTER 5

# Response Management

The goal of this domain is to develop and manage a capability to respond to and recover from disruptive and destructive information security events. The elements that comprise this capability are the following:

- Intrusion detection and response
- Business continuity and contingency planning
- Forensics

## Intrusion Detection and Response

Intrusion detection (ID) and response is the task of monitoring systems for evidence of intrusions or inappropriate usage and responding to this evidence. Response includes notifying the appropriate parties to take action in order to determine the severity of an incident and to remediate the incident's effects. ID is the detection of inappropriate, incorrect, or anomalous activity.

# Components of Incident Response Capability

An intrusion response capability has two primary components:

1. Creation and maintenance of intrusion detection systems (IDSs) and processes for host and network monitoring and event notification

2. Creation of a Computer Incident Response Team (CIRT) for the following:

   - Analysis of an event notification

   - Response to an incident if the analysis warrants it

   - Escalation path procedures

   - Resolution, post-incident follow-up, and reporting to the appropriate parties

An intrusion detection system (IDS) is a system that monitors network traffic and/or monitors host audit logs in order to determine whether any violations of an organization's security policy have taken place. An IDS can detect intrusions that have circumvented or passed through a firewall or that are occurring within the local area network behind the firewall.

Various types of IDS exist. The most common approaches to ID are statistical anomaly detection (also known as behavior-based) and pattern-matching (also known as knowledge-based or signature-based) detection. ID systems that operate on a specific host and detect malicious activity on that host only are called host-based ID systems. ID systems that operate on network segments and analyze that segment's traffic are called network-based ID systems. Because there are pros and cons for each, an effective IDS should use a combination of both network- and host-based intrusion detection systems. A truly effective IDS will detect common attacks, which include distributed attacks, as they occur. This type of IDS is called a network-based IDS because it monitors network traffic in real time. Conversely, a host-based IDS resides on centralized hosts.

## Network-Based ID

Network-based ID systems commonly reside on a discrete network segment and monitor the traffic on that network segment. They usually consist of a network appliance with a Network Interface Card (NIC) that is operating in promiscuous mode and is intercepting and analyzing the network packets in real time.

Network-based ID involves looking at the packets on the network as they pass by some sensor. The sensor can see only the packets that happen to be carried on the network segment to which it is attached. Network traffic on other segments, and traffic on other means of communication (like phone lines), can't be monitored properly by network-based IDS.

Packets are identified to be of interest if they match a signature. Three primary types of signatures are these:

**String signatures.**   String signatures look for a text string that indicates a possible attack.

**Port signatures.**   Port signatures watch for connection attempts to well-known, frequently attacked ports.

**Header condition signatures.**   Header signatures watch for dangerous or illogical combinations in packet headers.

A network-based IDS usually provides reliable, real-time information without consuming network or host resources. A network-based IDS is passive when acquiring data. Because a network-based IDS reviews packets and headers, it can also detect denial of service (DoS) attacks. Furthermore, because this IDS is monitoring an attack in real time, it can also respond to an attack in progress to limit damage.

A problem with a network-based IDS system is that it will not detect attacks against a host made by an intruder who is logged in at the host's terminal. If a network IDS, along with some additional support mechanism, determines that an attack is being mounted against a host, it is usually not capable of determining the type or effectiveness of the attack being launched.

## Host-Based ID

Host-based ID systems use small programs (intelligent agents), which reside on a host computer. They monitor the operating system detecting inappropriate activity, writing to log files, and triggering alarms. Host-based systems look for activity only on the host computer; they do not monitor the entire network segment.

A host-based IDS can review the system and event logs in order to detect an attack on the host and to determine whether the attack was successful. (It is also easier to respond to an attack from the host.) Detection capabilities of host-based ID systems are limited by the incompleteness of most host audit log capabilities.

Host-based ID systems do the following:

- Monitor accesses and changes to critical system files and changes in user privileges

- Detect trusted-insider attacks better than network-based IDSs

- Are relatively effective for detecting attacks from the outside

- Can be configured to look at all network packets, connection attempts, or login attempts to the monitored machine, including dial-in attempts or other nonnetwork-related communication ports

Figure 5.1 shows the host-based intrusion detection software RealSecure, from ISS (www.iss.net). This screen shows the discovery of critical vulnerabilities on the server after performing a baseline audit.

An IDS detects an attack through one of two conceptual approaches: a signature-based ID or a statistical anomaly-based ID. These two mechanisms are also referred to as knowledge-based and behavior-based IDS.

## Signature-Based ID

In a signature-based ID or knowledge-based ID system, signatures or attributes, which characterize an attack, are stored for reference. Then, when data about events is acquired from host audit logs or from network packet monitoring, this data is compared with the attack signature database. If there is a match, a response is initiated.

These systems use a database of previous attacks and known system vulnerabilities to look for current attempts to exploit their vulnerabilities, and they trigger an alarm if an attempt is found. These systems are more common than behavior-based ID systems. The advantages of signature-based ID systems include the following:

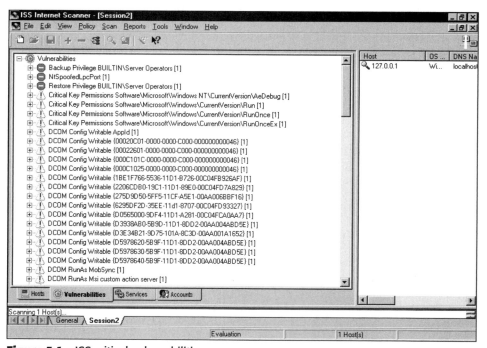

**Figure 5.1**   ISS critical vulnerabilities.

- The system is characterized by low false alarm rates (or positives).
- The alarms are standardized and are clearly understandable by security personnel.

A weakness of a signature-based ID or knowledge-based approach is the failure to characterize slow attacks that extend over a long time period. To identify these types of attacks, large amounts of information must be held for extended time periods. Another issue with signature-based IDs is that only attack signatures that are stored in their database are detected. The disadvantages of signature-based ID systems include the following:

- The system is resource-intensive. The knowledge database continually needs maintenance and updating with new vulnerabilities and environments to remain accurate.
- Because knowledge about attacks is very focused (dependent on the operating system, version, platform, and application), new, unique, or original attacks often go unnoticed.

### Statistical Anomaly-Based ID

Statistical anomaly-based or behavior-based ID systems dynamically detect deviations from the learned patterns of user behavior and trigger an alarm when an intrusive (outside of normal system use) activity occurs. Behavior-based ID systems are less common than knowledge-based ID systems. Behavior-based ID systems learn normal or expected behavior of the system or the users and assume that an intrusion can be detected by observing deviations from this norm.

With this method, an IDS acquires data and defines a "normal" usage profile for the network or host that is being monitored. This characterization is accomplished by taking statistical samples of the system over a period of normal use. Typical characterization information used to establish a normal profile includes memory usage, CPU utilization, and network packet types. With this approach, new attacks can be detected because they produce abnormal system statistics. The advantages of behavior-based ID systems include these:

- The system can dynamically adapt to new, unique, or original vulnerabilities.
- A behavior-based ID system is not as dependent on specific operating systems as a knowledge-based ID system.
- They help detect "abuse of privileges" types of attacks that do not actually involve exploiting any security vulnerability.

Some disadvantages of a statistical anomaly-based ID are that it will not detect an attack that does not significantly change the system operating characteristics, or it might falsely detect a nonattack event that had caused a momentary anomaly in the system. The disadvantages of behavior-based ID systems include these:

- They are characterized by high false alarm rates. High positives are the most common failure of behavior-based ID systems, and they can create data noise that can make the system unusable or difficult to use.

- Activity and behavior of the users while in the networked system might not be static enough to implement a behavior-based ID system effectively.

- The network may experience an attack at the same time the intrusion detection system is learning the behavior.

## Intrusion Detection Policies and Processes

A security policy defines the rules that regulate how your organization manages and protects computing resources to achieve security objectives. Well documented, communicated, and properly enforced intrusion detection policies and processes prepare the organization to respond to intrusions in a timely and controlled manner.

The networked systems security policy should require that designated system and network administrators and response team members are trained in the use of intrusion response tools and environments. This training should include participation in response practice drills or simulations using the tools and environments.

Also, the policy should require that the inventory of all applications software, operating systems, supporting tools, and hardware be kept up to date, and it should require quick access to backups in an emergency, even if they are stored at a remote site. This may include defining procedures that give specific managers the responsibility to authorize such access.

Often the policy will state that staff members dealing with an intrusion may need to gain access to restricted systems and data. This may include specifying how staff access is granted and how they will obtain administrator passwords and encryption keys, establishing the authority for staff access, establishing the authenticity of the staff member obtaining access, and requiring that all access is documented and tracked.

Intrusion detection processes must be planned and implemented to help organizations detect and respond to incidents before they occur. It's important to respond to incidents in an efficient and effective manner. For example, the ISSO must determine how the organization is going to monitor the IDS, who will monitor it, how alerts will be processed, and how the incident is remediated with what level of response. The critical issues involved are the following:

- Protecting the assets that could be compromised
- Protecting resources that could be utilized more profitably if an incident did not require their services
- Complying with (government or other) regulations
- Preventing the use of your systems in attacks against other systems (which could cause you to incur legal liability)
- Minimizing the potential for negative exposure

## *CERT/CC Practices*

The Carnegie Mellon University CERT Coordination Center (CERT/CC) recommends the following incident response practices:

### PREPARE

1. Establish policies and procedures for responding to intrusions.
2. Prepare to respond to intrusions.

### HANDLE

3. Analyze all available information to characterize an intrusion.
4. Communicate with all parties that need to be made aware of an intrusion and its progress.
5. Collect and protect information associated with an intrusion.
6. Apply short-term solutions to contain an intrusion.
7. Eliminate all means of intruder access.
8. Return systems to normal operation.

### FOLLOW UP

9. Identify and implement security lessons learned.

Let's look at these practices in more detail.

### Establish Response Policies and Procedures

Response procedures describe how the response policies will be implemented throughout your organization—for example, who to notify, at what point in the response procedure and with what types of information. From these procedures, all concerned parties are able to determine what operational steps they need to take to comply with your policies and, thereby, respond in a manner that upholds the security objectives for your organization's information and networked systems.

This practice describes a subset of the topics your intrusion response policies and procedures should address. Additional policy and procedure information is contained in the other practices of this module where it is most applicable. This language needs to be tailored to reflect the specific business objectives and security requirements of your organization and its computing environment. The details of procedures used to address specific types of intrusions may vary.

- Establish guidelines and rules at the management level for responding to intrusions and include these in your organization's networked systems security policy.

- Document your configuration redundancy policy.

- Document a response procedure that implements your intrusion response policies.

- Conduct a legal review of your policies and procedures.

- Train designated staff about your response policies and procedures.

### Prepare to Respond to Intrusions

Preparation includes selecting, installing, and becoming familiar with tools that will assist you in the response process and will help you collect and maintain data related to an intrusion. You need to perform these preparation steps well in advance of an intrusion:

- Build an archive of boot disks and distribution media for all applications and all operating systems and versions.

- Build an archive of security-related patches for all applications and all operating systems and versions.

- Identify and install tools that support the reinstallation of systems, applications, and patches.

- Ensure that your backup procedures are adequate to recover from any damage.

- Build an archive of test results that describe the expected state of your systems.

- Ensure that high-capacity, removable- and write-protected media and supporting equipment are available to make and restore system backups.

- Build and maintain a database of contact information.

- Set up secure communication mechanisms.

- Identify and install tools to access directories and other sources of contact information.

- Build a resource kit of tools and hardware devices.
- Ensure that test systems and networks are properly configured and available.

### Analyze All Available Information

Once you have been alerted by your intrusion detection mechanisms or another trusted site that an intrusion has been detected, you need to determine to what extent your systems and data have been compromised and you need to respond. Information, as collected and interpreted through analysis, is key to your decisions and actions throughout the response process.

The purpose of analysis is to find out the following:

- What attacks were used to gain access
- What systems and data were accessed by an intruder
- What an intruder did after obtaining access
- What an intruder is currently doing when an intrusion has not been contained or eliminated

The analysis process entails the following tasks:

- Back up the compromised systems.
- Isolate the compromised systems.
- Search on other systems for signs of intrusion.
- Examine logs generated by firewalls, network monitors, and routers.
- Identify the attacks used to gain access to your systems.
- Identify what an intruder did while accessing your systems.

### Communicate with All Parties

Those with key roles in responding to an intrusion need to be notified and kept informed at the appropriate times to fulfill their responsibilities. You need to immediately notify the responsible mid-level and senior managers, your local Computer Security Incident Response Team (CSIRT) if one exists, your public relations staff, and the affected system administrators (if they are not already involved) based on your organization's information dissemination policy. Executing your information dissemination procedures may include contacting users affected by an intrusion, security personnel, law enforcement agencies, vendors, and other CSIRTs external to your organization.

- Execute your information dissemination procedures, taking the specifics of an intrusion into account.
- Use secure communication mechanisms.
- Inform upstream and downstream sites of attacks and intrusions.

- Maintain a detailed contact log.
- Maintain current contact information for your systems and sites.

### Collect and Protect Information

All information about the compromised system(s) and cause(s) of an intrusion needs to be captured and securely stored. This may include system and network log files, network message traffic, user files, results produced by intrusion detection tools, analysis results, system administrator console logs and notes, and backup tapes that capture the before-intrusion and after-intrusion states of the affected system. All information must be carefully collected, labeled, cataloged, and securely stored at each stage of intrusion analysis.

- Collect all information related to an intrusion.
- Collect and preserve evidence.
- Ensure that evidence is captured and preserved securely.
- Preserve the chain of custody for all evidence.
- Contact law enforcement immediately if you decide to pursue and prosecute an intruder.

### Apply Short-Term Containment Solutions

Containment consists of short-term, tactical actions whose purpose is to stop an intruder's access to compromised systems, limit the extent of an intrusion, and prevent an intruder from causing further damage.

- Temporarily shut down the compromised system.
- Disconnect the compromised system from a network.
- Disable access to compromised file systems that are shared with other computers.
- Disable system services, if possible.
- Change passwords or disable accounts.
- Monitor system and network activities.
- Verify that redundant systems and data have not been compromised.

### Eliminate All Means of Intruder Access

Complete eradication of the root cause(s) of an intrusion is a long-term goal that can be achieved only by implementing an ongoing security improvement process. In response to a specific intrusion, you need to ensure that the affected systems are protected against the same or similar types of access and attacks in the future, once an intrusion is contained and systems are returned to normal operation.

- Change all passwords on all systems to which the attacker may have had access.

- Reinstall compromised systems if your preparation was insufficient.

- Remove any means for intruder access including changes made by an intruder.

- Restore executable programs (including application services) and binary files from original distribution media.

- Review system configurations.

- Determine if you have uncorrected system and network vulnerabilities and correct them.

- Improve protection mechanisms to limit the exposure of networks and systems.

- Improve detection mechanisms to enable better reporting of attacks.

### Return Systems to Normal Operation

Restoring and returning a compromised system to normal operation permits your staff to have access to that system again. This is best accomplished after all means of intruder access are eliminated. Doing so prevents the same or similar types of intrusions from occurring or, at the very least, ensures timely detection and notification by your updated intrusion detection mechanisms.

- Determine the requirements and time frame for returning the system to normal operations.

- Enable system and application services.

- Restore user data from trusted backup media.

- Reestablish the availability of previously disconnected file systems.

- Reconnect the restored system to the network.

- Validate the restored system.

- Watch for additional scans or probes that may signal the return of an intruder.

### Identify and Implement Security Lessons Learned

It is important to learn from the successful and unsuccessful actions taken in response to an intrusion. Capturing and disseminating what worked well and what did not will help reduce the likelihood of similar intrusions and will improve the security of your operation. This can be accomplished by performing a post-mortem review with all involved parties and then communicating the results of the review.

- If further notification is required (per policies and procedure), execute this notification.

- Manage ongoing press aspects of an intrusion, if any.

- Hold a post-mortem analysis and review meeting with all involved parties.

- Revise security plans, policies, procedures, and user and administrator training to prevent intrusion recurrence.

- Determine whether to perform a new risk analysis based on the severity and impact of an intrusion.

- Take a new inventory of your system and network assets.

- Participate in investigation and prosecution, if applicable.

Table 5.1 shows these practices in order.

### IETF

Additional guidance on incident handling is provided by the Internet Engineering Task Force (IETF) RFC 2196, *Site Security Handbook*. The handbook recommends the following approach to the handling of incidents:

1. Preparing and planning (what are the goals and objectives in handling an incident)
2. Notification (who should be contacted in the case of an incident)
    - Local managers and personnel
    - Law enforcement and investigative agencies
    - Computer security incident handling teams
    - Affected and involved sites
    - Internal communications
    - Public relations and press releases
3. Identifying an incident (is it an incident and how serious is it)
4. Handling (what should be done when an incident occurs)
    - Notification (who should be notified about the incident)
    - Protecting evidence and activity logs (what records should be kept from before, during, and after the incident)
    - Containment (how can the damage be limited)
    - Eradication (how to eliminate the reasons for the incident)
    - Recovery (how to reestablish service and systems)
    - Follow-up (what actions should be taken after the incident)
5. Aftermath (what are the implications of past incidents)
6. Administrative response to incidents

**Table 5.1**  Summary of Recommended Practices

| CATEGORY | RECOMMENDED PRACTICE |
|----------|----------------------|
| Prepare | 1. Establish policies and procedures for responding to intrusions.<br>2. Prepare to respond to intrusions. |
| Handle | 3. Analyze all available information to characterize an intrusion.<br>4. Communicate with all parties that need to be made aware of an intrusion and its progress.<br>5. Collect and protect information associated with an intrusion.<br>6. Apply short-term solutions to contain an intrusion.<br>7. Eliminate all means of intruder access.<br>8. Return systems to normal operation. |
| Follow up | 9. Identify and implement security lessons learned. |

### Layered Security and IDS

Computer security is most effective when multiple layers of security controls are used in an organization, and IDSs are best utilized when implemented using a "layered security" approach. This means that multiple steps are taken to secure the data, thereby increasing the workload and time required for an intruder to penetrate the network. While a firewall is an excellent perimeter security device, it is just one element of an effective security strategy. The more elements, or layers, of security that can be added to protect the data, the more secure the infrastructure will remain.

Elements of an effective layered security approach include the following:

- Security policies, procedures, standards, and guidelines, including high-level security policy
- Perimeter security, like routers, firewalls, and other edge devices
- Hardware and/or software host security products
- Auditing, monitoring, and intrusion detection and response

Each of these layers may be implemented independently of the others, yet each is interdependent when functioning. An IDS that alerts to unauthorized access attempts or port scanning is useless without a response plan to react to the problem. Because each layer provides elements of protection, the defeat of any one layer should not lead to a failure of protection.

## Computer Security and Incident Response Teams

Numerous Computer Security and Incident Response Teams (CSIRTs) have formed to address the issue of coordination and communication in response to security incidents. Response teams provide a coordinated and organized method of data sharing in their sphere of influence. This coordination may include the detection, prevention, and handling of security incidents, understanding the current state of security, and identifying trends in activity within their constituency. Because the Internet is a cooperative network, there does not exist one entity with the authority or responsibility for its security. Instead, authority is scattered across logical domains.

Table 5.2 shows some of the existing response teams in the government, military, university, and corporate sectors.

## CERT

The CERT Coordination Center (CERT/CC) is a unit of the Carnegie Mellon University Software Engineering Institute (SEI). SEI is a federally funded R&D center. CERT's mission is to alert the Internet community to vulnerabilities and attacks and to conduct research and training in the areas of computer security, including incident response.

As part of a structured program of intrusion detection and response, a Computer Emergency Response Team (CERT), or Computer Incident Response Team (CIRT), may be created. The prime directive of every CIRT is incident response management, which manages a company's response to events that pose a risk to its computing environment. This management often consists of the following:

- Coordinating the notification and distribution of information pertaining to the incident to the appropriate parties (those with a need to know) through a predefined escalation path

- Mitigating risk to the enterprise by minimizing the disruptions to normal business activities and the costs associated with remediating the incident (including public relations)

- Assembling teams of technical personnel to investigate the potential vulnerabilities and to resolve specific intrusions

Additional examples of CIRT activities include the following:

- Management of the network logs, including collection, retention, review, and analysis of data

- Management of the resolution of an incident, management of the remediation of a vulnerability, and post-event reporting to the appropriate parties

**Table 5.2** Examples of CSIRTs

| RESPONSE TEAM | CONSTITUENCY |
| --- | --- |
| AUSCERT | Australia (sites in .au domain) |
| CERT® Coordination Center (CERT/CC) | The Internet |
| Cisco-PSIRT | Commercial—Cisco customers |
| DFN-CERT | German sites |
| DOD-CERT | Department of Defense systems |
| Global Integrity (REACT) | Commercial and government customers |
| OSU-IRT | Ohio State University |
| OxCERT Oxford University IT Security Team | Oxford University |

## FedCIRC

The Federal Computer Incident Response Center (FedCIRC) is an organization that "establishes a collaborative partnership of computer incident response, security and law enforcement professionals who work together to handle computer security incidents and to provide both proactive and reactive security services for the U.S. Federal government." The FedCIRC charter states: "Fed-CIRC provides assistance and guidance in incident response and provides a centralized approach to incident handling across agency boundaries." The mission of FedCIRC is to do the following:

- Provide civil agencies with technical information, tools, methods, assistance, and guidance
- Be proactive and provide liaison activities and analytical support
- Encourage the development of quality products and services through collaborative relationships with federal civil agencies, Department of Defense, academia, and private industry
- Promote the highest security profile for government information technology (IT) resources
- Promote incident response and handling procedural awareness with the federal government

### FIRST

The Forum of Incident Response and Security Teams (FIRST) brings together a variety of computer security incident response teams from government, commercial, and academic organizations. FIRST aims to foster cooperation and coordination in incident prevention, to prompt rapid reaction to incidents, and to promote information sharing among members and the community at large.

The goals of FIRST are the following:

- To foster cooperation among information technology constituents in the effective prevention, detection, and recovery from computer security incidents

- To provide a means for the communication of alert and advisory information on potential threats and emerging incident situations

- To facilitate the actions and activities of the FIRST members, including research and operational activities

- To facilitate the sharing of security-related information, tools, and techniques

## Security Incident Notification Process

All potential, suspected, or known information security incidents should be reported to a Computer Security and Incident Response Team (CSIRT). The CSIRT will then assign personnel who will assemble all needed resources to handle the reported incident. The incident coordinator will make decisions as to the interpretation of policy, standards, and procedures when applied to the incident.

Law enforcement and investigative agencies will be notified, as needed and required, by the CSIRT. In the event of an incident that has legal consequences, it is important to establish contact with investigative agencies such as the FBI as soon as possible. Local law enforcement should also be informed as appropriate. Legal counsel should be notified of an incident as soon as it is reported. At a minimum, legal counsel should be involved to protect the legal and financial interests of your company.

The security incident notification process should provide some escalation mechanisms. In order to define such a mechanism, the CSIRT should create an internal classification scheme for incidents. Associated with each level of incident will be the appropriate procedures. The following list is an example of various levels of incidents.

**Priority One.**   Protect human life and people's safety; human life always has precedence over all other considerations.

**Priority Two.**   Protect restricted and/or internal data. Prevent exploitation of restricted systems, networks, or sites. Inform affected restricted sensitive systems, networks, or sites about already occurred penetrations while abiding by any applicable government regulations.

**Priority Three.**   Protect other data, including managerial data, because loss of data is costly in terms of resources. Prevent exploitations of other systems, networks, or sites, and inform already affected systems, networks, or sites about successful penetrations.

**Priority Four.**   Prevent damage to systems (for example, loss or alteration of system files, damage to disk drives, and so on). Damage to systems can result in costly down time and recovery.

**Priority Five.**   Minimize disruption of computing resources (including processes). It is better in many cases to shut a system down or disconnect from a network than to risk damage to data or systems. Each data and system owner must evaluate the trade-off between shutting down and disconnecting, and staying up. This decision must be made prior to an incident occurring. There may be service agreements in place that may require keeping the systems up even in light of further damage occurring. The damage and scope of an incident, though, may be so extensive that service agreements may have to be overridden.

## Automated Notice and Recovery Mechanisms

Automated notice and recovery mechanisms can provide automated capabilities in one or more of the following areas: intruder prevention, intruder detection, and damage assessment. A number of automated intruder responses have been implemented as part of intrusion detection systems. Some responses may be active, such as terminating processes, closing connections, and disabling accounts. Other responses are passive, such as sending an e-mail to the system administrator.

Damage assessment is normally performed after an attack. A number of vulnerability scanning tools, such as Tiger, may be used to perform damage assessment. Other tools, such as Tripwire, were specifically developed to aid in damage assessment. At Texas A&M, a prototype tool called the Automated Incident Response System (AIRS) was developed to perform damage control and damage assessment on individual hosts in a network.

The electronic quarantine concept requires the use of host-based intrusion detection systems, which perform real-time activity monitoring and maintain a suspicion level for each user as well as an overall suspicion level of the monitored host.

Although not absolutely required, the ability of host-based intrusion detection systems to cooperate and share information in order to track users as they connect to other monitored hosts is also important.

Automated notice and recovery are appealing because they do not require continuous human oversight, they can act more rapidly than humans, and they can be tailored to, and will consistently follow, specified policies. Common automated response capabilities includes session logging, session termination, posting events on the event console, and alerting personnel through e-mail, paging, and other means. The architecture to collect incident information consists of four crucial components: a sensor, a collector, a backing store, and an analysis engine.

Most IDSs require a human operator to be in the loop. Given the current maturity of IDS technology, the dangers of automated response are significant, and they outweigh the advantages just described. With the frequency of false positives that exists in the current generation of ID systems, the potential for inappropriate response to misdiagnosis is too high. In addition, automated response could be exploited by a perpetrator whose aim is to induce denial of service by spoofing an attack from a legitimate user. Also, many intrusion detection tools provide some form of automated intruder response, but few security tools perform any automated recovery.

CIDDS, the Common Intrusion Detection Director System (also knows as CID Director), is a dedicated hardware/software/operating system platform supporting the Air Force Information Warfare Center's (AFIWC) Intrusion Detection Tools (IDT) program. AFIWC is the U.S. Air Force Office of Primary Responsibility for the IDT program. Within AFIWC, the Air Force Computer Emergency Response Team (AFCERT) is charged with the responsibility for day-to-day administration and network security operations involving the IDT program.

CIDDS receives near-real-time connections data and associated transcripts from Automated Security Incident Measurement (ASIM) sensor host machines and selected other intrusion detection tools. It stores this data on a local database and allows for detailed (local, regional, or theater-wide) correlation and analysis by human analysts and other automated tools.

## IDS Issues

Many issues confront the effective use of IDS. Some of these include the following:

- Increases in the types of intruder goals, intruder abilities, tool sophistication, and diversity, as well as the use of more complex, subtle, and new attack scenarios.
- The use of encrypted messages to transport malicious information.

- The need to interoperate and correlate data across infrastructure environments with diverse technologies and policies.

- Ever-increasing network traffic.

- The lack of widely accepted ID terminology and conceptual structures.

- Volatility in the ID marketplace, which makes the purchase and maintenance of ID systems difficult.

- Risks inherent in taking inappropriate automated response actions.

- Attacks on the ID systems themselves.

- Unacceptably high levels of false positives and false negatives, making it difficult to determine true positives.

- The lack of objective ID system evaluation and test information.

- The fact that most computing infrastructures are not designed to operate securely.

- Limited network traffic visibility resulting from switched local area networks. Faster networks preclude effective real-time analysis of all traffic on large pipes.

An issue with the implementation of intrusion detection systems is the performance of the IDS when the network bandwidth begins to reach saturation levels. Obviously, there is a limit to the number of packets that a network intrusion detection sensor can accurately analyze in any given time period. The higher the network traffic level and the more complex the analysis, the more the IDS may experience high error rates, such as the premature discard of copied network packets.

Another issue with IDS is the proper implementation of IDS sensors in a switched environment. This issue arises from the basic differences between standard hubs and switches. Hubs exclude only the port the packet came in on and echo every packet to every port on the hub. Therefore, in networks employing only hubs, IDS sensors can be placed almost anywhere in the infrastructure.

When a packet comes into a switch, a temporary connection in the switch is first made to the destination port, and then the packets are forwarded. This means more care must be exerted when placing IDS sensors in a switched environment to ensure that the sensor is able to see all of the network traffic.

Some switches permit spanning port configuration, which configures the switch to behave like a hub only for a specific port. The switch can be configured to span the data from a specific port to the IDS port. Unfortunately, some switches cannot be guaranteed to pass all the traffic to the spanned port, and most switches allow only one port to be spanned at a time.

Another partial solution is to place a hub between the monitored connections, say between two switches, a router and a switch, or a server and a switch, for example. This allows traffic to still flow between the switch and the target but with traffic to be copied off to the IDS. This solution, however, spells the beginning of the end for the switched network, and it removes the benefits of a switched solution.

# Business Continuity and Contingency Planning

Business continuity and contingency planning addresses the preservation of business in the face of major disruptions to normal operations. Business continuity includes the preparation, testing, and updating of the actions required to protect critical business processes from the effects of major system and network failures. The ISSO must have an understanding of the preparation of specific actions required to preserve the business in the event of a major disruption to normal business operations.

Business continuity planning (BCP) is a strategy to minimize the effect of disturbances and to allow for the resumption of business processes. The aim of BCP is to minimize the effects of a disruptive event on a company. Business continuity plans are created to prevent interruptions to normal business activity. They are designed to protect critical business processes from natural or man-made failures or disasters and the resultant loss of capital due to the unavailability of normal business processes. Business continuity planning is a strategy to minimize the effect of disturbances and to allow for the resumption of business processes.

A disruptive event is any intentional or unintentional security violation that suspends normal operations. The aim of BCP is to minimize the effects of a disruptive event on a company. The primary purpose of business continuity plans is to reduce the risk of financial loss and enhance a company's capability to recover from a disruptive event promptly. The business continuity plan should also help minimize the cost associated with the disruptive event and mitigate the risk associated with it.

Business continuity plans should look at all critical information processing areas of the company, including, but not limited to, the following:

- LANs, WANs, and servers
- Telecommunications and data communication links
- Workstations and workspaces
- Applications, software, and data
- Media and records storage
- Staff duties and production processes

## CONTINUITY AND RECOVERY DEFINITIONS

♦ *Contingency Plans (CP).* **The documented, organized plan for emergency response, backup operations, and recovery maintained by an activity as part of its security program that will ensure the availability of critical resources and facilitates the continuity of operations in an emergency situation.**

♦ *Disaster Recovery Plans (DRP).* **The plans and procedures that have been developed to recover from a disaster that has made the system operations impossible.**

♦ *Continuity of Operations Plans (COOP).* **The plans and procedures documented to ensure continued critical operations during any period where normal operations are impossible.**

♦ *Business Continuity Plans (BCP).* **The plans and procedures developed that identify and prioritize the critical business functions that must be preserved; the procedures for continued operations of those critical business functions during any disruption (other than a disaster) to normal operations.**

The events that can affect business continuity and require disaster recovery can be categorized as to whether their origination was natural or human. Examples of natural events that can affect business continuity are as follows:

- Fires, explosions, or hazardous material spills of environmental toxins
- Earthquakes, storms, floods, and fires due to acts of nature
- Power outages or other utility failures

Examples of man-made events that can affect business continuity are as follows:

- Bombings, sabotage, or other intentional attacks
- Strikes and job actions
- Employee or operator unavailability due to emergency evacuation or other issues (these could be either man-made or naturally caused)
- Communications infrastructure failures or testing-related outages (including a massive failure of configuration management controls)

Business continuity plans are designed to protect critical business processes from these natural or man-made failures and the resultant loss of capital due to the unavailability of normal business processes. The business continuity plan should also help minimize the cost associated with the disruptive event and mitigate the risk associated with it.

There are four major elements of the BCP process:

**Scope and plan initiation.**   Creating the scope and the other elements needed to define the parameters of the plan.

**Business impact assessment.**   A process to help business units understand the impact of a disruptive event.

**Business continuity plan development.**   Developing the BCP. This process includes the areas of plan implementation, plan testing, and ongoing plan maintenance.

**Plan approval and implementation.**   Final senior management signoff, enterprise-wide awareness of the plan, and implementing a maintenance procedure for updating the plan as needed.

## Scope and Plan Initiation

This phase marks the beginning of the BCP process. It entails creating the scope and the other elements needed to define the parameters of the plan.

The scope and plan initiation phase is the first step to creating a business continuity plan. This phase marks the beginning of the BCP process. It entails creating the scope for the plan and the other elements needed to define the parameters of the plan. This phase embodies an examination of the company's operations and support services. Scope activities could include creating a detailed account of the work required, listing the resources to be used, and defining the management practices to be employed.

## Business Impact Assessment

A business impact assessment (BIA) is a process used to help business units understand the impact of a disruptive event. This phase includes the execution of a vulnerability assessment.

A BIA is an attempt to measure the effect of resource loss and escalating losses over time in order to provide the entity with reliable data on which to base decisions on hazard mitigation and continuity planning. A BIA is performed as one step during the creation of the BCP. It is similar to a risk assessment.

The purpose of a BIA is to create a document to be used to help understand what impact a disruptive event would have on the business. The impact might be financial (quantitative) or operational (qualitative, such as the inability to respond to customer complaints). A vulnerability assessment is often part of the BIA process.

BIA has three primary goals:

**Criticality prioritization.**   Every critical business unit process must be identified and prioritized, and the impact of a disruptive event must be evaluated. Obviously, non-time-critical business processes will require a lower priority rating for recovery than time-critical business processes.

**Down-time estimation.**   The BIA is used to help estimate the Maximum Tolerable Downtime (MTD) that the business can tolerate and still remain a viable company; that is, the longest period of time a critical process can remain interrupted before the company can never recover. It is often found during the BIA process that this time period is much shorter than expected—that is, the company can tolerate only a much briefer period of interruption than was previously thought.

**Resource requirements identification.**   The resource requirements for the critical processes are also identified at this time, with the most time-sensitive processes receiving the most resource allocation.

A BIA generally takes the form of these four steps:

1.  Gathering the needed assessment materials.
2.  Performing the vulnerability assessment.
3.  Analyzing the information compiled.
4.  Documenting the results and presenting recommendations.

## Gathering Assessment Materials

The initial step of the BIA is identifying which business units are critical to continuing an acceptable level of operations. Often, the starting point is a simple organizational chart that shows the business units' relationships to each other. Other documents might also be collected at this stage in an effort to define the functional interrelationships of the organization.

As the materials are collected and the functional operations of the business are identified, the BIA will examine these business function interdependencies with an eye toward several factors, such as the business success factors involved, establishing a set of priorities between the units, and what alternate processing procedures can be utilized.

## The Vulnerability Assessment

The vulnerability assessment is often part of a BIA. It is similar to a risk assessment in that there is a quantitative (financial) section and a qualitative (operational) section. It differs in that it is smaller than a full risk assessment and is focused on providing information that is used solely for the business continuity plan or disaster recovery plan.

A function of a vulnerability assessment is to conduct a loss impact analysis. Because there will be two parts to the assessment, a financial assessment and an operational assessment, it will be necessary to define loss criteria both quantitatively and qualitatively.

Quantitative loss criteria can be defined as follows:

- Incurring financial losses from loss of revenue, capital expenditure, or personal liability resolution

- The additional operational expenses incurred due to the disruptive event

- Incurring financial loss from resolution of violation of contract agreements

- Incurring financial loss from resolution of violation of regulatory or compliance requirements

Qualitative loss criteria can consist of the following:

- The loss of competitive advantage or market share

- The loss of public confidence or credibility, or incurring public embarrassment

During the vulnerability assessment, *critical support* areas must be defined in order to assess the impact of a disruptive event. A critical support area is defined as a business unit or function that must be present to sustain continuity of the business processes, maintain life safety, or avoid public relations embarrassment.

Critical support areas could include the following:

- Telecommunications, data communications, or information technology areas

- Physical infrastructure or plant facilities, transportation services

- Accounting, payroll, transaction processing, customer service, purchasing

The granular elements of these critical support areas will also need to be identified. By granular elements we mean the personnel, resources, and services the critical support areas need to maintain business continuity.

## Analyzing the Information

During the analysis phase of the BIA, several activities take place, such as documenting required processes, identifying interdependencies, and determining what an acceptable interruption period would be.

The goal of this section is to describe clearly what support the defined critical areas will require to preserve the revenue stream and maintain predefined processes, such as transaction processing levels and customer service levels. Therefore, elements of the analysis will have to come from many areas of the enterprise.

### Documentation and Recommendation

The last step of the BIA entails a full documentation of all of the processes, procedures, analysis, and results and the presentation of recommendations to the appropriate senior management.

The report will contain the previously gathered material, list the identified critical support areas, summarize the quantitative and qualitative impact statements, and provide the recommended recovery priorities generated from the analysis.

## Business Continuity Plan Development

Business continuity plan development refers to using the information collected in the BIA to create the recovery strategy plan to support these critical business functions. Here we take the information gathered from the BIA and begin to map out a strategy for creating a continuity plan. This process includes the areas of plan implementation, plan testing, and ongoing plan maintenance. This phase consists of defining and documenting the continuity strategy.

## Plan Approval and Implementation

This process involves getting the final senior management signoff, creating enterprise-wide awareness of the plan, and implementing a maintenance procedure for updating the plan as needed.

### Senior Management Approval

Senior management has the ultimate responsibility for all phases of the plan. Because they have the responsibility for supervision and execution of the plan during a disruptive event, they must have final approval. When a disaster strikes, senior management must be able to make informed decisions quickly during the recovery effort.

### Plan Awareness

Enterprise-wide awareness of the plan is important. There are several reasons for this, including the fact that the capability of the organization to recover from an event will most likely depend on the efforts of many individuals. Also, employee awareness of the plan will emphasize the organization's commitment to its employees. Specific training may be required for certain personnel to carry out their tasks, and quality training is perceived as a benefit that increases the interest and the commitment of personnel in the BCP process.

### Plan Maintenance

Business continuity plans often get out of date: A major similarity among recovery plans is how quickly they become obsolete, for many different reasons. The company may reorganize, and the critical business units may be different than when the plan was first created. Most commonly, the network or computing infrastructure changes, including the hardware, software, and other components. The reasons might be administrative: Cumbersome plans are not easily updated, personnel lose interest or forget, or employee turnover may affect involvement.

Whatever the reason, plan maintenance techniques must be employed from the outset to ensure that the plan remains fresh and usable. It's important to build maintenance procedures into the organization by using job descriptions that centralize responsibility for updates. Also, create audit procedures that can report regularly on the state of the plan. It's also important to ensure that multiple versions of the plan do not exist because they could create confusion during an emergency. Always replace older versions of the text with updated versions throughout the enterprise when a plan is changed or replaced.

## Roles and Responsibilities in the BCP Process

The BCP process involves many personnel from various parts of the enterprise. Creation of a BCP committee will represent the first enterprise-wide involvement of the major critical functional business units. All other business units will be involved in some way later, especially during the implementation and awareness phases.

### The BCP Committee

A BCP committee should be formed and given the responsibility to create, implement, and test the plan. The committee is made up of representatives from senior management, all functional business units, information systems, and security administration. The committee initially defines the scope of the plan, which should deal with how to recover promptly from a disruptive event and mitigate the financial and resource loss due to a disruptive event.

### Senior Management's Role

Senior management has the ultimate responsibility for all phases of the plan, which includes not only initiation of the plan process but also monitoring and management of the plan during testing and supervision and execution of the plan during a disruptive event. This support is essential, and without management being willing to commit adequate tangible and intangible resources, the plan will not be successful.

Because of the concept of due diligence, stockholders might hold senior managers as well as the board of directors personally responsible if a disruptive event causes losses that adherence to base industry standards of due care could have prevented. For this reason and others, it is in the senior managers' best interest to be fully involved in the BCP process.

Also, many elements of the BCP will address senior management, such as the statement of importance and priorities, the statement of organizational responsibility, and the statement of urgency and timing.

## Disaster Recovery Planning and Business Recovery

To preserve the C.I.A. tenets of confidentiality, integrity, and especially availability, disaster recovery and business continuity are vital security concerns. Disaster recovery planning involves the preparation, testing, and updating of the actions required to protect critical business processes from the effects of major system and network failures, by quickly recovering from an emergency with the minimum of impact to the organization.

Examples of natural events that can create a continuity-threatening event include the following:

- Fires, explosions, or hazardous material spills of environmental toxins
- Earthquakes, storms, floods, and fires due to acts of nature
- Power outages or other utility failures

Examples of man-made events include the following:

- Bombings, sabotage, or other attacks
- Strikes and job actions
- Communications infrastructure failures or testing-related outages (including a massive failure of configuration management controls)

A disaster recovery plan is a comprehensive statement of consistent actions to be taken before, during, and after a disruptive event that causes a significant loss of information systems resources. The major goal of a disaster recovery plan is to provide an organized way to make decisions if a disruptive event occurs. The purpose of the disaster recovery plan is to reduce confusion and enhance the ability of the organization to deal with the crisis. When a disruptive event occurs the organization will not have the luxury to create and execute a recovery plan on the spot; therefore, the amount of planning and testing that can be done beforehand will determine the capability of the organization to withstand a disaster.

Disaster recovery plans are the procedures for responding to an emergency, providing extended backup operations during the interruption, and managing recovery and salvage processes afterward, should an organization experience a substantial loss of processing capability. Another objective of a properly executed DRP is to provide the capability to implement critical processes at an alternate site and return to the primary site and normal processing within a time frame that minimizes the loss to the organization.

The objectives of the DRP include these:

- Protecting an organization from major computer services failure

- Minimizing the risk to the organization from delays in providing services

- Guaranteeing the reliability of standby systems through testing and simulation

- Minimizing the decision-making required by personnel during a disaster

Fundamentally, the DRP process is as follows:

1. Create the DRP.

2. Test and adjust the DRP.

3. Execute the DRP in the event of an emergency.

## Creating the DRP

This phase of the DRP process involves the development and creation of the recovery plans and defining the steps needed to perform to protect the business in the event of an actual disaster.

Several vendors distribute automated tools to create disaster recovery plans. These tools can improve productivity by providing formatted templates customized to the particular organization's needs. Also, some vendors offer specialized recovery software focused on a particular type of business or vertical market.

## Recovery Time Objectives

Early in the DRP process, all business functions and critical systems must be examined to determine their recovery time requirements. Recovery time objectives are assigned to each function or system, and this will guide the selection of alternate processing procedures. Table 5.3 shows a common matrix used to classify the recovery time frame needs of business functions or systems.

## Alternate Sites

The three most common types of remote off-site backup processing facilities are hot sites, warm sites, and cold sites. They are primarily differentiated by how much preparation is devoted to the site and, therefore, how quickly the site can be used as an alternate processing site.

**Cold site.** A designated computer operations room with HVAC, which may have few or no computing systems installed and therefore would require a substantial effort to install the hardware and software required to begin alternate processing. This type of site is rarely useful in an actual emergency.

**Warm site.** An alternate processing facility with most hardware and software installed, which would need a minor effort to be up and running as an alternate processing center. It may use cheaper or older equipment and create a degradation in processing performance, but it would be able to handle the most important processing tasks.

**Hot site.** A site with all required hardware and software installed to begin alternate processing either immediately or within an acceptably short time frame. This site would be 100 percent compatible with the original site and may need only an upgrade of the most current data to duplicate operations.

Other alternate processing concepts are as follows:

**Table 5.3** Recovery Time Objectives

| RATING CLASS | RECOVERY TIMEFRAME OBJECTIVE |
|---|---|
| AAA | Immediate recovery needed; no down time allowed. |
| AA | Full functional recovery required within 4 hours. |
| A | Same-business-day recovery required. |
| B | Up to 24 hours down time acceptable. |
| C | 24 to 72 hours down time acceptable. |
| D | Greater than 72 hours down time acceptable. |

**Mutual aid agreements.**    An arrangement with another company that may have similar computing needs. Both parties agree to support each other in the case of a disruptive event by providing alternative processing facilities to the other party. While appealing, this is not a good choice if the emergency affects both parties.

**Rolling or mobile backup.**    Contracting with a vendor to provide mobile power and HVAC facilitates sufficient to stage the alternate processing.

**Multiple centers.**    In a multiple-center concept, the processing is spread over several operations centers, creating a distributed approach to redundancy and sharing of available resources. These multiple centers could be owned and managed by the same organization (in-house sites) or used in conjunction with some sort of reciprocal agreement.

**Service bureaus.**    In rare cases, an organization may contract with a service bureau to fully provide all alternate backup-processing services. The big advantages to this type of arrangement are the quick response and availability of the service bureau, the possibility of testing, and that the service bureau may be available for more than backup. The disadvantages of this type of setup are primarily the expense and resource contention during a large emergency.

### Backup Viability

The availability of a reliable backup and data restoration system is a cornerstone of a viable disaster recovery process. The purpose of tape backup is to preserve and restore lost, corrupted, or deleted information, thereby preserving data integrity and ensuring network availability.

All backup systems share common issues and problems such as the following:

**Slow data transfer.**    The time required to restore the data must be factored into a disaster recovery plan.

**Disk space expansion.**    As the amount of data that needs to be copied increases, the length of time to run the backup proportionally increases and the demand on the system grows as more tapes are required.

Also, backup media security controls must be implemented to prevent the exposure of sensitive information when the media is stored off-site. These security controls include the following:

**Logging.**    Logging the use of backup media provides accountability and helps facilitate the recovery process.

**Access control.**    Physical access control to the media is used to prevent unauthorized personnel from accessing the media.

**Disposal.**    Proper disposal of the media after use is required to prevent data remanence.

Backup media viability controls should be used to protect the media from damage during handling and transportation or during short-term or long-term storage. Viability controls must ensure that the media is readily available and usable when needed for data restoration.

## Testing and Adjusting the DRP

Regular drills and tests are fundamental to a disaster recovery plan. Because no demonstrated recovery capability exists until the plan is tested, the plan must be tested on a regular basis.

Some reasons for regularly testing the DRP are these:

- Testing verifies the accuracy of the recovery procedures and identifies deficiencies.
- Testing prepares and trains the personnel to execute their emergency duties.
- Testing verifies the processing capability of the alternate backup site.

### DRP Testing Types

There are several types of DRP tests; some common ones are these:

**Checklist review.**   Plan is distributed and reviewed by business units for its thoroughness and effectiveness.

**Table-top exercise or structured walk-through test.**   Members of the emergency management group meet in a conference-room setting to discuss their responsibilities and how they would react to emergency scenarios by stepping through the plan.

**Walk-through drill or simulation test.**   The emergency management group and response teams actually perform their emergency response functions by walking through the test, without actually initiating recovery procedures. This approach is more thorough than the table-top exercise.

**Functional drill.**   This approach tests specific functions, such as medical response, emergency notifications, warning and communications procedures and equipment, although not necessarily all at once. It also includes evacuation drills, where personnel walk the evacuation route to a designated area where procedures for accounting for the personnel are tested.

**Parallel test or full-scale exercise.**   A real-life emergency situation is simulated as closely as possible. It involves all of the participants who would be responding to the real emergency, including community and external organizations. The test may involve ceasing some real production processing.

Table 5.4 lists the five disaster recovery plan testing types.

**Table 5.4**  Disaster Recovery Plan Testing Types

| LEVEL | TYPE | DESCRIPTION |
|-------|------|-------------|
| 1 | Checklist | Copies of plan are distributed to management for review. |
| 2 | Structured walk-through | Business unit management meets to review the plan. |
| 3 | Simulation | All support personnel meet in a practice execution session. |
| 4 | Parallel test | Critical systems are run at an alternate site. |
| 5 | Full-interruption test | Normal production is shut down, with real disaster recovery processes. |

### DRP Maintenance

Disaster recovery plans often get out of date. A similarity common to all recovery plans is how quickly they become obsolete, for many different reasons. The company may reorganize, and the critical business units may be different from when the plan was first created. Most commonly, changes in the network or computing infrastructure may change the location or configuration of hardware, software, and other components. The reasons might be administrative: Complex disaster recovery plans are not easily updated, personnel lose interest in the process, or employee turnover might affect involvement.

Whatever the reason, plan maintenance techniques must be employed from the outset to ensure that the plan remains fresh and usable. It's important to build maintenance procedures into the organization by using job descriptions that centralize responsibility for updates. Also, create audit procedures that can report regularly on the state of the plan. It's also important to ensure that multiple versions of the plan do not exist because they could create confusion during an emergency. Always replace older versions of the text with updated versions throughout the enterprise when a plan is changed or replaced.

### *Executing the DRP*

Like life insurance, these are the procedures that you hope you never have to implement. This part of the plan details what roles various personnel will take on, what tasks must be implemented to recover and salvage the site, how the company interfaces with external groups, and financial considerations. The DRP should contain the steps necessary to operate at alternate sites and return to normal operations at the primary site.

### Secure Recovery

There are three options for disaster recovery, based on the extent of the disaster and the organization's recovery ability:

1. Recover at the primary operating site
2. Recover to an alternate site for critical functions
3. Restore full system after a catastrophic loss

Two teams may be used to restore the system from a catastrophic loss, the recovery team and the salvage team:

**The recovery team.** The recovery team's primary task is to get the predefined critical business functions operating at the alternate backup processing site. The recovery team is concerned with rebuilding production processing and determining the criticality of data, for example.

**The salvage team.** The salvage team is different from the recovery team, and it has the mandate to quickly and safely clean, repair, salvage, and determine the viability of the primary processing infrastructure immediately after the disaster.

Other important elements of a DRP to be considered are the following:

- Interfacing with external groups, like police and fire
- Employee relations
- Fraud and crime
- Financial disbursement
- Media relations

## Emergency Management Practices

FEMA defines emergency management practices for federal, state, and local levels of government, as well as in the private and volunteer sectors through its "Partnerships in Preparedness—Exemplary Practices in Emergency Management" program. FEMA's Exemplary Practices in Emergency Management series provides an avenue for forging cooperation and leveraging emergency management talent and resources throughout the public and private sectors, and it pays tribute to those who have developed such practices.

According to the "Emergency Management Guide for Business and Industry," Federal Emergency Management Agency, August 1998, the proper order of steps in the emergency management planning process is as follows:

1. Establish a planning team.
2. Analyze capabilities and hazards.

3. Develop the plan.

4. Implement the plan.

Currently two organizations certify emergency managers:

- International Association of Emergency Managers (IAEM)
- Certified Emergency Manager (CEM) Program

# Forensics

The field of investigating computer crime is also known as computer forensics. *Computer forensics* is the collecting of information from and about computer systems that is admissible in a court of law. To address computer crime, many jurisdictions have expanded the definition of property to include electronic information.

Because information stored in a computer is intangible, special issues arise during an investigation and the collection of evidence associated with computer crime in an organization. Some of these issues include the following:

- The investigation might interfere with the normal conduct of business.
- Data associated with the criminal investigation is usually located on the same computers as the data required for the normal conduct of business (co-mingling of data). In some cases, computers may be seized.
- In many instances, the locations involved in the crime are geographically separated by long distances in different jurisdictions. The different locations usually have different laws, definitions and attitudes toward computer crimes.
- Evidence might be difficult to gather.
- Care must be exercised not to destroy or modify evidence during the collection process.
- Investigators and prosecutors usually have a compressed time frame for the investigation.
- A computer forensics expert is usually required to collect the evidence.

## Requirements for Collecting and Presenting Evidence

There are many issues involved in the conduct of an investigation of suspected computer crime. For example, in a corporate environment, an investigation should involve management, corporate security, human resources, the legal department, and other appropriate staff members. The act of investigating may also affect critical operations.

The gathering, control, storage, and preservation of evidence are extremely critical in any legal investigation. Because the evidence involved in a computer crime is subject to easy modification without a trace, evidence must be carefully handled and controlled throughout its entire life cycle.

## Rules for Evidence

Specifically, there is a chain of evidence that one must follow and protect. The following are the major components of this chain of evidence:

- Location of the evidence when obtained
- Time the evidence was obtained
- Identification of individual(s) who discovered the evidence
- Identification of individual(s) who secured the evidence
- Identification of individual(s) who controlled the evidence and/or who maintained possession of that evidence

Evidence has a life cycle that ranges from its initial discovery to its eventual return to its owner, if applicable. This life cycle has the following components:

- Discovery and recognition
- Protection
- Recording
- Collection
    - Collect all relevant storage media.
    - Make an image of the hard disk before removing power.
    - Print out the screen.
    - Avoid degaussing equipment.
- Identification (tagging and marking)
- Preservation
    - Protect magnetic media from erasure.
    - Store in a proper environment.
- Transportation
- Presentation in a court of law
- Return of evidence to owner

## Admissibility of Evidence

To be admissible in a court of law, evidence must meet certain stringent requirements. The evidence must be relevant, legally permissible, reliable, properly identified, and properly preserved. The principal elements of these requirements are as follows:

**Relevant.**   The evidence is related to the crime in that it shows that the crime has been committed, can provide information describing the crime, can provide information as to the perpetrator's motives, can verify what had occurred, and can fix the crime's time of occurrence.

**Legally permissible.**   The evidence was obtained in a lawful manner.

**Reliability.**   The evidence has not been tampered with or modified.

**Identification.**   The evidence is properly identified without changing or damaging the evidence. In computer forensics, this process includes the following:

- Labeling printouts with permanent markers
- Identifying the operating system used, the hardware types, and so on
- Recording serial numbers
- Marking evidence without damaging it or placing it in sealed containers that are marked

**Preservation.**   The evidence is not subject to damage or destruction. The following are the recommended procedures for preservation:

- Do not prematurely remove power.
- Back up the hard disk image by using disk imaging hardware or software.
- Avoid placing magnetic media in the proximity of sources of magnetic fields.
- Store media in a dust- and smoke-free environment at a proper temperature and humidity.
- Write-protect media.
- Authenticate the file system by creating a digital signature based on the contents of a file or disk sector. One-way hash algorithms, such as the Secure Hash Algorithm (SHA), as described in Chapter 1, "Cryptographic Techniques," can be used.

## Quality and Completeness of Evidence

Evidence can be divided into a number of categories, depending on its reliability, quality, and completeness. These categories are as follows:

**Best evidence.**   Original or primary evidence rather than a copy or duplicate of the evidence.

**Secondary evidence.**   A copy of the evidence or an oral description of its contents; not as reliable as best evidence.

**Direct evidence.**   Proves or disproves a specific act through oral testimony based on information gathered through the witness's five senses.

**Conclusive evidence.**   Incontrovertible evidence; overrides all other evidence.

**Opinions.**   The following are the two types of opinions:

- *Expert*. Can offer an opinion based on personal expertise and facts
- *Nonexpert*. Can testify only to facts.

**Circumstantial evidence.**   Inference of information from other, intermediate, relevant facts.

**Hearsay evidence (third-party evidence).**   Evidence that is not based on personal, first-hand knowledge of the witness, but that was obtained from another source. Under the U.S. Federal Rules of Evidence (803), hearsay evidence is generally not admissible in court. Computer-generated records and other business records fall under the category of hearsay evidence because these records cannot be proven accurate and reliable. This inadmissibility is known as the hearsay rule. There are certain exceptions to the hearsay rule for records that are the following:

- Made during the regular conduct of business and authenticated by witnesses familiar with their use
- Relied on in the regular course of business
- Made by a person with knowledge of the records
- Made by a person with information transmitted by a person with knowledge
- Made at or near the time of occurrence of the act being investigated
- In the custody of the witness on a regular basis

## Post-Incident Reviews and Follow-Up Procedures

If a computer crime is suspected, it is important not to alert the suspect. A preliminary investigation should be conducted to determine if a crime has been committed by examining the audit records and system logs, interviewing witnesses, and assessing the damage incurred. It is critical to determine if disclosure to legal authorities is required by law or regulation. U.S. Federal Sentencing Guidelines require organizations to report criminal acts. There are a number of pertinent issues to consider relative to outside disclosure. Negative publicity resulting in a lack of confidence in the business of the organization is an obvious concern. Once an outside entity such as law enforcement is involved, information dissemination is out of the hands of the organization. Law enforcement involvement necessarily involves support from the organization in terms of personnel time.

The timing of requesting outside assistance from law enforcement is another major issue. In the United States, law enforcement personnel are bound by the Fourth Amendment to the U.S. Constitution and must obtain a warrant to search for evidence. This amendment protects individuals from unlawful search and seizure. Search warrants are issued when there is probable cause for the search, and they provide legal authorization to search a location for specific evidence. Private citizens are not held to this strict requirement, and thus, in some cases, a private individual can conduct a search for possible evidence without a warrant. If a private individual were asked by a law enforcement officer to search for evidence, a warrant would be required because the private individual would be acting as an agent of law enforcement.

An exception to the search warrant requirement for law enforcement officers is the *Exigent Circumstances Doctrine*. Under this doctrine, if probable cause is present and destruction of the evidence is deemed imminent, the search can be conducted without the delay of having the warrant in-hand.

Thus, if law enforcement is called in too early when a computer crime is suspected, the law enforcement investigators will be held to a stricter standard than the organization's employees in regard to searching for and gathering evidence. There is a higher probability, though, that any evidence acquired by law enforcement personnel will be admissible in court because law officers are trained in preserving the chain of evidence. Good sources of evidence include telephone records, video cameras, audit trails, system logs, system backups, witnesses, results of surveillance, and emails.

A standard discriminator used to determine whether a subject may be the perpetrator of a crime is to evaluate whether the individual had a motive, the opportunity, and the means to commit the crime. This test is known as MOM.

If the investigation is undertaken internally, the suspect should be interviewed to acquire information and to determine who committed the offense. This interrogation should be planned in advance, and expert help should be obtained in the conduct of the interview. Obviously, the suspect is alerted when he or she is scheduled for interrogation; a common mistake in setting up and conducting the interview is providing the suspect with too much information. With this information, the suspect may try to alter additional evidence, leave the premises, or warn other co-conspirators. In the conduct of the interrogation, the pertinent information relative to the crime should be obtained and the questions should be scripted beforehand. Original documents should not be used in the conduct of the interview to avoid the possible destruction of critical information by the suspect.

# Sample Questions

Answers to the Sample Questions for this and the other chapters are found in Appendix C.

1. The type of evidence that proves or disproves a specific act through oral testimony based on information gathered through the witness's five senses is called what?

    a. Hearsay evidence

    b. Best evidence

    c. Conclusive evidence

    d. Direct evidence

2. Which of the following is a key principle in the evolution of computer crime laws in many countries?

    a. All members of the United Nations have agreed to uniformly define and prosecute computer crime.

    b. Existing laws against embezzlement, fraud, and wiretapping cannot be applied to computer crime.

    c. The definition of property was extended to include electronic information.

    d. Unauthorized acquisition of computer-based information without the intent to resell is not a crime.

3. In general, computer-based evidence is considered:

    a. Conclusive

    b. Circumstantial

    c. Secondary

    d. Hearsay

4. Investigating and prosecuting computer crimes is made more difficult because:

    a. Backups may be difficult to find.

    b. Evidence is mostly intangible.

    c. Evidence cannot be preserved.

    d. Evidence is hearsay and can never be introduced into a court of law.

5. Which of the following criteria are used to evaluate suspects in the commission of a crime?

    a. Motive, Intent, and Ability

    b. Means, Object, and Motive

    c. Means, Intent, and Motive

    d. Motive, Means, and Opportunity

6. Which of the following is NOT a computer investigation issue?

    a. Evidence is easy to obtain.

    b. The time frame for investigation is compressed.

    c. An expert may be required to assist.

    d. The information is intangible.

7. Conducting a search without the delay of obtaining a warrant if destruction of evidence seems imminent is possible under:

    a. Federal Sentencing Guidelines

    b. Proximate Causation

    c. Exigent Circumstances

    d. Prudent Man Rule

8. Discovery, recording, collection, and preservation are part of what process related to the gathering of evidence?

    a. Admissibility of evidence

    b. The chain of evidence

    c. The evidence life cycle

    d. Relevance of evidence

9. Relative to legal evidence, which one of the following correctly describes the difference between an expert and a nonexpert in delivering an opinion?

    a. An expert can offer an opinion based on personal expertise and facts, but a nonexpert can testify only as to facts.

    b. A nonexpert can offer an opinion based on personal expertise and facts, but an expert can testify only as to facts.

    c. An expert can offer an opinion based on personal expertise and facts, but a nonexpert can testify only as to personal opinion.

    d. An expert can offer an opinion based on facts only, but a nonexpert can testify only as to personal opinion.

10. The collecting of information from and about computer systems that is admissible in a court of law is called:

    a. Computer investigation

    b. Computer forensics

    c. Computer discovery

    d. Computer logistics

11. Which of the following items is NOT one of the requirement for evidence to be admissible in a court of law?

    a. It must be reliable.

    b. It must be legally permissible.

    c. It must be relevant.

    d. It must be approved by the affected organization.

12. If an organization brings in law enforcement to conduct an investigation of computer crime, which of the following does NOT occur?

    a. The organization can still control information dissemination.

    b. The chain of evidence will be better preserved.

    c. The organization may be required to supply supporting resources.

    d. Business may be affected because of investigation-related data residing on computers holding information needed to conduct day-to-day operations (co-location of data).

13. If an organization decides to interview an individual suspected of committing a computer crime, which one of the following should NOT be done?

    a. An expert should be brought in to assist in the investigation.

    b. Questions should be prepared beforehand.

    c. Original documents involved in the interview should be shown to the suspect.

    d. The minimum amount of information should be provided to the suspect.

14. If a private individual were asked by a law enforcement officer to search for evidence, which one of the following is true?

    a. A warrant would not be required because private citizens are not held to the strict requirements of the Fourth Amendment to the U.S. Constitution as law officers are.

    b. The chain of evidence would be broken.

    c. A warrant would be required because the private individual would be acting as an agent of law enforcement.

    d. The evidence would not be relevant.

15. Which choice is the BEST description of the criticality prioritization goal of the Business Impact Assessment (BIA) process?

    a. The identification and prioritization of every critical business unit process

    b. The identification of the resource requirements of the critical business unit processes

    c. The estimation of the maximum down time the business can tolerate

    d. The presentation of the documentation of the results of the BIA

16. Which choice is NOT an element of BCP plan approval and implementation?

    a. Creating an awareness of the plan

    b. Executing a disaster scenario and documenting the results

    c. Obtaining senior management approval of the results

    d. Updating the plan regularly and as needed

17. Which statement is the most accurate about the results of the disaster recovery plan test?

    a. If no deficiencies were found during the test, then the plan is probably perfect.

    b. The results of the test should be kept secret.

    c. If no deficiencies were found during the test, then the test was probably flawed.

    d. The plan should not be changed no matter what the results of the test.

18. Which statement is true regarding company/employee relations during and after a disaster?

   a. The organization has a responsibility to continue salaries or other funding to the employees and/or families affected by the disaster.

   b. The organization's responsibility to the employees' families ends when the disaster stops the business from functioning.

   c. Employees should seek any means of obtaining compensation after a disaster, including fraudulent ones.

   d. Senior-level executives are the only employees who should receive continuing salaries during the disruptive event.

19. Which statement is NOT true regarding the relationship of the organization with the media during and after a disaster?

   a. The organization should establish a unified organizational response to the media during and after the disruptive event.

   b. The organization must avoid dealing with the media at all costs during and after the disruptive event.

   c. The company's response should be delivered by a credible, informed spokesperson.

   d. The company should be honest and accurate about what it knows about the event and its effects.

20. Which choice is the MOST accurate description of a warm site?

   a. A backup processing facility with adequate electrical wiring and air conditioning, but no hardware or software installed

   b. A backup processing facility with most hardware and software installed, which can be operational within a matter of days

   c. A backup processing facility with all hardware and software installed and 100 percent compatible with the original site, operational within hours

   d. A mobile trailer with portable generators and air conditioning

21. Which disaster recovery/emergency management plan testing type is the most cost-effective and efficient way to identify areas of overlap in the plan before conducting more demanding training exercises?

   a. Full-scale exercise

   b. Walk-through drill

   c. Table-top exercise test

   d. Evacuation drill

22. Which choice is NOT a role or responsibility of the person designated to manage the contingency planning process?

    a. Providing direction to senior management

    b. Providing stress reduction programs to employees after an event

    c. Ensuring the identification of all critical business functions

    d. Integrating the planning process across business units

23. Which choice is NOT an emergency management procedure directly related to financial decision making?

    a. Establishing accounting procedures to track the costs of emergencies

    b. Establishing procedures for the continuance of payroll

    c. Establishing critical incident stress procedures

    d. Establishing program procurement procedures

24. Which choice is NOT an appropriate role for senior management in the business continuity and disaster recovery process?

    a. Delegate recovery roles

    b. Publicly praise successes

    c. Closely control media and analyst communications

    d. Assess the adequacy of information security during the disaster recovery

25. Which choice represents the most important first step in creating a business resumption plan?

    a. Performing a risk analysis

    b. Obtaining senior management support

    c. Analyzing the business impact

    d. Planning recovery strategies

26. Which choice is NOT a commonly accepted definition for a disaster?

    a. An occurrence that is outside the normal computing function

    b. An occurrence or imminent threat to the entity of widespread or severe damage, injury, loss of life, or loss of property

    c. An emergency that is beyond the normal response resources of the entity

    d. A suddenly occurring event that has a long-term negative impact on social life

27. Which choice most accurately describes a business continuity program?

    a. Ongoing process to ensure that the necessary steps are taken to identify the impact of potential losses and maintain viable recovery

    b. A program that implements the mission, vision, and strategic goals of the organization

    c. A determination of the effects of a disaster on human, physical, economic, and natural resources

    d. A standard that allows for rapid recovery during system interruption and data loss

28. Which choice is the correct definition of a mutual aid agreement?

    a. A management-level analysis that identifies the impact of losing an entity's resources

    b. An appraisal or determination of the effects of a disaster on human, physical, economic, and natural resources

    c. A prearranged agreement to render assistance to the parties of the agreement

    d. Activities taken to eliminate or reduce the degree of risk to life and property

29. In which order should the following steps be taken to create an emergency management plan?

    a. Implement the plan

    b. Form a planning team

    c. Develop a plan

    d. Conduct a vulnerability assessment

30. Which choice most accurately describes a business impact analysis (BIA)?

    a. A program that implements the strategic goals of the organization

    b. A management-level analysis that identifies the impact of losing an entity's resources

    c. A prearranged agreement between two or more entities to provide assistance

    d. Activities designed to return an organization to an acceptable operating condition

31. In which order should the following steps be taken to perform a vulnerability assessment?

    a. List potential emergencies

    b. Estimate probability

    c. Assess external and internal resources

    d. Assess potential impact

32. Which choice is NOT a recommended step to take when resuming normal operations after an emergency?

    a. Re-occupy the damaged building as soon as is possible

    b. Account for all damage-related costs

    c. Protect undamaged property

    d. Conduct an investigation

33. In developing an emergency or recovery plan, which choice would NOT be a short-term objective?

    a. Priorities for restoration

    b. Acceptable downtime before restoration

    c. Minimum resources needed to accomplish the restoration

    d. The organization's strategic plan

34. When should security isolation of the incident scene start?

    a. Immediately after the emergency is discovered

    b. As soon as the disaster plan is implemented

    c. After all personnel have been evacuated

    d. When hazardous materials have been discovered at the site

35. Which choice is incorrect regarding when a BCP, DRP, or emergency management plan should be evaluated and modified?

    a. Never, once it has been tested it should not be changed

    b. Annually, in a scheduled review

    c. After training drills, tests, or exercises

    d. After an emergency or disaster response

36. Which choice is NOT an example of a potential hazard resulting from a technological event?

    a. Structural collapse

    b. Hazardous materials release

    c. Mass hysteria

    d. Fuel shortage

37. When should the public and media be informed about a disaster?

    a. Whenever site emergencies extend beyond the facility

    b. When any emergency occurs at the facility, internally or externally

    c. When the public's health or safety is in danger

    d. When the disaster has been contained

38. Which choice is the first priority in an emergency?

    a. Communicating with employees' families regarding the status of the emergency.

    b. Notifying external support resources for recovery and restoration.

    c. Protecting the health and safety of everyone in the facility.

    d. Warning customers and contractors of a potential interruption of service.

39. A statistical anomaly-based intrusion detection system:

    a. Acquires data to establish a normal system operating profile

    b. Refers to a database of known attack signatures

    c. Will detect an attack that does not significantly change the system's operating characteristics

    d. Does not report an event that caused a momentary anomaly in the system

40. Intrusion detection systems can be all of the following types EXCEPT:

    a. Signature-based

    b. Statistical anomaly-based

    c. Network-based

    d. Defined-based

41. The organization that "establishes a collaborative partnership of computer incident response, security and law enforcement professionals who work together to handle computer security incidents and to provide both proactive and reactive security services for the U.S. federal government" is called:

    a. CERT®/CC

    b. Center for Infrastructure Protection

    c. Federal CIO Council

    d. Federal Computer Incident Response Center

42. The Carnegie Mellon University CERT Coordination Center (CERT/CC) recommends which of the following sets of incident response practices?

    a. Prepare, notify, follow-up

    b. Prepare, handle, follow-up

    c. Notify, handle, follow-up

    d. Prepare, handle, notify

# Glossary of Terms
# and Acronyms

**\* property (or star property)**   A Bell-LaPadula security model rule giving a subject write access to an object only if the security level of the object dominates the security level of the subject. Also called *confinement property*.

**1000BaseT**   1000 Mbps (1Gbps) baseband Ethernet using twisted-pair wire.

**100BaseT**   100 Mbps baseband Ethernet using twisted-pair wire.

**10Base2**   802.3 IEEE Ethernet standard for 10 Mbps Ethernet using coaxial cable (thinnet) rated to 185 meters.

**10Base5**   10 Mbps Ethernet using coaxial cable (thicknet) rated to 500 meters.

**10BaseF**   10 Mbps baseband Ethernet using optical fiber.

**10BaseT**   10 Mbps UTP Ethernet rated to 100 meters.

**10Broad36**   10 Mbps broadband Ethernet rated to 3600 meters.

**3DES**   Triple Data Encryption Standard.

**802.10**   IEEE standard that specifies security and privacy access methods for LANs.

**802.11**   IEEE standard that specifies 1 Mbps and 2 Mbps wireless connectivity. Defines aspects of frequency hopping and direct-sequence spread spectrum (DSSS) systems for use in the 2.4 MHz ISM (industrial, scientific, medical) band. Also refers to the IEEE committee responsible for setting wireless LAN standards.

**802.11a**  Specifies high-speed wireless connectivity in the 5 GHz band using *orthogonal frequency division multiplexing* (OFDM) with data rates up to 54 Mbps.

**802.11b**  Specifies high-speed wireless connectivity in the 2.4 GHz ISM band up to 11 Mbps.

**802.15**  Specification for Bluetooth LANs in the 2.4–2.5 GHz band.

**802.2**  Standard that specifies the *LLC (logical link control)*.

**802.3**  Ethernet bus topology using carrier sense medium access control/carrier detect (CSMA/CD) for 10 Mbps wired LANs. Currently, the most popular LAN topology.

**802.4**  Specifies a token-passing bus access method for LANs.

**802.5**  Specifies a token-passing ring access method for LANs.

**A**

**acceptance inspection**  The final inspection to determine whether a facility or system meets the specified technical and performance standards. Note: This inspection is held immediately after facility and software testing and is the basis for commissioning or accepting the information system.

**acceptance testing**  A type of testing used to determine whether the network is acceptable to the actual users.

**access**  A specific type of interaction between a subject and an object that results in the flow of information from one to the other.

**access control**  The process of limiting access to system resources only to authorized programs, processes, or other systems (on a network). This term is synonymous with *controlled access* and *limited access*.

**access control mechanism**  Hardware or software features, operating procedures, management procedures, and various combinations thereof that are designed to detect and prevent unauthorized access and to permit authorized access in an automated system.

**access level**  The hierarchical portion of the security level that is used to identify the sensitivity of data and the clearance or authorization of users. Note: The access level, in conjunction with the nonhierarchical categories, forms the sensitivity label of an object. See *category, security level*, and *sensitivity label*.

**access list**  A list of users, programs, and/or processes, and the specifications of access categories to which each is assigned; a list denoting which users have what privileges to a particular resource.

**access period**  A segment of time, generally expressed on a daily or weekly basis, during which access rights prevail.

**access point (AP)**   A wireless LAN transceiver interface between the wireless network and a wired network. Access points forward frames between wireless devices and hosts on the LAN.

**access port**   A logical or physical identifier that a computer uses to distinguish different terminal input/output data streams.

**access type**   The nature of an access right to a particular device, program, or file (for example, read, write, execute, append, modify, delete, or create).

**accountability**   The property that enables activities on a system to be traced to individuals who might then be held responsible for their actions.

**accreditation**   A formal declaration by the DAA that the AIS is approved to operate in a particular security mode by using a prescribed set of safeguards. Accreditation is the official management authorization for operation of an AIS and is based on the certification process as well as on other management considerations. The accreditation statement affixes security responsibility with the DAA and shows that due care has been taken for security.

**accreditation authority**   Synonymous with *Designated Approving Authority*.

**ACK**   Acknowledgment; a short-return indication of the successful receipt of a message.

**acknowledged connectionless service**   A datagram-style service that includes error-control and flow-control mechanisms.

**ACO**   Authenticated ciphering offset.

**adaptive routing**   A form of network routing whereby the path data packets traverse from a source to a destination node depending on the current state of the network by calculating the best path through the network.

**add-on security**   The retrofitting of protection mechanisms implemented by hardware or software.

**Address Resolution Protocol (ARP)**   A TCP/IP protocol that binds logical (IP) addresses to physical addresses.

**administrative security**   The management constraints and supplemental controls established to provide an acceptable level of protection for data. Synonymous with *procedural security*.

**Advanced Encryption Standard (AES) (Rijndael)**   A symmetric block cipher with a block size of 128 bits in which the key can be 128, 192, or 256 bits. The Advanced Encryption Standard replaces the Date Encryption Standard (DES) and was announced on November 26, 2001, as Federal Information Processing Standard Publication (FIPS PUB 197).

**AIS**   *Automated Information System.*

**analog signal**   An electrical signal with an amplitude that varies continuously.

**Application layer**   The top layer of the OSI model, which is concerned with application programs. It provides services such as file transfer and e-mail to the network's end users.

**application process**   An entity, either human or software, that uses the services offered by the Application layer of the OSI reference model.

**application program interface**   A software interface provided between a specialized communications program and an end-user application.

**application software**   Software that accomplishes functions such as database access, electronic mail, and menu prompts.

**architecture**   As refers to a computer system, describes the type of components, interfaces, and protocols the system uses and how they fit together.

**assurance**   A measure of confidence that the security features and architecture of an AIS accurately mediate and enforce the security policy. Grounds for confidence that an IT product or system meets its security objectives. See *DITSCAP*.

**asymmetric (public) key encryption**   Cryptographic system that employs two keys, a public key and a private key. The public key is made available to anyone wishing to send an encrypted message to an individual holding the corresponding private key of the public-private key pair. Any message encrypted with one of these keys can be decrypted with the other. The private key is always kept private. It should not be possible to derive the private key from the public key.

**Asynchronous Transfer Mode**   A cell-based connection-oriented data service offering high-speed data communications. ATM integrates circuit and packet switching to handle both constant and burst information at rates up to 2.488 Gbps. Also called *cell relay*.

**asynchronous transmission**   Type of communications data synchronization with no defined time relationship between transmission of data frames. *See synchronous transmission.*

**attachment unit interface (AUI)**   A 15-pin interface between an Ethernet Network Interface Card and a transceiver.

**attack**   The act of trying to bypass security controls on a system. An attack can be active, resulting in data modification, or passive, resulting in the release of data. Note: The fact that an attack is made does not necessarily mean that it will succeed. The degree of success depends on the vulnerability of the system or activity and the effectiveness of existing countermeasures.

**audit trail**   A chronological record of system activities that is sufficient to enable the reconstruction, reviewing, and examination of the sequence of environments and activities surrounding or leading to an operation, a procedure, or an event in a transaction from its inception to its final result.

**authenticate**   (1) To verify the identity of a user, device, or other entity in a computer system, often as a prerequisite to allowing access to system resources. (2) To verify the integrity of data that has been stored, transmitted, or otherwise exposed to possible unauthorized modification.

**authentication device**   A device whose identity has been verified during the lifetime of the current link based on the authentication procedure.

**authentication**   Generically, the process of verifying "who" is at the other end of a transmission.

**authenticator**   The means used to confirm the identity or verify the eligibility of a station, originator, or individual.

**authorization**   The granting of access rights to a user, program, or process.

**automated data processing security**   Synonymous with *automated information systems security.*

**automated information system (AIS)**   An assembly of computer hardware, software, and/or firmware that is configured to collect, create, communicate, compute, disseminate, process, store, and/or control data or information.

**automated information system security**   Measures and controls that protect an AIS against Denial of Service (DoS) and unauthorized (accidental or intentional) disclosure, modification, or destruction of AISs and data. AIS security includes consideration of all hardware and/or software functions, characteristics and/or features; operational procedures, accountability procedures, and access controls at the central computer facility, remote computers, and terminal facilities; management constraints; physical structures and devices; and personnel and communication controls that are needed to provide an acceptable level of risk for the AIS and for the data and information contained in the AIS. It includes the totality of security safeguards needed to provide an acceptable protection level for an AIS and for data handled by an AIS.

**automated security monitoring**   The use of automated procedures to ensure that security controls are not circumvented.

**availability of data**   The condition in which data is in the place needed by the user, at the time the user needs it, and in the form needed by the user.

## B

**backbone network**   A network that interconnects other networks.

**backdoor**   Synonymous with *trapdoor.*

**backup plan**   Synonymous with *contingency plan.*

**backward chaining**   In an expert system, the process of beginning with a possible solution and using the knowledge in the knowledge base to justify the solution based on the raw input data. Backward chaining is generally used when a large number of possible solutions exist relative to the number of inputs.

**bandwidth**   Specifies the amount of the frequency spectrum that is usable for data transfer. In other words, bandwidth identifies the maximum data rate a signal can attain on the medium without encountering significant attenuation (loss of power). Also, the amount of information one can send through a connection.

**baud rate**   The number of pulses of a signal that occur in one second. Thus, baud rate is the speed at which the digital signal pulses travel. Also, the rate at which data is transferred.

**Bell-LaPadula model**   A formal state transition model of computer security policy that describes a set of access control rules. In this formal model, the entities in a computer system are divided into abstract sets of subjects and objects. The notion of a secure state is defined, and it is proven that each state transition preserves security by moving from secure state to secure state, thereby inductively proving that the system is secure. A system state is defined to be secure if the only permitted access modes of subjects to objects are in accordance with a specific security policy. In order to determine whether a specific access mode is allowed, the clearance of a subject is compared to the classification of the object, and a determination is made as to whether the subject is authorized for the specific access mode. See *star property (\* property)* and *simple security property*.

**benign environment**   A nonhostile environment that might be protected from external hostile elements by physical, personnel, and procedural security countermeasures.

**between-the-lines entry**   Unauthorized access obtained by tapping the temporarily inactive terminal of a legitimate user. See *piggyback*.

**beyond A1**   A level of trust defined by the *DoD Trusted Computer System Evaluation Criteria* (TCSEC) that is beyond the state-of-the-art technology available at the time the criteria was developed. It includes all of the A1-level features plus additional features that are not required at the A1 level.

**binary digit**   See *bit*.

**biometrics**   Access control method in which an individual's physiological or behavioral characteristics are used to determine that individual's access to a particular resource.

**BIOS**   *Basic Input/Output System* The BIOS is the first program to run when the computer is turned on. BIOS initializes and tests the computer hardware, loads and runs the operating system, and manages Setup for making changes in the computer.

**bit**    Short for *binary digit*. A single-digit number in binary is 0 or 1.

**bit rate**    The transmission rate of binary symbols 0s and 1s. Bit rate is equal to the total number of bits transmitted in one second.

**blackboard**    An expert system reasoning methodology in which a solution is generated by the use of a virtual "blackboard" wherein information or potential solutions are placed on the blackboard by a plurality of individuals or expert knowledge sources. As more information is placed on the blackboard in an iterative process, a solution is generated.

**blind signature**    A form of digital signature where the signer is not privy to the content of the message.

**block cipher**    A symmetric key algorithm that operates on a fixed-length block of plaintext and transforms it into a fixed-length block of ciphertext. A block cipher is obtained by segregating plaintext into blocks of $n$ characters or bits and applying the identical same encryption algorithm and key to each block.

**Bluetooth**    An open specification for wireless communication of data and voice, based on a low-cost short-range radio link facilitating protected ad hoc connections for stationary and mobile communication environments.

**bridge**    A network device that provides internetworking functionality by connecting networks. Bridges can provide segmentation of data frames and can be used to connect LANs by forwarding packets across connections at the media access control (MAC) sublayer of the OSI model's Data Link layer.

**broadband**    A transmission system in which signals are encoded and modulated into different frequencies and then transmitted simultaneously with other signals (that is, having undergone a shift in frequency). A LAN broadband signal is commonly analog.

**browsing**    The act of searching through storage to locate or acquire information without necessarily knowing the existence or the format of the information being sought.

**BSI ISO/IEC 17799:2000,BS 7799-I: 2000, Information technology—Code of practice for information security management, British Standards Institution, London, UK**    A standard intended to "provide a comprehensive set of controls comprising best practices in information security." ISO refers to the International Organization for Standardization, and IEC is the International Electrotechnical Commission.

**bus topology**    A type of network topology wherein all nodes are connected to a single length of cabling with a terminator at each end.

**Business Software Alliance (BSA)**    An international organization representing leading software and e-commerce developers in 65 countries around the world. BSA efforts include educating computer users about software copyrights, advocating for public policy that fosters innovation and expands trade opportunities, and fighting software piracy.

**byte**    A set of bits, usually eight, that represent a single character.

## C

**call back**    A procedure for identifying a remote terminal. In a call back, the host system disconnects the caller and then dials the authorized telephone number of the remote terminal in order to re-establish the connection. Synonymous with *dial back*.

**capability**    A protected identifier that both identifies the object and specifies the access rights allowed to the accessor who possesses the capability. In a capability-based system, access to protected objects (such as files) is granted if the would-be accessor possesses a capability for the object.

**Capstone**    A Very Large Scale Integration (VLSI) chip that employs the Escrowed Encryption Standard and incorporates the Skipjack algorithm, similar to the Clipper Chip. As such, it has a Law Enforcement Access Field (LEAF). Capstone also supports public key exchange and digital signatures. At this time, Capstone products have their LEAF function suppressed and a Certificate authority provides for key recovery.

**Carnivore**    A device used by the U.S. FBI to monitor ISP traffic (S.P. Smith, et al., *Independent Technical Review of the Carnivore System*—Draft report, U.S. Department of Justice Contract # 00-C-328 IITRI, CR-022-216, November 17, 2000).

**carrier current LAN**    A LAN that uses power lines within the facility as a medium for data transport.

**carrier sense multiple access (CSMA)**    The technique used to reduce transmission contention by listening for contention before transmitting.

**carrier sense multiple access/collision detection (CSMA/CD)**    The most common Ethernet cable access method.

**category**    A restrictive label that has been applied to classified or unclassified data as a means of increasing the protection of the data and further restricting its access.

**category 1 twisted-pair wire**    Used for early analog telephone communications; not suitable for data.

**category 2 twisted-pair wire**    Rated for 4 Mbps and used in 802.5 token ring networks.

**category 3 twisted-pair wire**    Rated for 10 Mbps and used in 802.3 10Base-T Ethernet networks.

**category 4 twisted-pair wire**   Rated for 16 Mbps and used in 802.5 token ring networks.

**category 5 twisted-pair wire**   Rated for 100 Mbps and used in 100BaseT Ethernet networks.

**CBC**   Cipher block chaining, an encryption mode of the Data Encryption Standard (DES) that operates on plaintext blocks 64 bits in length.

**CC**   Common Criteria, a standard for specifying and evaluating the features of computer products and systems.

**Centronics**   A de facto standard 36-pin parallel 200 Kbps asynchronous interface for connecting printers and other devices to a computer.

**CERT Coordination Center (CERT®/CC)**   A unit of the Carnegie Mellon University Software Engineering Institute (SEI). SEI is a federally funded R&D Center. CERT's mission is to alert the Internet community to vulnerabilities and attacks and to conduct research and training in the areas of computer security, including incident response.

**certification**   The comprehensive evaluation of the technical and nontechnical security features of an AIS and other safeguards, made in support of the accreditation process, that establishes the extent to which a particular design and implementation meet a specified set of security requirements.

**Chinese Wall model**   Uses internal rules to "compartmentalize" areas in which individuals may work to prevent disclosure of proprietary information and to avoid conflicts of interest. The Chinese Wall model also incorporates the principle of separation of duty.

**cipher**   A cryptographic transformation that operates on characters or bits.

**ciphertext or cryptogram**   An unintelligible encrypted message.

**circuit-switched**   The application of a network wherein a dedicated line is used to transmit information; contrast with *packet-switched*.

**client**   A computer that accesses a server's resources.

**client/server architecture**   A network system design in which a processor or computer designated as a file server or database server provides services to other client processors or computers. Applications are distributed between a host server and a remote client.

**closed security environment**   An environment in which both of the following conditions hold true: (1) Application developers (including maintainers) have sufficient clearances and authorizations to provide an acceptable presumption that they have not introduced malicious logic, and (2) Configuration control provides sufficient assurance that applications and the equipment are protected against the introduction of malicious logic prior to and during the operation of system applications.

**closed shop**  Data processing area using physical access controls to limit access to authorized personnel.

**clustering**  Situation in which a plaintext message generates identical ciphertext messages using the same transformation algorithm, but with different cryptovariables or keys.

**coaxial cable (coax)**  Type of transmission cable consisting of a hollow outer cylindrical conductor that surrounds a single inner wire conductor for current flow. Because the shielding reduces the amount of electrical noise interference, coax can extend to much greater lengths than twisted-pair wiring.

**code division multiple access (CDMA)**  A spread spectrum digital cellular radio system that uses different codes to distinguish users.

**codes**  Cryptographic transformation that operates at the level of words or phrases.

**collision detection**  The detection of simultaneous transmission on the communications medium.

**Common Object Model (COM)**  A model that allows two software components to communicate with each other independent of their platforms' operating systems and languages of implementation. As in the object-oriented paradigm, COM works with encapsulated objects.

**Common Object Request Broker Architecture (CORBA)**  A standard that uses the Object Request Broker (ORB) to implement exchanges among objects in a heterogeneous, distributed environment.

**Communications Assistance for Law Enforcement Act (CALEA) of 1994**  An act that required all communications carriers to make wiretaps possible in ways approved by the FBI.

**communications security (COMSEC)**  Measures taken to deny unauthorized persons information derived from telecommunications of the U.S. government concerning national security and to ensure the authenticity of such telecommunications. Communications security includes cryptosecurity, transmission security, emission security, and physical security of communications security material and information.

**compartment**  A class of information that has need-to-know access controls beyond those normally provided for access to Confidential, Secret, or Top Secret information.

**compartmented security mode**  See *modes of operation*.

**compensating controls**  A combination of controls, such as physical and technical or technical and administrative (or all three).

**composition model**  An information security model that investigates the resultant security properties when subsystems are combined.

**compromise**    A violation of a system's security policy such that unauthorized disclosure of sensitive information might have occurred.

**compromising emanations**    Unintentional data-related or intelligence-bearing signals that, when intercepted and analyzed, disclose the information transmission that is received, handled, or otherwise processed by any information processing equipment. See *TEMPEST*.

**COMPUSEC**    Computer security.

**computer abuse**    The misuse, alteration, disruption, or destruction of data-processing resources. The key is that computer abuse is intentional and improper.

**computer cryptography**    The use of a crypto-algorithm in a computer, microprocessor, or microcomputer to perform encryption or decryption in order to protect information or to authenticate users, sources, or information.

**computer facility**    The physical structure housing data processing operations.

**computer forensics**    Information collection from and about computer systems that is admissible in a court of law.

**computer fraud**    Computer-related crimes involving deliberate misrepresentation, alteration, or disclosure of data in order to obtain something of value (usually for monetary gain). A computer system must have been involved in the perpetration or cover-up of the act or series of acts. A computer system might have been involved through improper manipulation of input data, output or results, applications programs, data files, computer operations, communications, or computer hardware, systems software, or firmware.

**computer security (COMPUSEC)**    Synonymous with *automated information systems security.*

**computer security subsystem**    A device that is designed to provide limited computer security features in a larger system environment.

**Computer Security Technical Vulnerability Reporting Program (CSTVRP)**    A program that focuses on technical vulnerabilities in commercially available hardware, firmware, and software products acquired by DoD. CSTVRP provides for the reporting, cataloging, and discrete dissemination of technical vulnerability and corrective measure information to DoD components on a need-to-know basis.

**COMSEC**    See *communications security.*

**concealment system**    A method of achieving confidentiality in which sensitive information is hidden by embedding it in irrelevant data.

**confidentiality**   The concept of holding sensitive data in confidence, limited to an appropriate set of individuals or organizations.

**configuration control**   The process of controlling modifications to the system's hardware, firmware, software, and documentation that provides sufficient assurance that the system is protected against the introduction of improper modifications prior to, during, and after system implementation. Compare with *configuration management.*

**configuration management**   The management of security features and assurances through control of changes made to a system's hardware, software, firmware, documentation, test, test fixtures, and test documentation throughout the development and operational life of the system. Compare with *configuration control.*

**confinement**   The prevention of the leaking of sensitive data from a program.

**confinement channel**   Synonymous with *covert channel.*

**confinement property**   Synonymous with *star property (\* property).*

**confusion**   A method of hiding the relationship between the plaintext and the ciphertext.

**connection-oriented service**   Service that establishes a logical connection that provides flow control and error control between two stations that need to exchange data.

**connectivity**   A path through which communications signals can flow.

**connectivity software**   A software component that provides an interface between the networked appliance and the database or application software located on the network.

**Construction Cost Model (COCOMO), basic version**   Estimates software development effort and cost as a function of the size of the software product in source instructions.

**containment strategy**   A strategy for containment (in other words, stopping the spread) of the disaster and the identification of the provisions and processes required to contain the disaster.

**contamination**   The intermixing of data at different sensitivity and need-to-know levels. The lower-level data is said to be contaminated by the higher-level data; thus, the contaminating (higher-level) data might not receive the required level of protection.

**contingency management**   Establishing actions to be taken before, during, and after a threatening incident.

**contingency plan**   A plan for emergency response, backup operations, and post-disaster recovery maintained by an activity as a part of its security program; this plan ensures the availability of critical resources and facilitates the continuity of operations in an emergency situation. Synonymous with *disaster plan* and *emergency plan*.

**continuity of operations**    Maintenance of essential IP services after a major outage.

**control zone**    The space, expressed in feet of radius, surrounding equipment processing sensitive information that is under sufficient physical and technical control to preclude an unauthorized entry or compromise.

**controlled access**    See *access control*.

**controlled sharing**    The condition that exists when access control is applied to all users and components of a system.

**Copper Data Distributed Interface (CDDI)**    A version of FDDI specifying the use of unshielded twisted pair wiring.

**cost-risk analysis**    The assessment of the cost of providing data protection for a system versus the cost of losing or compromising the data.

**countermeasure**    Any action, device, procedure, technique, or other measure that reduces the vulnerability of or threat to a system.

**countermeasure/safeguard**    An entity that mitigates the potential risk to an information system.

**covert channel**    A communications channel that enables two cooperating processes to transfer information in a manner that violates the system's security policy. Synonymous with *confinement channel*.

**covert storage channel**    A covert channel that involves the direct or indirect writing of a storage location by one process and the direct or indirect reading of the storage location by another process. Covert storage channels typically involve a finite resource (for example, sectors on a disk) that is shared by two subjects at different security levels.

**covert timing channel**    A covert channel in which one process signals information to another by modulating its own use of system resources (for example, CPU time) in such a way that this manipulation affects the real response time observed by the second process.

**CPU**    The central processing unit of a computer.

**criteria**    See *DoD Trusted Computer System Evaluation Criteria*.

**CRL**    Certificate Revocation List.

**cryptanalysis**    Refers to the ability to "break" the cipher so that the encrypted message can be read. Cryptanalysis can be accomplished by exploiting weaknesses in the cipher or in some fashion determining the key.

**crypto-algorithm**    A well-defined procedure or sequence of rules or steps used to produce a key stream or ciphertext from plaintext, and vice versa. Step-by-step procedure that is used to encipher plaintext and decipher ciphertext. Also called a *cryptographic algorithm*.

**cryptographic algorithm**   See *crypto-algorithm.*

**cryptographic application programming interface (CAPI)**   An interface to a library of software functions that provide security and cryptography services. CAPI is designed for software developers to call functions from the library, which makes it easier to implement security services.

**cryptography**   The principles, means, and methods for rendering information unintelligible and for restoring encrypted information to intelligible form. The word *cryptography* comes from the Greek *kryptos,* meaning "hidden," and *graphein*, "to write."

**cryptosecurity**   The security or protection resulting from the proper use of technically sound cryptosystems.

**cryptosystem**   A set of transformations from a message space to a ciphertext space. This system includes all cryptovariables (keys), plaintexts, and ciphertexts associated with the transformation algorithm.

**cryptovariable**   See *key.*

**CSMA/CA**   Carrier sense multiple access/collision avoidance, commonly used in 802.11 Ethernet and LocalTalk.

**CSMA/CD**   Carrier sense multiple access/collision detection, used in 802.3 Ethernet.

**CSTVRP**   See *Computer Security Technical Vulnerability Reporting Program.*

**cyclic redundancy check (CRC)**   A common error-detection process. A mathematical operation is applied to the data when transmitted. The result is appended to the core packet. Upon receipt, the same mathematical operation is performed and checked against the CRC. A mismatch indicates a very high probability that an error has occurred during transmission.

**D**

**DAA**   See designated approving authority.

**DAC**   See discretionary access control.

**data dictionary**   A database that comprises tools to support the analysis, design, and development of software and to support good software engineering practices.

**Data Encryption Standard (DES)**   A cryptographic algorithm for the protection of unclassified data, published in Federal Information Processing Standard (FIPS) 46. The DES, which was approved by the National Institute of Standards and Technology (NIST), is intended for public and government use.

**data flow control**   See information flow control.

**data integrity**   When data meet a prior expectation of quality.

**Data Link layer**   The OSI level that performs the assembly and transmission of data packets, including error control.

**data mart**   A database that comprises data or relations that have been extracted from the data warehouse. Information in the data mart is usually of interest to a particular group of people.

**data mining**   The process of analyzing large data sets in a data warehouse to find nonobvious patterns.

**data scrubbing**   Maintenance of a data warehouse by deleting information that is unreliable or no longer relevant.

**data security**   The protection of data from unauthorized (accidental or intentional) modification, destruction, or disclosure.

**Data service unit/channel service unit (DSU/CSU)**   A set of network components that reshape data signals into a form that can be effectively transmitted over a digital transmission medium, typically a leased 56 Kbps or T1 line.

**data warehouse**   A subject-oriented, integrated, time-variant, nonvolatile collection of data in support of management's decision-making process.

**database**   A persistent collection of data items that form relations among each other.

**database shadowing**   A data redundancy process that uses the live processing of remote journaling but creates even more redundancy by duplicating the database sets to multiple servers.

**datagram service**   A connectionless form of packet switching whereby the source does not need to establish a connection with the destination before sending data packets.

**DB-15**   A standard 15-pin connector commonly used with RS-232 serial interfaces, Ethernet transceivers, and computer monitors.

**DB-25**   A standard 25-pin connector commonly used with RS-232 serial interfaces. The DB-25 connector supports all RS-232 functions.

**DB-9**   A standard 9-pin connector commonly used with RS-232 serial interfaces on portable computers. The DB-9 connector does not support all RS-232 functions.

**de facto standard**   A standard based on broad usage and support but not directly specified by the IEEE.

**decipher**   To unscramble the encipherment process in order to make the message human-readable.

**declassification of AIS storage media**   An administrative decision or procedure to remove or reduce the security classification of the subject media.

**DeCSS**   A program that bypasses the Content Scrambling System (CSS) software used to prevent the viewing of DVD movie disks on unlicensed platforms.

**dedicated security mode**   See *modes of operation*.

**default**   A value or option that is automatically chosen when no other value is specified.

**default classification**   A temporary classification reflecting the highest classification being processed in a system. The default classification is included in the caution statement that is affixed to the object.

**Defense Information Technology Systems Certification and Accreditation Process (DITSCAP)**   Establishes for the defense entities, a standard process, set of activities, general task descriptions, and a management structure to certify and accredit IT systems that will maintain the required security posture. The process is designed to certify that the IT system meets the accreditation requirements and that the system will maintain the accredited security posture throughout the system lifecycle. The four phases to the DITSCAP are Definition, Verification, Validation, and Post Accreditation.

**degauss**   The purpose of degaussing magnetic storage media.

**Degausser Products List (DPL)**   A list of commercially produced degaussers that meet National Security Agency specifications. This list is included in the NSA Information Systems Security Products and Services Catalogue and is available through the Government Printing Office.

**degraded fault tolerance**   Specifies which capabilities the TOE will still provide after a system failure. Examples of general failures are flooding of the computer room, short-term power interruption, breakdown of a CPU or host, software failure, or buffer overflow. Only functions specified must be available.

**Denial of Service (DoS)**   Any action (or series of actions) that prevents any part of a system from functioning in accordance with its intended purpose. This action includes any action that causes unauthorized destruction, modification, or delay of service. Synonymous with interdiction.

**DES**   See Data Encryption Standard.

**Descriptive Top-Level Specification (DTLS)**   A top-level specification that is written in a natural language (for example, English), an informal design notation, or a combination of the two.

**designated approving authority**   The official who has the authority to decide on accepting the security safeguards prescribed for an AIS, or the official who might be responsible for issuing an accreditation statement that records the decision to accept those safeguards.

**dial back**   Synonymous with call back.

**dialup**   The service whereby a computer terminal can use the telephone to initiate and effect communication with a computer.

**diffusion**   A method of obscuring redundancy in plaintext by spreading the effect of the transformation over the ciphertext.

**Digital Millennium Copyright Act (DMCA) of 1998**   In addition to addressing licensing and ownership information, the DMCA prohibits trading, manufacturing, or selling in any way that is intended to bypass copyright protection mechanisms.

**Direct-sequence spread spectrum (DSSS)**   A method used in 802.11b to split the frequency into 14 channels, each with a frequency range, by combining a data signal with a chipping sequence. Data rates of 1, 2, 5.5, and 11 Mbps are obtainable. DSSS spreads its signal continuously over this wide-frequency band.

**disaster**   A sudden, unplanned, calamitous event that produces great damage or loss; any event that creates an inability on the organization's part to provide critical business functions for some undetermined period of time.

**disaster plan**   Synonymous with contingency plan.

**disaster recovery plan**   Procedure for emergency response, extended backup operations, and post-disaster recovery when an organization suffers a loss of computer resources and physical facilities.

**discovery**   In the context of legal proceedings and trial practice, a process in which the prosecution presents information it has uncovered to the defense. This information may include potential witnesses, reports resulting from the investigation, evidence, and so on. During an investigation, discovery refers to the following:

- The process undertaken by the investigators to acquire evidence needed for prosecution of a case
- A step in the computer forensic process

**discretionary access control**   A means of restricting access to objects based on the identity and need to know of the user, process, and/or groups to which they belong. The controls are discretionary in the sense that a subject that has certain access permissions is capable of passing that permission (perhaps indirectly) on to any other subject. Compare with *mandatory access control*.

**disk image backup**   Conducting a bit-level copy, sector –by sector of a disk, which provides the capability to examine slack space, undeleted clusters, and, possibly, deleted files.

**Distributed Component Object Model (DCOM)**   A distributed object model that is similar to the Common Object Request Broker Architecture (CORBA). DCOM is the distributed version of COM that supports remote objects as if the objects reside in the client's address space. A COM client can access a COM object through the use of a pointer to one of the object's interfaces and then invoke methods through that pointer.

**Distributed Queue Dual Bus (DQDB)**   The IEEE 802.6 standard that provides full-duplex 155 Mbps operation between nodes in a metropolitan area network.

**distributed routing**   A form of routing wherein each router on the network periodically identifies neighboring nodes, updates its routing table, and, with this information, sends its routing table to all of its neighbors. Because each node follows the same process, complete network topology information propagates through the network and eventually reaches each node.

**DITSCAP**   See *Defense Information Technology Systems Certification and Accreditation Process.*

**DoD**   U.S. Department of Defense.

**DoD Trusted Computer System Evaluation Criteria (TCSEC)**   A document published by the National Computer Security Center containing a uniform set of basic requirements and evaluation classes for assessing degrees of assurance in the effectiveness of hardware and software security controls built into systems. These criteria are intended for use in the design and evaluation of systems that process and/or store sensitive or classified data. This document is Government Standard DoD 5200.28-STD and is frequently referred to as "The Criteria" or "The Orange Book."

**DoJ**   U.S. Department of Justice.

**domain**   The unique context (for example, access control parameters) in which a program is operating; in effect, the set of objects that a subject has the ability to access. See *process* and *subject.*

**dominate**   Security level S1 is said to *dominate* security level S2 if the hierarchical classification of S1 is greater than or equal to that of S2 and if the nonhierarchical categories of S1 include all those of S2 as a subset.

**DoS attack**   Denial of Service attack.

**DPL**   Degausser Products List.

**DT**   Data terminal.

**DTLS**   Descriptive Top-Level Specification.

**due care**   That care that an ordinary prudent person would have exercised under the same or similar circumstances. The terms *due care* and *reasonable care* are used interchangeably.

**Dynamic Host Configuration Protocol (DHCP)**   A protocol that issues IP addresses automatically within a specified range to devices such as PCs when they are first powered on. The device retains the use of the IP address for a specific license period that the system administrator can define.

**E**

**EAP**   Extensible Authentication Protocol. Cisco proprietary protocol for enhanced user authentication and wireless security management.

**EBCDIC**   Extended Binary-Coded Decimal Interchange Code. An 8-bit character representation developed by IBM in the early 1960s.

**ECC**   Elliptic curve cryptography.

**ECDSA**   Elliptic curve digital signature algorithm.

**Echelon**   A cooperative, worldwide signal intelligence system that is run by the NSA of the United States, the Government Communications Head Quarters (GCHQ) of England, the Communications Security Establishment (CSE) of Canada, the Australian Defense Security Directorate (DSD), and the General Communications Security Bureau (GCSB) of New Zealand.

**Electronic Communications Privacy Act (ECPA) of 1986**   An act that prohibited eavesdropping or the interception of message contents without distinguishing between private or public systems.

**Electronic Data Interchange (EDI)**   A service that provides communications for business transactions. ANSI standard X.12 defines the data format for EDI.

**electronic vaulting**   A term that refers to the transfer of backup data to an off-site location. This process is primarily a batch process of dumping the data through communications lines to a server at an alternate location.

**Electronics Industry Association (EIA)**   A U.S. standards organization that represents a large number of electronics firms.

**emanations**   See *compromising emanations*.

**embedded system**   A system that performs or controls a function, either in whole or in part, as an integral element of a larger system or subsystem.

**emergency plan**   Synonymous with *contingency plan*.

**emission security**   The protection resulting from all measures that are taken to deny unauthorized persons information of value that might be derived from intercept and from an analysis of compromising emanations from systems.

**encipher**   To make the message unintelligible to all but the intended recipients.

**Endorsed Tools List (ETL)**   The list of formal verification tools endorsed by the NCSC for the development of systems that have high levels of trust.

**end-to-end encryption**   Encrypted information sent from the point of origin to the final destination. In symmetric key encryption, this process requires the sender and receiver to have the identical key for the session.

**Enhanced Hierarchical Development Methodology**   An integrated set of tools designed to aid in creating, analyzing, modifying, managing, and documenting program specifications and proofs. This methodology includes a specification parser and typechecker, a theorem prover, and a multilevel security checker. Note: This methodology is not based on the Hierarchical Development Methodology.

**entrapment**   The deliberate planting of apparent flaws in a system for the purpose of detecting attempted penetrations.

**environment**   The aggregate of external procedures, conditions, and objects that affect the development, operation, and maintenance of a system.

**EPL**   Evaluated Products List.

**erasure**   A process by which a signal recorded on magnetic media is removed. Erasure is accomplished in two ways: (1) by alternating current erasure, by which the information is destroyed when an alternating high and low magnetic field is applied to the media, or (2) by direct current erasure, in which the media is saturated by applying a unidirectional magnetic field.

**Ethernet**   An industry-standard local area network media access method that uses a bus topology and CSMA/CD. IEEE 802.3 is a standard that specifies Ethernet.

**Ethernet repeater**   A component that provides Ethernet connections among multiple stations sharing a common collision domain. Also referred to as a *shared Ethernet hub*.

**Ethernet switch**   More intelligent than a hub, with the capability to connect the sending station directly to the receiving station.

**ETL**   Endorsed Tools List.

**ETSI**   European Telecommunications Standards Institute.

**Evaluated Products List (EPL)**   A list of equipment, hardware, software, and/or firmware that has been evaluated against, and found to be technically compliant with, a particular level of trust with the DoD TCSEC by the NCSC. The EPL is included in the National Security Agency Information Systems Security Products and Services Catalogue, which is available through the Government Printing Office (GPO).

**Evaluation**   Assessment of an IT product or system against defined security functional and assurance criteria performed by a combination of testing and analytic techniques.

**Evaluation Assurance Level (EAL)**   In the Common Criteria, the degree of examination of the product to be tested. EALs range from EA1 (functional testing) to EA7 (detailed testing and formal design verification). Each numbered package represents a point on the CC's predefined assurance scale. An EAL can be considered a level of confidence in the security functions of an IT product or system.

**executive state**   One of several states in which a system can operate and the only one in which certain privileged instructions can be executed. Such instructions cannot be executed when the system is operating in other (for example, user) states. Synonymous with *supervisor state*.

**exigent circumstances doctrine**   Specifies that a warrantless search and seizure of evidence can be conducted if there is probable cause to suspect criminal activity or destruction of evidence.

**expert system shell**   An off-the-shelf software package that implements an inference engine, a mechanism for entering knowledge, a user interface, and a system to provide explanations of the reasoning used to generate a solution. It provides the fundamental building blocks of an expert system and supports the entering of domain knowledge.

**exploitable channel**   Any information channel that is usable or detectable by subjects that are external to the trusted computing base whose purpose is to violate the security policy of the system. See *covert channel*.

**exposure**   An instance of being exposed to losses from a threat.

**F**

**fail over**   Operations automatically switching over to a backup system when one system/application fails.

**fail safe**   A term that refers to the automatic protection of programs and/or processing systems to maintain safety when a hardware or software failure is detected in a system.

**fail secure**   A term that refers to a system that preserves a secure state during and after identified failures occur.

**fail soft**   A term that refers to the selective termination of affected nonessential processing when a hardware or software failure is detected in a system.

**failure access**   An unauthorized and usually inadvertent access to data resulting from a hardware or software failure in the system.

**failure control**   The methodology that is used to detect and provide fail-safe or fail-soft recovery from hardware and software failures in a system.

**fault**   A condition that causes a device or system component to fail to perform in a required manner.

**fault-resilient systems**   Systems designed without redundancy; in the event of failure, they result in a slightly longer down time.

**FCC**   Federal Communications Commission.

**FDMA**   Frequency division multiple access. A spectrum-sharing technique whereby the available spectrum is divided into a number of individual radio channels.

**FDX**   Full-duplex.

**Federal Intelligence Surveillance Act (FISA) of 1978**   An act that limited wiretapping for national security purposes as a result of the Nixon Administration's history of using illegal wiretaps.

**fetch protection**   A system-provided restriction to prevent a program from accessing data in another user's segment of storage.

**Fiber-Distributed Data Interface (FDDI)**   An ANSI standard for token-passing networks. FDDI uses optical fiber and operates at 100 Mbps in dual, counter-rotating rings.

**Fiestel cipher**   An iterated block cipher that encrypts by breaking a plaintext block into two halves and, with a subkey, applying a "round" transformation to one of the halves. The output of this transformation is then XOR'd with the remaining half. The round is completed by swapping the two halves.

**FIFO**   Acronym for "first in, first out."

**file server**   A computer that provides network stations with controlled access to sharable resources. The network operating system (NOS) is loaded on the file server, and most sharable devices, including disk subsystems and printers, are attached to it.

**file protection**   The aggregate of all processes and procedures in a system designed to inhibit unauthorized access, contamination, or elimination of a file.

**file security**   The means by which access to computer files is limited to authorized users only.

**File Transfer Protocol (FTP)**   A TCP/IP protocol for file transfer.

**FIPS**   Federal Information Processing Standard.

**firewall**   A network device that shields the trusted network from unauthorized users in the untrusted network by blocking certain specific types of traffic. Many types of firewalls exist, including packet filtering and stateful inspection.

**firmware** Executable programs stored in nonvolatile memory.

**flaw hypothesis methodology** A systems analysis and penetration technique in which specifications and documentation for the system are analyzed and then hypotheses made regarding flaws in the system. The list of hypothesized flaws is prioritized on the basis of the estimated probability that a flaw exists, and—assuming that a flaw does exist—on the ease of exploiting it and on the extent of control or compromise that it would provide. The prioritized list is used to direct a penetration attack against the system.

**flow control** See *information flow control*.

**frequency modulation (FM)** A method of transmitting information over a radio wave by changing frequencies.

**formal access approval** Documented approval by a data owner to allow access to a particular category of information.

**Formal Development Methodology** A collection of languages and tools that enforces a rigorous method of verification. This methodology uses the Ina Jo specification language for successive stages of system development, including identification and modeling of requirements, high-level design, and program design.

**formal proof** A complete and convincing mathematical argument presenting the full logical justification for each proof step for the truth of a theorem or set of theorems.

**formal security policy model** A mathematically precise statement of a security policy. To be adequately precise, such a model must represent the initial state of a system, the way in which the system progresses from one state to another, and a definition of a secure state of the system. To be acceptable as a basis for a TCB, the model must be supported by a formal proof that if the initial state of the system satisfies the definition of a secure state and if all assumptions required by the model hold, then all future states of the system will be secure. Some formal modeling techniques include state transition models, denotational semantics models, and algebraic specification models. *See Bell-LaPadula model.*

**Formal Top-Level Specification (FTLS)** A top-level specification that is written in a formal mathematical language to enable theorems showing the correspondence of the system specification to its formal requirements to be hypothesized and formally proven.

**formal verification** The process of using formal proofs to demonstrate the consistency between a formal specification of a system and a formal security policy model (design verification) or between the formal specification and its high-level program implementation (implementation verification).

**forward chaining** The reasoning approach that can be used when a small number of solutions exist relative to the number of inputs. The input data is used to reason "forward" to prove that one of the possible solutions in a small solution set is correct.

**fractional T-1** A 64 Kbps increment of a T1 frame.

**frame relay** A packet-switching interface that operates at data rates of 56 Kbps to 2 Mbps. Frame relay is minus the error control overhead of X.25, and it assumes that a higher-layer protocol will check for transmission errors.

**frequency division multiple access (FDMA)** A digital radio technology that divides the available spectrum into separate radio channels. Generally used in conjunction with time division multiple access (TDMA) or code division multiple access (CDMA).

**frequency hopping multiple access (FHMA)** A system using frequency hopping spread spectrum (FHSS) to permit multiple, simultaneous conversations or data sessions by assigning different hopping patterns to each.

**frequency hopping spread spectrum (FHSS)** A method used to share the available bandwidth in 802.11b WLANs. FHSS takes the data signal and modulates it with a carrier signal that hops from frequency to frequency on a cyclical basis over a wide band of frequencies. FHSS in the 2.4 GHz frequency band will hop between 2.4 GHz and 2.483 GHz. The receiver must be set to the same hopping code.

**frequency shift keying (FSK)** A modulation scheme for data communications using a limited number of discrete frequencies to convey binary information.

**front-end security filter** A security filter that could be implemented in hardware or software that is logically separated from the remainder of the system in order to protect the system's integrity.

**FTLS** Formal Top-Level Specification.

**functional programming** A programming method that uses only mathematical functions to perform computations and solve problems.

**functional testing** The segment of security testing in which the advertised security mechanisms of the system are tested, under operational conditions, for correct operation.

## G

**gateway**    A network component that provides interconnectivity at higher network layers.

**genetic algorithms**    Part of the general class known as *evolutionary computing*, which uses the Darwinian principles of survival of the fittest, mutation, and the adaptation of successive generations of populations to their environment. The genetic algorithm implements this process through iteration of generations of a constant-size population of items or individuals.

**Gigabyte (GB, GByte)**    A unit of measure for memory or disk storage capacity; 1,073,741,824 bytes.

**Gigahertz (GHz)**    A measure of frequency; one billion hertz.

**Global System for Mobile (GSM) communications**    The wireless analog of the ISDN landline system.

**Gramm-Leach-Bliley (GLB) Act of November 1999**    An act that removes Depression-era restrictions on banks that limited certain business activities, mergers, and affiliations. It repeals the restrictions on banks affiliating with securities firms contained in sections 20 and 32 of the Glass-Steagall Act. GLB became effective on November 13, 2001. GLB also requires health plans and insurers to protect member and subscriber data in electronic and other formats. These health plans and insurers will fall under new state laws and regulations that are being passed to implement GLB because GLB explicitly assigns enforcement of the health plan and insurer regulations to state insurance authorities (15 U.S.C. §6805). Some of the privacy and security requirements of Gramm-Leach-Bliley are similar to those of HIPAA.

**granularity**    An expression of the relative size of a data object; for example, protection at the file level is considered coarse granularity, whereas protection at field level is considered to be of a finer granularity.

**guard**    A processor that provides a filter between two disparate systems operating at different security levels or between a user terminal and a database in order to filter out data that the user is not authorized to access.

**Gypsy Verification Environment**    An integrated set of tools for specifying, coding, and verifying programs written in the Gypsy language—a language similar to Pascal that has both specification and programming features. This methodology includes an editor, a specification processor, a verification condition generator, a user-directed theorem prover, and an information flow tool.

H

**handshaking procedure**   A dialogue between two entities (for example, a user and a computer, a computer and another computer, or a program and another program) for the purpose of identifying and authenticating the entities to one another.

**HDX**   Half duplex.

**Hertz (Hz)**   A unit of frequency measurement; one cycle of a periodic event per second. Used to measure frequency.

**Hierarchical Development Methodology**   A methodology for specifying and verifying the design programs written in the Special specification language. The tools for this methodology include the Special specification processor, the Boyer-Moore theorem prover, and the Feiertag information flow tool.

**high-level data link control**   An ISO protocol for link synchronization and error control.

**HIPAA**   See *Kennedy-Kassebaum Act of 1996.*

**host to front-end protocol**   A set of conventions governing the format and control of data that is passed from a host to a front-end machine.

**host**   A time-sharing computer accessed via terminals or terminal emulation; a computer to which an expansion device attaches.

**HTTP**   Hypertext Transfer Protocol.

**Hypertext Markup Language (HTML)**   A standard used on the Internet for defining hypertext links between documents.

I

**I&A**   Identification and authentication.

**IAC**   Inquiry access code; used in inquiry procedures. The IAC can be one of two types: a dedicated IAC for specific devices or a generic IAC for all devices.

**IAW**   Acronym for "in accordance with."

**ICV**   Integrity check value. In WEP encryption, the frame is run through an integrity algorithm, and the ICV generated is placed at the end of the encrypted data in the frame. Then the receiving station runs the data through its integrity algorithm and compares it to the ICV received in the frame. If it matches, the unencrypted frame is passed to the higher layers. If it does not match, the frame is discarded.

**ID**   Common abbreviation for "identifier" or "identity."

**identification**   The process that enables a system to recognize an entity, generally by the use of unique machine-readable user names.

**IDS**   Intrusion detection system.

**IETF**   Internet Engineering Task Force.

**IKE**   Internet key exchange.

**impersonating**   Synonymous with *spoofing*.

**incomplete parameter checking**   A system design flaw that results when all parameters have not been fully anticipated for accuracy and consistency, thus making the system vulnerable to penetration.

**individual accountability**   The ability to positively associate the identity of a user with the time, method, and degree of access to a system.

**industrial, scientific, and medicine (ISM) bands**   Radio frequency bands authorized by the Federal Communications Commission (FCC) for wireless LANs. The ISM bands are located at 902 MHz, 2.400 GHz, and 5.7 GHz. The transmitted power is commonly less than 600mw; therefore, no FCC license is required.

**inference engine**   A component of an artificial intelligence system that takes inputs and uses a knowledge base to infer new facts and solve a problem.

**information flow control**   A procedure undertaken to ensure that information transfers within a system are not made from a higher security level object to an object of a lower security level. See *covert channel*, *simple security property*, and *star property (* property)*. Synonymous with *data flow control* and *flow control*.

**information flow model**   Information security model in which information is categorized into classes and rules define how information can flow between the classes.

**Information System Security Officer (ISSO)**   The person who is responsible to the DAA for ensuring that security is provided for and implemented throughout the life cycle of an AIS, from the beginning of the concept development plan through its design, development, operation, maintenance, and secure disposal.

**Information Systems Security Products and Services Catalogue**   A catalogue issued quarterly by the National Security Agency that incorporates the DPL, EPL, ETL, PPL, and other security product and service lists. This catalogue is available through the U.S. Government Printing Office, Washington, D.C., 20402.

**infrared (IR) light**   Light waves that range in length from about 0.75 to 1000 microns—this is a lower frequency than the spectral colors, but a higher frequency than radio waves.

**inheritance (in object-oriented programming)**   When all the methods of one class, called a *superclass*, are inherited by a subclass. Thus, all messages understood by the superclass are understood by the subclass.

**Institute of Electrical and Electronics Engineers (IEEE)**  A U.S.–based standards organization participating in the development of standards for data transmission systems. The IEEE has made significant progress in the establishment of standards for LANs, namely the IEEE 802 series.

**Integrated Services Digital Network (ISDN)**  A collection of CCITT standards specifying WAN digital transmission services. The overall goal of ISDN is to provide a single physical network outlet and transport mechanism for the transmission of all types of information, including data, video, and voice.

**integration testing**  Testing process used to verify the interface between network components as the components are installed. The installation crew should integrate components into the network one-by-one and perform integration testing when necessary to ensure proper, gradual integration of components.

**integrity**  A term that refers to a sound, unimpaired, or perfect condition.

**interdiction**  See *Denial of Service*.

**Interface Definition Language (IDL)**  A standard interface language that is used by clients to request services from objects.

**internal security controls**  Hardware, firmware, and software features within a system that restrict access to resources (hardware, software, and data) to authorized subjects only (persons, programs, or devices).

**International Standards Organization (ISO)**  A non-treaty standards organization active in the development of international standards, such as the Open System Interconnection (OSI) network architecture.

**International Telecommunications Union (ITU)**  An intergovernmental agency of the United States responsible for making recommendations and standardization regarding telephone and data communications systems for public and private telecommunication organizations and for providing coordination for the development of international standards.

**International Telegraph and Telephone Consultative Committee (CCITT)**  An international standards organization that is part of the ITU and dedicated to establishing effective and compatible telecommunications among members of the United Nations. CCITT develops the widely used V-series and X-series standards and protocols.

**Internet Protocol (IP)**  The Internet standard protocol that defines the Internet datagram as the information unit passed across the Internet. IP provides the basis of a best-effort packet delivery service. The Internet protocol suite is often referred to as TCP/IP because IP is one of the two fundamental protocols; the other is the Transfer Control Protocol.

**Internet**   The largest network in the world. Successor to ARPANET, the Internet includes other large internetworks. The Internet uses the TCP/IP protocol suite and connects universities, government agencies, and individuals around the world.

**Internetwork Packet Exchange (IPX)**   NetWare protocol for the exchange of message packets on an internetwork. IPX passes application requests for network services to the network drives and then to other workstations, servers, or devices on the internetwork.

**IPSec**   Secure Internet Protocol.

**Isochronous transmission**   Type of synchronization whereby information frames are sent at specific times.

**isolation**   The containment of subjects and objects in a system in such a way that they are separated from one another as well as from the protection controls of the operating system.

**ISP**   Internet service provider.

**ISSO**   Information System Security Officer.

**ITA**   Industrial Telecommunications Association.

**IV**   Initialization vector; for WEP encryption.

**J**

**joint application design (JAD)**   A parallel team design process simultaneously defining requirements composed of users, sales people, marketing staff, project managers, analysts, and engineers. Members of this team are used to simultaneously define requirements.

**K**

**Kennedy-Kassebaum Health Insurance Portability and Accountability Act (HIPAA) of 1996**   A set of regulations that mandate the use of standards in health care record keeping and electronic transactions. The act requires that health care plans, providers, insurers, and clearinghouses do the following:

- Provide for restricted access by the patient to personal health care information
- Implement administrative simplification standards
- Enable the portability of health insurance
- Establish strong penalties for health care fraud

**Kerberos**   A trusted, third party authentication protocol that was developed under Project Athena at MIT. In Greek mythology, Kerberos is a three-headed dog that guards the entrance to the underworld. Using symmetric key cryptography, Kerberos authenticates clients to other entities on a network of which a client requires services.

**key clustering**   A situation in which a plaintext message generates identical ciphertext messages by using the same transformation algorithm but with different cryptovariables.

**key**   Information or sequence that controls the enciphering and deciphering of messages. Also known as a *cryptovariable*. Used with a particular algorithm to encipher or decipher the plaintext message.

**key schedule**   A set of subkeys derived from a secret key.

**Kilobyte (KB, Kbyte)**   A unit of measurement, of memory or disk storage capacity; a data unit of $2^{10}$ (1,024) bytes.

**Kilohertz (kHz)**   A unit of frequency measurement equivalent to 1,000 Hertz.

**knowledge acquisition system**   The means of identifying and acquiring the knowledge to be entered into an expert system's knowledge base.

**knowledge base**   Refers to the rules and facts of the particular problem domain in an expert system.

**L**

**least privilege**   The principle that requires each subject to be granted the most restrictive set of privileges needed for the performance of authorized tasks. The application of this principle limits the damage that can result from accident, error, or unauthorized use.

**Light-emitting diode (LED)**   Used in conjunction with optical fiber, an LED emits incoherent light when current is passed through it. Its advantages include low cost and long lifetime, and LEDs are capable of operating in the Mbps range.

**limited access**   Synonymous with *access control*.

**limited fault tolerance**   Specifies against what type of failures the Target of Evaluation (TOE) must be resistant. Examples of general failures are flooding of the computer room, short-term power interruption, breakdown of a CPU or host, software failure, or buffer overflow. Requires all functions to be available if specified failure occurs.

**Link Access Procedure**   An ITU error correction protocol derived from the HDLC standard.

**link encryption**   Each entity has keys in common with its two neighboring nodes in the chain of transmission. Thus, a node receives the encrypted message from its predecessor neighboring node, decrypts it, and re-encrypts it with another key that is common to the successor node. Then, the encrypted message is sent on to the successor node, where the process is repeated until the final destination is reached. Obviously, this mode provides no protection if the nodes along the transmission path are subject to compromise.

**list-oriented**   A computer protection system in which each protected object has a list of all subjects that are authorized to access it. Compare *ticket-oriented*.

**LLC**   Logical Link Control; the IEEE layer 2 protocol.

**local area network (LAN)**   A network that interconnects devices in the same office, floor, or building, or close buildings.

**lock-and-key protection system**   A protection system that involves matching a key or password with a specific access requirement.

**logic bomb**   A resident computer program that triggers the perpetration of an unauthorized act when particular states of the system are realized.

**Logical Link Control layer**   The highest layer of the IEEE 802 reference model; provides similar functions to those of a traditional data link control protocol.

**loophole**   An error of omission or oversight in software or hardware that permits circumventing the system security policy.

**LSB**   Least-significant bit.

**M**

**MAC**   Mandatory Access Control if used in the context of a type of access control; MAC also refers to the Media Access Control address assigned to a network interface card on an Ethernet network.

**magnetic remanence**   A measure of the magnetic flux density that remains after removal of the applied magnetic force. Refers to any data remaining on magnetic storage media after removal of the power.

**mail gateway**   A type of gateway that interconnects dissimilar e-mail systems.

**maintenance hook**   Special instructions in software to enable easy maintenance and additional feature development. These instructions are not clearly defined during access for design specification. Hooks frequently enable entry into the code at unusual points or without the usual checks, so they are a serious security risk if they are not removed prior to live implementation. Maintenance hooks are special types of trapdoors.

**malicious logic**   Hardware, software, or firmware that is intentionally included in a system for an unauthorized purpose (for example, a Trojan horse).

**MAN**   Metropolitan area network.

**management information base (MIB)**   A collection of managed objects residing in a virtual information store.

**mandatory access control (MAC)**   A means of restricting access to objects based on the sensitivity (as represented by a label) of the information contained in the objects and the formal authorization (in other words, clearance) of subjects to access information of such sensitivity. Compare *discretionary access control*.

**MAPI**   Microsoft's mail application programming interface.

**masquerading**   See *spoofing*.

**Media access control (MAC)**   An IEEE 802 standards sublayer used to control access to a network medium, such as a wireless LAN. Also deals with collision detection. Each computer has its own unique MAC address.

**Medium access**   The Data Link layer function that controls how devices access a shared medium. IEEE 802.11 uses either CSMA/CA or contention-free access modes. Also, a data link function that controls the use of a common network medium.

**Megabits per second (Mbps)**   One million bits per second.

**Megabyte (MB, Mbyte)**   A unit of measurement for memory or disk storage capacity. $2^{20}$ (usually 1,048,576) bytes; sometimes interpreted as 1 million bytes.

**Megahertz (MHz)**   A measure of frequency equivalent to one million cycles per second.

**Middleware**   An intermediate software component located on the wired network between the wireless appliance and the application or data residing on the wired network. Middleware provides appropriate interfaces between the appliance and the host application or server database.

**mimicking**   See *spoofing*.

**Mobile IP**   A protocol developed by the IETF that enables users to roam to parts of the network associated with a different IP address than the one loaded in the user's appliance. Also refers to any mobile device that contains the IEEE 802.11 MAC and physical layers.

**modes of operation**   A description of the conditions under which an AIS functions, based on the sensitivity of data processed and the clearance levels and authorizations of the users. Four modes of operation are authorized:

1. Dedicated mode—An AIS is operating in the dedicated mode when each user who has direct or indirect individual access to the AIS, its peripherals, remote terminals, or remote hosts has all of the following:

    a. A valid personnel clearance for all information on the system

    b. Formal access approval and signed nondisclosure agreements for all the information stored and/or processed (including all compartments, subcompartments, and/or special access programs)

    c. A valid need-to-know for all information contained within the system

2. System-high mode—An AIS is operating in the system-high mode when each user who has direct or indirect access to the AIS, its peripherals, remote terminals, or remote hosts has all of the following:

    a. A valid personnel clearance for all information on the AIS

    b. Formal access approval, and signed nondisclosure agreements, for all the information stored and/or processed (including all compartments, subcompartments, and/or special access programs)

    c. A valid need-to-know for some of the information contained within the AIS

3. Compartmented mode—An AIS is operating in the compartmented mode when each user who has direct or indirect access to the AIS, its peripherals, remote terminals, or remote hosts has all of the following:

    a. A valid personnel clearance for the most restricted information processed in the AIS

    b. Formal access approval and signed nondisclosure agreements for that information that he or she will be able to access

    c. A valid need-to-know for that information that he or she will be able to access

4. Multilevel mode—An AIS is operating in the multilevel mode when all of the following statements are satisfied concerning the users who have direct or indirect access to the AIS, its peripherals, remote terminals, or remote hosts:

    a. Some do not have a valid personnel clearance for all the information processed in the AIS.

    b. All have the proper clearance and the appropriate formal access approval for that information to which they are to have access.

    c. All have a valid need-to-know for that information to which they are to have access.

**Modulation**   The process of translating the baseband digital signal to a suitable analog form. Any of several techniques for combining user information with a transmitter's carrier signal.

**MSB**   Most significant bit.

**multilevel device**   A device that is used in a manner that permits it to simultaneously process data of two or more security levels without the risk of compromise. To accomplish this, sensitivity labels are normally stored on the same physical medium and in the same form (for example, machine-readable or human-readable) as the data being processed.

**multilevel secure** A class of system containing information with different sensitivities that simultaneously permits access by users with different security clearances and needs-to-know but that prevents users from obtaining access to information for which they lack authorization.

**multilevel security mode** See *modes of operation*.

**Multipath** The signal variation caused when radio signals take multiple paths from transmitter to receiver.

**Multipath fading** A type of fading caused by signals taking different paths from the transmitter to the receiver and consequently interfering with each other.

**multiple access rights terminal** A terminal that can be used by more than one class of users; for example, users who have different access rights to data.

**multiple inheritance** In object-oriented programming, a situation where a subclass inherits the behavior of multiple superclasses.

**multiplexer** A network component that combines multiple signals into one composite signal in a form suitable for transmission over a long-haul connection, such as leased 56 Kbps or T1 circuits.

**Multistation access unit (MAU)** A multiport wiring hub for token ring networks.

**multiuser mode of operation** A mode of operation designed for systems that process sensitive, unclassified information in which users might not have a need-to-know for all information processed in the system. This mode is also used for microcomputers processing sensitive unclassified information that cannot meet the requirements of the stand-alone mode of operation.

**Musical Instrument Digital Interface (MIDI)** A standard protocol for the interchange of musical information between musical instruments and computers.

**mutually suspicious** A state that exists between interacting processes (subsystems or programs) in which neither process can expect the other process to function securely with respect to some property.

**MUX** Multiplexing sublayer; a sublayer of the L2CAP layer.

**N**

**NACK or NAK** Negative acknowledgment. This can be a deliberate signal that the message was received in error or can be inferred by a time-out.

**National Computer Security Assessment Program**   A program designed to evaluate the interrelationship of empirical data of computer security infractions and critical systems profiles while comprehensively incorporating information from the CSTVRP. The assessment builds threat and vulnerability scenarios that are based on a collection of facts from relevant reported cases. Such scenarios are a powerful, dramatic, and concise form of representing the value of loss experience analysis.

**National Computer Security Center (NCSC)**   Originally named the *DoD Computer Security Center,* the NCSC is responsible for encouraging the widespread availability of trusted computer systems throughout the federal government. It is a branch of the National Security Agency (NSA) that also initiates research and develops and publishes standards and criteria for trusted information systems.

**National Information Assurance Certification and Accreditation Process (NIACAP)**   Provides a standard set of activities, general tasks, and a management structure to certify and accredit systems that will maintain the information assurance and security posture of a system or site. The NIACAP is designed to certify that the information system meets documented accreditation requirements and continues to maintain the accredited security posture throughout the system life cycle.

**National Security Decision Directive 145 (NSDD 145)**   Signed by President Ronald Reagan on September 17, 1984, this directive is entitled "National Policy on Telecommunications and Automated Information Systems Security." It provides initial objectives, policies, and an organizational structure to guide the conduct of national activities toward safeguarding systems that process, store, or communicate sensitive information; establishes a mechanism for policy development; and assigns implementation responsibilities.

**National Telecommunications and Information System Security Directives (NTISSD)**   NTISS directives establish national-level decisions relating to NTISS policies, plans, programs, systems, or organizational delegations of authority. NTISSDs are promulgated by the executive agent of the government for telecommunications and information systems security or by the chairman of the NTISSC when so delegated by the executive agent. NTISSDs are binding on all federal departments and agencies.

**National Telecommunications and Information Systems Security Advisory Memoranda/Instructions (NTISSAM, NTISSI)**   NTISS Advisory Memoranda and Instructions provide advice, assistance, or information on telecommunications and systems security that is of general interest to applicable federal departments and agencies. NTISSAMs/NTISSIs are promulgated by the National Manager for Telecommunications and Automated Information Systems Security.

**NCSC** National Computer Security Center.

**need-to-know** The necessity for access to, knowledge of, or possession of specific information that is required to carry out official duties.

**Network Basic Input/Output System (NetBIOS)** A standard interface between networks and PCs that enables applications on different computers to communicate within a LAN. NetBIOS was created by IBM for its early PC network, was adopted by Microsoft, and has since become a de facto industry standard. It is not routable across a WAN.

**network file system (NFS)** A distributed file system enabling a set of dissimilar computers to access each other's files in a transparent manner.

**network front end** A device that implements the necessary network protocols, including security-related protocols, to enable a computer system to be attached to a network.

**Network Interface Card (NIC)** A network adapter inserted into a computer that enables the computer to be connected to a network.

**Network monitoring** A form of operational support enabling network management to view the network's inner workings. Most network monitoring equipment is nonobtrusive and can be used to determine the network's utilization and to locate faults.

**Network re-engineering** A structured process that can help an organization proactively control the evolution of its network. Network re-engineering consists of continually identifying factors influencing network changes, analyzing network modification feasibility, and performing network modifications as necessary.

**network service access point (NSAP)** A point in the network where OSI network services are available to a transport entity.

**NIST** National Institute of Standards and Technology.

**node** Any network-addressable device on the network, such as a router or Network Interface Card. Any network station.

**noninterference model** The information security model that addresses a situation wherein one group is not affected by another group using specific commands.

**NSA** National Security Agency.

**NSDD 145** See *National Security Decision Directive 145*.

**NTISSC** National Telecommunications and Information Systems Security.

**Number Field Sieve (NFS)** A general-purpose factoring algorithm that can be used to factor large numbers.

## O

**object**   A passive entity that contains or receives information. Access to an object potentially implies access to the information that it contains. Examples of objects include records, blocks, pages, segments, files, directories, directory trees, and programs, as well as bits, bytes, words, fields, processors, video displays, keyboards, clocks, printers, and network nodes.

**Object Request Broker (ORB)**   The fundamental building block of the Object Request Architecture (ORA), which manages the communications between the ORA entities. The purpose of the ORB is to support the interaction of objects in heterogeneous, distributed environments. The objects may be on different types of computing platforms.

**object reuse**   The reassignment and reuse of a storage medium (for example, page frame, disk sector, and magnetic tape) that once contained one or more objects. To be securely reused and assigned to a new subject, storage media must contain no residual data (data remanence) from the object(s) that were previously contained in the media.

**object services**   Services that support the ORB in creating and tracking objects as well as performing access control functions.

**OFDM**   Orthogonal frequency division multiplexing; a set of frequency-hopping codes that never use the same frequency at the same time. Used in IEEE 802.11a for high-speed data transfer.

**One-time pad**   Encipherment operation performed using each component ki of the key, K, only once to encipher a single character of the plaintext. Therefore, the key has the same length as the message. The popular interpretation of one-time pad is that the key is used only once and never used again. Ideally, the components of the key are truly random and have no periodicity or predictability, making the ciphertext unbreakable.

**Open Database Connectivity (ODBC)**   A standard database interface enabling interoperability between application software and multivendor ODBC-compliant databases.

**Open Data-Link Interface (ODI)**   Novell's specification for Network Interface Card device drivers, allowing simultaneous operation of multiple protocol stacks.

**open security environment**   An environment that includes those systems in which at least one of the following conditions holds true: (1) Application developers (including maintainers) do not have sufficient clearance or authorization to provide an acceptable presumption that they have not introduced malicious logic. (2) Configuration control does not provide sufficient assurance that applications are protected against the introduction of malicious logic prior to and during the operation of system applications.

**Open Shortest Path First (OSPF)**   A TCP/IP routing protocol that bases routing decisions on the least number of hops from source to destination.

**open system authentication**   The IEEE 802.11 default authentication method, which is a very simple, two-step process: First, the station that wants to authenticate with another station sends an authentication management frame containing the sending station's identity. The receiving station then sends back a frame alerting whether it recognizes the identity of the authenticating station.

**Open System Interconnection (OSI)**   An ISO standard specifying an open system capable of enabling the communications between diverse systems. OSI has the following seven layers of distinction: Physical, Data Link, Network, Transport, Session, Presentation, and Application. These layers provide the functions that enable standardized communications between two application processes.

**operations security**   Controls over hardware and media and operators who have access; protects against asset threats, baseline, or selective mechanisms.

**Operations Security (OPSEC)**   An analytical process by which the U.S. government and its supporting contractors can deny to potential adversaries information about capabilities and intentions by identifying, controlling, and protecting evidence of the planning and execution of sensitive activities and operations.

**operator**   An individual who supports system operations from the operator's console: monitors execution of the system, controls the flow of jobs, and mounts input/output volumes (be alert for shoulder surfing).

**OPSEC**   See *Operations Security*.

**Orange Book**   Alternate name for *DoD Trusted Computer Security Evaluation Criteria*.

**original equipment manufacturer (OEM)**   A manufacturer of products for integration in other products or systems.

**OS**   Commonly used abbreviation for "operating system."

**overt channel**   A path within a computer system or network that is designed for the authorized transfer of data. Compare with *covert channel*.

**overwrite procedure**   A stimulation to change the state of a bit followed by a known pattern. See *magnetic remanence*.

**P**

**packet**   A basic message unit for communication across a network. A packet usually includes routing information, data, and (sometimes) error-detection information.

**packet-switched**   A network that routes data packets based on an address contained in the data packet. Multiple data packets can share the same network resources. A communications network that uses shared facilities to route data packets from and to different users. Unlike a circuit-switched network, a packet-switched network does not set up dedicated circuits for each session.

**PAD**   Acronym for *packet assembly/disassembly*.

**partitioned security mode**   A mode of operation wherein all personnel have the clearance but not necessarily formal access approval and need-to-know for all information contained in the system. Not to be confused with *compartmented security mode*.

**password**   A protected/private character string that is used to authenticate an identity.

**PCMCIA**   Personal Computer Memory Card International Association. The industry group that defines standards for PC cards (and the name applied to the cards themselves). These roughly credit-card-sized adapters for memory and modem cards come in three thicknesses: 3.3, 5, and 10.5 mm.

**PDN**   Public data network.

**PED**   Personal electronic device.

**Peer-to-peer network**   A network in which a group of devices can communicate between a group of equal devices. A peer-to-peer LAN does not depend on a dedicated server, but it allows any node to be installed as a nondedicated server and share its files and peripherals across the network.

**pen register**   A device that records all the numbers dialed from a specific telephone line.

**penetration**   The successful act of bypassing a system's security mechanisms.

**penetration signature**   The characteristics or identifying marks that might be produced by a penetration.

**penetration study**   A study to determine the feasibility and methods for defeating the controls of a system.

**penetration testing**   The portion of security testing in which the evaluators attempt to circumvent the security features of a system. The evaluators might be assumed to use all system design and implementation documentation, which can include listings of system source code, manuals, and circuit diagrams. The evaluators work under the same constraints that are applied to ordinary users.

**performance modeling**   The use of simulation software to predict network behavior, allowing developers to perform capacity planning. Simulation makes it possible to model the network and impose varying levels of utilization to observe the effects.

**performance monitoring**   Activity that tracks network performance during normal operations. Performance monitoring includes real-time monitoring, during which metrics are collected and compared against thresholds; recent-past monitoring, in which metrics are collected and analyzed for trends that may lead to performance problems; and historical data analysis, in which metrics are collected and stored for later analysis.

**periods processing**   The processing of various levels of sensitive information at distinctly different times. Under periods processing, the system must be purged of all information from one processing period before transitioning to the next, when there are different users who have differing authorizations.

**permissions**   A description of the type of authorized interactions that a subject can have with an object. Examples of permissions types include read, write, execute, add, modify, and delete.

**permutation**   A method of encrypting a message also known as transposition; operates by rearranging the letters of the plaintext.

**personnel security**   The procedures that are established to ensure that all personnel who have access to sensitive information possess the required authority as well as appropriate clearances. Procedures to ensure a person's background; provides assurance of necessary trustworthiness.

**PGP**   Pretty Good Privacy; a form of encryption.

**Physical layer (PHY)**   The layer of the OSI model that provides the transmission of bits through a communication channel by defining electrical, mechanical, and procedural specifications and establishes protocols for voltage and data transmission timing and rules for "handshaking."

**physical security**   The application of physical barriers and control procedures as preventive measures or countermeasures against threats to resources and sensitive information.

**piconet**   A collection of devices connected via Bluetooth technology in an ad hoc fashion. A piconet starts with two connected devices, such as a portable PC and cellular phone, and can grow to eight connected devices.

**piggyback**   Gaining unauthorized access to a system via another user's legitimate connection. See *between-the-lines entry*.

**pipelining**   In computer architecture, a design in which the decode and execution cycles of one instruction are overlapped in time with the fetch cycle of the next instruction.

**PKI**   Public key infrastructure.

**plain old telephone system (POTS)**   The original common analog telephone system, which is still in widespread use today.

**plaintext**   Message text in cleartext, human-readable form.

**Platform for Privacy Preferences (P3P)**   Proposed standards developed by the World Wide Web Consortium (W3C) to implement privacy practices on Web sites.

**Point-to-Point Protocol (PPP)**   A protocol that provides router-to-router and host-to-network connections over both synchronous and asynchronous circuits. PPP is the successor to SLIP.

**portability**   Defines network connectivity that can be easily established, used, and then dismantled.

**PPL**   Preferred Products List.

**PRBS**   Pseudorandom bit sequence.

**Preferred Products List (PPL)**   A list of commercially produced equipment that meets TEMPEST and other requirements prescribed by the National Security Agency. This list is included in the NSA Information Systems Security Products and Services Catalogue, issued quarterly and available through the Government Printing Office.

**Presentation layer**   The layer of the OSI model that negotiates data transfer syntax for the Application layer and performs translations between different data types, if necessary.

**print suppression**   Eliminating the displaying of characters in order to preserve their secrecy; for example, not displaying a password as it is keyed at the input terminal.

**private key encryption**   See *symmetric key encryption*.

**privileged instructions**   A set of instructions (for example, interrupt handling or special computer instructions) to control features (such as storage protection features) that are generally executable only when the automated system is operating in the executive state.

**PRNG**   Pseudo-random number generator.

**procedural language**   Implies sequential execution of instructions based on the von Neumann architecture of a CPU, memory, and input/output device. Variables are part of the sets of instructions used to solve a particular problem, and therefore, the data is not separate from the statements.

**procedural security**   Synonymous with *administrative security.*

**process**   A program in execution. See *domain* and *subject.*

**Protected Health Information (PHI)**   Individually identifiable health information that is as follows:

- Transmitted by electronic media

- Maintained in any medium described in the definition of electronic media (under HIPAA)

- Transmitted or maintained in any other form or medium

**protection philosophy**   An informal description of the overall design of a system that delineates each of the protection mechanisms employed. A combination, appropriate to the evaluation class, of formal and informal techniques is used to show that the mechanisms are adequate to enforce the security policy.

**Protection Profile (PP)**   In the Common Criteria, an implementation-independent specification of the security requirements and protections of a product that could be built.

**protection ring**   One of a hierarchy of privileged modes of a system that gives certain access rights to user programs and processes authorized to operate in a given mode.

**protection-critical portions of the TCB**   Those portions of the TCB whose normal function is to deal with access control between subjects and objects. Their correct operation is essential to the protection of the data on the system.

**protocols**   A set of rules and formats, semantic and syntactic, that permits entities to exchange information.

**prototyping**   A method of determining or verifying requirements and design specifications. The prototype normally consists of network hardware and software that support a proposed solution. The approach to prototyping is typically a trial-and-error experimental process.

**pseudo-flaw**   An apparent loophole deliberately implanted in an operating system program as a trap for intruders.

**PSTN**   Public-switched telephone network; the general phone network.

**public key cryptography**   See *asymmetric key encryption.*

**Public Key Cryptography Standards (PKCS)**   A set of public key cryptography standards that support algorithms such as Diffie-Hellman and RSA, as well as algorithm-independent standards.

**Public Law 100-235 (P.L. 100-235)**  Also known as the *Computer Security Act of 1987*, this law creates a means for establishing minimum acceptable security practices for improving the security and privacy of sensitive information in federal computer systems. This law assigns to the National Institute of Standards and Technology responsibility for developing standards and guidelines for federal computer systems processing unclassified data. The law also requires establishment of security plans by all operators of federal computer systems that contain sensitive information.

**pump**  In a multilevel security system, or MLS, a one-way information flow device or data diode. In an analog to a pump operation, it permits information flow in one direction only, from a lower level of security classification or sensitivity to a higher level. The pump is a convenient approach to multilevel security in that it can be used to put together systems with different security levels.

**purge**  The removal of sensitive data from an AIS, AIS storage device, or peripheral device with storage capacity at the end of a processing period. This action is performed in such a way that there is assurance proportional to the sensitivity of the data that the data cannot be reconstructed. An AIS must be disconnected from any external network before a purge. After a purge, the medium can be declassified by observing the review procedures of the respective agency.

**R**

**RADIUS**  Remote Authentication Dial-In User Service.

**RC4**  RSA cipher algorithm 4.

**read**  A fundamental operation that results only in the flow of information from an object to a subject.

**read access**  Permission to read information.

**recovery planning**  The advance planning and preparations that are necessary to minimize loss and to ensure the availability of the critical information systems of an organization.

**recovery procedures**  The actions that are necessary to restore a system's computational capability and data files after a system failure or outage/ disruption.

**Red Book**  A document of the United States *National Security Agency* (NSA) defining criteria for secure networks.

**Reduced Instruction Set Computer (RISC)**  A computer architecture designed to reduce the number of cycles required to execute an instruction. A RISC architecture uses simpler instructions, but it makes use of other features, such as optimizing compilers, to reduce the number of instructions required, large numbers of general-purpose registers in the processor, and data caches.

**reference monitor concept**   An access-control concept that refers to an abstract machine that mediates all accesses to objects by subjects.

**reference validation mechanism**   An implementation of the reference monitor concept. A security kernel is a type of reference-validation mechanism.

**reliability**   The probability of a given system performing its mission adequately for a specified period of time under expected operating conditions.

**remote bridge**   A bridge connecting networks separated by longer distances. Organizations use leased 56 Kbps circuits, T1 digital circuits, and radio waves to provide long-distance connections between remote bridges.

**remote journaling**   Refers to the parallel processing of transactions to an alternate site, as opposed to a batch dump process such as electronic vaulting. A communications line is used to transmit live data as it occurs, which enables the alternate site to be fully operational at all times and introduces a very high level of fault tolerance.

**repeater**   A network component that provides internetworking functionality at the Physical layer of a network's architecture. A repeater amplifies network signals, extending the distance they can travel.

**residual risk**   The portion of risk that remains after security measures have been applied.

**residue**   Data left in storage after processing operations are complete but before degaussing or rewriting has taken place.

**resource encapsulation**   The process of ensuring that a resource not be directly accessible by a subject but that it be protected so that the reference monitor can properly mediate access to it.

**restricted area**   Any area to which access is subject to special restrictions or controls for reasons of security or safeguarding of property or material.

**RFC**   Acronym for request for comment.

**RFP**   Acronym for request for proposal.

**ring topology**   A topology in which a set of nodes is joined in a closed loop.

**risk**   The probability that a particular threat will exploit a particular vulnerability of the system.

**risk analysis**   The process of identifying security risks, determining their magnitude, and identifying areas needing safeguards. Risk analysis is a part of risk management. Synonymous with *risk assessment*.

**risk assessment**   See *risk analysis*.

**risk index**   The disparity between the minimum clearance or authorization of system users and the maximum sensitivity (for example, classification and categories) of data processed by a system. See CSC-STD-003-85 and CSC-STD-004-85 for a complete explanation of this term.

**risk management**   The total process of identifying, controlling, and eliminating or minimizing uncertain events that might affect system resources. It includes risk analysis, a cost/benefit analysis, selection, implementation and tests, a security evaluation of safeguards, and an overall security review.

**ROM**   Read-only memory.

**router**   A network component that provides internetworking at the Network layer of a network's architecture by allowing individual networks to become part of a WAN. A router works by using logical and physical addresses to connect two or more separate networks. It determines the best path by which to send a packet of information.

**Routing Information Protocol (RIP)**   A common type of routing protocol. RIP bases its routing path on the distance (number of hops) to the destination. RIP maintains optimum routing paths by sending out routing update messages if the network topology changes.

**RS-232**   A serial communications interface. Serial communication standards are defined by the Electronic Industries Association (EIA). The ARS-232n EIA standard specifies up to 20 Kbps, 50 foot, serial transmission between computers and peripheral devices.

**RS-422**   An EIA standard specifying electrical characteristics for balanced circuits (in other words, both transmit and return wires are at the same voltage above ground). RS-422 is used in conjunction with RS-449.

**RS-423**   An EIA standard specifying electrical characteristics for unbalanced circuits (in other words, the return wire is tied to the ground). RS-423 is used in conjunction with RS-449.

**RS-449**   An EIA standard specifying a 37-pin connector for high-speed transmission.

**RS-485**   An EIA standard for multipoint communications lines.

**S**

**S/MIME**   A protocol that adds digital signatures and encryption to Internet MIME (Multipurpose Internet Mail Extensions).

**safeguards**   See security safeguards.

**SAISS**   Subcommittee on Automated Information Systems Security of NTISSC.

**sandbox**   An access-control-based protection mechanism. It is commonly applied to restrict the access rights of mobile code that is downloaded from a Web site as an applet. The code is set up to run in a "sandbox" that blocks its access to the local workstation's hard disk, thus preventing the code from malicious activity. The sandbox is usually interpreted by a virtual machine such as the Java Virtual Machine (JVM).

**SBU**   Abbreviation for *sensitive but unclassified*; an information designation.

**scalar processor**   A processor that executes one instruction at a time.

**scavenging**   Searching through object residue to acquire unauthorized data.

**SDLC**   Synchronous data link control.

**secure configuration management**   The set of procedures that are appropriate for controlling changes to a system's hardware and software structure for the purpose of ensuring that changes will not lead to violations of the system's security policy.

**secure state**   A condition in which no subject can access any object in an unauthorized manner.

**secure subsystem**   A subsystem that contains its own implementation of the reference monitor concept for those resources it controls. The secure subsystem, however, must depend on other controls and the base operating system for the control of subjects and the more primitive system objects.

**security critical mechanisms**   Those security mechanisms whose correct operation is necessary to ensure that the security policy is enforced.

**security evaluation**   An evaluation that is performed to assess the degree of trust that can be placed in systems for the secure handling of sensitive information. One type, a product evaluation, is an evaluation performed on the hardware and software features and assurances of a computer product from a perspective that excludes the application environment. The other type, a system evaluation, is made for the purpose of assessing a system's security safeguards with respect to a specific operational mission; it is a major step in the certification and accreditation process.

**security fault analysis**   A security analysis, usually performed on hardware at the gate level, to determine the security properties of a device when a hardware fault is encountered.

**security features**   The security-relevant functions, mechanisms, and characteristics of system hardware and software. Security features are a subset of system security safeguards.

**security filter**   A trusted subsystem that enforces a security policy on the data that passes through it.

**security flaw**   An error of commission or omission in a system that might enable protection mechanisms to be bypassed.

**security flow analysis**   A security analysis performed on a formal system specification that locates the potential flows of information within the system.

**security functional requirements**   Requirements, preferably from the Common Criteria, Part 2, that when taken together specify the security behavior of an IT product or system.

**security kernel**   The hardware, firmware, and software elements of a Trusted Computer Base (TCB) that implement the reference monitor concept. The security kernel must mediate all accesses, be protected from modification, and be verifiable as correct.

**security label**   A piece of information that represents the security level of an object.

**security level**   The combination of a hierarchical classification and a set of nonhierarchical categories that represents the sensitivity of information.

**security measures**   Elements of software, firmware, hardware, or procedures that are included in a system for the satisfaction of security specifications.

**security objective**   A statement of intent to counter specified threats and/or satisfy specified organizational security policies and assumptions.

**security perimeter**   The boundary where security controls are in effect to protect assets.

**security policy**   The set of laws, rules, and practices that regulates how an organization manages, protects, and distributes sensitive information.

**security policy model**   A formal presentation of the security policy enforced by the system. It must identify the set of rules and practices that regulate how a system manages, protects, and distributes sensitive information. See *Bell-LaPadula model* and *formal security policy model*.

**security range**   The highest and lowest security levels that are permitted in or on a system, system component, subsystem, or network.

**security requirements**   The types and levels of protection that are necessary for equipment, data, information, applications, and facilities to meet security policy.

**security requirements baseline**   A description of minimum requirements necessary for a system to maintain an acceptable level of security.

**security safeguards**   The protective measures and controls that are prescribed to meet the security requirements specified for a system. Those safeguards can include (but are not necessarily limited to) the following:

hardware and software security features, operating procedures, accountability procedures, access and distribution controls, management constraints, personnel security, and physical structures, areas, and devices. Also called *safeguards*.

**security specifications** A detailed description of the safeguards required to protect a system.

**Security Target (ST)** In the Common Criteria, a listing of the security claims for a particular IT security product. A set of security functional and assurance requirements and specifications to be used as the basis for evaluating an identified product or system.

**security test and evaluation** An examination and analysis of the security safeguards of a system as they have been applied in an operational environment to determine the security posture of the system.

**security testing** A process that is used to determine that the security features of a system are implemented as designed. This process includes hands-on functional testing, penetration testing, and verification.

**sensitive information** Information that, if lost, misused, modified, or accessed by unauthorized individuals, could affect the national interest or the conduct of federal programs or the privacy to which individuals are entitled under Section 552a of Title 5, U.S. Code, but that has not been specifically authorized under criteria established by an executive order or an act of Congress to be kept classified in the interest of national defense or foreign policy.

**sensitivity label** A piece of information that represents the security level of an object. Sensitivity labels are used by the TCB as the basis for mandatory access control decisions.

**serial interface** An interface to provide serial communications service.

**Serial Line Internet Protocol (SLIP)** An Internet protocol used to run IP over serial lines and dial-up connections.

**Session layer** One of the seven OSI model layers. Establishes, manages, and terminates sessions between applications.

**shared key authentication** A type of authentication that assumes each station has received a secret shared key through a secure channel, independent from an 802.11 network. Stations authenticate through shared knowledge of the secret key. Use of shared key authentication requires implementation of the 802.11 Wireless Equivalent Privacy (WEP) algorithm.

**Simple Mail Transfer Protocol (SMTP)** The Internet e-mail protocol.

**Simple Network Management Protocol (SNMP)** The network management protocol of choice for TCP/IP-based Internets. Widely implemented with 10BASE-T Ethernet. A network management protocol that defines information transfer between management information bases (MIBs).

**simple security condition**   See *simple security property*.

**simple security property**   A Bell-LaPadula security model rule giving a subject read access to an object only if the security level of the subject dominates the security level of the object. Synonymous with *simple security condition*.

**single-user mode**   OS loaded without security front end.

**single-level device**   An automated information systems device that is used to process data of a single security level at any one time.

**SMS**   Short (or small) message service.

**SNR**   Signal-to-noise ratio.

**software development methodologies**   Methodologies for specifying and verifying design programs for system development. Each methodology is written for a specific computer language. See *Enhanced Hierarchical Development Methodology*, *Formal Development Methodology*, *Gypsy Verification Environment*, and *Hierarchical Development Methodology*.

**software engineering**   The science and art of specifying, designing, implementing, and evolving programs, documentation, and operating procedures whereby computers can be made useful to man.

**software process**   A set of activities, methods, and practices that are used to develop and maintain software and associated products.

**software process capability**   Describes the range of expected results that can be achieved by following a software process.

**software process maturity**   The extent to which a software process is defined, managed, measured, controlled, and effective.

**software process performance**   The result achieved by following a software process.

**software security**   General-purpose (executive, utility, or software development tools) and applications programs or routines that protect the data handled by a system.

**software system test and evaluation process**   A process that plans, develops, and documents the quantitative demonstration of the fulfillment of all baseline functional performance and operational and interface requirements.

**spoofing**   An attempt to gain access to a system by posing as an authorized user. Synonymous with *impersonating, masquerading*, or *mimicking*.

**SSL**   Secure Sockets Layer.

**SSO**   System Security Officer.

**Subcommittee on Automated Information Systems Security**   The SAISS is composed of one voting member from each organization that is represented on the NTISSC.

**ST connector**   An optical fiber connector that uses a bayonet plug and socket.

**standalone (shared system)**   A system that is physically and electrically isolated from all other systems and is intended to be used by more than one person, either simultaneously (for example, a system that has multiple terminals) or serially, with data belonging to one user remaining available to the system while another user uses the system (for example, a personal computer that has nonremovable storage media, such as a hard disk).

**standalone (single-user system)**   A system that is physically and electrically isolated from all other systems and is intended to be used by one person at a time, with no data belonging to other users remaining in the system (for example, a personal computer that has removable storage media, such as a floppy disk).

**star property**   See * *property*.

**Star topology**   A topology wherein each node is connected to a common central switch or hub.

**State Delta Verification System**   A system that is designed to give high confidence regarding microcode performance by using formulae that represent isolated states of a computation to check proofs concerning the course of that computation.

**state variable**   A variable that represents either the state of the system or the state of some system resource.

**storage object**   An object that supports both read and write access.

**Structured Query Language (SQL)**   An international standard for defining and accessing relational databases.

**STS**   Subcommittee on Telecommunications Security of NTISSC.

**Subcommittee on Telecommunications Security (STS)**   NSDD-145 authorizes and directs the establishment, under the NTISSC, of a permanent subcommittee on Telecommunications Security. The STS is composed of one voting member from each organization that is represented on the NTISSC.

**subject**   An active entity, generally in the form of a person, process, or device, that causes information to flow among objects or that changes the system state. Technically, a process/domain pair.

**subject security level**   A subject's security level is equal to the security level of the objects to which it has both read and write access. A subject's security level must always be dominated by the clearance of the user with which the subject is associated.

**superscalar processor**   A processor that allows concurrent execution of instructions in the same pipelined stage. The term *superscalar* denotes multiple, concurrent operations performed on scalar values, as opposed to vectors or arrays that are used as objects of computation in array processors.

**supervisor state**   See *executive state.*

**Switched Multimegabit Digital Service (SMDS)**   A packet-switching connectionless data service for WANs.

**symmetric (private) key encryption**   Cryptographic system in which the sender and receiver both know a secret key that is used to encrypt and decrypt the message.

**Synchronous Optical NETwork (SONET)**   A fiber optic transmission system for high-speed digital traffic. SONET is part of the B-ISDN standard.

**Synchronous transmission**   Type of communications data synchronization whereby frames are sent within defined time periods. It uses a clock to control the timing of bits being sent. See *asynchronous transmission.*

**system**   Data processing facility.

**System Development Methodologies**   Methodologies developed through software engineering to manage the complexity of system development. Development methodologies include software engineering aids and high-level design analysis tools.

**system high security mode**   System and all peripherals *protected in accordance with* (IAW) requirements for highest security level of material in system; personnel with access have security clearance but not need-to-know. See *modes of operation.*

**system integrity**   A characteristic of a system when it performs its intended function in an unimpaired manner, free from deliberate or inadvertent unauthorized manipulation of the system.

**system low**   The lowest security level supported by a system at a particular time or in a particular environment.

**System Security Officer (SSO)**   See *Information System Security Officer.*

**system testing**   Type of testing that verifies the installation of the entire network. Testers normally complete system testing in a simulated production environment, simulating actual users in order to ensure the network meets all stated requirements.

**Systems Network Architecture (SNA)**   IBM's proprietary network architecture.

**Systems Security Steering Group**    The senior government body established by NSDD-145 to provide top-level review and policy guidance for the telecommunications security and automated information systems security activities of the United States government. This group is chaired by the assistant to the President for National Security Affairs and consists of the Secretary of State, Secretary of Treasury, Secretary of Defense, Attorney General, Director of the Office of Management and Budget, and Director of Central Intelligence.

**T**

**T1**    A standard specifying a time division multiplexing scheme for point-to-point transmission of digital signals at 1.544 Mbps.

**tampering**    An unauthorized modification that alters the proper functioning of an equipment or system in a manner that degrades the security or functionality that it provides.

**Target of Evaluation (TOE)**    In the Common Criteria, TOE refers to the product to be tested.

**TCB**    See *Trusted Computing Base.*

**TCSEC**    See *DoD Trusted Computer System Evaluation Criteria.*

**technical attack**    An attack that can be perpetrated by circumventing or nullifying hardware and software protection mechanisms, rather than by subverting system personnel or other users.

**technical vulnerability**    A hardware, firmware, communication, or software flaw that leaves a computer processing system open for potential exploitation, either externally or internally—thereby resulting in a risk to the owner, user, or manager of the system.

**TELNET**    A virtual terminal protocol used in the Internet, enabling users to log in to a remote host. A terminal emulation defined as part of the TCP/IP protocol suite.

**TEMPEST**    The study and control of spurious electronic signals emitted by electrical equipment.

**terminal identification**    The means used to uniquely identify a terminal to a system.

**test case**    An executable test with a specific set of input values and a corresponding expected result.

**threat**    Any circumstance or event that can cause harm to a system in the form of destruction, disclosure, modification of data, and/or denial of service.

**threat agent**    A method that is used to exploit a vulnerability in a system, operation, or facility.

**threat analysis**    The examination of all actions and events that might adversely affect a system or operation.

**threat monitoring**    The analysis, assessment, and review of audit trails and other data that are collected for the purpose of searching for system events that might constitute violations or attempted violations of system security.

**ticket-oriented**    A computer protection system in which each subject maintains a list of unforgeable bit patterns, called *tickets*, one for each object the subject is authorized to access. Compare with *list-oriented*.

**time-dependent password**    A password that is valid only at a certain time of day or during a specified interval of time.

**Time-domain reflectometer (TDR)**    Mechanism used to test the effectiveness of network cabling.

**TLA**    Top-level architecture.

**TLS**    Transport layer security.

**Token bus**    A network that uses a logical token-passing access method. Unlike in a token-passing ring, permission to transmit is usually based on the node address rather than the position in the network. A token bus network uses a common cable set with all signals broadcast across the entire LAN.

**token ring**    A local area network (LAN) standard developed by IBM that uses tokens to control access to the communication medium. A medium access method that provides multiple access to a ring-type network through the use of a token. FDDI and IEEE 802.5 are token ring standards.

**top-level specification**    A nonprocedural description of system behavior at the most abstract level; typically, a functional specification that omits all implementation details.

**topology**    A description of the network's geographical layout of nodes and links.

**tranquility**    A security model rule stating that an object's security level cannot change while the object is being processed by an AIS.

**transceiver**    A device for transmitting and receiving packets between the computer and the medium.

**Transmission Control Protocol (TCP)**    A commonly used protocol in wide use for establishing and maintaining communications between applications on different computers. TCP provides full-duplex, acknowledged, and flow-controlled service to upper-layer protocols and applications.

**Transmission Control Protocol/ Internet Protocol (TCP/IP)**    A de facto, industry-standard protocol for interconnecting disparate networks. Standard protocols that define both the reliable full-duplex transport level and the connectionless, "best effort" unit of information passed across an Internet.

**Transport layer**   OSI model layer that provides mechanisms for the establishment, maintenance, and orderly termination of virtual circuits while shielding the higher layers from the network implementation details.

**trapdoor**   A hidden software or hardware mechanism that can be triggered to permit system protection mechanisms to be circumvented. It is activated in a manner that appears innocent—for example, a special "random" key sequence at a terminal. Software developers often introduce trapdoors in their code to enable them to reenter the system and perform certain functions. Synonymous with *backdoor*.

**Trojan horse**   A computer program that has an apparently or actually useful function that contains additional (hidden) functions that surreptitiously exploit the legitimate authorizations of the invoking process to the detriment of security or integrity.

**trusted computer system**   A system that employs sufficient hardware and software assurance measures to enable its use for simultaneous processing of a range of sensitive or classified information.

**Trusted Computing Base (TCB)**   The totality of protection mechanisms in a computer system, including hardware, firmware, and software, the combination of which is responsible for enforcing a security policy. A TCB consists of one or more components that together enforce a unified security policy over a product or system. The ability of a TCB to correctly enforce a unified security policy depends solely on the mechanisms in the TCB and on the correct input of parameters by system administrative personnel (for example, a user's clearance level) related to the security policy.

**trusted distribution**   A trusted method for distributing the TCB hardware, software, and firmware components, both originals and updates, that provides methods for protecting the TCB from modification during distribution and for the detection of any changes to the TCB that might occur.

**trusted identification forwarding**   An identification method used in networks whereby the sending host can verify that an authorized user on its system is attempting a connection to another host. The sending host transmits the required user authentication information to the receiving host. The receiving host can then verify that the user is validated for access to its system. This operation might be transparent to the user.

**trusted path**   A mechanism by which a person at a terminal can communicate directly with the TCB. This mechanism can be activated only by the person or by the TCB and cannot be imitated by untrusted software.

**trusted process**   A process whose incorrect or malicious execution is capable of violating system security policy.

**trusted software**   The software portion of the TCB.

**twisted-pair wire**   Type of medium using metallic-type conductors twisted together to provide a path for current flow. The wire in this medium is twisted in pairs to minimize the electromagnetic interference between one pair and another.

**U**

**U.S Federal Computer Incident Response Center (FedCIRC)**   FedCIRC provides assistance and guidance in incident response and provides a centralized approach to incident handling across U.S. government agency boundaries.

**U.S. Patriot Act of October 26, 2001**   A law that permits the following:

- Subpoena of electronic records

- Monitoring of Internet communications

- Search and seizure of information on live systems (including routers and servers), backups, and archives

- Reporting of cash and wire transfers of $10,000 or more

   Under the Patriot Act, the government has new powers to subpoena electronic records and to monitor Internet traffic. In monitoring information, the government can require the assistance of ISPs and network operators. This monitoring can even extend into individual organizations.

**U.S. Uniform Computer Information Transactions Act (UCITA) of 1999**
A model act that is intended to apply uniform legislation to software licensing.

**UART**   Universal asynchronous receiver transmitter. A device that converts parallel data into serial data for transmission or converts serial data into parallel data for receiving data.

**untrusted process**   A process that has not been evaluated or examined for adherence to the security policy. It might include incorrect or malicious code that attempts to circumvent the security mechanisms.

**user**   A person or process that is accessing an AIS either by direct connections (for example, via terminals) or by indirect connections (in other words, prepare input data or receive output that is not reviewed for content or classification by a responsible individual).

**User datagram protocol**   UDP uses the underlying Internet protocol (IP) to transport a message. This is an unreliable, connectionless delivery scheme. It does not use acknowledgments to ensure that messages arrive, and it does not provide feedback to control the rate of information flow. UDP messages can be lost, duplicated, or arrive out of order.

**user ID**   A unique symbol or character string that is used by a system to identify a specific user.

**user profile**   Patterns of a user's activity that can be used to detect changes in normal routines.

**V**

**V.21**   An ITU standard for asynchronous 0-300 bps full-duplex modems.

**V.21FAX**   An ITU standard for facsimile operations at 300 bps.

**V.34**   An ITU standard for 28,800 bps modems.

**validation (in software engineering)**   To establish the fitness or worth of a software product for its operational mission.

**vaulting**   Running mirrored data centers in separate locations.

**verification**   The process of comparing two levels of system specification for proper correspondence (for example, a security policy model with top-level specification, top-level specification with source code, or source code with object code). This process might or might not be automated.

**very-long-instruction word (VLIW) processor**   A processor in which multiple, concurrent operations are performed in a single instruction. The number of instructions is reduced relative to those in a scalar processor. For this approach to be feasible, however, the operations in each VLIW instruction must be independent of each other.

**VIM**   Lotus's vendor-independent messaging system.

**virus**   A self-propagating Trojan horse composed of a mission component, a trigger component, and a self-propagating component.

**vulnerability**   A weakness in system security procedures, system design, implementation, internal controls, and so on that could be exploited to violate system security policy.

**vulnerability analysis**   The systematic examination of systems in order to determine the adequacy of security measures, identify security deficiencies, and provide data from which to predict the effectiveness of proposed security measures.

**vulnerability assessment**   A measurement of vulnerability that includes the susceptibility of a particular system to a specific attack and the opportunities that are available to a threat agent to mount that attack.

## W

**WAP**   Wireless Application Protocol. A standard commonly used for the development of applications for wireless Internet devices.

**wide area network (WAN)**   A network that interconnects users over a wide area, usually encompassing different metropolitan areas.

**Wired Equivalency Privacy (WEP)**   The algorithm of the 802.11 wireless LAN standard that is used to protect transmitted information from disclosure. WEP is designed to prevent the violation of the confidentiality of data transmitted over the wireless LAN. WEP generates secret shared encryption keys that both source and destination stations use to alter frame bits to avoid disclosure to eavesdroppers.

**wireless**   Describes any computing device that can access a network without a wired connection.

**wireless metropolitan area network (wireless MAN)**   Provides communications links between buildings, avoiding the costly installation of cabling or leasing fees and the down time associated with system failures.

**WLAN**   Wireless local area network.

**Work breakdown structure (WBS)**   A diagram of the way a team will accomplish the project at hand by listing all tasks the team must perform and the products they must deliver.

**work factor**   An estimate of the effort or time needed by a potential intruder who has specified expertise and resources to overcome a protective measure.

**work function (factor)**   The difficulty in recovering the plaintext from the ciphertext, as measured by cost and/or time. The security of the system is directly proportional to the value of the work function. The work function need only be large enough to suffice for the intended application. If the message to be protected loses its value after a short period of time, the work function need only be large enough to ensure that the decryption would be highly infeasible in that period of time.

**write**   A fundamental operation that results only in the flow of information from a subject to an object.

**write access**   Permission to write to an object.

## X

**X.12**   An ITU standard for EDI.

**X.121**   An ITU standard for international address numbering.

**X.21**   An ITU standard for a circuit-switching network.

**X.25**   An ITU standard for an interface between a terminal and a packet-switching network. X.25 was the first public packet-switching technology, developed by the CCITT and offered as a service during the 1970s and still available today. X.25 offers connection-oriented (virtual circuit) service; it operates at 64 Kbps, which is too slow for some high-speed applications.

**X.400**   An ITU standard for OSI messaging.

**X.500**   An ITU standard for OSI directory services.

**X.75**   An ITU standard for packet switching between public networks.

# CISM Area Tasks and Knowledge Statements

This appendix highlights the tasks and statements of knowledge for each area that a CISM should know to prepare for the CISM examination and professional practice.

## Information Security Governance

Establish and maintain a framework to provide assurance that information security strategies are aligned with business objectives and consistent with applicable laws and regulations.

### Tasks

- Develop the information security strategy in support of business strategy and direction.
- Obtain senior management commitment and support for information security throughout the enterprise.
- Ensure that definitions of roles and responsibilities throughout the enterprise include information security governance activities.
- Establish reporting and communication channels that support information security governance activities.

- Identify current and potential legal and regulatory issues affecting information security and access their impact on the enterprise.
- Establish and maintain information security policies that support business goals and objectives.
- Ensure the development of procedures and guidelines that support information security policies.
- Develop business case and enterprise value analyses that support information security program investments.

## Knowledge Statements

- Knowledge of information security concepts
- Knowledge of the relationship between information security and business operations
- Knowledge of techniques used to secure senior management commitment and support of information security management
- Knowledge of methods of integrating information security governance into the overall enterprise governance framework
- Knowledge of practices associated with an overall policy directive that captures senior-management-level direction and expectations for information security in laying the foundation for information security management within an organization
- Knowledge of an information security steering group function
- Knowledge of information security management roles, responsibilities, and organizational structure
- Knowledge of areas of governance (for example, risk management, data classification management, network security, and system access)
- Knowledge of centralized and decentralized approaches to coordinating information security
- Knowledge of legal and regulatory issues associated with Internet businesses, global transmissions, and transborder data flows (for example, privacy, tax laws and tariffs, data import/export restrictions, restrictions on cryptography, warranties, patents, copyrights, trade secrets, national security)
- Knowledge of common insurance policies and imposed conditions (for example, crime or fidelity insurance, business interruptions)
- Knowledge of the requirements for the content and retention of business records and compliance

- Knowledge of the process for linking policies to enterprise business objectives

- Knowledge of the function and content of essential elements of an information security program (for example, policy statements, procedures and guidelines)

- Knowledge of techniques for developing an information security process improvement model for sustainable and repeatable information security policies and procedures

- Knowledge of information security process improvement and its relationship to traditional process management

- Knowledge of information security process improvement and its relationship to security architecture development and modeling

- Knowledge of information security process improvement and its relationship to security infrastructure

- Knowledge of generally accepted international standards for information security management and related process improvement models

- Knowledge of the key components of cost benefit analysis and enterprise transformation/migration plans (for example, architectural alignment, organizational positioning, change management, benchmarking, market/competitive analysis)

- Knowledge of methodology for business case development and computing enterprise value proposition

# Risk Management

Identify and manage information security risks to achieve business objectives.

## Tasks

- Develop a systematic, analytical, and continuous risk management process.

- Ensure that risk identification, analysis, and mitigation activities are integrated into life cycle processes.

- Apply risk identification and analysis methods.

- Define strategies and prioritize options to mitigate risk to levels acceptable to the enterprise.

- Report significant changes in risk to appropriate levels of management on both a periodic and an event-driven basis.

## Knowledge Statements

- Knowledge of information resources used in support of business processes
- Knowledge of information resource valuation methodologies
- Knowledge of information classification
- Knowledge of the principles of development of baselines and their relationship to risk-based assessments of control requirements
- Knowledge of life cycle-based risk management principles and practices
- Knowledge of threats, vulnerabilities, and exposures associated with confidentiality, integrity, and availability of information resources
- Knowledge of quantitative and qualitative methods used to determine sensitivity and criticality of information resources and the impact of adverse events
- Knowledge of use of gap analysis to assess generally accepted standards of good practice for information security management against current state
- Knowledge of recovery time objectives (RTO) for information resources and how to determine RTO
- Knowledge of RTO and how it relates to business continuity and contingency planning objectives and processes
- Knowledge of risk mitigation strategies used in defining security requirements for information resources supporting business applications
- Knowledge of cost/benefit analysis techniques in assessing options for mitigating risks, threats, and exposures to acceptable levels
- Knowledge of managing and reporting status of identified risks

# Information Security Program Management

Design, develop, and manage an information security program to implement the information security governance framework.

## Tasks

- Create and maintain plans to implement the information security governance framework.
- Develop information security baseline(s).

- Develop procedures and guidelines to ensure business processes address information security risk.

- Develop procedures and guidelines for IT infrastructure activities to ensure compliance with information security policies.

- Integrate information security program requirements into the organization's life cycle activities.

- Develop methods of meeting information security policy requirements that recognize their impact on end users.

- Promote accountability by business process owners and other stakeholders in managing information security risks.

- Establish metrics to manage the information security governance framework.

- Ensure that internal and external resources for information security are identified, appropriated, and managed.

## Knowledge Statements

- Knowledge of methods to develop an implementation plan that meets security requirements identified in risk analyses

- Knowledge of project management methods and techniques

- Knowledge of the components of an information security governance framework for integrating security principles, practices, management, and awareness into all aspects and all levels of the enterprise

- Knowledge of security baselines and configuration management in the design and management of business applications and the infrastructure

- Knowledge of information security architectures (for example, single sign-on, rules-based as opposed to list-based system access control for systems, limited points of systems administration)

- Knowledge of information security technologies (for example, cryptographic techniques and digital signatures, to enable management to select appropriate controls)

- Knowledge of security procedures and guidelines for business processes and infrastructure activities

- Knowledge of the systems development life cycle methodologies (for example, traditional SDLC, prototyping)

- Knowledge of planning, conducting, reporting, and follow-up of security testing

- Knowledge of certifying and accrediting the compliance of business applications and infrastructure to the enterprise's information security governance framework

- Knowledge of the relative benefits and costs of physical, administrative, and technical controls

- Knowledge of planning, designing, developing, testing, and implementing information security requirements into an enterprise's business processes

- Knowledge of security metrics design, development, and implementation

- Knowledge of acquisition management methods and techniques (for example, evaluation of vendor service level agreements, preparation of contracts)

# Information Security Management

Oversee and direct information security activities to execute the information security program.

## Tasks

- Ensure that the rules of use for information systems comply with the enterprise's information security policies.

- Ensure that the administrative procedures for information systems comply with the enterprise's information security policies.

- Ensure that services provided by other enterprises including outsourced providers are consistent with established information security policies.

- Use metrics to measure, monitor, and report on the effectiveness and efficiency of information security controls and compliance with information security policies.

- Ensure that information security is not compromised throughout the change management process.

- Ensure that vulnerability assessments are performed to evaluate the effectiveness of existing controls.

- Ensure that noncompliance issues and other variances are resolved in a timely manner.

- Ensure the development and delivery of the activities that can influence culture and behavior of staff including information security education and awareness.

## Knowledge Statements

- Knowledge of how to interpret information security policies into operational use

- Knowledge of information security administration process and procedures

- Knowledge of methods for managing the implementation of the enterprise's information security program through third parties including trading partners and security services providers

- Knowledge of continuous monitoring of security activities in the enterprise's infrastructure and business applications

- Knowledge of the methods used to manage success/failure in information security investments through data collection and periodic review of key performance indicators

- Knowledge of change and configuration management activities

- Knowledge of information security management due diligence activities and reviews of the infrastructure

- Knowledge of liaison activities with internal/external assurance providers performing information security reviews

- Knowledge of due diligence activities, reviews, and related standards for managing and controlling access to information resources

- Knowledge of external vulnerability reporting sources, which provide information that may require changes to the information security in applications and infrastructure

- Knowledge of events affecting security baselines that may require risk reassessments and changes to information security requirements in security plans, test plans and reperformance

- Knowledge of information security problem management practices

- Knowledge of information security manager facilitative roles as change agents, educators, and consultants

- Knowledge of the ways in which culture and cultural differences affect the behavior of staff

- Knowledge of the activities that can change culture and behavior of staff

- Knowledge of methods and techniques for security awareness training and education

# Response Management

Develop and manage a capability to respond to and recover from disruptive and destructive information security events.

## Tasks

- Develop and implement processes for detecting, identifying, and analyzing security-related events.
- Develop response and recovery plans including organizing, training, and equipping the teams.
- Ensure periodic testing of the response and recovery plans where appropriate.
- Ensure the execution of response and recovery plans as required.
- Establish procedures for documenting an event as a basis for subsequent action including forensics when necessary.
- Manage post-event reviews to identify causes and corrective actions.

## Knowledge Statements

- Knowledge of the components of an incident response capability
- Knowledge of information security emergency management practices (for example, production change control activities and development of computer emergency response team)
- Knowledge of disaster recovery planning and business recovery processes
- Knowledge of disaster recovery testing for infrastructure and critical business applications
- Knowledge of escalation process for effective security management
- Knowledge of intrusion detection policies and processes
- Knowledge of help desk processes for identifying security incidents reported by users and distinguishing them from other issues dealt with by the help desks
- Knowledge of the notification process in managing security incidents and recovery (for example, automated notice and recovery mechanisms in response to virus alerts in a real-time fashion)
- Knowledge of the requirements for collecting and presenting evidence—rules for evidence, admissibility of evidence, quality and completeness of evidence
- Knowledge of post-incident reviews and follow-up procedures

# Answers to Sample Questions

## Chapter 1: Information Security Governance

1. The difficulty of finding the prime factors of very large numbers is the strong, one-way function used in which of the following public key cryptosystems?

   a. El Gamal

   b. Diffie-Hellman

   c. RSA

   d. Elliptic curve

   *Answer*: c

   The correct answer is c. The other answers are based on the difficulty of finding discrete logarithms in a finite field.

2. Elliptic curve cryptosystems:

   a. Have a higher strength per bit than an RSA cryptosystem

   b. Have a lower strength per bit than an RSA cryptosystem

   c. Cannot be used to implement digital signatures

   d. Cannot be used to implement encryption

   *Answer*: a

The correct answer is a. It is more difficult to compute elliptic curve discrete logarithms than conventional discrete logarithms or factoring. Smaller key sizes in the elliptic curve implementation can yield higher levels of security. Therefore, answer b is incorrect. Answers c and d are incorrect because elliptic curve cryptosystems can be used for digital signatures and encryption.

3. Digital certificates, certification authority, timestamping, Lightweight Directory Access Protocol (LDAP), and non-repudiation support a portion of what services?

   a. Cryptanalysis

   b. Public Key Infrastructure

   c. Steganography

   d. Disaster recovery

   *Answer*: b

   The correct answer is b, PKI, which describes the integration of digital certificates, digital signatures, and other services necessary to support e-commerce. The other answers are distracters.

4. A *reference monitor* is a system component that enforces access controls on an object. Specifically, the *reference monitor concept* is an abstract machine that mediates all access of subjects to objects. What do you call the hardware, firmware, and software elements of a Trusted Computing Base that implement the reference monitor concept?

   a. The authorization database

   b. Identification and authentication (I & A) mechanisms

   c. The auditing subsystem

   d. The security kernel

   *Answer*: d

   The *security kernel* implements the reference monitor concept. The reference monitor must exhibit the following characteristics:

   - It must mediate all accesses.
   - It must be protected from modification.
   - It must be verifiable as correct.

   Answer a, the authorization database, is used by the reference monitor to mediate accesses by subjects to objects. When a request for access is received, the reference monitor refers to entries in the authorization database to verify that the operation requested by a subject for application to an object is permitted. The authorization database has entries, or *authorizations*, of the form subject, object, access mode. In answer b, the

I & A operation is separate from the reference monitor. The user enters his or her identification to the I & A function. Then the user must be authenticated. *Authentication* is verification that the user's claimed identity is valid. Authentication is based on the following three factor types:

- *Type 1*. Something you know, such as a PIN or password.
- *Type 2*. Something you have, such as an ATM card or smart card.
- *Type 3*. Something you are (physically), such as a fingerprint or retina scan.

Answer c, the auditing subsystem, is a key complement to the reference monitor. The reference monitor uses the auditing subsystem to keep track of the reference monitor's activities. Examples of such activities include the date and time of an access request, identification of the subject and objects involved, the access privileges requested, and the result of the request.

5. Access control that is based on an individual's duties or title in an organization is known as:

   a. Rule-based access control

   b. Discretionary access control

   c. Role-based access control

   d. Mandatory access control

   *Answer*: c

   Answer a, rule-based access control, is a type of mandatory access control where access is determined by specified rules. Answer b refers to access control where a specified entity has the authority, within certain limitations, to specify access rights that can be assigned to an individual. Mandatory access control, answer d, is dependent on labels that indicate the subject's clearance level and the classification assigned to objects.

6. The * (star) property of the Bell-LaPadula model states what?

   a. Reading of information by a subject at a lower sensitivity level from an object at a higher sensitivity level is not permitted (no read up).

   b. Writing of information by a subject at a higher level of sensitivity to an object at a lower level of sensitivity is not permitted (no write down).

   c. An access matrix is used to specify discretionary access control.

   d. Reading or writing is permitted at a particular level of sensitivity, but not to either higher or lower levels of sensitivity.

   *Answer*: b

   Answer a describes the simple security property, and answer c describes the discretionary security property. Answer d is the Strong * (star) property.

7. An ATM card and a PIN are an example of what?

   a. Multi-factor identification

   b. Single-factor authentication

   c. Two-factor authentication

   d. Single-factor identification

   *Answer*: c

   A PIN and an ATM card are something you know and something you have, respectively. Answers a and d are incorrect because the factors are used for authentication, not identification only. Answer b is incorrect because a PIN and an ATM card are two authentication factors.

8. A token that generates a unique password at fixed time intervals is called:

   a. An asynchronous dynamic password token

   b. A time-sensitive token

   c. A synchronous dynamic password token

   d. A challenge-response token

   *Answer*: c

   The correct answer is c. An asynchronous dynamic password token, answer a, generates a new password that does not have to fit into a fixed time window for authentication, as is the case for a synchronous dynamic password token. Answer b is a distracter. Answer d, a challenge-response token, generates a random challenge string as the owner enters the string into the token along with a PIN. Then, the token generates a response that the owner enters into the workstation for authentication.

9. Elliptic curves, which are applied to public key cryptography, employ modular exponentiation that characterizes the:

   a. Elliptic curve discrete logarithm problem

   b. Prime factors of very large numbers

   c. Elliptic curve modular addition

   d. Knapsack problem

   *Answer*: a

   The correct answer is a. Modular exponentiation in elliptic curves is the analog of the modular discreet logarithm problem. Answer b is incorrect because prime factors are involved with RSA public key systems; answer c is incorrect because modular addition in elliptic curves is the analog of modular multiplication; answer d is incorrect because the knapsack problem is not an elliptic curve problem.

10. In the discretionary portion of the Bell-LaPadula model that is based on the access matrix, how the access rights are defined and evaluated is called:

    a. Authentication

    b. Authorization

    c. Identification

    d. Validation

    *Answer*: b

    The correct answer is b because authorization is concerned with how access rights are defined and how they are evaluated.

11. The Biba model axiom "an object at one level of integrity is not permitted to modify (write to) an object of a higher level of integrity (no write up)" is called:

    a. The Constrained Integrity Axiom

    b. The * (star) Integrity Axiom

    c. The Simple Integrity Axiom

    d. The Discretionary Integrity Axiom

    *Answer*: b

    The correct answer is b. Answers a and d are distracters. Answer c, the Simple Integrity Axiom, states "a subject at one level of integrity is not permitted to observe (read) an object of lower integrity (no read down)."

12. A trade secret:

    a. Provides the owner with a legally enforceable right to exclude others from practicing the art covered for a specified time period

    b. Protects "original" works of authorship

    c. Secures and maintains the confidentiality of proprietary technical or business-related information that is adequately protected from disclosure by the owner

    d. Is a word, name, symbol, color, sound, product shape, or device used to identify goods and to distinguish them from those made or sold by others

    *Answer*: c

    The correct answer is c. It defines a trade secret. Answer a refers to a patent. Answer b refers to a copyright. Answer d refers to a trademark.

13. The chain of evidence relates to:

    a. Securing laptops to desks during an investigation

    b. DNA testing

    c. Handling and controlling evidence

    d. Making a disk image

*Answer*: c

The correct answer is c. Answer a relates to physical security; answer b is a type of biological testing; answer d is part of the act of gathering evidence.

14. The concept of due care states that senior organizational management must ensure that:

    a. All risks to an information system are eliminated

    b. Certain requirements must be fulfilled in carrying out their responsibilities to the organization

    c. Other management personnel are delegated the responsibility for information system security

    d. The cost of implementing safeguards is greater than the potential resultant losses resulting from information security breaches

*Answer*: b

The correct answer is b. Answer a is incorrect because all risks to information systems cannot be eliminated; answer c is incorrect because senior management cannot delegate its responsibility for information system security under due care; answer d is incorrect because the cost of implementing safeguards should be less than or equal to the potential resulting losses relative to the exercise of due care.

15. Which one of the following items is NOT TRUE concerning the Platform for Privacy Preferences (P3P) developed by the World Wide Web Consortium (W3C)?

    a. It allows Web sites to express their privacy practices in a standard format that can be retrieved automatically and interpreted easily by user agents.

    b. It allows users to be informed of site practices in human-readable format.

    c. It does not provide the site privacy practices to users in machine-readable format.

    d. It automates decision-making based on the site's privacy practices, when appropriate.

*Answer*: c

The correct answer is c. In addition to the capabilities in answers a, b, and d, P3P does provide the site privacy practices to users in machine-readable format.

16. Kerberos is an authentication scheme that can be used to implement:

    a. Public key cryptography

    b. Digital signatures

    c. Hash functions

    d. Single Sign-On

    *Answer*: d

    The correct answer is d. Kerberos is a third-party authentication protocol that can be used to implement Single Sign-On. Answer a is incorrect because public key cryptography is not used in the basic Kerberos protocol. Answer b is a public key-based capability, and answer c is a one-way transformation used to disguise passwords or to implement digital signatures.

17. In biometrics, a "one-to-one" search to verify an individual's claim of an identity is called:

    a. Audit trail review

    b. Authentication

    c. Accountability

    d. Aggregation

    *Answer*: b

    The correct answer is b. Answer a is a review of audit system data, usually done after the fact. Answer c is holding individuals responsible for their actions, and answer d is obtaining higher-sensitivity information from a number of pieces of information of lower sensitivity.

18. Biometrics is used for identification in the physical controls and for authentication in the:

    a. Detective controls

    b. Preventive controls

    c. Logical controls

    d. Corrective controls

    *Answer*: c

    The correct answer is c. The other answers are different categories of controls where preventive controls attempt to eliminate or reduce vulnerabilities before an attack occurs; detective controls attempt to determine that an attack is taking place or has taken place; and corrective controls involve taking action to restore the system to normal operation after a successful attack.

19. What part of an access control matrix shows one user's capabilities to multiple resources?

    a. Columns

    b. Rows

    c. Rows and columns

    d. Access control list

    *Answer*: b

    The rows of an access control matrix indicate the capabilities that users have to a number of resources. Answer a, columns in the access control matrix, defines the access control list. Answer c is incorrect because capabilities involve only the rows of the access control matrix. Answer d is incorrect because an ACL, again, is a column in the access control matrix.

20. The Secure Hash Algorithm–1 (SHA–1) is specified in the:

    a. Data Encryption Standard

    b. Digital Signature Standard

    c. Digital Encryption Standard

    d. Advanced Encryption Standard

    *Answer*: b

    The correct answer is b. Answer a refers to DES, a symmetric encryption algorithm; answer c is a distracter; answer d is the Advanced Encryption Standard, which has replaced DES.

21. The Digital Signature Standard (DSS) uses which digital signature algorithm(s)?

    a. Either the RSA digital signature algorithm or the Digital Signature Algorithm (DSA)

    b. DSA only

    c. RSA only

    d. Either the El Gamal digital signature algorithm or the Digital Signature Algorithm (DSA)

    *Answer*: a

    The correct answer is a. DSS specifies that either the RSA or DSA algorithms can be used.

22. The U.S. Escrowed Encryption Standard employed which of the following symmetric key algorithms?

    a. IDEA

    b. DES

c. 3 DES

d. SKIPJACK

*Answer*: d

The SKIPJACK algorithm is specified in the Clipper Chip. Answers a, b, and c are other symmetric key algorithms.

23. Key clustering is:

a. The condition where many keys in use are very similar

b. When one key encrypts a plaintext message into two different ciphertexts

c. When two different keys encrypt a plaintext message into the same ciphertext

d. Escrowing of keys

*Answer*: c

The other answers are distracters.

24. Which of the following is NOT an asymmetric key algorithm?

a. Knapsack

b. RSA

c. Diffie-Hellman

d. Rijndael

*Answer*: d

The correct answer is d, the Advanced Encryption Standard (AES). The other answers are examples of asymmetric key systems.

25. A hybrid cryptosystem employs which of the following methodologies?

a. Private key encryption to encrypt and send the secret key that will be used to encrypt and send the message using public key encryption

b. Public key encryption to encrypt and send the secret key that will be used to encrypt and send the message using private key encryption

c. Public key encryption to encrypt and send the secret key that will be used to encrypt and send the message using public key encryption

d. Private key encryption to encrypt and send the secret key that will be used to encrypt and send the message using private key encryption

*Answer*: b

The correct answer is b; therefore, all the other answers are incorrect. Public key encryption is slower than private key encryption. In a hybrid system, public key encryption is used to encrypt and send the smaller secret key, while private key encryption uses that secret key to encrypt much larger volumes of data to be securely transmitted.

26. In public key cryptography, which of the following statements is NOT true?

    a. A message encrypted with Bob's public key can be decrypted only with Bob's private key.

    b. A message encrypted with Bob's private key can be decrypted only with Bob's public key.

    c. A message encrypted with Bob's public key can be decrypted with Bob's public key.

    d. Given Bob's public key, it is very difficult or impossible to determine his private key.

    *Answer*: c

    The correct answer is c. All the other answers are true.

27. Which of the following is NOT one of the AES key sizes?

    a. 128 bits

    b. 512 bits

    c. 192 bits

    d. 256 bits

    *Answer*: b

    The correct answer b. AES is made up of three key sizes, 128, 192, and 256 bits, with a fixed block size of 128 bits. Depending on which of the three keys is used, the standard may be referred to as "AES-128," "AES-192," or "AES-256."

28. A polyalphabetic cipher is also known as:

    a. One-time pad

    b. Vernam cipher

    c. Steganography

    d. Vigenère cipher

    *Answer*: d

    The correct answer is d. The Vigenère cipher substitutes letters from multiple alphabets instead of a single alphabet, as in monoalphabetic substitution. The use of multiple alphabets thwarts attacks based on the frequency of letters used in a given alphabet. Answer a is incorrect because a one-time pad uses a random key with a length equal to the plaintext message and is used only once. Answer b is incorrect because it applies to stream ciphers that are XORed with a random key string. Answer c is the process of sending a message with no indication that a message even exists.

29. A method that is used to securely transmit secret messages and that is based on keeping the existence of the messages unknown is called:

    a. Private key encryption

    b. Blind signatures

    c. Steganography

    d. A zero-knowledge proof

    *Answer*: c

    The correct answer is c. Examples of steganography include imbedding data into digital images and shrinking information into microdots.

30. Which of the following characteristics does NOT apply to a one-time pad, if it is used properly?

    a. The key is truly random with no repeating sequences or patterns.

    b. It can be used, carefully, more than once.

    c. It is unbreakable.

    d. The key must be of the same length as the message to be encrypted.

    *Answer*: b

    The correct answer is b. The one-time pad should be used only once, lest the key become compromised. If the one-time-pad is used only once and its corresponding key is truly random and does not have repeating characters, it is unbreakable. The key must be the same length as the message.

31. The key length of the DES key is:

    a. 128 bits

    b. 56 bits

    c. 64 bits

    d. 256 bits

    *Answer*: b

    The correct answer is b.

32. In generating a digitally signed message using a hash function:

    a. The message is encrypted in the public key of the sender

    b. The message digest is encrypted in the private key of the sender

    c. The message digest is encrypted in the public key of the sender

    d. The message is encrypted in the private key of the sender

    *Answer*: b

    The correct answer is b. The hash function generates a message digest from the message. The message digest is encrypted with the private key of the sender and sent along with the message. Thus, if the message digest can be opened at the receiving end with the sender's public key (known to all), the message must have come from the sender. The message is not encrypted with the private key because the message is usually longer than the message digest and would take more computing resources to encrypt and decrypt. Because the message digest uniquely characterizes the message, it can also be used to verify the integrity of the message.

Answers a and c are not correct because a message encrypted in the public key of the sender can be read only by using the sender's private key. Because the sender is the only one who knows this key, no one else can read the message. Answer d is incorrect because the message is not encrypted, but the message digest is encrypted.

33. The theft of a laptop poses a threat to which tenet of the C.I.A. triad?

   a. Confidentiality

   b. Integrity

   c. Availability

   d. All of the above

   *Answer*: d

   The correct answer is d: confidentiality, because the data can now be read by someone outside of a monitored environment; availability, because the user has lost the computing ability provided by the unit; integrity, because the data residing on and any telecommunications from the portable are now suspect.

34. Which choice MOST accurately describes the difference between the role of a data owner versus the role of a data custodian?

   a. The custodian implements the information classification scheme after the initial assignment by the owner.

   b. The data owner implements the information classification scheme after the initial assignment by the custodian.

   c. The custodian makes the initial information classification assignments, and the operations manager implements the scheme.

   d. The custodian implements the information classification scheme after the initial assignment by the operations manager.

   *Answer*: a

35. Which choice is usually the number one-used criterion to determine the classification of an information object?

   a. Value

   b. Useful life

c. Age

d. Personal association

*Answer*: a

The correct answer is a. Value of the information asset to the organization is usually the first and foremost criterion used in determining its classification. Answer b is a common criterion used for declassification of an information object.

36. Which choice BEST describes the type of control that a firewall exerts on a network infrastructure?

a. Corrective control

b. Preventive control

c. Detective control

d. Application control

*Answer*: b

The correct answer is b. A firewall is primarily intended to prevent unauthorized access.

37. Which choice is NOT a concern of policy development at the high level?

a. Identifying the key business resources

b. Identifying the type of firewalls to be used for perimeter security

c. Defining roles in the organization

d. Determining the capability and functionality of each role

*Answer*: b

Answers a, c, and d are elements of policy development at the highest level. Key business resources would have been identified during the risk assessment process. The various roles are then defined to determine the various levels of access to those resources. Answer d is the final step in the policy creation process and combines steps a and c. It determines which group gets access to each resource and what access privileges its members are assigned. Access to resources should be based on roles, not on individual identity.

38. Which firewall type uses a dynamic state table to inspect the content of packets?

a. A packet filtering firewall

b. An application-level firewall

c. A circuit-level firewall

d. A stateful inspection firewall

*Answer*: d

A stateful inspection firewall intercepts incoming packets at the network level, then uses an inspection engine to extract state-related information from upper layers. It maintains the information in a dynamic state table and evaluates subsequent connection attempts.

39. Which choice is NOT considered an information classification role?

   a. Data owner

   b. Data custodian

   c. Data alterer

   d. Data user

*Answer*: c

The correct answer is c. Data owners, custodians, and users all have defined roles in the process of information classification. Answer c is a distracter.

40. Which PPP authentication method sends passwords in cleartext?

   a. PAP

   b. CHAP

   c. MS-CHAP

   d. MS-CHAP v2

*Answer*: a

Password Authentication Protocol (PAP) is a cleartext authentication scheme. When the network access server (NAS) requests the username and the password, PAP returns them in unencrypted "clear" text. The other three answers all use a hash variation to encrypt the transmitted password.

41. Which choice is NOT one of the legal IP address ranges specified by RFC1976 and reserved by the Internet Assigned Numbers Authority (IANA) for nonroutable private addresses?

   a. 10.0.0.0–10.255.255.255

   b. 127.0.0.0–127.0.255.255

   c. 172.16.0.0–172.31.255.255

   d. 192.168.0.0–192.168.255.255

*Answer*: b

The other three address ranges can be used for Network Address Translation (NAT). While NAT is, in itself, not a very effective security measure, a large network can benefit from using NAT with Dynamic Host Configuration Protocol (DHCP) to help prevent certain internal routing information from being exposed. The address 127.0.0.1 is called the "loopback" address.

42. Which statement is correct regarding VLANs?

    a. A VLAN restricts flooding to only those ports included in the VLAN.

    b. A VLAN is a network segmented physically, not logically.

    c. A VLAN is less secure when implemented in conjunction with private port switching.

    d. A "closed" VLAN configuration is the least secure VLAN configuration.

    *Answer*: a

    A virtual local area network (VLAN) allows ports on the same or different switches to be grouped so that traffic is confined to members of that group only, and it restricts broadcast, unicast, and multicast traffic. Answer b is incorrect because a VLAN is segmented logically, rather than physically. Answer c is incorrect. When a VLAN is implemented with private port, or single-user, switching, it provides fairly stringent security because broadcast vulnerabilities are minimized. Answer d is incorrect, as a "closed" VLAN authenticates a user to an access control list on a central authentication server, where they are assigned authorization parameters to determine their level of network access.

# Chapter 2: Risk Management

1. What is the prime directive of Risk Management?

    a. Reduce the risk to a tolerable level

    b. Reduce all risk regardless of cost

    c. Transfer any risk to external third parties

    d. Prosecute any employees that are violating published security policies

    *Answer*: a

    Risk can never be eliminated, and Risk Management must find the level of risk the organization can tolerate and still function effectively.

2. Which choice MOST closely depicts the difference between qualitative and quantitative risk analysis?

    a. A quantitative RA does not use the hard costs of losses, and a qualitative RA does.

    b. A quantitative RA uses less guesswork than a qualitative RA.

    c. A qualitative RA uses many complex calculations.

    d. A quantitative RA cannot be automated.

*Answer*: b

The other answers are incorrect.

3. What is the BEST description of risk reduction?

    a. Altering elements of the enterprise in response to a risk analysis

    b. Removing all risk to the enterprise at any cost

    c. Assigning any costs associated with risk to a third party

    d. Assuming all costs associated with the risk internally

*Answer*: a

Answer b is not possible or desirable, c is risk transference, and d is risk acceptance.

4. How is an SLE derived?

    a. (Cost – Benefit) × (% of Asset Value)

    b. AV × EF

    c. ARO × EF

    d. % of AV – Implementation Cost

*Answer*: b

A Single Loss Expectancy is derived by multiplying the Asset Value with its Exposure Factor. The other answers do not exist.

5. What is an ARO?

    a. A dollar figure assigned to a single event

    b. The annual expected financial loss to an organization from a threat

    c. A number that represents the estimated frequency of an occurrence of an expected threat

    d. The percentage of loss that a realized threat event would have on a specific asset

*Answer*: c

Answer a is the definition of SLE, b is an ALE, and d is an EF.

6. What does an Exposure Factor (EF) describe?

    a. A dollar figure that is assigned to a single event

    b. A number that represents the estimated frequency of the occurrence of an expected threat

    c. The percentage of loss that a realized threat event would have on a specific asset

    d. The annual expected financial loss to an organization from a threat

*Answer*: c

Answer a is a SLE, b is an ARO, and d is an ALE.

7. Which choice is the BEST description of a vulnerability?

    a. A weakness in a system that could be exploited

    b. A company resource that could be lost due to an incident

    c. The minimization of loss associated with an incident

    d. A potential incident that could cause harm

*Answer*: a

Answer b describes an asset, answer c describes risk management, and answer d describes a threat.

8. Which choice is NOT a common result of a risk analysis?

    a. A detailed listing of relevant threats

    b. Valuations of critical assets

    c. Likelihood of a potential threat

    d. Definition of business recovery roles

*Answer*: d

The first three answers are common results of a risk analysis to determine the probability and effect of threats to company assets. Answer d is a distracter.

9. Which statement BEST describes the primary purpose of risk analysis?

    a. To create a clear cost-to-value ratio for implementing security controls

    b. To influence the system design process

    c. To influence site selection decisions

    d. To quantify the impact of potential threats

*Answer*: d

The main purpose of performing a risk analysis is to put a hard cost or value on the loss of a business function. The other answers are benefits of risk management but not its main purpose.

10. Put the following steps in the qualitative scenario procedure in order:

    a. The team prepares its findings and presents them to management.

    b. A scenario is written to address each identified threat.

   c. Business unit managers review the scenario for a reality check.

   d. The team works through each scenario by using a threat, asset, and safeguard.

*Answer*: b, c, d, and a.

11. Which statement is NOT correct about safeguard selection in the risk analysis process?

   a. Maintenance costs need to be included in determining the total cost of the safeguard.

   b. The best possible safeguard should always be implemented, regardless of cost.

   c. The most commonly considered criteria is the cost effectiveness of the safeguard.

   d. Many elements need to be considered in determining the total cost of the safeguard.

*Answer*: b

Performing a cost/benefit analysis of the proposed safeguard before implementation is vital. The level of security afforded could easily outweigh the value of a proposed safeguard. Other factors need to be considered in the safeguard selection process, such as accountability, auditability, and the level of manual operations needed to maintain or operate the safeguard.

12. Which choice most accurately reflects the goals of risk mitigation?

   a. Defining the acceptable level of risk the organization can tolerate and reducing risk to that level

   b. Analyzing and removing all vulnerabilities and threats to security within the organization

   c. Defining the acceptable level of risk the organization can tolerate, and assigning any costs associated with loss or disruption to a third party, such as an insurance carrier

   d. Analyzing the effects of a business disruption and preparing the company's response

*Answer*: a

The goal of risk mitigation is to reduce risk to a level acceptable to the organization. Therefore, risk needs to be defined for the organization through risk analysis, business impact assessment, and/or vulnerability assessment. Answer b is not possible. Answer c is called risk transference. Answer d is a distracter.

13. Which answer is the BEST description of a Single Loss Expectancy (SLE)?

    a. An algorithm that represents the magnitude of a loss to an asset from a threat

    b. An algorithm that expresses the annual frequency with which a threat is expected to occur

    c. An algorithm used to determine the monetary impact of each occurrence of a threat

    d. An algorithm that determines the expected annual loss to an organization from a threat

    *Answer*: c

    The Single Loss Expectancy (or Exposure) figure may be created as a result of a Business Impact Assessment (BIA). The SLE represents only the estimated monetary loss of a single occurrence of a specified threat event. The SLE is determined by multiplying the value of the asset by its exposure factor. This gives the expected loss the threat will cause for one occurrence.

    Answer a describes the Exposure Factor (EF). The EF is expressed as a percentile of the expected value or functionality of the asset to be lost due to the realized threat event. This figure is used to calculate the SLE. Answer b describes the Annualized Rate of Occurrence (ARO). This is an estimate of how often a given threat event may occur annually. For example, a threat expected to occur weekly would have an ARO of 52. A threat expected to occur once every five years has an ARO of 1/5 or .2. This figure is used to determine the ALE. Answer d describes the Annualized Loss Expectancy (ALE). The ALE is derived by multiplying the SLE by its ARO. This value represents the expected risk factor of an annual threat event. This figure is then integrated into the risk management process.

14. Which choice is the BEST description of an Annualized Loss Expectancy?

    a. The expected risk factor of an annual threat event, derived by multiplying the SLE by its ARO

    b. An estimate of how often a given threat event may occur annually

    c. The percentile of the value of the asset expected to be lost, used to calculate the SLE

    d. A value determined by multiplying the value of the asset by its exposure factor

    *Answer*: a

    Answer b describes the Annualized Rate of Occurrence (ARO). Answer c describes the Exposure Factor (EF). Answer d describes the algorithm to determine the Single Loss Expectancy (SLE) of a threat.

15. Which choice is NOT a common information-gathering technique when performing a risk analysis?

    a. Distributing a questionnaire

    b. Employing automated risk assessment tools

    c. Reviewing existing policy documents

    d. Interviewing terminated employees

    *Answer*: d

    Any combination of the following techniques can be used in gathering information relevant to the IT system within its operational boundary:

    - *Questionnaire.* The questionnaire should be distributed to the applicable technical and nontechnical management personnel who are designing or supporting the IT system.

    - *On-site interviews.* On-site visits also allow risk assessment personnel to observe and gather information about the physical, environmental, and operational security of the IT system.

    - *Document review.* Policy documents, system documentation, and security-related documentation can provide good information about the security controls used by and planned for the IT system.

    - *Use of automated scanning tools.* Proactive technical methods can be used to collect system information efficiently.

16. Which statement is NOT accurate regarding the process of risk assessment?

    a. The likelihood of a threat must be determined as an element of the risk assessment.

    b. The level of impact of a threat must be determined as an element of the risk assessment.

    c. Risk assessment is the first process in the risk management methodology.

    d. Risk assessment is the final result of the risk management methodology.

    *Answer*: d

    Risk is a function of the likelihood of a given threat-source's exercising a particular potential vulnerability and the resulting impact of that adverse event on the organization. Risk assessment is the first process in the risk management methodology. The risk assessment process helps organizations identify appropriate controls for reducing or eliminating risk during the risk mitigation process.

    To determine the likelihood of a future adverse event, threats to an IT system must be analyzed in conjunction with the potential vulnerabilities and the controls in place for the IT system. The likelihood that a potential vulnerability could be exercised by a given threat-source can be described as high, medium, or low. Impact refers to the magnitude of harm that could be caused by a threat's exploitation of a vulnerability. The determination of the level of impact produces a relative value for the IT assets and resources affected.

17. Which formula accurately represents an Annualized Loss Expectancy (ALE) calculation?

    a. $SLE \times ARO$

    b. Asset Value $(AV) \times EF$

    c. $ARO \times EF - SLE$

    d. % of $ARO \times AV$

    *Answer*: a

    Answer b is the formula for an SLE, and answers c and d are distracters.

18. What is the MOST accurate definition of a safeguard?

    a. A guideline for policy recommendations

    b. A step-by-step instructional procedure

    c. A control designed to counteract a threat

    d. A control designed to counteract an asset

    *Answer*: c

    Answer a is a guideline, b is a procedure, and d is a distracter.

19. Three things that must be considered for the planning and implementation of access control mechanisms are:

    a. Threats, assets, and objectives

    b. Threats, vulnerabilities, and risks

    c. Vulnerabilities, secret keys, and exposures

    d. Exposures, threats, and countermeasures

    *Answer:* b

    Threats define the possible source of security policy violations; vulnerabilities describe weaknesses in the system that might be exploited by the threats; the risk determines the probability of threats being realized. All three items must be present to apply access control meaningfully. Therefore, the other answers are incorrect.

20. Which choice BEST describes a threat?

    a. A potential incident that could cause harm

    b. A weakness in a system that could be exploited

   c. A company resource that could be lost due to an incident

   d. The minimization of loss associated with an incident

*Answer:* a

Answer b describes a vulnerability, answer c describes an asset, and answer d describes risk management.

21. Which choice is an incorrect description of a control?

   a. Detective controls discover attacks and trigger preventative or corrective controls.

   b. Corrective controls reduce the likelihood of a deliberate attack.

   c. Corrective controls reduce the effect of an attack.

   d. Controls are the countermeasures for vulnerabilities.

*Answer:* b

Controls are the countermeasures for vulnerabilities. There are many kinds, but generally they are categorized into four types:

- Deterrent controls reduce the likelihood of a deliberate attack.
- Preventive controls protect vulnerabilities and make an attack unsuccessful or reduce its impact. Preventive controls inhibit attempts to violate security policy.
- Corrective controls reduce the effect of an attack.
- Detective controls discover attacks and trigger preventive or corrective controls. Detective controls warn of violations or attempted violations of security policy and include such controls as audit trails, intrusion detection methods, and checksums.

22. Which of the following would NOT be a component of a general enterprise security architecture model for an organization?

   a. Information and resources to ensure the appropriate level of risk management

   b. Consideration of all the items that make up information security, including distributed systems, software, hardware, communications systems and networks

   c. A systematic and unified approach for evaluating the organization's information systems security infrastructure and defining approaches to implementation and deployment of information security controls

   d. IT system auditing

*Answer:* d

The auditing component of the IT system should be independent and distinct from the information system security architecture for a system.

In answer a, the resources to support intelligent risk management decisions include technical expertise, applicable evaluation processes, refinement of business objectives, and delivery plans. Answer b promotes an enterprise-wide view of information system security issues. For answer c, the intent is to show that a comprehensive security architecture model includes all phases involved in information system security including planning, design, integrating, testing, and production.

23. Access control must consider which of the following?

    a. Vulnerabilities, biometrics, and exposures

    b. Threats, assets, and safeguards

    c. Exposures, threats, and countermeasures

    d. Threats, vulnerabilities, and risks

    *Answer*: d

    Threats are an event or situation that may cause harm to an information system; vulnerabilities describe weaknesses in the system that might be exploited by the threats; the risk determines the probability of threats being realized. All three items must be considered to apply access control meaningfully. Therefore, the other answers are incorrect.

24. What are high-level policies?

    a. They are recommendations for procedural controls.

    b. They are the instructions on how to perform a quantitative risk analysis.

    c. They are statements that indicate a senior management's intention to support InfoSec.

    d. They are step-by-step procedures to implement a safeguard.

    *Answer*: c

    High-level policies are senior management statements of recognition of the importance of InfoSec controls.

25. Which choice is NOT a good criterion for selecting a safeguard?

    a. The ability to recover from a reset with the permissions set to "allow all"

    b. Comparing the potential dollar loss of an asset to the cost of a safeguard

    c. The ability to recover from a reset without damaging the asset

    d. Accountability features for tracking and identifying operators

    *Answer*: a

    Permissions should be set to "deny all" during reset.

26. Which statement is accurate about the reasons to implement a layered security architecture?

    a. A layered security approach is not necessary when using COTS products.

    b. A good packet-filtering router will eliminate the need to implement a layered security architecture.

    c. A layered security approach is intended to increase the work factor for an attacker.

    d. A layered approach doesn't really improve the security posture of the organization.

    *Answer*: c

    Security designs should consider a layered approach to address or protect against a specific threat or to reduce a vulnerability. For example, the use of a packet-filtering router in conjunction with an application gateway and an intrusion detection system combine to increase the work factor an attacker must expend to attack the system successfully. The need for layered protections is important when commercial off-the-shelf (COTS) products are used. The current state-of-the-art for security quality in COTS products does not provide a high degree of protection against sophisticated attacks. It is possible to help mitigate this situation by placing several controls in levels, requiring additional work by attackers to accomplish their goals.

27. Which choice describes a control?

    a. Competitive advantage, credibility, or good will

    b. Events or situations that could cause a financial or operational impact to the organization

    c. Personnel compensation and retirement programs

    d. Protection devices or procedures in place that reduce the effects of threats

    *Answer*: d

    Protection devices or procedures are controls that can reduce the effect of a threat, such as a UPS, sprinkler systems, or generators. Answer a describes an asset. Answer b is a definition of a threat. Answer c is a distracter.

28. According to NIST, which choice is not an accepted security self-testing technique?

    a. War dialing

    b. Virus distribution

    c. Password cracking

d. Virus detection

*Answer*: b

Common types of self-testing techniques include the following:

- Network mapping
- Vulnerability scanning
- Penetration testing
- Password cracking
- Log review
- Virus detection
- War dialing

Some testing techniques are predominantly human initiated and conducted, while other tests are highly automated and require less human involvement. The staff that initiates and implements in-house security testing should have significant security and networking knowledge. These testing techniques are often combined to gain a more comprehensive assessment of the overall network security posture. For example, penetration testing almost always includes network mapping and vulnerability scanning to identify vulnerable hosts and services that may be targeted for later penetration. None of these tests by themselves will provide a complete picture of the network or its security posture.

29. What is the BEST reason for the security administrator to initiate internal vulnerability scanning?

   a. Vulnerability scanning can replicate a system crash.

   b. Vulnerability scanning can identify exposed ports.

   c. Vulnerability scanning can return false positives.

   d. Vulnerability scanning can return false negatives.

   *Answer*: b

Vulnerability scanning should be conducted on a periodic basis to identify compromised or vulnerable systems. Conducting scans is one way to identify and track several types of potential problems, such as unused ports or unauthorized software. The other three answers are distracters.

30. What are the detailed instructions on how to perform or implement a control called?

   a. Procedures

   b. Policies

   c. Guidelines

   d. Standards

   *Answer*: a

31. Which of the following is a reason to institute output controls?

    a. To preserve the integrity of the data in the system while changes are being made to the configuration

    b. To protect the output's confidentiality

    c. To detect irregularities in the software's operation

    d. To recover damage after an identified system failure

    *Answer:* b

    The correct answer is b. In addition to being used as a transaction control verification mechanism, output controls are used to ensure that output, such as printed reports, is distributed securely. Answer a is an example of Configuration or Change control, c is an example of Application controls, and d is an example of Recovery controls.

32. Why are maintenance accounts a threat to operations controls?

    a. Maintenance personnel could slip and fall and sue the organization.

    b. Maintenance accounts are commonly used by hackers to access network devices.

    c. Maintenance account information could be compromised if printed reports are left out in the open.

    d. Maintenance might require physical access to the system by vendors or service providers.

    *Answer:* b

    Maintenance accounts are login accounts to systems resources, primarily networked devices. They often have the factory-set passwords that are frequently distributed through the hacker community.

33. Who has the final responsibility for the preservation of the organization's information?

    a. Technology providers

    b. Senior management

    c. Users

    d. Application owners

    *Answer:* b

    Various officials and organizational offices are typically involved with computer security. They include the following groups:

    - Senior management
    - Program/functional managers/application owners
    - Computer security management
    - Technology providers

- Supporting organizations
- Users

Senior management has the final responsibility through due care and due diligence to preserve the capital of the organization and further its business model through the implementation of a security program. While senior management does not have the functional role of managing security procedures, it has the ultimate responsibility to see that business continuity is preserved.

34. Which choice represents an application or system demonstrating a need for a high level of confidentiality protection and controls?

   a. Unavailability of the system could result in inability to meet payroll obligations and could cause work stoppage and failure of user organizations to meet mission-critical requirements. The system requires 24-hour access.

   b. The application contains proprietary business information and other financial information, which, if disclosed to unauthorized sources, could cause unfair advantage for vendors, contractors, or individuals and could result in financial loss or adverse legal action to user organizations.

   c. Destruction of the information would require significant expenditures of time and effort to replace. Although corrupted information would present an inconvenience to the staff, most information, and all vital information, is backed up either by paper documentation or on disk.

   d. The mission of this system is to produce local weather forecast information that is made available to the news media forecasters and the general public at all times. None of the information requires protection against disclosure.

*Answer*: b

Although elements of all of the systems described could require specific controls for confidentiality, given the descriptions here, system b fits the definition most closely of a system requiring a very high level of confidentiality. Answer a is an example of a system requiring high availability. Answer c is an example of a system that requires medium integrity controls. Answer d is a system that requires only a low level of confidentiality.

A system may need protection for one or more of the following reasons:

- *Confidentiality*. The system contains information that requires protection from unauthorized disclosure.

- *Integrity*. The system contains information that must be protected from unauthorized, unanticipated, or unintentional modification.

■ *Availability.* The system contains information or provides services that must be available on a timely basis to meet mission-critical requirements or to avoid substantial losses.

35. Using prenumbered forms to initiate a transaction is an example of what type of control?

    a. Deterrent control

    b. Preventive control

    c. Detective control

    d. Application control

    *Answer*: b

    Prenumbered forms are an example of preventive controls. They can also be considered a transaction control and input control.

# Chapter 3: Information Security Program Management

1. The simplistic model of software life cycle development assumes that:

    a. Iteration will be required among the steps in the process.

    b. Each step can be completed and finalized without any effect from the later stages that may require rework.

    c. Each phase is identical to a completed milestone.

    d. Software development requires reworking and repeating some of the phases.

    *Answer*: b

    The correct answer is b. Each step can be completed and finalized without any effect from the later stages that might require rework. Answer a is incorrect because no iteration is allowed for in the model. Answer c is incorrect because it applies to the modified Waterfall model. Answer d is incorrect because no iteration or reworking is considered in the model.

2. What does the Spiral model depict?

    a. A spiral that incorporates various phases of software development

    b. A spiral that models the behavior of biological neurons

    c. The operation of expert systems

    d. Information security checklists

*Answer*: a

The correct answer is a. A Spiral model incorporates various phases of software development. The other answers are distracters.

3. In the software life cycle, verification:

   a. Evaluates the product in development against real-world requirements

   b. Evaluates the product in development against similar products

   c. Evaluates the product in development against general baselines

   d. Evaluates the product in development against the specification

*Answer*: d

The correct answer is d. In the software life cycle, verification evaluates the product in development against the specification. Answer a defines validation. Answers b and c are distracters.

4. In the modified Waterfall model:

   a. Unlimited backward iteration is permitted.

   b. The model was reinterpreted to have phases end at project milestones.

   c. The model was reinterpreted to have phases begin at project milestones.

   d. Product verification and validation are not included.

*Answer*: b

The correct answer is b. The modified Waterfall model was reinterpreted to have phases end at project milestones. Answer a is false because unlimited backward iteration is not permitted in the modified Waterfall model. Answer c is a distracter, and answer d is false because verification and validation are included.

5. In a system life cycle, information security controls should be:

   a. Designed during the product implementation phase

   b. Implemented prior to validation

   c. Part of the feasibility phase

   d. Specified after the coding phase

*Answer*: c

The correct answer is c. In the system life cycle, information security controls should be part of the feasibility phase. The other answers are incorrect because the basic premise of information system security is that controls should be included in the earliest phases of the system life cycle and not added later in the cycle or as an afterthought.

6. In configuration management, what is a software library?

   a. A set of versions of the component configuration items

   b. A controlled area accessible only to approved users who are restricted to the use of an approved procedure

   c. A repository of backup tapes

   d. A collection of software build lists

   *Answer*: b

   The correct answer is b. In configuration management, a software library is a controlled area accessible only to approved users who are restricted to the use of an approved procedure. Answer a is incorrect because it defines a build list. Answer c is incorrect because it defines a backup storage facility. Answer d is a distracter.

7. What is configuration control?

   a. Identifying and documenting the functional and physical characteristics of each configuration item

   b. Controlling changes to the configuration items and issuing versions of configuration items from the software library

   c. Recording the processing of changes

   d. Controlling the quality of the configuration management procedures

   *Answer*: b

   The correct answer is b. Configuration control is controlling changes to the configuration items and issuing versions of configuration items from the software library. Answer a is the definition of configuration identification. Answer c is the definition of configuration status accounting, and answer d is the definition of configuration audit.

8. Which one of the following is NOT one of the maturity levels of the Software Capability Maturity Model (CMM)?

   a. Fundamental

   b. Repeatable

   c. Defined

   d. Managed

   *Answer*: a

   The correct answer is a, a distracter. The first level of the Software CMM is the Initiating level. At this level, processes are performed on an ad hoc basis. Answer b, the Repeatable level, is the second maturity level in the model. In the third level, Defined, or answer c, management practices are institutionalized and technical procedures are integrated into the organizational structure. The Managed level of answer d has both product and processes quantitatively controlled. The fifth level of the Software CMM is the Optimized level, where continuous process improvement is institutionalized.

9. What does the Bell-LaPadula model NOT allow?

    a. Subjects to read from a higher level of security relative to their level of security

    b. Subjects to read from a lower level of security relative to their level of security

    c. Subjects to write to a higher level of security relative to their level of security

    d. Subjects to read at their same level of security

    *Answer*: a

    The correct answer is a. The other options are not prohibited by the model.

10. In the * (star) property of the Bell-LaPadula model:

    a. Subjects cannot read from a higher level of security relative to their level of security

    b. Subjects cannot read from a lower level of security relative to their level of security

    c. Subjects cannot write to a lower level of security relative to their level of security

    d. Subjects cannot read from their same level of security

    *Answer*: c

    The correct answer is c by definition of the star property.

11. The Clark-Wilson model focuses on data's:

    a. Integrity

    b. Confidentiality

    c. Availability

    d. Format

    *Answer*: a

    The correct answer is a. The Clark-Wilson model is an integrity model.

12. The * (star) property of the Biba model states:

    a. Subjects cannot write to a lower level of integrity relative to their level of integrity.

    b. Subjects cannot write to a higher level of integrity relative to their level of integrity.

    c. Subjects cannot read from a lower level of integrity relative to their level of integrity.

    d. Subjects cannot read from a higher level of integrity relative to their level of integrity.

*Answer*: b

13. Which of the following does the Clark-Wilson model NOT involve?

    a. Constrained data items

    b. Transformational procedures

    c. Confidentiality items

    d. Well-formed transactions

*Answer*: c

The correct answer is c. The Clark-Wilson model does not address confidentiality. Answers a, b, and d are parts of the Clark-Wilson model.

14. Which one of the following is NOT a type of prototyping?

    a. Incremental

    b. Architectural

    c. Evolutionary

    d. Throw-away

*Answer:* b

The correct answer is b.

15. The basic version of the Construction Cost Model (COCOMO), which proposes quantitative, life-cycle relationships, performs what function?

    a. Estimates software development effort based on user function categories

    b. Estimates software development effort and cost as a function of the size of the software product in source instructions

    c. Estimates software development effort and cost as a function of the size of the software product in source instructions modified by manpower buildup and productivity factors

    d. Estimates software development effort and cost as a function of the size of the software product in source instructions modified by hardware and input functions

*Answer*: b

The correct answer is b. The Basic COCOMO Model (B.W. Boehm, *Software Engineering Economics*, Englewood Cliffs, NJ: Prentice-Hall, 1981). In addition, Boehm has developed an intermediate COCOMO Model that also takes into account hardware constraints, personnel quality, use of modern tools, and other attributes and their aggregate impact on overall project costs. A detailed COCOMO Model, by Boehm, accounts for the effects of the additional factors used in the intermediate model on the costs of individual project phases.

Answer a describes a function point measurement model that does not require the user to estimate the number of delivered source instructions. In this model, functions are tallied and weighted according to complexity and used to determine the software development effort.

Answer c describes the Rayleigh curve applied to software development cost and effort estimation. Answer d is a distracter.

16. A refinement to the basic Waterfall model that states that software should be developed in increments of functional capability is called:

    a. Functional refinement

    b. Functional development

    c. Incremental refinement

    d. Incremental development

    *Answer*: d

    The correct answer is d. The advantages of incremental development include the ease of testing increments of functional capability and the opportunity to incorporate user experience into a successively refined product. Answers a, b, and c are distracters.

17. The Spiral model of the software development process (B.W. Boehm, "A Spiral Model of Software Development and Enhancement," *IEEE Computer,* May 1988) uses the following metric relative to the spiral:

    a. The radial dimension represents the cost of each phase

    b. The radial dimension represents progress made in completing each cycle

    c. The angular dimension represents cumulative cost

    d. The radial dimension represents cumulative cost

    *Answer*: d

    The correct answer is d. The radial dimension represents cumulative cost, and the angular dimension represents progress made in completing each cycle of the spiral. The spiral model is actually a meta-model for software development processes. A summary of the stages in the spiral is as follows:

    - The spiral begins in the top, left-hand quadrant by determining the objectives of the portion of the product being developed, the alternative means of implementing this portion of the product, and the constraints imposed on the application of the alternatives.

- Next, the risks of the alternatives are evaluated based on the objectives and constraints. Following this step, the relative balances of the perceived risks are determined.

- The spiral then proceeds to the lower right-hand quadrant where the development phases of the projects begin. A major review completes each cycle, and then the process begins anew for succeeding phases of the project. Typical succeeding phases are software product design, integration and test plan development, additional risk analyses, operational prototype, detailed design, code, unit test, acceptance test, and implementation.

Answers a, b, and c are distracters.

18. In the Capability Maturity Model (CMM) for software, the definition "describes the range of expected results that can be achieved by following a software process" is that of:

a. Structured analysis/structured design (SA/SD)

b. Software process capability

c. Software process performance

d. Software process maturity

*Answer*: b

The correct answer is b. A software process is a set of activities, methods, and practices that are used to develop and maintain software and associated products. Software process capability is a means of predicting the outcome of the next software project conducted by an organization. Answer c, software process performance, is the result achieved by following a software process. Thus, software capability is aimed at expected results while software performance is focused on results that have been achieved. Software process maturity, answer d, is the extent to which a software process is the following:

- Defined

- Managed

- Measured

- Controlled

- Effective

Software process maturity then provides for the potential for growth in capability of an organization. An immature organization develops software in a crisis mode, usually exceeds budgets and time schedules, and develops software processes in an ad hoc fashion during the project. In a mature organization, the software process is effectively communicated to staff, the required processes are documented and consistent, software quality is evaluated, and roles and responsibilities are understood for the project.

Answer a is a distracter.

19. Which of the following composes the four phases of the National Information Assurance Certification and Accreditation Process (NIACAP)?

    a. Definition, Verification, Validation, and Confirmation

    b. Definition, Verification, Validation, and Post Accreditation

    c. Verification, Validation, Authentication, and Post Accreditation

    d. Definition, Authentication, Verification, and Post Accreditation

    *Answer*: b

    The correct answer is b.

20. Which of the following are the three types of NIACAP accreditation?

    a. Site, type, and location

    b. Site, type, and system

    c. Type, system, and location

    d. Site, type, and general

    *Answer*: b

    The correct answer is b.

21. In the Common Criteria, a Protection Profile:

    a. Specifies the mandatory protection in the product to be evaluated

    b. Is also known as the Target of Evaluation (TOE)

    c. Is also known as the Orange Book

    d. Specifies the security requirements and protections of the products to be evaluated

    *Answer*: d

    The correct answer is d. Answer a is a distracter. Answer b is the product to be evaluated. Answer c refers to TCSEC.

22. In a ring protection system, where is the security kernel usually located?

    a. Highest ring number

    b. Arbitrarily placed

    c. Lowest ring number

    d. Middle ring number

    *Answer*: c

    The correct answer is c.

23. What are the hardware, firmware, and software elements of a Trusted Computing Base (TCB) that implement the reference monitor concept called?

    a. The trusted path

    b. A security kernel

    c. An Operating System (OS)

    d. A trusted computing system

    *Answer:* b

    The correct answer is b.

24. The standard process to certify and accredit U.S. defense critical information systems is called:

    a. DITSCAP

    b. NIACAP

    c. CIAP

    d. DIACAP

    *Answer:* a

    The correct answer is a, the Defense Information Technology Security Certification and Accreditation Process. Answer b refers to the U.S. government, non-defense Certification and Accreditation (C &A) process— the National Information Assurance Certification and Accreditation Process. CIAP, answer c, refers to the Commercial Information Security Analysis Process that is under development for application to commercial systems. Answer d is a distracter.

25. What information security model formalizes the U.S. Department of Defense multilevel security policy?

    a. Clark-Wilson

    b. Stark-Wilson

    c. Biba

    d. Bell-LaPadula

    *Answer:* d

    The correct answer is d. The Bell-LaPadula model addresses the confidentiality of classified material. Answers a and c are integrity models, and answer b is a distracter.

26. The Biba model axiom "an object at one level of integrity is not permitted to modify (write to) an object of a higher level of integrity (no write up)" is called:

a.  The Constrained Integrity Axiom

b.  The * (star) Integrity Axiom

c.  The Simple Integrity Axiom

d.  The Discretionary Integrity Axiom

*Answer*: b

The correct answer is b. Answers a and d are distracters. Answer c, the Simple Integrity Axiom, states " a subject at one level of integrity is not permitted to observe (read) an object of lower integrity (no read down)."

27. The property that states "reading or writing is permitted at a particular level of sensitivity, but not to either higher or lower levels of sensitivity" is called the:

a.  Strong * (star) Property

b.  Discretionary Security Property

c.  Simple * (star) Property

d.  * (star) Security Property

*Answer*: a

The correct answer is a. Answer b, the Discretionary Security Property, specifies discretionary access control in the Bell-LaPadula model by the use of an access matrix. Answer c is distracter. Answer d, in the Bell-LaPadula model, states "the writing of information by a subject at a higher level of sensitivity to an object at a lower level of sensitively is not permitted (no write down)."

28. Which one the following is NOT one of the three major parts of the Common Criteria (CC)?

a.  Introduction and General Model

b.  Security Evaluation Requirements

c.  Security Functional Requirements

d.  Security Assurance Requirements

*Answer*: b

The correct answer is b, a distracter. Answer a is Part 1 of the CC. It defines general concepts and principles of information security and defines the contents of the Protection Profile (PP), Security Target (ST), and the Package. The Security Functional Requirements, answer c, are Part 2 of the CC, which contains a catalog of well-defined standard means of expressing security requirements of IT products and systems. Answer d is Part 3 of the CC and comprises a catalog of a set of standard assurance components.

29. Configuration management control best refers to:

    a. The concept of "least control" in operations

    b. Ensuring that changes to the system do not unintentionally diminish security

    c. The use of privileged-entity controls for system administrator functions

    d. Implementing resource protection schemes for hardware control

    *Answer*: b

    The correct answer is b. Configuration Management Control (and Change Control) are processes to ensure that any changes to the system are managed properly and do not inordinately affect either the availability or security of the system.

30. The SEI Software Capability Maturity Model is based on the premise that:

    a. Good software development is a function of the number of expert programmers in the organization

    b. The maturity of an organization's software processes cannot be measured

    c. The quality of a software product is a direct function of the quality of its associated software development and maintenance processes

    d. Software development is an art that cannot be measured by conventional means

    *Answer*: c

    The correct answer is c. The quality of a software product is a direct function of the quality of its associated software development and maintenance processes. Answer a is false because the SEI Software CMM relates the production of good software to having the proper processes in place in an organization and not to expert programs or heroes. Answer b is false because the Software CMM provides means to measure the maturity of an organization's software processes. Answer d is false for the same reason as answer b.

31. In configuration management, a configuration item is:

    a. The version of the operating system, which is operating on the workstation, that provides information security services

    b. A component whose state is to be recorded and against which changes are to be progressed

    c. The network architecture used by the organization

    d. A series of files that contain sensitive information

*Answer*: b

The correct answer is b, a component whose state is to be recorded and against which changes are to be progressed. Answers a, c, and d are incorrect by the definition of a configuration item.

32. What is the formula for the Annualized Loss Expectancy or ALE that is used in risk analysis to estimate the potential losses to an information system as a result of the exploitation of a vulnerability?

   a. ALE = Single Loss Expectancy (SLE) × Annualized Rate of Occurrence (ARO)

   b. ALE = Multiple Loss Expectancy (MLE) × Annualized Rate of Occurrence (ARO)

   c. ALE = Single Loss Expectancy (SLE) × Modified Annualized Rate of Occurrence (MARO)

   d. ALE = Multiple Loss Expectancy (MLE) × Modified Annualized Rate of Occurrence (ARO)

*Answer*: a

The correct answer is a, where the SLE is the dollar figure that represents an organization's loss from the occurrence of a single threat and the ARO is a number that represents the estimated annual frequency with which a threat is expected to occur.

The SLE, in turn, is derived from the following formula:

Asset Value ($) × Exposure Factor (EF) = SLE

where the EF represents the percentage of loss that a realized threat event would have on a specific asset.

33. Which one of the following items is NOT one of the System Development Life Cycle (SDLC) phases discussed in NIST Special Publication 800-18, *Guide for Developing Security Plans for Information Technology Systems*?

   a. Initiation Phase

   b. Development/Acquisition Phase

   c. Organizing Phase

   d. Disposal Phase

*Answer*: c

The correct answer is c. The other SDLC phases discussed in Special Publication 800-18 are the Operations and Maintenance phase and the Implementation phase.

34. Management techniques for prototyping projects differ from those used in conventional development projects. Which one of the following statements is NOT true with respect to prototyping project management techniques?

    a. One of the three types of prototypes should be decided on at the beginning of the project.

    b. Evaluation criteria should be defined up front.

    c. Configuration management is not required.

    d. Prototyping objectives should be stated and agreed upon early in the project.

    *Answer*: c

    The correct answer is c. Configuration management is an important component of prototyping and should be applied to manage the changes inherent in such a project approach.

35. The comprehensive evaluation of the technical and nontechnical security features of an information system and the other safeguards to establish the extent to which a particular design and implementation meet the set of specified security requirements is called:

    a. Accreditation

    b. Validation

    c. Verification

    d. Certification

    *Answer*: d

    The correct answer is d. Answer a, accreditation, is the formal declaration by a Designated Approving Authority (DAA) where an information system is approved to operate in a particular security mode by using a prescribed set of safeguards at an acceptable level of risk. Validation, answer b, establishes the fitness or worth of a software product for its operational mission, and verification, answer c, is the process of establishing the truth of correspondence between a software product and its specification.

36. Which one of the following is NOT a phase of the National Security Agency INFOSEC Assessment Methodology (NSA-IAM)?

    a. Post-assessment

    b. Operational

    c. Pre-assessment

    d. On-site

    *Answer*: b

The correct answer is b. There is no operational phase in the NSA-IAM.

37. Which self-assessment methodology defines the terms "managers," "reporters," "subject matter experts," and "collectors"?

    a. The National Security Agency INFOSEC Assessment Methodology (NSA-IAM)

    b. The Systems Security Engineering Capability Maturity Model (SSE-CMM)

    c. The Defense-Wide Information Assurance Program (DIAP) Information Assurance Readiness Assessment

    d. The NIST Automated Security Self Evaluation Tool (ASSET)

    *Answer*: d

    The correct answer is d.

38. Which information security assessment method includes Manager and System Applications?

    a. The NIST Automated Security Self Evaluation Tool (ASSET)

    b. The National Security Agency INFOSEC Assessment Methodology (NSA-IAM)

    c. The Systems Security Engineering Capability Maturity Model (SSE-CMM)

    d. The Defense-Wide Information Assurance Program (DIAP) Information Assurance Readiness Assessment

    *Answer*: a

    The correct answer is a. ASSET comprises two separate host-based applications, the ASSET Manager and the ASSET System. The ASSET Manager houses the Recorder role, and the ASSET System incorporates the Collector Role. The questionnaire used in the assessment described in NIST Special Publication 800-26 is presented in the ASSET System.

39. When a computer or network component fails and the computer or the network continues to function, it is called a:

    a. Fail-safe system

    b. Fail-soft system

    c. Fault-tolerant system

    d. Resilient system

    *Answer*: c

    The correct answer is c. For fault tolerance to operate, the system must be capable of detecting that a fault has occurred, and the system must then have the ability to correct the fault or operate around it. Answer a, a fail-safe system, terminates the program execution. The system is thus protected from being compromised when a hardware or software failure occurs and is detected. Answers b and d refer to the same type of system, fail soft or resilient. This type of system terminates selected, noncritical processing when a hardware or software failure occurs and is detected. The computer or network then continues to function in a degraded mode.

40. In a PERT chart, the critical path is:

a. The path along dependent project tasks that takes the shortest time to complete

b. The path along dependent project tasks that has the most slack time

c. The path along dependent project tasks that takes the longest time to complete

d. The path along dependent project tasks that is the average of all the completion times

*Answer*: c

The correct answer is c. Answer a therefore is incorrect. The shortest path is not the critical path because the project cannot be completed until the tasks in the longest time path are completed. Answer b is incorrect because there is no slack time in the critical path. Answer d is a distracter.

# Chapter 4: Information Security Management

1. As stated in the National Security Agency/Central Security Service (NSA/CSS) Circular No. 500R, the objective of acquisition management is to manage a project by applying a number of techniques. Which one of the following is NOT one of these techniques?

a. Functional analysis

b. Design synthesis

c. Freezing requirements early in the design cycle

d. Verification

*Answer*: c

The correct answer is c. The circular states that the requirements shall be reviewed at key decision points and, if necessary, refined to meet cost, schedule, and performance objectives.

2. In addressing software engineering projects, the NSA/CSS circular emphasizes good practices to use in acquisition management of these

projects. Which one of the following items is NOT one of these recommended practices?

a. Employ software reuse

b. Apply software metrics

c. Assess and mitigate information assurance risks

d. Avoid the use of commercial off-the-shelf (COTS) products

*Answer*: d

The correct answer is d. In many cases, COTS products might be technically more advanced and less costly than MIL SPEC products.

3. Which one of the following is NOT one of the maturity levels of the Software Acquisition Capability Maturity Model® (SA-CMM®)?

a. Quantitative

b. Repeatable

c. Defined

d. Standardized

*Answer*: d

The correct answer is d. The remaining two maturity levels of the SA-CMM are Initial and Optimizing.

4. The following focus points are associated with what maturity level of the SA-CMM?

- Evaluation
- Contract tracking and oversight
- Project management
- Requirements development and management
- Software acquisition planning

a. Defined

b. Repeatable

c. Quantitative

d. Optimizing

*Answer*: b

The correct answer is b.

5. The following principles are taken from which one of the following documents?

- Reduce cost of ownership
- Expand the use of commercial products and processes

- Evaluate bids and proposals on a total-cost-of-ownership basis
- Manage contracts for end results

a. SA-CMM

b. NSA/CSS Circular No. 500R

c. Office of the Secretary of Defense (OSD) Principles of Acquisition Reform

d. DoD Standard Service Level Agreement (DoD-SLA)

*Answer*: c

The correct answer is c. Answers a and c are valid documents, but answer d is a distracter.

6. An acquisition strategy in which the required final functionality of the target deliverable is defined at the start of the program and increments during the program to take advantage of technological developments is called:

a. Developmental acquisition

b. Evolutionary acquisition

c. Conditional acquisition

d. Relative acquisition

*Answer*: b

The correct answer is b. The other answers are distracters.

7. A contract between a customer and provider that specifies a minimum level of service that will be supplied by the provider is called a:

a. Quality of service agreement

b. Service level agreement

c. Measured service agreement

d. Service legal agreement

*Answer*: b

The correct answer is b. The other answers are distracters.

8. Which one of the following does NOT describe the terms under which a contractual agreement must be made?

a. Mutual

b. Free

c. Communicated to each other

d. Unilateral

*Answer*: d

The correct answer is d. The terms must have mutual assent and understanding by all parties entering into a contract, a contract must be entered into without duress, and the terms must be communicated to all parties.

9. Which one of the following best describes an express contract?

   a. Exists in writing

   b. Inferred from the conduct of the involved parties

   c. An oral agreement

   d. A voided contract

   *Answer*: a

   The correct answer is a. Answer b defines an implied contract. Answers c and d are distracters.

10. Which one of the following is NOT a condition under which a contract may be unenforceable in court?

    a. Excessively harsh

    b. Entered into under duress

    c. Contrary to express statutes

    d. Mutual assent

    *Answer*: d

    The correct answer is d. Mutual assent is a requirement for contractual agreement.

11. Which one of the following statements is NOT true regarding recovery of contractual damages?

    a. Injured parties may normally recover an amount to compensate for any damage caused by breach of contract.

    b. Injured parties may normally recover an amount to compensate for any damage that would result from breach of contract.

    c. Injured parties may recover punitive damages.

    d. Injured parties may recover loss of profits that were a direct result of the breach of contract.

    *Answer*: c

    The correct answer is c. Punitive damages are not generally recoverable in a breach-of-contract case.

12. A repudiation of a contract that occurs before the time when performance is due is called a(n):

    a. Anticipatory breach

    b. Actual breach

c. Expected breach

d. Nonperforming breach

*Answer*: a

The correct answer is a. Answer b, an actual breach, is an unwarranted failure to perform a contract at the time performance is due. Answers c and d are distracters.

13. A set of policies, procedures, and tools to manage and resolve problems is defined as:

a. Project management

b. Problem management

c. Problem resolution

d. Problem prevention

*Answer*: b

The correct answer is b. The other answers are distracters.

14. Which one of the following is NOT usually associated with problems among individuals?

a. Conflict

b. Argument

c. Dissolution

d. Competition

*Answer*: c

The correct answer is c. Answer c is a distracter. Conflict, argument, and competition are the three most common situations relating to problems among individuals. Competition can be used in a positive manner, argument can be a positive or negative condition, and conflict is usually negative. One method of resolving conflict is to change it into a competitive or positive argument situation.

15. A third-party liability in which an individual may be responsible for an action by another party is called:

a. Contributory liability

b. Relational liability

c. Engaged liability

d. Vicarious liability

*Answer*: d

The correct answer is d. Vicarious liability is based on the doctrine of respondeat superior, where a superior is responsible for the actions of a subordinate. Conditional liability involves knowledge and participation by the offender.

16. Clipping levels are used to:

   a. Limit the number of letters in a password

   b. Set thresholds for voltage variations

   c. Reduce the amount of data to be evaluated in audit logs

   d. Limit errors in callback systems

   *Answer*: c

   The correct answer is c, reducing the amount of data to be evaluated by definition. Answer a is incorrect because clipping levels do not relate to letters in a password. Answer b is incorrect because clipping levels in this context have nothing to do with controlling voltage levels. Answer d is incorrect because they are not used to limit callback errors.

17. Which of the following is NOT a use of an audit trail?

   a. Provides information about additions, deletions, or modifications to the data

   b. Collects information such as passwords or infrastructure configurations

   c. Assists the monitoring function by helping to recognize patterns of abnormal user behavior

   d. Enables the security practitioner to trace a transaction's history

   *Answer*: b

   Auditing should not be used to collect user's passwords. It is used for the other three examples, however.

18. An audit trail is an example of what type of control?

   a. Deterrent control

   b. Preventive control

   c. Detective control

   d. Application control

   *Answer*: c

   An audit trail is a record of events to piece together what has happened and allow enforcement of individual accountability by creating a reconstruction of events. They can be used to assist in the proper implementation of the other controls, however.

19. Which of the following would be the BEST description of clipping levels?

   a. A baseline of user errors above which violations will be recorded

   b. A listing of every error made by users to initiate violation processing

c. Variance detection of too many people with unrestricted access

d. Changes to a system's stored data characteristics

*Answer*: a

This description of a clipping level is the best. It is not b because the reason for creating a clipping level is to prevent auditors from having to examine every error. The answer c is a common use for clipping levels but is not a definition. Answer d is a distracter.

20. Which choice would NOT be a common element of a transaction trail?

    a. The date and time of the transaction

    b. Who processed the transaction

    c. Why the transaction was processed

    d. At which terminal the transaction was processed

    *Answer*: c

    Why the transaction was processed is not initially a concern of the audit log, but we will investigate it later. The other three elements are all important information that the audit log of the transaction should record.

21. Which task would normally be a function of the security administrator, not the system administrator?

    a. Installing system software

    b. Adding and removing system users

    c. Reviewing audit data

    d. Managing print queues

    *Answer*: c

    Reviewing audit data should be a function separate from the day-to-day administration of the system.

22. What does an audit trail or access log usually NOT record?

    a. How often a diskette was formatted

    b. Who attempted access

    c. The date and time of the access attempt

    d. Whether the attempt was successful

    *Answer*: a

    The other three answers are common elements of an access log or audit trail.

23. Which choice is an accurate statement about the difference between monitoring and auditing?

a. Monitoring is a one-time event to evaluate security.

b. A system audit is a ongoing "real-time" activity that examines the system.

c. A system audit cannot be automated.

d. Monitoring is an ongoing activity that examines either the system or the users.

*Answer*: d

System audits and monitoring are the two methods organizations use to maintain operational assurance. Although the terms are used loosely within the computer security community, a system audit is a one-time or periodic event to evaluate security, whereas monitoring refers to an ongoing activity that examines either the system or the users. In general, the more "real-time" an activity is, the more it falls into the category of monitoring.

24. Which choice is the BEST description of an audit trail?

a. Audit trails are used to detect penetration of a computer system and to reveal usage that identifies misuse.

b. An audit trail is a device that permits simultaneous data processing of two or more security levels without risk of compromise.

c. An audit trail mediates all access to objects within the network by subjects within the network.

d. Audit trails are used to prevent access to sensitive systems by unauthorized personnel.

*Answer*: a

An audit trail is a set of records that collectively provide documentary evidence of processing used to aid in tracing from original transactions forward to related records and reports, and/or backward from records and reports to their component source transactions. Audit trails may be limited to specific events or may encompass all of the activities on a system.

User audit trails can usually log the following:

- All commands directly initiated by the user
- All identification and authentication attempts
- Files and resources accessed

It is most useful if options and parameters are also recorded from commands. It is much more useful to know that a user tried to delete a log file (for example, to hide unauthorized actions) than to know the user merely issued the delete command, possibly for a personal data file.

Answer b is a description of a multilevel device, which a device used in a manner that permits it to process data of two or more security levels simultaneously without risk of compromise. To accomplish this, sensitivity labels are normally stored on the same physical medium and in the same form (that is, machine-readable or human-readable) as the data being processed.

Answer c refers to a network reference monitor, an access control concept that refers to an abstract machine that mediates all access to objects in the network by subjects in the network.

Answer d is incorrect because audit trails are detective, and answer d describes a preventive process, access control.

25. Which choice is NOT a security goal of an audit mechanism?

   a. Deter perpetrators' attempts to bypass the system protection mechanisms

   b. Review employee production output records

   c. Review patterns of access to individual objects

   d. Discover when a user assumes a functionality with privileges greater than his or her own

   *Answer*: b

   The audit mechanism of a computer system has five important security goals:

   ■ The audit mechanism must "allow the review of patterns of access to individual objects, access histories of specific processes and individuals, and the use of the various protection mechanisms supported by the system and their effectiveness."*

   ■ Allow discovery of both users' and outsiders' repeated attempts to bypass the protection mechanisms.

   ■ Allow discovery of any use of privileges that may occur when a user assumes a functionality with privileges greater than his or her own—that is, programmer to administrator. In this case, there may be no bypass of security controls, but nevertheless a violation is made possible.

   ■ Act as a deterrent against perpetrators' habitual attempts to bypass the system protection mechanisms. To act as a deterrent, the perpetrator must be aware of the audit mechanism's existence and its active use to detect any attempts to bypass system protection mechanisms.

---

*Gligor, Virgil D., "Guidelines for Trusted Facility Management and Audit," University of Maryland, 1985.

- Supply "an additional form of user assurance that attempts to bypass the protection mechanisms are recorded and discovered." Even if the attempt to bypass the protection mechanism is successful, the audit trail will still provide assurance by its ability to aid in assessing the damage done by the violation, thus improving the system's ability to control the damage.

Answer b is a distracter.

26. Which statement is NOT correct about reviewing user accounts?

a. User account reviews cannot be conducted by outside auditors.

b. User account reviews can examine conformity with "least privilege."

c. User account reviews may be conducted on a system-wide basis.

d. User account reviews may be conducted on an application-by-application basis.

*Answer*: a

It is necessary to review user accounts on a system regularly. Such reviews may examine the levels of access each individual has, conformity with the concept of least privilege, whether all accounts are still active, whether management authorizations are up-to-date, or whether required training has been completed, for example. These reviews can be conducted on at least two levels: on an application-by-application basis or on a system-wide basis. Both kinds of reviews can be conducted by, among others, in-house systems personnel (a self-audit), the organization's internal audit staff, or external auditors.

27. During the investigation of a computer crime, audit trails can be very useful. To ensure that the audit information can be used as evidence, certain procedures must be followed. Which of the following is NOT one of these procedures?

a. The audit trail information must be used during the normal course of business.

b. There must be a valid organizational security policy in place and in use that defines the use of the audit information.

c. Mechanisms should be in place to protect the integrity of the audit trail information.

d. Audit trails should be viewed prior to the image backup.

*Answer*: d

The image backup should be done first in order not to modify any information on the hard disk. For example, the authentication process applied to a hard disk can change the time of last access information on files. Thus, authentication should be applied to a disk image copy.

28. Which one of the following conditions must be met if legal electronic monitoring of employees is conducted by an organization?

    a. Employees must be unaware of the monitoring activity.

    b. All employees must agree with the monitoring policy.

    c. Results of the monitoring cannot be used against the employee.

    d. The organization must have a policy stating that all employees are regularly notified that monitoring is being conducted.

    *Answer*: d

    Answer a is incorrect because employees must be made aware of the monitoring if it is to be legal; answer b is incorrect because employees do not have to agree with the policy; answer c is incorrect because the results of monitoring might be used against the employee if the corporate policy is violated.

29. Which one of the following is NOT a recommended practice regarding electronic monitoring of employees' email?

    a. Apply monitoring in a consistent fashion

    b. Provide individuals being monitored with a guarantee of email privacy

    c. Inform all that email is being monitored by means of a prominent login banner

    d. Explain who is authorized to read monitored email

    *Answer*: b

    No guarantee of email privacy should be provided or implied by the employer.

30. Configuration management control best refers to:

    a. The concept of "least control" in operations

    b. Ensuring that changes to the system do not unintentionally diminish security

    c. The use of privileged-entity controls for system administrator functions

    d. Implementing resource protection schemes for hardware control

    *Answer*: b

    Configuration management control (and change control) are processes to ensure that any changes to the system are managed properly and do not inordinately affect either the availability or security of the system.

31. In configuration management, a configuration item is:

    a. The version of the operating system that is operating on the workstation that provides information security services

    b. A component whose state is to be recorded and against which changes are to be progressed

    c. The network architecture used by the organization

    d. A series of files that contain sensitive information

    *Answer*: b

    Answers a, c, and d are incorrect by the definition of a configuration item.

32. Which choice does NOT accurately describe a task of the Configuration Control Board?

    a. The CCB should meet periodically to discuss configuration status accounting reports.

    b. The CCB is responsible for documenting the status of configuration control activities.

    c. The CCB is responsible for ensuring that changes made do not jeopardize the soundness of the verification system.

    d. The CCB ensures that the changes made are approved, tested, documented, and implemented correctly.

    *Answer*: b

    All analytical and design tasks are conducted under the direction of the vendor's corporate entity called the Configuration Control Board (CCB). The CCB is headed by a chairperson who is responsible for ensuring that changes made do not jeopardize the soundness of the verification system and that the changes made are approved, tested, documented, and implemented correctly.

    The members of the CCB should interact periodically, either through formal meetings or other available means, to discuss configuration management topics such as proposed changes, configuration status accounting reports, and other topics that may be of interest to the different areas of the system development. These interactions should be held to keep the entire system team updated on all advances or alterations in the verification system.

    Answer b describes configuration accounting. Configuration accounting documents the status of configuration control activities and, in general, provides the information needed to manage a configuration effectively. The configuration accounting reports are reviewed by the CCB.

33. Which element of Configuration Management involves the use of Configuration Items (CIs)?

    a. Configuration accounting

    b. Configuration audit

    c. Configuration control

    d. Configuration identification

    *Answer*: d

    Configuration management entails decomposing the verification system into identifiable, understandable, manageable, trackable units known as Configuration Items (CIs). A CI is a uniquely identifiable subset of the system that represents the smallest portion to be subject to independent configuration control procedures. The decomposition process of a verification system into CIs is called configuration identification. CIs can vary widely in size, type, and complexity. Although there are no hard and fast rules for decomposition, the granularity of CIs can have great practical importance. A favorable strategy is to designate relatively large CIs for elements that are not expected to change over the life of the system and small CIs for elements likely to change more frequently.

    Answer a, configuration accounting, documents the status of configuration control activities and in general provides the information needed to manage a configuration effectively. It allows managers to trace system changes and establish the history of any developmental problems and associated fixes.

    Answer b, configuration audit, is the quality assurance component of configuration management. It involves periodic checks to determine the consistency and completeness of accounting information and to verify that all configuration management policies are being followed.

    Answer c, configuration control, is a means of ensuring that system changes are approved before being implemented, only the proposed and approved changes are implemented, and the implementation is complete and accurate.

34. The discipline of identifying the components of a continually evolving system for the purposes of controlling changes to those components and maintaining integrity and traceability throughout the life cycle is called:

    a. Change control

    b. Request control

    c. Release control

    d. Configuration management

*Answer*: d

This is demonstrated in *Configuration management of computer-based systems,* British Standards Institution, 1984. Answers a, b, and c are components of the maintenance activity of software life cycle models. In general, one can look at the maintenance phase as the progression from request control, to change control, to release control. Answer b, *request control*, is involved with the users' requests for changes to the software. *Change control*, answer a, involves the analysis and understanding of the existing code, the design of changes, and corresponding test procedures. Answer c, *release control*, involves deciding which requests are to be implemented in the new release, performing the changes, and conducting testing.

35. Which choice best describes the function of change control?

    a. To ensure that system changes are implemented in an orderly manner

    b. To guarantee that an operator is given only the privileges needed for the task

    c. To guarantee that transaction records are retained in accordance with compliance requirements

    d. To assign parts of security-sensitive tasks to more than one individual

    *Answer*: a

    Answer b describes "least privilege," answer c describes "record retention," and answer d describes "separation on duties."

36. A purpose of a security awareness program is to improve:

    a. The security of vendor relations

    b. The performance of a company's intranet

    c. The possibility for career advancement of the IT staff

    d. The company's attitude about safeguarding data

    *Answer*: d

37. Which choice is an example of a cost-effective way to enhance security awareness in an organization?

    a. Train every employee in advanced InfoSec.

    b. Create an award or recognition program for employees.

    c. Calculate the cost/benefit ratio of the asset valuations for a risk analysis.

    d. Train only managers in implementing InfoSec controls.

    *Answer*: b

38. Which choice is not an example of appropriate security management practice?

    a. Reviewing access logs for unauthorized behavior

    b. Monitoring employee performance in the workplace

    c. Researching information on new intrusion exploits

    d. Promoting and implementing security awareness programs

    *Answer*: b

    Monitoring employee performance is not an example of security management or the Information Security Officer. Employee performance issues are the domain of human resources and the employee's manager. The other three choices are appropriate practice for the information security area.

39. Which statement is NOT true about security awareness, training, and educational programs?

    a. Awareness and training help users become more accountable for their actions.

    b. Security education assists management in determining who should be promoted.

    c. Security improves the users' awareness of the need to protect information resources.

    d. Security education assists management in developing the in-house expertise to manage security programs.

    *Answer*: b

    The purpose of computer security awareness, training, and education is to enhance security by:

    - Improving awareness of the need to protect system resources.

    - Developing skills and knowledge so computer users can perform their jobs more securely.

    - Building in-depth knowledge, as needed, to design, implement, or operate security programs for organizations and systems.

    - Making computer system users aware of their security responsibilities and teaching them correct practices, which helps users change their behavior. It also supports individual accountability because without the knowledge of the necessary security measures and how to use them, users cannot be truly accountable for their actions.

40. Which choice is NOT a generally accepted benefit of security awareness, training, and education?

a. A security awareness program can help operators understand the value of the information.

b. A security education program can help system administrators recognize unauthorized intrusion attempts.

c. A security awareness and training program will help prevent natural disasters from occurring.

d. A security awareness and training program can help an organization reduce the number and severity of errors and omissions.

*Answer*: c

An effective computer security awareness and training program requires proper planning, implementation, maintenance, and periodic evaluation.

In general, a computer security awareness and training program should encompass the following seven steps:

- Identify program scope, goals, and objectives.
- Identify training staff.
- Identify target audiences.
- Motivate management and employees.
- Administer the program.
- Maintain the program.
- Evaluate the program.

41. Which statement most accurately describes the difference between security awareness, security training, and security education?

a. Security training teaches the skills that will help employees to perform their jobs more securely.

b. Security education is required for all system operators.

c. Security awareness is not necessary for high-level senior executives.

d. Security training is more in-depth than security education.

*Answer*: a

Awareness is used to reinforce the fact that security supports the mission of the organization by protecting valuable resources. The purpose of training is to teach people the skills that will enable them to perform their jobs more securely. Security education is more in depth than security training and is targeted for security professionals and those whose jobs require expertise in security. Management commitment is necessary because of the resources used in developing and implementing the program and also because the program affects their staff.

42. Which statement is true about security awareness and educational programs?

    a. Awareness and training help users become more accountable for their actions.

    b. Security education assists management in determining who should be promoted.

    c. A security awareness and training program helps prevent the occurrence of natural disasters.

    d. Security awareness is not necessary for high-level senior executives.

    *Answer*: b

    Making computer system users aware of their security responsibilities and teaching them correct practices helps users change their behavior. It also supports individual accountability because without the knowledge of the necessary security measures and how to use them, users cannot be truly accountable for their actions.

43. Which choice would NOT be considered a benefit of employing incident-handling capability?

    a. An individual acting alone would not be able to subvert a security process or control.

    b. It enhances internal communications and the readiness of the organization to respond to incidents.

    c. It assists an organization in preventing damage from future incidents.

    d. Security training personnel would have a better understanding of users' knowledge of security issues.

    *Answer*: a

    The primary benefits of employing an incident-handling capability are containing and repairing damage from incidents and preventing future damage. Additional benefits related to establishing an incident-handling capability are the following:

    - Enhancement of the risk assessment process. An incident-handling capability will allow organizations to collect threat data that may be useful in their risk assessment and safeguard selection processes (for example, in designing new systems). Statistics on the numbers and types of incidents in the organization can be used in the risk assessment process as an indication of vulnerabilities and threats.

    - Enhancement of internal communications and the readiness of the organization to respond to any type of incident, not just computer security incidents. Internal communications will be improved, management will be better organized to receive communications, and contacts within public affairs, legal staff, law enforcement, and other groups will have been pre-established.

- Security training personnel will have a better understanding of users' knowledge of security issues. Trainers can use actual incidents to illustrate the importance of computer security vividly. Training that is based on current threats and controls recommended by incident-handling staff provides users with information more specifically directed to their current needs, thereby reducing the risks to the organization from incidents.

Answer a is a benefit of employing "separation of duties" controls.

# Chapter 5: Response Management

1. The type of evidence that proves or disproves a specific act through oral testimony based on information gathered through the witness's five senses is called what?

   a. Hearsay evidence

   b. Best evidence

   c. Conclusive evidence

   d. Direct evidence

   *Answer*: d

   Answer a, hearsay or third-party evidence, is evidence that is not based on personal, first-hand knowledge of the witness, but was obtained from another source. Answer b, best evidence, is original or primary evidence rather than a copy or duplicate of the evidence. Conclusive evidence, answer c, is evidence that is incontrovertible; it overrides all other evidence.

2. Which of the following is a key principle in the evolution of computer crime laws in many countries?

   a. All members of the United Nations have agreed to uniformly define and prosecute computer crime.

   b. Existing laws against embezzlement, fraud, and wiretapping cannot be applied to computer crime.

   c. The definition of property was extended to include electronic information.

   d. Unauthorized acquisition of computer-based information without the intent to resell is not a crime.

   *Answer:* c

Answer a is incorrect because all nations do not agree on the definition of computer crime and corresponding punishments. Answer b is incorrect because existing laws can be applied against computer crime. Answer d is incorrect because, in some countries, possession without intent to sell is considered a crime.

3. In general, computer-based evidence is considered:

   a. Conclusive

   b. Circumstantial

   c. Secondary

   d. Hearsay

*Answer:* d

Answer a refers to incontrovertible evidence; answer b refers to inference from other, intermediate facts; answer c refers to a copy of evidence or an oral description of its content.

4. Investigating and prosecuting computer crimes is made more difficult because:

   a. Backups may be difficult to find.

   b. Evidence is mostly intangible.

   c. Evidence cannot be preserved.

   d. Evidence is hearsay and can never be introduced into a court of law.

*Answer:* b

Answer a is incorrect because if backups are done, they usually can be located. Answer c is incorrect because evidence can be preserved using the proper procedures. Answer d is incorrect because there are exceptions to the hearsay rule.

5. Which of the following criteria are used to evaluate suspects in the commission of a crime?

   a. Motive, Intent, and Ability

   b. Means, Object, and Motive

   c. Means, Intent, and Motive

   d. Motive, Means, and Opportunity

*Answer:* d

6. Which of the following is NOT a computer investigation issue?

   a. Evidence is easy to obtain.

   b. The time frame for investigation is compressed.

   c. An expert may be required to assist.

   d. The information is intangible.

*Answer*: a

In many instances, evidence is difficult to obtain in computer crime investigations. Answers b, c, and d are computer investigation issues.

7. Conducting a search without the delay of obtaining a warrant if destruction of evidence seems imminent is possible under:

   a. Federal Sentencing Guidelines

   b. Proximate Causation

   c. Exigent Circumstances

   d. Prudent Man Rule

   *Answer*: c

   The other answers refer to other principles, guidelines, or rules.

8. Discovery, recording, collection, and preservation are part of what process related to the gathering of evidence?

   a. Admissibility of evidence

   b. The chain of evidence

   c. The evidence life cycle

   d. Relevance of evidence

   *Answer*: c

   The evidence life cycle covers the evidence gathering and application process. Answer a refers to certain requirements that evidence must meet to be admissible in court. Answer b, the chain of evidence, comprises steps that must be followed to protect the evidence. Relevance of evidence, answer d, is one of the requirements of evidence admissibility.

9. Relative to legal evidence, which one of the following correctly describes the difference between an expert and a nonexpert in delivering an opinion?

   a. An expert can offer an opinion based on personal expertise and facts, but a nonexpert can testify only as to facts.

   b. A nonexpert can offer an opinion based on personal expertise and facts, but an expert can testify only as to facts.

   c. An expert can offer an opinion based on personal expertise and facts, but a nonexpert can testify only as to personal opinion.

   d. An expert can offer an opinion based on facts only, but a nonexpert can testify only as to personal opinion.

   *Answer*: a

   The other answers are distracters.

10. The collecting of information from and about computer systems that is admissible in a court of law is called:

    a. Computer investigation

    b. Computer forensics

    c. Computer discovery

    d. Computer logistics

    *Answer*: b

    The other answers are distracters.

11. Which of the following items is NOT one of the requirements for evidence to be admissible in a court of law?

    a. It must be reliable.

    b. It must be legally permissible.

    c. It must be relevant.

    d. It must be approved by the affected organization.

    *Answer*: d

    Answers a, b, and c are requirements for evidence admissibility. Other requirements are proper identification and preservation of the evidence.

12. If an organization brings in law enforcement to conduct an investigation of computer crime, which of the following does NOT occur?

    a. The organization can still control information dissemination.

    b. The chain of evidence will be better preserved.

    c. The organization may be required to supply supporting resources.

    d. Business may be affected because of investigation-related data residing on computers holding information needed to conduct day-to-day operations (co-location of data).

    *Answer*: a

    When an outside law enforcement agency is brought in to investigate a computer crime, control of the investigation and dissemination of information is out of the hands of the affected organization.

13. If an organization decides to interview an individual suspected of committing a computer crime, which one of the following should NOT be done?

    a. An expert should be brought in to assist in the investigation.

    b. Questions should be prepared beforehand.

    c. Original documents involved in the interview should be shown to the suspect.

    d. The minimum amount of information should be provided to the suspect.

*Answer*: c

The other answers describe good interview practices.

14. If a private individual were asked by a law enforcement officer to search for evidence, which one of the following is true?

    a. A warrant would not be required because private citizens are not held to the strict requirements of the Fourth Amendment to the U.S. Constitution as law officers are.

    b. The chain of evidence would be broken.

    c. A warrant would be required because the private individual would be acting as an agent of law enforcement.

    d. The evidence would not be relevant.

*Answer*: c

In answer a, U.S. citizens are not held to the strict requirements of the Fourth Amendment to the U.S. Constitution as law officers are IF they are not acting as agents of law enforcement. The other answers are false.

15. Which choice is the BEST description of the criticality prioritization goal of the Business Impact Assessment (BIA) process?

    a. The identification and prioritization of every critical business unit process

    b. The identification of the resource requirements of the critical business unit processes

    c. The estimation of the maximum down time the business can tolerate

    d. The presentation of the documentation of the results of the BIA

*Answer*: a

The three primary goals of a BIA are criticality prioritization, maximum down-time estimation, and identification of critical resource requirements. Answer d is a distracter.

16. Which choice is NOT an element of BCP plan approval and implementation?

    a. Creating an awareness of the plan

    b. Executing a disaster scenario and documenting the results

    c. Obtaining senior management approval of the results

    d. Updating the plan regularly and as needed

*Answer*: b

Answer b is a distracter, although it could be a loose description of disaster recovery plan testing. The other three choices are primary elements of BCP approval, implementation, and maintenance.

17. Which statement is the most accurate about the results of the disaster recovery plan test?

    a. If no deficiencies were found during the test, then the plan is probably perfect.

    b. The results of the test should be kept secret.

    c. If no deficiencies were found during the test, then the test was probably flawed.

    d. The plan should not be changed no matter what the results of the test.

    *Answer*: c

    The purpose of the test is to find weaknesses in the plan. Every plan has weaknesses. After the test, all parties should be advised of the results and the plan updated to reflect the new information.

18. Which statement is true regarding company/employee relations during and after a disaster?

    a. The organization has a responsibility to continue salaries or other funding to the employees and/or families affected by the disaster.

    b. The organization's responsibility to the employees' families ends when the disaster stops the business from functioning.

    c. Employees should seek any means of obtaining compensation after a disaster, including fraudulent ones.

    d. Senior-level executives are the only employees who should receive continuing salaries during the disruptive event.

    *Answer*: a

    The organization has an inherent responsibility to its employees and their families during and after a disaster or other disruptive event. The company must be insured to the extent that it can properly compensate its employees and families. Alternatively, employees do not have the right to obtain compensatory damages fraudulently if the organization cannot compensate.

19. Which statement is NOT true regarding the relationship of the organization with the media during and after a disaster?

    a. The organization should establish a unified organizational response to the media during and after the disruptive event.

    b. The organization must avoid dealing with the media at all costs during and after the disruptive event.

   c. The company's response should be delivered by a credible, informed spokesperson.

   d. The company should be honest and accurate about what it knows about the event and its effects.

*Answer*: b

20. Which choice is the MOST accurate description of a warm site?

   a. A backup processing facility with adequate electrical wiring and air conditioning, but no hardware or software installed

   b. A backup processing facility with most hardware and software installed, which can be operational within a matter of days

   c. A backup processing facility with all hardware and software installed and 100 percent compatible with the original site, operational within hours

   d. A mobile trailer with portable generators and air conditioning

*Answer*: b

The three most common types of remote off-site backup processing facilities are hot sites, warm sites, and cold sites. They are primarily differentiated by how much preparation is devoted to the site, and therefore how quickly the site can be used as an alternate processing site. Answer c is an example of a "cold" site, which is a designated computer operations room with HVAC that may have few or no computing systems installed and therefore would require a substantial effort to install the hardware and software required to begin alternate processing. This type of site is rarely useful in an actual emergency.

Answer b, a warm site, is a backup processing facility with most hardware and software installed, which would need a minor effort to be up and running as an alternate processing center. It may use cheaper or older equipment and create a degradation in processing performance, but it would be able to handle the most important processing tasks. A hot site, answer c, has all required hardware and software installed to begin alternate processing either immediately or within an acceptably short time frame. This site would be 100 percent compatible with the original site and would need only an upgrade of the most current data to duplicate operations.

21. Which disaster recovery/emergency management plan testing type is the most cost-effective and efficient way to identify areas of overlap in the plan before conducting more demanding training exercises?

   a. Full-scale exercise

   b. Walk-through drill

   c. Table-top exercise test

   d. Evacuation drill

*Answer*: c

In a table-top exercise, members of the emergency management group meet in a conference room setting to discuss their responsibilities and how they would react to emergency scenarios. Disaster recovery/emergency management plan testing scenarios have several levels, and they can be called different things. The primary hierarchy of disaster/emergency testing plans type is as follows:

- *Checklist review.* Plan is distributed and reviewed by business units for its thoroughness and effectiveness.

- *Table-top exercise or structured walk-through test.* Members of the emergency management group meet in a conference room setting to discuss their responsibilities and how they would react to emergency scenarios, by stepping through the plan.

- *Walk-through drill or simulation test.* The emergency management group and response teams actually perform their emergency response functions by walking through the test, without actually initiating recovery procedures. This approach is more thorough than the table-top exercise.

- *Functional drills.* Test specific functions such as medical response, emergency notifications, warning, and communications procedures and equipment, although not necessarily all at once. Also includes evacuation drills, where personnel walk the evacuation route to a designated area where procedures for accounting for the personnel are tested.

- *Parallel test or full-scale exercise.* A real-life emergency situation is simulated as closely as possible. Involves all of the participants who would be responding to the real emergency, including community and external organizations. The test may involve ceasing some real production processing.

22. Which choice is NOT a role or responsibility of the person designated to manage the contingency planning process?

   a. Providing direction to senior management

   b. Providing stress reduction programs to employees after an event

   c. Ensuring the identification of all critical business functions

   d. Integrating the planning process across business units

*Answer:* b

Contingency planners have many roles and responsibilities when planning business continuity, disaster recovery, emergency management, or business resumption processes. In addition to answers a, c, and d, some of these roles and responsibilities can include the following:

- Ensuring executive management compliance with the contingency plan program
- Providing periodic management reports and status
- Coordinating and integrating the activation of emergency response organizations

Answer b, providing stress reduction programs to employees after an event, is a responsibility of the human resources area.

23. Which choice is NOT an emergency management procedure directly related to financial decision making?

   a. Establishing accounting procedures to track the costs of emergencies

   b. Establishing procedures for the continuance of payroll

   c. Establishing critical incident stress procedures

   d. Establishing program procurement procedures

   *Answer:* c

   Answers a, b, and d are all examples of emergency management procedures that must be established by the financial department to ensure that fiscal decisions are executed in accordance with authority levels and accounting practices. Answer c is an example of a procedure that should be developed by the human resources department. The quality of employee morale and well-being can include psychological needs as well as physical needs, and the role of the human resources department is critical in monitoring and managing immediate, short-term, and long-term employee stress.

24. Which choice is NOT an appropriate role for senior management in the business continuity and disaster recovery process?

   a. Delegate recovery roles

   b. Publicly praise successes

   c. Closely control media and analyst communications

   d. Assess the adequacy of information security during the disaster recovery

   *Answer*: d

   The tactical assessment of information security is a role of information management or technology management, not senior management. In addition to the elements of answers a, b, and c, senior management has many very important roles in the process of disaster recovery, including the following:

- Remaining visible to employees and stakeholders
- Directing, managing, and monitoring the recovery
- Rationally amending business plans and projections
- Clearly communicating new roles and responsibilities

Senior management must resist the temptation to participate hands-on in the recovery effort, as these efforts should be delegated.

25. Which choice represents the most important first step in creating a business resumption plan?

    a. Performing a risk analysis

    b. Obtaining senior management support

    c. Analyzing the business impact

    d. Planning recovery strategies

    *Answer*: b

    The business resumption, or business continuity plan, must have total, highly visible senior management support. Senior management must agree on the scope of the project, delegate resources for the success of the project, and support the time line and training efforts.

26. Which choice is NOT a commonly accepted definition for a disaster?

    a. An occurrence that is outside the normal computing function

    b. An occurrence or imminent threat to the entity of widespread or severe damage, injury, loss of life, or loss of property

    c. An emergency that is beyond the normal response resources of the entity

    d. A suddenly occurring event that has a long-term negative impact on social life

    *Answer*: a

    The disaster/emergency management and business continuity community consists of many different types of entities, such as governmental (federal, state, and local), nongovernmental (business and industry), and individuals. Each entity has its own focus and its own definition of a disaster. Answers b, c, and d are examples of these various definitions of disasters.

27. Which choice most accurately describes a business continuity program?

    a. Ongoing process to ensure that the necessary steps are taken to identify the impact of potential losses and maintain viable recovery

b. A program that implements the mission, vision, and strategic goals of the organization

c. A determination of the effects of a disaster on human, physical, economic, and natural resources

d. A standard that allows for rapid recovery during system interruption and data loss

*Answer*: a

A business continuity program is an ongoing process supported by senior management and funded to ensure that the necessary steps are taken to identify the impact of potential losses, maintain viable recovery strategies and recovery plans, and ensure continuity of services through personnel training, plan testing, and maintenance. Answer b describes a disaster/emergency management program. A disaster/emergency management program, like a disaster recovery program, is a program that implements the mission, vision, and strategic goals and objectives as well as the management framework of the program and organization. Answer c describes a damage assessment. A damage assessment is an appraisal or determination of the effects of a disaster on human, physical, economic, and natural resources. Answer d is a distracter.

28. Which choice is the correct definition of a mutual aid agreement?

a. A management-level analysis that identifies the impact of losing an entity's resources

b. An appraisal or determination of the effects of a disaster on human, physical, economic, and natural resources

c. A prearranged agreement to render assistance to the parties of the agreement

d. Activities taken to eliminate or reduce the degree of risk to life and property

*Answer:* c

A mutual aid agreement is used by two or more parties to provide for assistance if one of the parties experiences an emergency. It is expected that the other parties will assist the affected party in various ways, perhaps by making office space available, or offering computing time or resources, or supplying manpower if needed. While mutual aid agreements may be a very cost-effective solution for disaster recovery, they do not provide for full operations redundancy. An example of a problem with a total reliance on mutual aid would be the event that affects all parties to the agreement, thereby rendering the agreement useless. While they are an effective means to provide some resources to the organization in an emergency, they in themselves are not a replacement for a full disaster recovery plan, including alternate computer processing sites.

Answer a describes a business continuity plan. Answer b describes a damage assessment, and answer d describes risk mitigation.

29. In which order should the following steps be taken to create an emergency management plan?

a. Implement the plan

b. Form a planning team

c. Develop a plan

d. Conduct a vulnerability assessment

*Answer:* b, d, c, and a.

The proper order of steps in the emergency management planning process is the following:

- Establish a planning team
- Analyze capabilities and hazards
- Develop the plan
- Implement the plan

30. Which choice most accurately describes a business impact analysis (BIA)?

a. A program that implements the strategic goals of the organization

b. A management-level analysis that identifies the impact of losing an entity's resources

c. A prearranged agreement between two or more entities to provide assistance

d. Activities designed to return an organization to an acceptable operating condition

*Answer:* b

A business impact analysis (BIA) measures the effect of resource loss and escalating losses over time in order to provide the entity with reliable data on which to base decisions on hazard mitigation and continuity planning. A BIA is performed as one step during the creation of a Business Continuity Plan (BCP). A common five-step approach to a BCP could consist of the following:

- BCP project scope creation
- Business impact assessment
- Recovery strategy development

- Recovery plan development
- Implementation, testing, and maintenance

Answer a is a definition of a disaster/emergency management program. Answer c describes a mutual aid agreement. Answer d is the definition of a recovery program.

31. In which order should the following steps be taken to perform a vulnerability assessment?

    a. List potential emergencies

    b. Estimate probability

    c. Assess external and internal resources

    d. Assess potential impact

    *Answer*: a, b, d, and c

    Common steps to performing a vulnerability assessment could be the following:

    - List potential emergencies, both internally to your facility and externally to the community. Natural, man-made, technological, and human error are all categories of potential emergencies and errors.
    - Estimate the likelihood that each emergency could occur, in a subjective analysis.
    - Assess the potential impact of the emergency on the organization in the areas of human impact (death or injury), property impact (loss or damage), and business impact (market share or credibility).
    - Assess external and internal resources required to deal with the emergency, and determine if they are located internally or if external capabilities or procedures are required.

32. Which choice is NOT a recommended step to take when resuming normal operations after an emergency?

    a. Re-occupy the damaged building as soon as is possible

    b. Account for all damage-related costs

    c. Protect undamaged property

    d. Conduct an investigation

    *Answer*: a

    Re-occupying the site of a disaster or emergency should not be undertaken until a full safety inspection has been done, an investigation into the cause of the emergency has been completed, and all damaged property has been salvaged and restored. During and after an emergency, the safety of personnel must be monitored, any remaining hazards must be assessed, and security must be maintained at the scene. After all safety precautions have been taken, an inventory of damaged and undamaged property must be done to begin salvage and restoration tasks. Also, the site must not be re-occupied until all investigative processes have been completed. Detailed records must be kept of all disaster-related costs, and valuations must be made of the effect of the business interruption.

33. In developing an emergency or recovery plan, which choice would NOT be a short-term objective?

    a. Priorities for restoration

    b. Acceptable downtime before restoration

    c. Minimum resources needed to accomplish the restoration

    d. The organization's strategic plan

    *Answer*: d

The organization's strategic plan is a long-term goal. In developing plans, consideration should be given to both short-term and long-term goals and objectives. Short-term goals can include the following:

- Vital personnel, systems, operations, and equipment
- Priorities for restoration and mitigation
- Acceptable downtime before restoration to a minimum level of operations
- Minimum resources needed to accomplish the restoration

Long-term goals and objectives can include the following:

- The organization's strategic plan
- Management and coordination of activities
- Funding and fiscal management
- Management of volunteer, contractual, and entity resources

34. When should security isolation of the incident scene start?

    a. Immediately after the emergency is discovered

    b. As soon as the disaster plan is implemented

    c. After all personnel have been evacuated

    d. When hazardous materials have been discovered at the site

    *Answer*: a

Isolation of the incident scene should begin as soon as the emergency has been discovered. Authorized personnel should attempt to secure the scene and control access; however, no one should be placed in physical danger to perform these functions. It's important for life safety that access be controlled immediately at the scene, and only by trained personnel directly involved in the disaster response. Additional injury or exposure to recovery personnel after the initial incident must be tightly controlled.

35. Which choice is incorrect regarding when a BCP, DRP, or emergency management plan should be evaluated and modified?

    a. Never, once it has been tested it should not be changed

    b. Annually, in a scheduled review

    c. After training drills, tests, or exercises

    d. After an emergency or disaster response

    *Answer*: a

    Emergency management plans, business continuity plans, and disaster recovery plans should be regularly reviewed, evaluated, modified, and updated. At a minimum, the plan should be reviewed at an annual audit. It should also be reevaluated in these circumstances:

    ■ After tests or training exercises, to adjust any discrepancies between the test results and the plan

    ■ After a disaster response or an emergency recovery, as this is an excellent time to amend the parts of the plan that were not effective

    ■ When personnel, their responsibilities, their resources, or organizational structures change, to familiarize new or reorganized personnel with procedures

    ■ When polices, procedures, or infrastructures change

36. Which choice is NOT an example of a potential hazard resulting from a technological event?

    a. Structural collapse

    b. Hazardous materials release

    c. Mass hysteria

    d. Fuel shortage

    *Answer*: c

    According to the NFPA, mass hysteria is a potential hazard resulting from a human event. Of the three categories of potential hazards (natural, technological, and human), technological events include the following:

    ■ Hazard material release (HazMat)

    ■ Explosion or fire (not arson)

    ■ Fuel shortage

    ■ Structure collapse

- Utility failure
- Severe air pollution

Human events include the following:

- General strikes
- Terrorism
- Sabotage
- Mass hysteria
- Civil unrest

37. When should the public and media be informed about a disaster?

   a. Whenever site emergencies extend beyond the facility

   b. When any emergency occurs at the facility, internally or externally

   c. When the public's health or safety is in danger

   d. When the disaster has been contained

   *Answer*: a

   When an emergency occurs that could potentially have an impact outside the facility, the public must be informed, regardless of whether there is any immediate threat to public safety. The disaster recovery plan should include determinations of the audiences that may be affected by an emergency and procedures to communicate with them. Information the public will want to know could include public safety or health concerns, the nature of the incident, the remediation effort, and future prevention steps.

   Because the media is such an important link to the public, disaster plans and tests must contain procedures for addressing the media and communicating important information. A trained spokesperson should be designated, and established communications procedures should be prepared. Accurate and approved information should be released in a timely manner, without speculation, blame, or obfuscation.

38. Which choice is the first priority in an emergency?

   a. Communicating with employees' families regarding the status of the emergency.

   b. Notifying external support resources for recovery and restoration.

   c. Protecting the health and safety of everyone in the facility.

   d. Warning customers and contractors of a potential interruption of service.

   *Answer*: c

Life safety, or protecting the health and safety of everyone in the facility, is the first priority in an emergency or disaster. Evacuation routes, assembly areas, and accounting for personnel (head counts and last-known locations) are the most important function of emergency procedures, before anything else. Once all personnel have been accounted for and emergency teams have arrived to prevent further damage or hazard, family members should be notified of the status of the event. Providing restoration and recovery and implementing alternative production methods also come later.

39. A statistical anomaly-based intrusion detection system:

    a. Acquires data to establish a normal system operating profile

    b. Refers to a database of known attack signatures

    c. Will detect an attack that does not significantly change the system's operating characteristics

    d. Does not report an event that caused a momentary anomaly in the system

    *Answer*: a

    A statistical anomaly-based intrusion detection system acquires data to establish a normal system operating profile. Answer b is incorrect because it is used in signature-based intrusion detection. Answer c is incorrect because a statistical anomaly-based intrusion detection system will not detect an attack that does not significantly change the system operating characteristics. Similarly, answer d is incorrect because the statistical anomaly-based IDS is susceptible to reporting an event that caused a momentary anomaly in the system.

40. Intrusion detection systems can be all of the following types EXCEPT:

    a. Signature-based

    b. Statistical anomaly-based

    c. Network-based

    d. Defined-based

    *Answer*: d

    All the other answers are types of intrusion detection systems.

41. The organization that "establishes a collaborative partnership of computer incident response, security and law enforcement professionals who work together to handle computer security incidents and to provide both proactive and reactive security services for the U.S. federal government" is called:

a. CERT®/CC

b. Center for Infrastructure Protection

c. Federal CIO Council

d. Federal Computer Incident Response Center

*Answer*: d

To quote the FedCIRC charter, "FedCIRC provides assistance and guidance in incident response and provides a centralized approach to incident handling across agency boundaries." Answer a, the CERT Coordination Center (CERT/CC) is a unit of the Carnegie Mellon University Software Engineering Institute (SEI). SEI is a federally funded R&D Center. CERT's mission is to alert the Internet community to vulnerabilities and attacks and to conduct research and training in the areas of computer security, including incident response. Answer b is a distracter, and answer c, the Federal Chief Information Officers' Council, is the sponsor of FedCIRC.

42. The Carnegie Mellon University CERT Coordination Center (CERT/CC) recommends which of the following sets of incident response practices?

a. Prepare, notify, follow up

b. Prepare, handle, follow up

c. Notify, handle, follow up

d. Prepare, handle, notify

*Answer*: b

The other answers are distracters.

# Index

# Wiley Publishing, Inc.
# End-User License Agreement

**READ THIS.** You should carefully read these terms and conditions before opening the software packet(s) included with this book "Book". This is a license agreement "Agreement" between you and Wiley Publishing, Inc. "WPI". By opening the accompanying software packet(s), you acknowledge that you have read and accept the following terms and conditions. If you do not agree and do not want to be bound by such terms and conditions, promptly return the Book and the unopened software packet(s) to the place you obtained them for a full refund.

1. **License Grant.** WPI grants to you (either an individual or entity) a nonexclusive license to use one copy of the enclosed software program(s) (collectively, the "Software" solely for your own personal or business purposes on a single computer (whether a standard computer or a workstation component of a multi-user network). The Software is in use on a computer when it is loaded into temporary memory (RAM) or installed into permanent memory (hard disk, CD-ROM, or other storage device). WPI reserves all rights not expressly granted herein.

2. **Ownership.** WPI is the owner of all right, title, and interest, including copyright, in and to the compilation of the Software recorded on the disk(s) or CD-ROM "Software Media". Copyright to the individual programs recorded on the Software Media is owned by the author or other authorized copyright owner of each program. Ownership of the Software and all proprietary rights relating thereto remain with WPI and its licensers.

3. **Restrictions On Use and Transfer.**

   **(a)** You may only (i) make one copy of the Software for backup or archival purposes, or (ii) transfer the Software to a single hard disk, provided that you keep the original for backup or archival purposes. You may not (i) rent or lease the Software, (ii) copy or reproduce the Software through a LAN or other network system or through any computer subscriber system or bulletin- board system, or (iii) modify, adapt, or create derivative works based on the Software.

   **(b)** You may not reverse engineer, decompile, or disassemble the Software. You may transfer the Software and user documentation on a permanent basis, provided that the transferee agrees to accept the terms and conditions of this Agreement and you retain no copies. If the Software is an update or has been updated, any transfer must include the most recent update and all prior versions.

4. **Restrictions on Use of Individual Programs.** You must follow the individual requirements and restrictions detailed for each individual program in the "What's on the CD-ROM" appendix of this Book. These limitations are also contained in the individual license agreements recorded on the Software Media. These limitations may include a requirement that after using the program for a specified period of time, the user must pay a registration fee or discontinue use. By opening the Software packet(s), you will be agreeing to abide by the licenses and restrictions for these individual programs that are detailed in the "What's on the CD-ROM" appendix and on the Software Media. None of the material on this Software Media or listed in this Book may ever be redistributed, in original or modified form, for commercial purposes.

5. **Limited Warranty.**

   **(a)** WPI warrants that the Software and Software Media are free from defects in materials and workmanship under normal use for a period of sixty (60) days from the date of purchase of this Book. If WPI receives notification within the warranty period of defects in materials or workmanship, WPI will replace the defective Software Media.

**(b)** WPI AND THE AUTHOR OF THE BOOK DISCLAIM ALL OTHER WARRANTIES, EXPRESS OR IMPLIED, INCLUDING WITHOUT LIMITATION IMPLIED WARRANTIES OF MERCHANTABILITY AND FITNESS FOR A PARTICULAR PURPOSE, WITH RESPECT TO THE SOFTWARE, THE PROGRAMS, THE SOURCE CODE CONTAINED THEREIN, AND/OR THE TECHNIQUES DESCRIBED IN THIS BOOK. WPI DOES NOT WARRANT THAT THE FUNCTIONS CONTAINED IN THE SOFTWARE WILL MEET YOUR REQUIREMENTS OR THAT THE OPERATION OF THE SOFTWARE WILL BE ERROR FREE.

**(c)** This limited warranty gives you specific legal rights, and you may have other rights that vary from jurisdiction to jurisdiction.

6. **Remedies.**

   **(a)** WPI's entire liability and your exclusive remedy for defects in materials and workmanship shall be limited to replacement of the Software Media, which may be returned to WPI with a copy of your receipt at the following address: Software Media Fulfillment Department, Attn.: *The CISM Prep Guide: Mastering the Five Domains of Information Security Management*, Wiley Publishing, Inc., 10475 Crosspoint Blvd., Indianapolis, IN 46256, or call 1-800-762-2974. Please allow four to six weeks for delivery. This Limited Warranty is void if failure of the Software Media has resulted from accident, abuse, or misapplication. Any replacement Software Media will be warranted for the remainder of the original warranty period or thirty (30) days, whichever is longer.

   **(b)** In no event shall WPI or the author be liable for any damages whatsoever (including without limitation damages for loss of business profits, business interruption, loss of business information, or any other pecuniary loss) arising from the use of or inability to use the Book or the Software, even if WPI has been advised of the possibility of such damages.

   **(c)** Because some jurisdictions do not allow the exclusion or limitation of liability for consequential or incidental damages, the above limitation or exclusion may not apply to you.

7. **U.S. Government Restricted Rights.** Use, duplication, or disclosure of the Software for or on behalf of the United States of America, its agencies and/or instrumentalities "U.S. Government" is subject to restrictions as stated in paragraph (c)(1)(ii) of the Rights in Technical Data and Computer Software clause of DFARS 252.227-7013, or subparagraphs (c) (1) and (2) of the Commercial Computer Software - Restricted Rights clause at FAR 52.227-19, and in similar clauses in the NASA FAR supplement, as applicable.

8. **General.** This Agreement constitutes the entire understanding of the parties and revokes and supersedes all prior agreements, oral or written, between them and may not be modified or amended except in a writing signed by both parties hereto that specifically refers to this Agreement. This Agreement shall take precedence over any other documents that may be in conflict herewith. If any one or more provisions contained in this Agreement are held by any court or tribunal to be invalid, illegal, or otherwise unenforceable, each and every other provision shall remain in full force and effect.

# What's on the CD-ROM

This appendix provides you with information on the contents of the CD that accompanies this book. For the latest and greatest information, please refer to the ReadMe file located at the root of the CD. Here is what you will find:

- System Requirements
- Using the CD with Windows
- What's on the CD
- Troubleshooting

## System Requirements

Make sure that your computer meets the minimum system requirements listed in this section. If your computer doesn't match up to most of these requirements, you may have a problem using the contents of the CD.

**For Windows 9x, Windows 2000, Windows NT4 (with SP 4 or later), Windows Me, or Windows XP:**

- PC with a Pentium processor running at 120 Mhz or faster
- At least 32 MB of total RAM installed on your computer; for best performance, we recommend at least 64 MB

- Ethernet network interface card (NIC) or modem with a speed of at least 28,800 bps
- A CD-ROM drive

## Using the CD with Windows

To install the items from the CD to your hard drive, follow these steps:

1. Insert the CD into your computer's CD-ROM drive.
2. A window will appear with the following options: Install, Explore, and Exit.
   - **Install:** Gives you the option to install the Wiley test engine powered by Boson software.
   - **Explore:** Allows you to view the contents of the CD-ROM in its directory structure.
   - **Exit:** Closes the autorun window.

If you do not have autorun enabled or if the autorun window does not appear, follow the steps below to access the CD.

1. Click Start → Run.
2. In the dialog box that appears, type *d:*\**setup.exe**, where *d* is the letter of your CD-ROM drive. This will bring up the autorun window described above.
3. Choose the Install, Explore, or Exit option from the menu. (See Step 2 in the preceding list for a description of these options.)

## What's on the CD

Included on the CD-ROM is a testing engine that is powered by Boson Software. This program resembles the testing engine that will be used by the testing center where you will be taking your exam. The goal of the testing engine is to make you comfortable with the testing interface so that taking your exam will not be the first time you see that style of exam.

The questions that will be used in the testing engine are those presented in the book, and cover all 5 domains of the exam. When installed and run, the test engine presents you with a multiple-choice, question-and-answer format. Each question deals directly with exam-related material.

Once you select what you believe to be the correct answer for each question, the test engine not only notes whether you are correct or not, but also provides information as to why the right answer is right and the wrong answers are wrong, providing you with valuable information for further review. Thus, the test engine gives not only valuable simulated exam experience, but useful tutorial direction as well.

## Troubleshooting

If you have difficulty installing or using any of the materials on the companion CD, try the following solutions:

**Turn off any anti-virus software that you may have running.**  Installers sometimes mimic virus activity and can make your computer incorrectly believe that it is being infected by a virus. (Be sure to turn the anti-virus software back on later.)

**Close all running programs.**  The more programs you're running, the less memory is available to other programs. Installers also typically update files and programs; if you keep other programs running, installation may not work properly.

**Reference the ReadMe.**  Please refer to the ReadMe file located at the root of the CD-ROM for the latest product information at the time of publication.

If you still have trouble with the CD, please call the Wiley Customer Care phone number: (800) 762-2974. Outside the United States, call 1 (317) 572-3994. You can also contact Wiley Customer Service by e-mail at techsupdum@ wiley.com. Wiley will provide technical support only for installation and other general quality control items; for technical support on the applications themselves, consult the program's vendor or author.